The Elements
of Parapsychology

The Elements of Parapsychology

K. RAMAKRISHNA RAO

McFarland & Company, Inc., Publishers
Jefferson, North Carolina

ALSO OF INTEREST AND FROM K.R. RAO AND McFARLAND
J.B. Rhine: On the Frontiers of Science, Edited by K. Ramakrishna Rao
(1982; paperback 2011)
Consciousness Studies: Cross-Cultural Perspectives, K. Ramakrishna Rao
(2002; paperback 2005)
Basic Research in Parapsychology, 2d ed., Compiled and edited by
K. Ramakrishna Rao (2001)
*Charles Honorton and the Impoverished State of Skepticism: Essays on
a Parapsychological Pioneer*, Edited by K. Ramakrishna Rao (1994)
*Case Studies in Parapsychology: Papers in Honor of Dr. Louisa E. Rhine
Presented November 12, 1983, at Duke University*, Edited by
K. Ramakrishna Rao (1985)

LIBRARY OF CONGRESS CATALOGUING-IN-PUBLICATION DATA

Names: Rao, K. Ramakrishna, author.
Title: The elements of parapsychology / K. Ramakrishna Rao.
Description: Jefferson, North Carolina : McFarland & Company, Inc.,
    Publishers, 2017. | Includes bibliographical references and index.
Identifiers: LCCN 2017035744 | ISBN 9781476671222 (softcover :
    acid free paper) ∞
Subjects: LCSH: Parapsychology.
Classification: LCC BF1031 .R229 2017 | DDC 130—dc23
LC record available at https://lccn.loc.gov/2017035744

BRITISH LIBRARY CATALOGUING DATA ARE AVAILABLE

ISBN (print) 978-1-4766-7122-2
ISBN (ebook) 978-1-4766-3120-2

Front cover images © 2017 iStock

Printed in the United States of America

*McFarland & Company, Inc., Publishers
    Box 611, Jefferson, North Carolina 28640
    www.mcfarlandpub.com*

To Sri Nara Chandrababu Naidu,
Chief Minister of Andhra Pradesh,
with much respect and admiration for the way
he is developing the new state of Andhra Pradesh

Table of Contents

Preface

About fifty years ago, on a flight to New Delhi, I happened to sit next to Sir C.V. Raman, Nobel laureate in physics. During the course of our conversation, I told him about my interest in parapsychology and the work of the Rhines at Duke University. Dr. Raman nodded his head approvingly of their work and remarked spontaneously, "Then, they must have made this subject a science." There was no surprise or skepticism implied; it was just a matter of fact statement. Such ready acceptance was possible because, there was in him no *a priori* disbelief in these phenomena, but a culturally driven openness to the possibility of their existence. My cultural roots are similar to those of Dr. Raman; therefore, there were no reservations or apprehensions on my part when I chose to work in the area of parapsychology for my M.A. (Hons.) dissertation way back in 1953.

Even during my Duke University days and later at Rhine's Foundation for Research on the Nature of Man, unlike many of my colleagues, I tended to be more self-assertive and less defensive about my involvement in parapsychological study and research. This positive attitude gave me an advantage over my colleagues when I spoke about the subject. It made me appear more authentic and convincing than they, who probably had more factual information and data in their hands.

However, my prolonged stay in the U.S. and the leadership roles I had to play as the head of Rhine's Institute for Parapsychology, as the editor of the *Journal of Parapsychology*, and as president of the Parapsychological Association have created a mindset quite similar to that of my Western counterparts. It continues to drive my thoughts and work. The present exercise is a product of that mindset, resulting in a book that reviews parapsychology as it is pursued in the West.

I attempt in this volume to present an overall picture of the parapsychological landscape as I am accustomed to see it with my Western glasses. It is a descriptive account of parapsychology—now frequently called psi research—as it is currently understood in the West. It is also a statement of my own position as a student and research professional in parapsychology for over half a century, notwithstanding the fact that my cultural roots are essentially Eastern. The concluding chapter is not merely a personal history but also something meant to help those wishing to foray afresh into this challenging field still struggling for scientific recognition and acceptance.

The Center for Studies in Civilizations headed by the distinguished scholar Dr. D.P. Chattopadhyaya honored me by awarding a fellowship to do a book on parapsychology and yoga. This has led me to undertake a project that resulted in the publication of the book *Cognitive Anomalies, Consciousness and Yoga* (Rao, 2011). An offshoot of undertaking this project is a revival of my interest in parapsychology, resulting in this book.

There are some good reasons why I think the publication of this volume is timely. First, there is need for those who have an intrinsic belief in such phenomena as pursued in parapsychology to know the rational and scientific justification behind their beliefs, and at the same time see the distinction between scientifically warranted beliefs in their culture and those that are merely faith based. In countries like India, there is a revival of nationalism and a tendency to assert native culture and beliefs associated with it. In this context, becoming aware of the scientific basis of these beliefs would have significant positive ramifications. Further, the field itself would benefit much by way of receiving needed academic and other kinds of support in this part of the world.

Second, I believe, the current exercise is likely to have some authenticity as it represents the account of Western parapsychology by a person with Eastern cultural roots. Third, I offer this volume with the hope that it would help bring Western science to bear on some of the sacred Eastern beliefs.

Robbie Franklin, the founder and the sustaining spirit behind McFarland, has been a dear friend for a very long time. In a significant way, I see him as my spiritual twin. We have shared values; and our lifestyles have much in common.

There are others who helped me in other ways. These include Md. Rafi, a full time companion, Dr. Rositta Joseph, who did much of the copy editing, and Smt. Prasanna, a dedicated secretary who spares no effort to see me complete my work on schedule. My wife Sarojini cheerfully allowed me to use part of the time that justly belonged to her to pursue my professional interests beyond the call of duty.

I have received much encouragement and help from Dr. M.V.V.S. Murthi, president of GITAM University. My grateful thanks go to him.

Besides honoring me as GITAM's Chancellor, Dr. Murthi extended all kinds of support. I share with him visions to reshape higher education in the country along the *swadeshi* lines of Mahatma Gandhi.

This book is offered to a worldwide audience to bring awareness of the importance of scientific study of psychic phenomena. It is my hope that such awareness would help to initiate a process to realize the enormous human potentials that remain hidden. In today's troubled world, the focus on the spiritual side of human nature made possible by parapsychological research is necessary in order to step back from the precipice of potential global conflict. This book is a humble contribution in the direction of providing a possible check on the mad rush for material goods and eventual destruction, by rekindling interest in a subject that can throw significant light on the spiritual side of human nature.

1

Background and Beginnings

What Is Parapsychology?

Contrary to some common misconceptions, parapsychology is not palmistry, astrology or tarot card reading. It is not searching for the Big Foot, the Loch Ness Monster or UFOs. However, in the pursuit of some of the above, there may be an element of the paranormal. For example, a successful palmist or tarot card reader may actually be using her ESP.

In the Indian tradition, parapsychology is the science of *siddhis*. In contemporary Western scientific tradition, it is the study of putative paranormal phenomena such as extrasensory perception (ESP) and psychokinesis (PK). ESP is the alleged ability to have access to information shielded from the senses and is beyond inference and rational imagination. ESP is further classified into telepathy, which consists in knowing another person's thoughts paranormally, and clairvoyance, which is awareness of events and objects beyond one's sensory range without the use of any physical device. Telepathy and clairvoyance may be time displaced in that they may relate to thoughts, objects or events that were in the past or will be in the future. The former is called retrocognition and the latter precognition. So we have precognitive or retrocognitive ESP. PK or psychokinesis is the alleged ability of the mind to directly influence events outside with no sensory-motor mediation. Psi (Ψ) is the generic rubric that includes both ESP and PK, a term chosen to refer to paranormal phenomena and to avoid their nonscientific connotations. In recent years, new terms have been used to refer to parapsychological phenomena. For example, Cardena *et al.* (2015) prefer to use anomalous mental phenomena to avoid some of the theoretical assumptions underlying the term parapsychology.

Parapsychological concepts and practices have had a long history. *Yoga-Sūtras* as well as some Jaina texts explicitly speak of telepathy (*manaḥ-paryāya*) and clairvoyance (*divya dṛṣṭi*). There are numerous stories about extra-ordinary abilities of yogins and *ṛṣis* (sages) in Indian epics, *ithihāsas* and *purāṇas*. Even in the West, though the birth of parapsychology as a science took place roughly 150 years ago, the subject matter of psychical research itself has its origins in antiquity.

It is in the nature of humans to raise questions about the phenomena they encounter and attempt to provide satisfactory answers. Thus, science begins in human experience. It arises in our quest to understand what we encounter in our experience. The felt anomalies and observed incongruities between what we believe to be the case and what is actually found in experience are often the triggers that start further inquiry which, when successful, help reduce felt tensions and satisfy aroused curiosities.

If a rubber ball bounces up by hitting the ground while a piece of rock does not, here is an incongruity in experience that can only be resolved by postulating a set of physical laws. If a person reacts sharply to an affront hurled at him while another person pockets a similar insult unruffled, we have a comparable experiential anomaly that needs to be explained. The reason why the science of psychology has not taken as firm a hold as physics lies in the fact that the investigation into and the understanding of the reasons for divergent behavior patterns of humans are made difficult by the sheer number of interacting variables, which prevent a simple statement of law. The so-called subjectivity is in fact inherent in human experience inasmuch as the human situation is too complex and the intervening variables too numerous to formulate simple laws or to make confident predictions. Consequently, subjectivity is an inescapable impasse that all psychologies must confront.

This state of affairs leads to a quandary, which may be called the psychologist's predicament. On the one hand, any attempt to explain human behavior in terms of simple mechanical laws involves the denial of a great deal that is primarily psychological. It is likely to lead to a reductionist exercise that robs psychology of its essence, viz., the subjectivity. If, on the other hand, we admit that human behavior cannot be accounted for in terms of laws comparable to those found in other sciences, it is feared there may be no *science* of psychology at all.

One way to escape from this predicament is to resist reductionist temptations and realize that people operate at different levels—some levels being predictable, others not so predictable. Some may even be completely unpredictable. At each level we may have to postulate a set of assumptions, which may or may not be mutually congruous. The greater the incongruity, the less predictable becomes one's behavior insofar as one's actions and thoughts are not determined exclusively by any single set of behavioral determinants.

The dominant reductionist model in psychology is comparable to classical physics of the Newtonian kind. The uncertainties that abound in the human situations are more similar to the quantum postulates of uncertainty than the absolute assertions of a deterministic model. There are numerous reports of subjective experiences that seem to provide a *prima facie* basis for questioning some of our secure assumptions concerning the nature of humankind and the way we acquire information and influence the environment. If these experiences are genuine, they point to an aspect of our nature that seems to go far beyond what can be reasonably inferred from a reductionist model. The primary focus of parapsychology is on such experiences that appear in principle incongruent and conflict with known limits of knowing and being. For this reason parapsychology is considered to be the study of psychological or more precisely cognitive anomalies.

Intuition and Scientific Insight

There are usually two ways in which hypotheses occur to scientific thinkers. Sometimes scientists are patiently and consciously led, step by step. They observe phenomena, analyze the results and draw generalizations concerning them, which are also predictive of outcomes to be ascertained in the future. A few scientists have reported that sometimes a sudden insight into the nature of certain phenomena occurs to them and that their further work then consists of systematically developing the idea drawing verifiable hypotheses and obtaining evidence for them. In such cases it cannot be reasonably maintained that the insight itself is caused by the awareness of the problem by the scientist, because the scientist does not report any such awareness. The context of discovery and the context of its justification as discussed long ago by Reichenbach (1938) may still be fully relevant here. To argue that the scientists must have "noticed" the relationships at the level of the unconscious adds little to our understanding of the scientist's insight.

We know that the scientist requires something beyond mere intellect. Writing on the intellectual abilities of *Six Great Scientists,* Crowther (1955) tells us that the factor common among the great scientists "was the imagination to conceive a great idea." Introducing the English edition of Poincaré's book *Science and Hypothesis,* Professor Laumor says, "The aspect of the subject which has here been dwelt on is that scientific progress, considered historically, is not a strictly logical progress, and does not proceed by syllogisms. New ideas emerge dimly into intuition, come into consciousness from nobody knows where, and become the material on which the mind operates, forging them gradually into consistent doctrine, which can be welded onto existing domains of knowledge (Poincaré, 1952, p. xviii).

An interesting case of a great scientist whose discoveries, emerging from little or no formal training, baffled the commonsense canons of scientific process is that of the Indian mathematician Ramanujan. Professor Hardy who took Ramanujan to England and worked with him for a number of years characterized Ramanujan as a man whose career seems full of paradoxes and contradictions, who defies almost all the canons by which we are accustomed to judge one another, and about whom all of us will probably agree on one judgment only, that he was in some sense a very great mathematician.

> ... He was, at the best, a half-educated Indian; he never had the advantages, such as they are, of an orthodox Indian training; he never was able to pass the "First Arts Examination" of an Indian university, and never could raise even to be a "Failed B.A." he worked, for most of his life, in practically complete ignorance of Modern European mathematics, and died when he was a little over thirty and when his mathematical education had in some ways hardly begun. He published abundantly—his published papers make a volume of nearly 400 pages—but he also left a mass of unpublished work, which had never been analyzed properly until the last few years. This work includes a great deal that is new, but much more that is rediscovery and often imperfect rediscovery; and it is sometimes still impossible to distinguish between what he must have rediscovered and what he may somehow have learnt. I cannot imagine anybody saying with any confidence, even now, just how great a mathematician he was and still less how great a mathematician he might have been [Hardy, 1959, p. 1].

How did Ramanujan achieve what he did? According to his biographers, Ramanujan used to say that the goddess of Namakkal inspired him with the formulae in dreams. We are told that frequently, on rising from bed, Ramanujan would note down the formulae and rapidly verify them. Sometimes he was not able to supply a rigorous proof.

Professor S.R. Ranganathan reports that on a morning in 1913, Prof. Ross, a professor of mathematics at Madras Christian College, entered the classroom "with his eyes glittering and his lips throbbing." He asked Ranganathan, "Does Ramanujan know Polish?" to which he replied that it was not at all likely. The professor, pulling out from his pocket a university envelope containing the quarterly report of Ramanujan as a research student of the university exclaimed:

Look at this beautiful theorem. In the issue of a Polish periodical brought by today's mail, something of this kind appears. Surely, Ramanujan could not have divined what the Polish mathematician was thinking. What is more, Ramanujan's theorem is much deeper. Ramanujan has certainly anticipated the Polish mathematician. He is extraordinary. Is he not? [Ranganathan, 1967, p. 13].

We referred at some length to Ramanujan in order to focus on the similarity between the way he discovered solutions to mathematical problems and some of the "psychic" experiences that are not uncommonly reported. One may question with some justification whether Ramanujan's mathematical genius is mediated by psi. Scientific discoveries are made by those who were working on the problem. It is not unreasonable to think that the emergence of a sudden insight suggesting a solution to the problem or finding a solution in a dream may indicate no more than that sometimes a period of "incubation" may be necessary for the emergence of insight or that a dissociative state like dream may aid in bringing into consciousness solutions worked out at the unconscious level. However, it would not be difficult to see that, assuming the possibility of psychic phenomena on the basis of other evidence, the hypothesis that sometimes scientists obtain their solutions intuitively may be a simpler and more parsimonious explanation of Ramanujan's startling discoveries. Consider, for example, its similarity to the following case.

This is an experience recorded by a retired and respected engineer known to the present author, and reported to have occurred on June 28, 1940.

I was intending to go to Bezawada on 29th morning to do some work for a firm with which my friend Mr. S.K. Subrahmaniam is importantly connected. At dawn of 28th night, I heard the usual "voice" "Mr. S.K.S. is dead." I felt very sorry, commented on the sudden end, and also on the large number of people whose living was in his hands, who will now be thrown over in all probability—all this during the experience. Then, the voice seemed to laugh lightheartedly and said "It is not so bad as all that." I remembered this experience clearly at 7 a.m. and thought it was a freakish idea due to my projected journey that morning, connected with Mr. S.K.S. The daily paper that morning was seen by me at 8:30 a.m. and there, the obituary notice was given of Mr. S.K. Subrahmaniam, but he is all together a different gentleman connected with an Insurance Co. in Ceylon, of whose existence even I was not aware! [This is an excerpt from a recorded document given to the author.]

The similarities between Ramanujan's case and the one narrated above are obvious. Ramanujan believed he obtained his formulae in dreams through the inspiration of the goddess of Namakkal. The engineer heard "the usual voice" informing him of the death of Mr. S.K.S. In both cases partial verification is obtained through published reports. What is interesting is that both these experiences went beyond what was contained in the published reports. They are distortions of the actually available facts. For example, Ramanujan's theorem was much deeper than the Polish version. The deceased man was not the same S.K.S. known to the experiencer. These similarities are of course insufficient to establish that Ramanujan's discoveries are psi-mediated. It would be premature indeed to dub them as paranormal or consider them simply as no different from ordinary outcomes of diligent scientific pursuit.

Antecedents of Scientific Studies

Attempts at controlled observation of psi, like the episodes of its very occurrence, may be traced back to antiquity. King Croesus of Lydia (Dodds, 1971) sent his agents to the oracles in Egypt and Greece to check on their alleged paranormal abilities. The agents were instructed to ask the oracles to tell what the King was doing at a given time. To test the Oracle at Delphi, the King moved into a kitchen in the role of a cook at the specified time, and the Oracle, it was said, described accurately the King's unusual actions at that moment. Thus a field experiment was carried out some twenty-five centuries ago. Yet, it was only during the last quarter of the nineteenth century that we find the beginnings of serious scientific inquiry into psi.

Charles Richet (1923), a Nobel Prize winner in physiology, and one of the earliest to carry out experimental investigations of psi, divided the field into four stages before him. The first was the mythical stage which lasted up to Mesmer—a period in which miracles and prophecies played a part in and were at the root of several religious systems. The second, the magnetic stage, began with Mesmer (1779) and his doctrine of animal magnetism and lasted until the advent of the spiritistic stage in 1848 with the Fox sisters and the widespread interest in the so-called spiritistic manifestations represented by raps and such. Richet credited Sir William Crookes as having ushered in the fourth, the scientific stage in 1872 and expressed the hope that the publication of his own book *Thirty Years of Psychical Research* would "help to inaugurate a fifth, that of recognition as a science" (Richet, 1923, p. 15).

The Mythical Period

A firm belief in our ability to interact with our environment beyond the confines of the sensory-motor system is implicit in some of the practices of many tribal and primitive societies. Magical and shamanistic practices were widespread among primitive communities. Often spirits, angels, demons and gods were invoked to bring about and account for all kinds of psychic effects, e.g., to cause rain or cure illness, to cast a spell or to curse a foe. Diverse rituals were developed to achieve trance-like states believed to be conducive to invoking spirits. A variety of devices were employed to affect divination. Underlying the multiplicity of these practices and belief systems is the possibility that information could be acquired through nonsensory means and that we could influence and be influenced by causally remote events. Anthropologist Ronald Rose (1957) noted, for example, that telepathic communication was very much a part of the Australian aborigines he had studied. Henry Callaway (1868) reported how the Zulu aspirants for divination roles should first prove their clairvoyant abilities before they were initiated. The Melanesian islanders believed in a special force called *mana* that could be harnessed to achieve our intentions and realize the goals. Similar beliefs in the existence of mysterious forces, the spirits that can use them, and the human ability to invoke spirits to exploit these forces were common among primitive communities.

The supernatural beliefs of the primitives spilled over into organized religions. They were duly incorporated into early philosophical traditions as well. Descriptions of a variety of psychic phenomena abound in the Old Testament. The lives of Moses and other prophets are filled with stories of psychic events that lead Mircea Eliade (1959) to observe "a perfect continuity" in the occurrence of psychic experiences from the primitive to the highly evolved. On the authority of the Bible, Jesus Christ was clearly one of the most successful psychic practitioners of all times. He could turn water into wine, feed thousands of people with four loaves of bread, perform countless cures and even walk on water. Similarly St. Paul showed psychic powers, including materializations. The dispensation of Christianity during the period of the New Testament and Early Church was foreshadowed by "signs and wonders" that are believed to attest the authority and grace of God.

Miracles are not confined only to the Judeo-Christian tradition. Buddhistic, Hindu and Muslim scriptures, like the Bible, contain numerous reports of psychic occurrences. Krishna was a miracle maker. The life of Gautama the Buddha is filled with extraordinary legends of supernatural occurrences. Similarly, Muhammad, the Muslim prophet, was credited with numerous miracles.

The close resemblances between parapsychology and religious phenomena have led some to regard parapsychology as basic to understanding the religious phenomena (Eliot, 1959). "Parapsychology," wrote J.B. Rhine (1968), "is as close in principle to the doctrines of the religions as biology was to the early systems of medicine; it is the science underlying the systems of practices" (p. 60). All the orthodox systems of Indian philosophy with the sole exception of the Mīmāṃsā school regard psychic ability or yogic perception as a valid source of knowledge (Rao, 1957). Buddhistic thinkers as well as Jaina philosophers have also provided for psychic abilities in their epistemological systems. In fact the writings of some of the Buddhistic scholars such as Buddhaghoṣa of the fifth century CE provided possibly the most detailed and phenomenologically rich accounts of the various states of consciousness that emerge in one's pursuit of psychic excellence from the mundane state of *saṃsāra* until she reaches a state of *nirvāṇa* (Rao, 1988).

As E.R. Dodds (1971) points out in his scholarly review of psychical phenomena in classical antiquity, that not only are experiences indicative of telepathic, clairvoyant and precognitive forms of psi referred to in classical writings, but there are also attempts to explain them as well as interesting descriptions of states believed to be conducive to their occurrence. These explanations and descriptions astonishingly parallel some of the modern attempts to understand psychic phenomena. There were diviners like Kalchas in Homer's *Iliad*, who had knowledge of the events of the past, present and future. There were mediums, as in the Pythian tradition, who entered into trance-like states through prescribed rituals and produced veridical information via apparent nonsensory sources. There were then those professionals who could interpret dreams for their prophetic significance. It is said that Esarhadom of the seventh century BCE thought it worthwhile to kidnap some of these dream professionals. Socrates was credited with hearing a voice that guided him and on occasions provided premonitions. We learn from Plutarch that Democritus (about 400 BCE) had a theory of telepathy as well as psychokinesis (see Dodds, 1971). Though more cautious and less believing than Democritus and later stoics, Aristotle also saw it necessary to account for veridical dreams.

Brian Inglis (1977) suggests that as Christianity spread and had to deal with pagan rituals there arose a need to specify authority and endorse orthodoxy. The practice of divination became a suspect because one could propagate heresy as something inspired by the Holy Spirit. Consequently the institution of oracles was suppressed by the politically powerful Christian orthodoxy. Mediumistic practices and inspirational utterances tended to be regarded as the work of demons, which acquired the connotation of evil spirits. Therefore, we find very little positive emerging from the early fathers of the Christian church. Thus the Middle Ages were also dark ages for psychic studies.

One important exception, however, is St. Augustine, who, as Dodds says, "deserves a more honorable place in the history of psychical research than any other thinker between Aristotle and Kant" (1971, p. 205). St. Augustine provides some of "the most careful and sober" descriptions of psychic phenomena that have come down to us from antiquity. One of the examples is the case of a man who had to pay his deceased father's debt. One night the young man had a dream in which he saw his father who told him that the debt was paid. Further, he was shown in the dream by his father where he would find the receipt. The young man found the receipt at the place shown in the dream and was able to get his money back.

If the Church and Christian tradition tended to ignore, discourage and even suppress free exercise of psychic abilities for the fear that their authority might undermine the faith in the organized religion, the growing rationalism in Europe cast increasing intellectual skepticism on the very possibility of the existence of such abilities. Together they acted as a powerful inhibitor of public discussion of psychic experiences, regarded either as the work of the devil by the orthodox or as mere superstitious behavior unworthy of inquiry by the rationalist scholars. Again, the development of Newtonian mechanics that seemed to account fully for all natural events within a deterministic system of force and motion and Darwinism that sought to explain the diversity of species and the process of their evolution by the principle of natural selection, led to the rejection of non-natural phenomena in physical science as well as to a retreat of vitalism in biology.

There were, however, two other forces that left a feeling of uneasiness without any summary dismissal of reported psychic occurrences. First, Cartesian dualism which affirmed a basic duality in nature, mind and body, created an impasse between the extended body and the unextended mind that coexisted in humans. Descartes' solution that the pineal gland is the seat of the soul is unconvincing to all but his ardent followers. However, Cartesian dualism gave an added impetus for seeking a better understanding of the mind if the humans were to be considered any more than automatons. Also the spirit of science demanded that we offer appropriate explanations to all mental phenomena, including psychic experiences, and not limit its application to physical phenomena alone. The spread of spiritualism as well as the rise of Mesmerism may be understood against this background.

Emanuel Swedenborg (1688–1772) earned his reputation in Sweden as a scientist, religious teacher and clairvoyant. He claimed to communicate with spirits and wrote many volumes purported to have come from his contact with spirits. His "illuminations" received in trance states became the basis of a new theology. Swedenborg claimed clairvoyant visions that impressed no less an intellectual than Kant who was not known to be credulous or "to have an inclination to be marvelous." For example, Kant recounts what he had heard from several respected citizens in Gothenburg. Swedenborg sitting in Gothenburg was believed to have accurately described to about fifteen people gathered at his friend's house a terrible fire raging in Stockholm at the time several hundred kilometers away with no apparent means of receiving that information in any normal way. While accounts like this did puzzle and disturb him enough to write about them, Kant, the rationalist that he was, did not quite openly endorse their genuineness. (For an interesting discussion of Kant's views on the paranormal see C.D. Broad, 1953).

Mesmer and Animal Magnetism

Anton Friedrick Mesmer (1734–1815), a German physician educated in Vienna, practiced mostly in Paris. As a medical student, he wrote a dissertation in which he theorized that the sun, moon and stars influenced our bodies through the medium of a subtle fluid that is believed to encompass the entire universe. Speculations concerning such magnetic fluid were made before him by others like Paracelsus and Van Helmont. As Podmore (1902) points out, "not only did Mesmer borrow his theories ready-made from earlier mystics, but even the name 'magnetic' was in common use in the seventeenth and eighteenth centuries to denote the sympathetic system of medicine which was founded on those mystical doctrines" (p. 44). But Mesmer went beyond mere speculation. His experiments convinced him that he had a technique of far reaching therapeutic implications. First, he observed that he could influence a number of physiological functions such as blood flow by passing magnets over his patient's body. He later found that the magnets were not necessary and that the same effects could be obtained by pointing his forefinger at the patient or by passing any other object which he "magnetized."

In the course of the therapeutic sessions, the patients manifested a variety of bizarre behaviors. Some went into convulsions. Some were seen in a dissociative state. Catalepsy and violent movements were not uncommon. These were regarded as *crisis* states, which were believed to accelerate healing. During the crisis states, Mesmer noted the instances of what we now call ESP. Patients responded to signals hidden from them. They had veridical visions, and they caused physical effects in non-normal ways. Instances of self-diagnosis and diagnosing the illness of others by psychic means were not uncommon.

Mesmer's technique soon became popular among the rich and the fashionable circles and his practice flourished in Paris. The medical establishment remained, however, skeptical and even hostile. But Mesmer was successful in converting a few prominent people to his enticing art. Among them was Charles d'Eslon, physician to the Count d'Artois, brother of Louis XVI. This royal connection eventually led to the appointment of a commission in 1784 to inquire into the claims of animal magnetism.

The commission—consisting of four members each from the Faculty of Medicine and the Société Royale de Médicine and five delegates from the Academy of Sciences including Benjamin Franklin, then American Ambassador in France—observed the practice of animal magnetism by d'Eslon, a friend and disciple of Mesmer.

The commission did not evaluate the curative effects of mesmeric trance, but concerned itself with examining the evidence for the existence of a physical force which Mesmer and his followers regarded as the agent involved in the healing process. Nine members of the commission in the first report found no evidence for the existence of such a force and that the effects might be produced by the patient's imagination alone. In a confidential note, the commission even warned of the harmful effects of the practices.

The second report signed five days later belonging to the Société Royale de Médicine said much the same. One of the members, M. de Jussieu, however, disagreed. He thought that the commission should look also into the alleged physiological and curative aspects of these practices through careful observations and experiments with individual patients. He himself noted what seemed to be cases of action at a distance in which patients responded to the movement of a magnetized object that was not seen by them. These observations indicated that these effects seemed to be independent of the patient's imagination. This was of course a minority view. The findings of the commission and their implications were unambiguously negative.

The publication of the commission reports had the expected effect of removing the theories of Mesmer from the arena of scientific inquiry. However, it did not stop public interest in animal magnetism or the purported practice of it by a few. Among prominent such practitioners were de Puyseger and J.P.F. Deleuze. Puysegur, a pupil of Mesmer, "magnetized" a huge tree on his estate and the patients attached themselves to the tree with ropes. Like Mesmer's patients with the tub, the *baquet,* Puysegur's patients too were being magnetized by their connection to the tree and experienced similar *crisis* period. He also noted the special *rapport* that existed between the patient and the operator so that the former responded only to the latter and no one else in the trance period. Delueze, who believed that the magnetized patients could receive information independent of the conventional senses, thought that the magnetic fluid conveyed the information directly to the mind without the mediation of the senses. It is important to note that neither Puysegur nor Delueze was inclined to attribute the phenomena to anything but natural causes. There were of course others, however, who thought that the trance effects were due to the spiritual world.

A young physician in Paris, Alexander Bertrand, published two important books in 1823 and 1826, which reviewed the trance phenomena and the various theories offered to explain them. He concluded that the belief in the existence of a fluid, whether celestial or magnetic, is a myth and that the trance effects are due to suggestion. His own observations of trance behavior led him to believe that on occasions the somnambulists exhibited phenomena indicating action at a distance and a faculty of paranormal perception. Some of them were able to accurately describe the symptoms of various ailments in great detail when placed in *rapport* with the sick person. Bertrand, unlike Delueze, rejected the physical explanations of trance phenomena and preferred a psychological interpretation.

After an acrimonious debate in December of 1825, the Société Royale de Médicine at Paris appointed the second French commission to examine the somnambulistic trance phenomena. This commission presented its report in June of 1831, which essentially upheld the genuineness of the somnambulistic trance state and suggested that it could be an important adjunct to medical practice. This was an important step in reviving Mesmerism. The history of hypnosis, as it has come to be known, shows, however, a series of ups and downs before it finally came to be accepted as a genuine phenomenon worthy of scientific study.

Modern Spiritualism

In a sense, Mesmerism was a precursor to modern spiritualism as it first arose in the United States and later in the British Isles and Europe.

While many of the practitioners of Mesmer's art adhered to a naturalistic interpretation of the trance phenomena, there were others who attributed the somnambulistic utterances of entranced patients to spirit agencies.

Some philosophers in Germany readily saw in trance phenomena more cogent evidence for mystical belief in spirits. In Sweden, attempts were made to show how the spiritistic interpretation of trance utterances is consistent with the Swedenborgian view of man's intercourse with the spirit world.

First, Joseph du Commun and a few years later Charles Poyen, two French men, introduced Mesmerism in America. Their lectures, especially those of Poyen in Boston in 1836, attracted the attention of a few physicians and some medical students. Soon the strange phenomena were spread across the country by "traveling magnetists" who were no more than stage entertainers who demonstrated the phenomena for a fee. At the same time there arose magnetic healers some of whom proclaimed the intervention of spirits in their practice. Prominent among them was Andrew Jackson Davis who published in 1847 a treatise entitled *Nature's Divine Revelations* that at once became a sourcebook of spiritualism.

Davis was 17 years old and was apprenticing in a shoe shop when a traveling magnetist Stanley Grimes came in the fall of 1843 to Poughkeepsie, New York, Davis' hometown. Grimes' visit created a lot of excitement. Davis met Grimes who did not find Davis a good magnetic subject. Davis soon came into contact with a local tailor and amateur mesmerist by name William Levington, who not only "magnetized" Davis but also discovered that Davis had clairvoyant abilities and that he could, in a trance state, diagnose ailments in people. Encouraged by their success they soon gave up their trades to become full-time magnetic healers. Davis, in addition to diagnosing the disease of those present, practiced remote diagnosis. By holding the hand of a friend or relation of an absent patient, Davis attempted to diagnose the ailment and prescribed a remedy. This he did while he was magnetized and put in a trance state by Levington.

In 1845, Davis broke up with Levington and began working with Silas Lyon as his magnetizer until the spring of 1847 when he realized that he could exercise his clairvoyant and diagnostic skills without being magnetized and that he could at will receive and recall messages from the other "world."

Convinced that he was an instrument for transmitting divine revelation, Davis arranged to transcribe his trance utterances bearing on philosophical and spiritual issues. William Fishbough, a Universalist minister was hired for this purpose. Davis, who had little schooling and obviously no great learning, gave a series of philosophical and theological lectures. Fishbough edited and put them in a publishable form. They were published in 1847 under the title *The Principles of Nature, Her Divine Revelations and a Voice to Mankind*. The book, which ran through four editions in the first year of its publication, received considerable attention and made Davis a minor celebrity.

Davis claimed to be in communion with spirits of deceased persons and that he was inspired while in a trance state by the spirits of the Greek physician Yalen and Emanuel Swedenborg to practice healing and preach spiritual philosophy. He was clearly instrumental in many ways in promoting spiritistic philosophy through his writings and magazines like *The Universoleum* and *Spiritual Philosopher* he had helped to establish. The birth of modern spiritualism, however, is not traced to Andrew Jackson Davis, but to the strange happenings in 1848 in an obscure hamlet in upstate New York.

John D. Fox moved in December of 1847 with his wife and children, to a farmhouse in Hydesville, New York. The Foxes had seven children. Four of them, Margaret, Kate and Catherine, who were living with them at the time, and Leah, who lived in Rochester and taught for a living, were involved in the happenings that led to the outbreak of spiritualism across the United States.

Margaret was about ten years old and Kate her sister was seven when strange happenings began at their house in March of 1848. Noises of unknown origin were heard in all parts of the house during nights, but not during the day. These strange sounds included light rappings, knocks, footsteps and walking noise. The family felt that the house was haunted. One night, as we are told, Kate challenged the spirit, Mr. Splitfoot, to do what she did, count one, two, three by clapping with her hands. Raps appeared following Kate's command. When asked to count ten, there appeared ten strokes from apparently nowhere. The family was convinced that the source of the sounds was the spirit of a peddler who was believed to be murdered and buried in the cellar of the house.

Convinced that the problem was connected with the house, the family moved to the house of David Fox, which was about two miles away. But the raps followed them to David's house. They soon discovered that the raps occurred only in the presence of Catherine. Then, they decided to send Kate to live with her elder sister Leah in Rochester. The very first night Kate and Leah arrived in Rochester, the disturbances appeared there also. Soon the "spirits" began answering questions by an ingenious method. Someone would recite the alphabet. The spirit would rap to indicate the proper letter and thus slowly spell a message. The alphabets so retrieved would give a message ostensibly from the controlling spirit. Back in Hydesville the rappings did not stop with Kate leaving for Rochester. They continued, but now in the presence of Margaret.

As one would expect, the happenings in Hydesville and Rochester attracted the attention of a lot of people, and some of them did believe that spirits were behind these strange events. Leah, sensing the prospects of commercializing the phenomena associated with her sisters Margaret and Kate, arranged private sittings with clients for a fee. She also hired a large auditorium in the city of Rochester to demonstrate the "spiritist" phenomena to the public. Each night a committee was selected to inquire into the phenomena. The first two committees heard the raps and found no evidence of fraud. The third committee too found no way of explaining the raps even though it felt that trickery was a strong possibility. The final meeting itself ended in pandemonium when rowdies took over and the police had to escort the Foxes home. This incident did not, however, prevent the Fox sisters from going around Auburn, Albany, New York and Buffalo giving sittings and holding public demonstrations and collecting handsome fees.

The public interest in the phenomena exhibited by the Fox sisters was high. Reports of similar happenings had sprung up in many parts of the country. But then there were also skepticism and allegations of trickery and deceit. For example, three professors from the University of Buffalo who observed Leah and Margaret had no doubt that it was all fraud. They believed that the raps emanated from the knee joints of the sisters. When cushions were placed under the heels and legs stretched full length, they observed no raps. These observations they thought, were sufficient proof that the raps came from the voluntary action of muscles on knee joints. The Rev. Potts gave a demonstration on the stage to show how he could snap his toes to produce strange sounds. C.C. Burr and his brother Herman went on lecturing to expose the Foxes until Leah sued them for slander. The skepticism was reinforced when Mrs. Norman Culver who was related to the Fox family signed a sworn affidavit claiming that Kate had confessed to her of trickery in producing the manifestations. There were also those like E.W. Capron who defended the sisters by alleging that Culver's statement was a fabrication. Again, there were other manifestations in the sittings of the Fox sisters that cannot be explained by the knee joint hypothesis.

Several important and influential persons who witnessed the performances of Margaret and Kate were duly convinced that the Foxes were not hoaxes. Among them were those who seemed to believe in the spiritual origin of those raps such as Judge J.W. Edmonds of New York and Governor Nathaniel Tallmadge of Wisconsin. Though Horace Greeley of *New York Tribune* did not fully accept spiritualism, he had visited the Foxes, arranged for their sittings in his home and could never find a normal explanation for the phenomena he witnessed.

Despite the notoriety and ridicule in some quarters, the interest in the phenomena manifested in the presence of the Fox sisters was no doubt high. The interest spread well beyond New York state to at least St. Louis. Mediums began appearing in various parts of the country, sometimes producing far more interesting phenomena than the raps and knocks. Trance speaking and automatic writing became more common and popular than rappings. Even musical spirits and drawing mediums appeared. Speaking in languages unknown to the medium was also not uncommon. Thus there was a growing variety of "spiritual" phenomena by the mid–1850s.

As the decade came to a close, spiritualism was still flourishing, but the fame of the Fox sisters faded, partly because Leah got married and retired from spiritual practices and Margaret had withdrawn. Also there were too many mediums producing far more dramatic phenomena than the Fox sisters. As the sisters went into the background, Davis emerged as the main spokesperson for spiritualism. He traveled and lectured extensively and organized the Harmonial Brotherhood to promote spiritualism. He gave up magnetic healing and concentrated on the discussion of the philosophical and theological implications of spiritualism. He feared that the popular preoccupation with mediumistic phenomena might undermine the basic tenets of spiritualism and their benefits to humankind.

Beginnings of Empirical Investigations

Sir William Crookes was a scientist of eminence. A fellow of the Royal Society, he was elected its president in 1913. He declared in the July 1870 issue of the *Quarterly Journal of Science:* "That certain physical phenomena, such as the movement of material substances, and the production of sounds resembling electrical discharges, occur under circumstances in which they cannot be explained by any physical law at present known, is a fact of which I am as certain as I am of the most elementary fact in chemistry" (p. 8).

Crookes designed special apparatuses to test the claims of the celebrated medium D.D. Home and the results of these investigations, which were originally published in the *Quarterly Journal of Science,* were collectively reissued, posthumously, in one volume under the title *Researches in the Phenomena of Spiritualism* (1926). He was also involved in tests with Kate and Florence Cook. The things that distinguish Crookes as the originator of a new era in psychical research are not so much his personal credentials or the results of his own investigation as his forthright statement drawing the lines that divide spiritualism and the scientific research into extraordinary phenomena. He wrote:

> The spiritualist tells of bodies weighing 50 or 100 lbs. being lifted up into the air without the intervention of any known force; but the scientific chemist is accustomed to use a balance which will render sensible a weight so small that it would take ten thousand of them to weigh one grain; he is, therefore, justified in asking that a power professing to be guided by intelligence, which will toss a heavy body up to the ceiling, shall also cause his delicately-poised balance to move under the test conditions.
>
> The Spiritualist tells of rapping sounds, which are produced in different parts of the room when two or more persons sit quietly around a table. The scientific experimenter is entitled to ask that these taps shall be produced on the stretched membrane of his phonograph.
>
> The spiritualist tells of rooms and houses being shaken, even to injury, by super human power. The man of science merely asks for a pendulum to be set vibrating when it is in a glass case and supported on solid masonry.
>
> The spiritualist tells of heavy articles of furniture moving from one room to another without any human agency. But the man of science has made instruments, which will divide an inch into a million parts; and he is justified in doubting the accuracy of the former observations if the same force is powerless to move the index of his instrument one poor degree.
>
> The spiritualist tells of flowers with the fresh dew on them, of fruit and living objects being carried through closed windows, and even solid brick-walls. The scientific investigator naturally asks that an additional weight (if it be only the 1,000th part of a grain) be deposited on one pan of his balance when the case is locked. And the chemist asks for the 1,000th of a grain of arsenic to be carried through the sides of a glass tube in which pure water is hermetically sealed.
>
> The spiritualist tells of manifestations of power, which would be equivalent to many thousands of "foot-pounds," taking place without known agency. The man of science, believing firmly in the conservation of force, and that it is never produced without a corresponding exhaustion of something to replace it, asks for some such exhibitions of power to be manifested in his laboratory, where he can weigh, measure and submit it to proper tests [Crookes, 1926, pp. 10–12].

Crookes set out diligently to examine the claims of the spiritualists in the same manner, as he would test hypotheses in his own discipline of chemistry. He tells us that he began his investigations with the usual skepticism, believing "that the whole affair was a superstition or at least unexplained trick" (Medhurst *et al.,* 1972, p. 19). But his work with the celebrated physical medium D.D. Home soon convinced him of "the existence of a new force, in some unknown manner connected with the human organization, which for convenience may be called the "psychic force" (p. 22). Crookes was quick to note the "capricious manner" in which this "force" is exerted, as "it has but seldom happened that a result obtained on one occasion could be subsequently confirmed and tested with apparatus specially contrived for the purpose" (p. 23). Among the anomalous physical effects that Crookes observed with Home include the playing of musical instruments such as an accordion with no discernible human intervention. The reporting of Crookes' investigations with Home in the *Quarterly Journal of Science* reveals the scrupulous care with which he apparently carried out his work.

His subsequent work with Florence Cook, however, did not help to enhance his reputation as a careful investigator of mediumistic phenomena. For one thing, his account of his work with Florence Cook is less rigorous and one is left with the impression that the conditions were lax. Critics had accused Crookes of having an affair with Florence and having aided her in her fraudulent manifestations as Katie King (Hall, 1962). While there can be little doubt that Florence Cook was a fraudulent medium, it is arguable whether Crookes had colluded with her. Thouless (1963), for example, has persuasively argued that it was unlikely that Crookes was an accomplice of Florence Cook and that Hall's surmises were defective on many points.

The phenomenon of mediumship that became popular with the spread of spiritualism had a checkered history. Many mediums who were subjects of investigations proved to be fraudulent (Sargent, 1869; Seybert Commission, 1887). But D.D. Home, who was associated with some of the most impressive phenomena, was never found to have engaged in any fraudulent act. The famous Italian medium Eusapia Palladino, who was caught cheating on some occasions, did produce phenomena that convinced skeptics who challenged her (Lombroso, 1909). Similarly the Australian medium Rudi Schneider is known to have produced some impressive physical phenomena under controlled conditions (Osty, 1931).

While ostensible paraphysical effects, such as raps, object movements and materializations, manifest in the presence of physical mediums, in mental mediumship, the medium communicates by speech or writing, providing alleged paranormal information, usually attributed to a deceased entity. Boston medium Leonore Piper and the British medium Gladys Osbourne Leonard were among the better known mental mediums. Mrs. Piper was investigated among others by William James and Richard Hodgson. James not only believed in her honesty and the genuineness of her trance, but he also believed "her to be in possession of a power as yet unexplained" (Myers *et al.*, 1889–90, p. 653). Mrs. Piper's principal communicators were Dr. Phinuit, who claimed to be a French physician, and George Pellew, an acquaintance of Hodgson who had been killed in New York. A trance medium, Mrs. Piper's communications came through her speech as well as her writing. Careful and extensive recordings of her sittings were made by Hodgson, and there is a wealth of information that could not have been available to her in normal ways. Frank Podmore (1898–99), who was quite skeptical of mediumistic phenomena in general, in his careful evaluation of Mrs. Piper's mediumship refers not only to the "strictest precautions" taken to exclude fraud but also to the nature of the information obtained in her sittings which is not of the kind that one is likely to obtain through private inquiry.

Mrs. Leonard was made famous by the book *Raymond* by Sir Oliver Lodge (1916), which contains the communications, which were received through her mediumship, purported to be from her son who was killed in the war. The mediumship of Mrs. Leonard is similar to that of Mrs. Piper in many ways. Two distinguishing characteristics, however, are the book tests and proxy sittings done with her. In the book test the medium will direct the sitter to a book and a page number, which will contain a passage relevant to the needs of the sitter. The Rev. Drayton Thomas participated in a number of proxy sittings with Mrs. Leonard in which Thomas acted as a sitter for a third party who was not present at the sitting.

The fact that several mediums were exposed to be tricksters and frauds leads many to suspect that mediumistic phenomena are generally due to fraud. Several parapsychologists seem to share such a suspicion and are therefore generally wary of mediumistic phenomena. There are, however, a few highly regarded parapsychologists who think that a summary dismissal of all mediumistic phenomena as fraudulent is to abdicate scientific responsibility. John Beloff (1989), for example, writes, "I would say … that the records we have relating to the careers of the outstanding psychic individuals of the period, such as, for example, D.D. Home, Eusapia Palladino, Leonore Piper, Gladys Ossowiecki, or Rudi Schneider, represent the most convincing evidence we have for the reality of the paranormal" (p. 174).

Whether or not the mediumistic phenomena are genuinely paranormal, it is these strange and bizarre phenomena that attracted the attention of many laymen who attended the séances as well as the interest of a few scientists who attempted to investigate them. Thus, they provide the main background and constitute the immediate antecedents for the birth of a new science which was both bold and bizarre. It is bold because, like Crookes, a scientist has to put his reputation "on the mat" when undertaking to research these areas with any sense of sincerity. The emerging area of inquiry is clearly bizarre because of the very nature of the phenomena investigated; it lacked control, public observation, replicability and explanation within the bounds of science. How can we have a convincing science of phenomena that are conventionally outside the scope of science? If science is an inquiry into naturalistic phenomena, how can science deal with supernatural phenomena except by ignoring or denying them? However, the persistence of the claims and the bold initiatives of a few have combined to lead to a systematic investigation of psychic phenomena in an attempt to demystify them; and in the process was born the bold, new science called parapsychology.

The S.P.R. and the Early Experimental Work

While Crookes thus brought his scientific training and outlook to bear on parapsychological phenomena, it was the Society for Psychical Research (S.P.R.), established in England in 1882, that was to cradle the burden of the newborn science of psychical research. Several of the famous mediums were investigated by members of the S.P.R. The objective of the Society was "to investigate that large group of debatable phenomena designated by such terms as mesmeric, psychical and spiritualistic.... without prejudice or prepossession of any kind, and in the same spirit of exact and unimpassioned inquiry which has enabled science to solve so many problems, once not less obscure nor less hotly debated." Henry Sidgwick was the first president of the S.P.R. and Frederick Myers and Edmund Gurney were his close associates. Associated with the Society were the scholars, scientists and distinguished public figures, including two Prime Ministers of Great Britain, several fellows of the Royal Society and outstanding literary figures like Tennyson and Ruskin. Apart from testing mediums and collecting and documenting spontaneously occurring psychic events, S.P.R. members conducted some important experimental studies.

The early experiments by the members of the S.P.R. were concerned with the testing of the possibility of "thought-transference" or telepathy. The first volume of the *Proceedings* of the S.P.R. contains the account of experiments with the family of the Reverend Creery in which Creery's five daughters acted as subjects. The procedure was simple. One of the daughters acted as a subject attempting to guess a target (an image in the mind of the agent attempting to transmit it) while the rest acted as agents concentrating on and trying to mentally communicate the target to their sister. At the time of target selection, however, the subject was not in the room. The targets included names, two-figure numbers, playing cards or objects in the house chosen at random. Startling success was reported in these experiments conducted in different places with different agents (Barrett *et al.*, 1882). It is of course easy to see that the experimental conditions were far from ideal and that the reported success could have been due to non-telepathic factors. In fact, two of the sisters were later found to be using some sort of code.

In the Guthrie experiments, the subjects (two employees of M. Guthrie) attempted to reproduce a drawing placed on a wooden stand in the same room. The subject was blindfolded and the conditions were reported to be such that the subject could not have seen the picture even if she was not blindfolded. Several of these reproductions were strikingly similar to the originals (Guthrie *et al.*, 1883).

In the experiments carried out by P.H. Newnham in 1871 and reported in 1885, his wife was able to respond to the questions written down by him in a notebook from a position where she could not observe his face or see the notebook. The subject made her responses automatically with the aid of a planchette. The answers seemed to be appropriate to the questions even though she presumably had no knowledge of them.

Among the early S.P.R. experiments, those carried out by Sidgwick and Gurney to test the possibility of telepathy under hypnosis are important. In some of these, the subject's finger was anesthetized by telepathic suggestion. The hypnotist would look at a particular finger of the subject (which was selected as the target by the experimenter) and the finger would become anesthetized. In other tests by Mrs. Sidgwick, the hypnotized subjects attempted to guess two-figure numbers. In her first series, significant success was reported when the subject and the agent were in the same room and not when they were in separate rooms. In the second series, however, the subject was successful even when she and the agent were not in the same room (Sidgwick, 1889).

In France, Pierre Janet carried out experiments to test the possibility of inducing hypnosis at a distance by telepathic suggestion. It was reported (Gurney, 1888) that not only was telepathic induction of hypnosis possible at a considerable distance, but on occasions the hypnotist was able to influence the behavior of the subject telepathically.

By far, some the most important experimental investigations of psi during this period were by Charles Richet. These experiments (Richet,

1884) are methodologically important insofar as they involve the application of the calculus of probabilities. The subjects in these experiments were not gifted in any sense and claimed no extraordinary abilities. In some of these experiments, the subject attempted to guess a playing card randomly drawn from a pack and looked at by an agent. In the total of 2,927 trials at guessing the suit, the subjects obtained 789 hits, 57 more than what you would expect on the basis of chance. (Richet in his book *Thirty Years of Psychical Research* gives these figures as "on 2,103 guesses of playing cards there were 552 success as against a probable 525," p. 85). Richet also noted that the subject's performance declined when a large number of trials were made in the same session.

Richet was perhaps the earliest psychical researcher to see the importance of applying statistical techniques to ESP data. He wrote "these methods are not emotional or dramatic like experiments made with powerful mediums, or records on monitions of death, but are precise, and, when the experiment is well designed, undeniable" (p. 98).

While Richet thus saw the importance of applying the calculus of probability of investigating psychic phenomena, he did not extend his techniques far enough to estimate the probabilities for rejecting the hypothesis of chance. Nor was this done satisfactorily by Richet's counterparts in England who enthusiastically endorsed Richet's attempts. The mainstream of psychical research continued to favor qualitative studies, more dramatic and picturesque tasks, than the repeated card calling that would permit quantification. What Richet had initiated in the direction of quantitative measurement was not, however, completely lost. In fact, his methods and the efforts of S.P.R. members such as Lodge and Sidgwick have made it possible for academic psychologists to attempt to study psi in their laboratories. The first of such attempts was made at Stanford University.

Aided by a grant made to the University for the investigation of psychical phenomena by Thomas W. Stanford, John Edgar Coover carried out experimental investigations from 1912 to 1917. His results were published in a voluminous monograph of 641 pages. It was not without hesitation that the Department of Psychology at Stanford had accepted the responsibility of administering the endowment. Professor Frank Angell, head of the Department of Psychology, in his introduction to the monograph wrote: "...before coming to any final decision in the matter, letters were sent to the psychology departments of other universities asking their opinion of the probable worth of investigations in this field. The answers were uniformly favorable to the undertaking and from two especially, Cornell University and the University of California, there came valuable suggestions in regard to problems and to methods of investigation" (p. xx).

The experiments of Coover are a typical example of a psychologist's attempt to study psi without the necessary appreciation of the nature of the phenomena. It has since come increasingly to be realized that one should begin with simple and straightforward design uncomplicated by large numbers of variables and build on this progressively step by step. Coover's project was far too ambitious for a first attempt. His design was as complex as is the following sentence in which he sets forth the objectives of his card guessing experiments:

> In order to test the hypothesis of a common "suggestion mentale"; to analyze out the conditions of experimentation responsible for success, if found; to make a psychological study of the mental processes of the reagent in the thought-transference situation; to get material with which to make a comparison between inductive and theoretical probability; and to establish a "norm" for a definite test for thought-transference or clairvoyance: this investigation, continuing through four years and involving over 110 sets of 100 experiments each, was made [Coover, 1917, p. 50].

The subjects (n=100) in these experiments were largely students who were normal people without any claims of being "psychic." He also tested a group of ten "psychics." The test materials were 40 playing cards (without the jacks, queens, or kings). The probability of guessing the whole card correctly would be 1 in 40; the number, 1/10; the suit, 1/4, and the color, 1/2. The following procedure for testing was employed:

> The experimenter with a watch before him, (1) shuffles the deck of 40 playing cards (the face cards being discarded), cuts the pack, and holds cards concealed; (2) shakes the dice-box, to determine a control or regular experiment, he turns over the pack, exposing to his view the under card, taps once to signal the reagent that the experimental period begins, holds the mental content of the card and wills the content to be projected into the mind of the reagent, and, after 15 or 20 or more seconds taps twice to signal the close of the interval. After he notes that the reagent has recorded his guess, and has turned to his introspections, he records the color, number and suit of the card and the number of the die-spot which conditioned the form of the experiment (as, R5H I, for red, Five of hearts, Die-spot I—i.e., held in visual impression). The control experiments ran off in precisely the same form as the regular, except that the card remained until the reagent had recorded his guess [Coover, 1917, pp. 53–54].

Coover's normal subjects made 10,000 guesses and the psychics 1,000. Half of these were made when the agent looked at the target and half without his looking at it. In other words, half of the trials permitted telepathy and the other half did not. The non-telepathic trials did not preclude the possibility of clairvoyance, but Coover preferred to regard them as controls. It is not clear why Coover did that when he himself was not unaware of the possibility of clairvoyance. His normal subjects obtained in 5,000 clairvoyance trials 141 hits on whole cards and 153 hits in the same number of telepathic trials. His "psychic" subjects obtained 11 hits in 500 clairvoyance trials and 18 hits in 500 telepathic trials. These results led him to conclude that "no trace of an objective thought-transference is found..." (p. 124). This conclusion is misleading in some ways. It is pointed out that the "not imaged" (clairvoyance) trials may not be considered as true controls. If one treats these controls also as ESP trials, the total number of hits obtained significantly differs from the number expected by chance (p < .005). Even if we discard the clairvoyance trials, the number of hits obtained under the telepathic condition alone is significantly more than what one would expect on the basis of chance (p < .05). Thus, what was a promising beginning was completely overlooked and treated as support for the null hypothesis.

Among the early ESP experiments in American universities mention may be made of the work of L.T. Troland and George Estabrooks at Harvard University. Troland in 1924 asked his subjects to guess which of the two sides of a box would be illuminated. In this experiment consisting of 605 trials, the subjects scored 284 hits (p = 1/2), 18.5 fewer than chance expectation. Clearly the results give no evidence of psi. But it is important to note that Troland attempted to mechanize the whole test to every extent possible. Estabrooks (1927) carried out in 1924–25 a series of experiments in which the subjects attempted to guess the color and suit of the playing cards looked at by an agent. The subject and the agent sat in a double room, which consisted of an inner room separated from the main room by a double door. While the subject and the agent could not see each other with the doors closed, "scraping of the chair, or loud talking" could be heard between the two rooms. In three series of experiments conducted with the subject and the agent in the double-room set up, the subjects obtained 938 hits with color as target, where one expects 830 hits by chance. It is obvious that chance would not account for the excess hits. In the fourth series the agent sat in another room 60 feet away. The subjects obtained 130 hits on suits where 160 are expected. Estabrooks wrote off these results as "wholly negative." But the fact is that his subjects in series four seem to miss the targets to a significant degree while the subjects in other three series tended to hit the targets. This fact now makes sense in light of the evidence for psi-missing, which has accumulated over the years. Estabrooks also became skeptical about his positive results as he became aware of the possibility of auditory and other cues, which could have accounted for the results. But the internal evidence in the data renders the sensory cues hypothesis less than likely. For example, his subjects scored significantly more hits during the first half than on the second half of the run. If the subjects were using a code, it is difficult to explain why they did not succeed during the second half of the run. Also, it is difficult to explain why the subjects should use their code to miss in the fourth series.

We have not referred to all the experiments done during the early period of parapsychology. *Extrasensory Perception After Sixty Years* (Rhine *et al.*, 1940) lists 75 experiments reported before Estabrooks' publication of his results in 1927. There is, however, one experiment carried out by Brugmans (1921) at the University of Groningen in Holland which deserves particular mention here.

In the Groningen study, the experimenter's task was to guide by means of telepathy the hand of the subject to the right square on a checker board in front of him which corresponded to a letter (A to H) and a number (1 to 6). The experimenters who acted as agents selected at random a letter from one bag and a number from another and tried to "transmit" them to the subject who was in a room one floor below them. The subject, who was blindfolded, responded by pointing to one of the squares on a checkerboard screened from his vision. This indicated a letter and a number by cross reference. The experimenter, who could see this operation through a double-glazed aperture from the floor immediately above, recorded the response. In the total of 187 trials, the subject successfully indicated the correct letter and figure on 60 occasions, when he was expected to succeed fewer than 4 times on the hypothesis of coincidence. The experimenters reported that they could not conceive of the possibility that the subject was obtaining the information by any sensory cues.

Such a large percentage of success clearly rules out the possibility that all or most of the successful responses were mere coincidences. But a critical inquirer may raise questions relating to the recording procedures, which were not clearly reported. Since the subject was blindfolded and did not see the checkerboard when he made the responses, there may have been occasions when the subject pointed to no particular square but the line between the two squares. In such situations, as Gardner Murphy (1961) asked, what did the experimenters do? There were also questions about the recording: If the experimenter knew the target before recording the subject's response, could his recording of the response have been influenced by his knowledge of the target? Or if the target was recorded after the response was made, might the recording of the target not have been influenced by the subject's response? Similar questions about the adequacy of experimental conditions to rule out sensory cues and recording errors could be raised against most of the experiments of the early period.

The First Systematic Research Program

The publication of the Estabrooks' results of experimental telepathy coincided with J.B. Rhine's joining Duke University in Durham, North Carolina, where he carried out experimental investigations into psi uninterruptedly for nearly forty years. The year 1927 marks the beginning of a new era for the study of psi. One might say that it was the year of the conception for the science of psi. The publication of Rhine's results in his monograph of 1934 *Extrasensory Perception* marked the birth of a new science, parapsychology. Brian MacKenzie, writing on the history of parapsychology, states that the scientific stage of parapsychology began "with the founding of the Parapsychology Laboratory at Duke University in 1927, or perhaps with the first major output of this laboratory, Rhine's *Extrasensory Perception* in 1934" (1977, p. 28). The book provided a paradigm for experimental parapsychology. It gave "a shared language, methods and problems" (McVaugh and Mauskopf, 1976) which made a systematic scientific search for psi (putative paranormal phenomena) possible. Sociologist Paul D. Allison (1973) finds four innovative elements in Rhine's work. First, Rhine developed materials and methods for the quantitative assessment of psi. Second, the research focus shifted from testing psychic celebrities to ordinary college students. The third innovation, according to Allison, "was to refocus attention from telepathy to clairvoyance" (p. 39). Finally, Rhine sought to establish general laws of psi phenomena and provided a blueprint for future research activity. Thus he laid the foundation on which the science of psi was to be built. Allison finds in Rhine's work the two conditions necessary "for the development of a highly cohesive scientific group ... a radical innovation and a high potential for elaboration" (p. 39).

By restricting his inquiry to workable problems, problems to which scientific method could be applied, Rhine has contributed more than anyone else to the "naturalization" of psychical research, as William McDougall called it. His methods had become the standard procedures for the testing of psi throughout the world. His work has received more acclaim, both critical and appreciative, than that of any one else in the field, and he, in many respects, reflects the frontier spirit of a pioneering American with his rugged individualism, unflagging devotion, and resoluteness. In this work he was ably assisted by his wife, Louisa E. Rhine, and colleagues like Charles Stuart and J.G. Pratt.

The first objective of his researches into extrasensory perception was to answer by means of mathematically indisputable evidence the question of the occurrence and range of psi. For this purpose, he set out to develop materials and methods that would permit easy handling and precise measurement and evaluation. He used an especially designed deck of cards, which later came to be known as ESP cards. A set of these ESP cards contains 25 cards inscribed with five symbols: a plus sign, a circle, a square, a five-pointed star, and wavy lines. A deck of cards known to contain an equal number of cards of each kind is called a *closed* deck as distinguished from an *open* deck in which the number of cards bearing each of these symbols is not necessarily equal but random. A series of 25 trials in an ESP test is called a *run*. A successful trial is called a *hit*. Five hits is the expected average or the *mean chance expectation* (MCE) per run. When an expected number of hits in a given series of trials are subtracted from the actually observed number of hits, the deviation is obtained. Rhine used appropriate but simple statistical methods in his experimental studies to determine the probability that a deviation would occur by chance, i.e., without any apparent cause.

Using ESP cards, Rhine (1934) tested a number of subjects at Duke University. In his first three years of experimentation, he was able to find eight good subjects. In the total of 85,724 trials he conducted with them, he obtained 24,364 hits, i.e., 7,219 hits more than expected by chance, a deviation which is highly significant rendering chance coincidence as a nonviable explanation for the observed results. But critics raised several questions. The major criticisms were that (a) shuffling of the cards might not have been random; (b) the subjects could have obtained sensory clues from the backs of the cards since the same deck of cards was used more than once; (c) the experimenter or the agent could have unconsciously whispered what the card being guessed at was; and (d) the experimenter could have unconsciously committed errors in recording the subject's guess so as to obtain higher scores. While it could not be established that any of these did in fact happen, the possibility that any or all of these could account for some of the results is not ruled out. Rhine maintained, however, that in some of his experiments such as the Pearce-Pratt experiment he was able to control against the possibility of any of the above possible artifacts and yet the results were highly significant, leaving ESP as the only viable explanation.

In 1934, at the suggestion of a young gambler, Rhine began to investigate psychokinesis (PK) or the power of the mind to influence matter directly, without the involvement of the musculoskeletal system, using dice as target objects. Initially, Rhine investigated the ability of human subjects to influence dice to roll in such a way that a given "target" face would come up. Later other investigators had subjects attempt to influence the direction or speed of mechanically thrown dice so that they come to rest at specific target locations. Such tests became known as "placement tests." Because of the controversy surrounding his ESP results, Rhine withheld publication of his PK research until 1943.

Rhine's work is important in the history of parapsychology for many reasons. Even though he was not the first to use experimental method to obtain evidence for psychic phenomena, he is rightly regarded as the founding father of experimental parapsychology. As Brian Mackenzie pointed out, it was under Rhine's leadership that parapsychology began

> to acquire the unity of outlook necessary for any kind of cumulative development. This is what is meant in saying that Rhine established a distinct discipline of scientific parapsychology. He was the nucleus of what became a reference group of professional parapsychologists, one who agreed not only on the application of scientific method in general, but also in detail on the choice of the procedures, problems, standards, language, and audience [1982, p. 221].

For more than half a century Rhine was the undisputed leader of the field. He gave it its concepts and methods, defined its scope, mapped out its territory and helped to create the instrumentalities necessary for its professionalization—including the establishment of the *Journal of Parapsychology* in 1937 and twenty years later the formation of the Parapsychological Association. The history of parapsychology, to quote Mackenzie again, "is the history of the work and the influence of one individual" (1982, p. 231). The present author personally knew and worked with J.B. Rhine and his wife Louisa for a quarter of a century and had the privilege of heading his Institute for Parapsychology for two decades.

Rhine had a comprehensive view of the field and a *Weltanschauung* that governed his research. Some have labeled it as Rhinean paradigm (Nilsson, 1975). Rhine's worldview is Cartesian, a kind of dualistic interactionism. Inasmuch as psi phenomena are unconstrained by time/space variables and are known to be unrelated to our sensory or motor functions, they suggest the existence of a nonphysical mind which can exchange energy and interact with a physical body. Again, as an essential characteristic of a mind, psi is normal and is present in all humans and possibly even in animals. There is nothing supernatural about the mind or psi and therefore they can be studied scientifically. Rhine did not see any conflict between his concept of science as one involving the use of truly objective methods and the basic assumption underlying his worldview that distinguished between nonphysical mind and physical body.

Though his basic commitment was to the experimental method and quantitative research, Rhine did not discredit or reject qualitative studies of psi as manifesting in real life situations. He acknowledged the importance of spontaneous case studies as a rich source for generating hypotheses that could be experimentally verified. He therefore encouraged his wife Louisa Rhine, who like him had her training and background in biological science and shared his unswerving allegiance to experimental method, as she carried out extensive and highly influential case studies. Rhinean tradition, if not their paradigm, continued to influence psi research for several decades after them.

Rhine was of course not alone. He was aided by a group of committed and competent researchers at Duke University. These include Charles Stuart, Betty Humphrey and J.G. Pratt. As Rhine's work received national and international attention, the attempts to replicate his work were undertaken by a number of researchers in other places. Some of these were successful and some were not. When Rhine retired from Duke in 1965, parapsychology moved out of the Duke campus to be housed at the Foundation for Research on the Nature of Man (FRNM), which Rhine established to find a permanent home for parapsychology. The FRNM was later renamed the Rhine Research Center (RRC). The struggle to gain academic approval for research in this area and to establish parapsychology as a scientific discipline continued until Rhine's death in 1980. Rhine died as a man with unfinished business and unsure whether his many decades of solid effort to do science with psychic phenomena would succeed as he had hoped when he started this long journey on the frontiers of human science. The controversy over whether parapsychology is a science continues. The place of psychic research in academia remains uncertain. Notwithstanding the widespread public interest and belief in paranormal phenomena, financial support for scientific investigations in the field is sparse and sporadic. The RRC itself is fighting for its survival.

Whether parapsychology is a science depends as much on what we mean by science as it does on the subject matter of this unusual science. Parapsychologists collect data as other scientists do. The problem is that the data they seek appear to question the very assumptive base of science as it is understood today. The unconventionality of the conclusions generally drawn from the data has led to different descriptions and assessments of the field. Parapsychology is variously described as a frontier science (Rhine and Pratt, 1957), protoscience (Truzzi, 1980), elusive science (Mauskopf and McVaugh, 1980), anomalous science, parascience, deviant science (McClenon, 1981), pathological science (Hyman, 1980), pseudoscience (Alcock, 1981) and so on. It is probably all of these; for in many ways it is unusual and bizarre. Its most unusual feature is that it claims to be a science and pledges its unswerving adherence to scientific method; and yet as pointed out by Brian and Lynne (1980), it "constitutes an attack not merely on present scientific theories, but on the conviction of the accessibility of the world of human reason, and thereby on the potential of reason and science themselves" (p. 134). Such historically perceived incompatibility between science and psychic phenomena is what gives many a distorted and often incomprehensible picture of this field and results in the plethora of diverse descriptions of parapsychology.

This unreserved commitment to objectivity and scientific method in exploring psychic abilities for over one hundred years, culminating in the Rhines' research at Duke, marks more than a beginning and birth of a new science. The data accumulated and the controversies that ensued have posed a challenge to science itself, its methods and limits.

2

Concepts and Methods

As we have seen in the previous chapter, the history of parapsychology is as long as, if not longer than, that of academic psychology. However, unlike psychology, its progress has been sporadic and halting with few centers carrying out sustained research. The sporadic and unsustained nature of the work, notwithstanding the Rhines' determined efforts, resulted in a lack of coherent conceptual framework, and repeated attempts to reinvent the wheel, as it were, from different perspectives at different times in different places. Despite the widespread conceptual confusions and the consequent ambiguities characterizing what parapsychology really is, even among those who wrote on the subject, there is a general consensus among those involved in psi research on the broad contours of the field and the methodological requirements to scientifically investigate psychic phenomena.

Subject Matter

The immediate antecedents of psychical research are the widely popular spiritualist movements, the mediumistic phenomena and the establishment of societies for psychical research in England and the United States. Parapsychology itself, however, sprouted out of the seeds of the experiences people reported throughout the world. J.B. Rhine, with his small contingent of workers, attempted to systematically cultivate them in the field he called parapsychology, a term adapted from the German word *Parapsychologie*. He preferred "parapsychology" to others in vogue at the time such as psychical research (British) and *métapsychique* (French) because he thought that "parapsychology" was less ambiguous than the others and conveyed the spirit of science. It might simply be, however, that Rhine needed a new term that suited his agenda and the assumptions that governed his research. As noted previously, Rhine began with a comprehensive worldview, a *Weltanschauung*, that was to govern the so-called Rhinean paradigm.

It is Rhine's contention that parapsychological phenomena are first of all natural events; therefore, their study belongs to natural science. The rules that govern the investigation of parapsychological phenomena are necessarily the same as those that govern other natural sciences. In other words, their observations and experiments must strictly adhere to the established norms of scientific (method) inquiry. What comes out of these investigations is then as much a natural law as the organized knowledge in other areas of science.

Second, all parapsychological phenomena manifest among living organisms; more precisely, among "behaving" organisms. Therefore, parapsychology belongs to the realm of biological sciences in general and to psychology in particular. Rhine goes further to argue that the association with psychology suggests that parapsychology is "concerned with persons, personality, or personal agency within the living world" (Rhine and Pratt, 1957). It would seem that Rhine was inclined to favor some kind of vitalism, a kind of mental force behind psychic abilities.

Third, what marks off parapsychology from psychology, according to Rhine, is that the former deals with "nonphysical" phenomena. Rhine appears to have assumed that the phenomena which parapsychology investigates are manifestly of nonphysical character, because the methods that are designed to study them rule out at the outset all physical explanations. While recognizing the fact that parapsychological phenomena involve physical events or objects either as stimuli or effects, he argued that "*a completely physical interpretation of them is manifestly inadequate*" (Rhine and Pratt, 1957, p. 6). By definition, for Rhine, a parapsychological event is one which is not mediated by physical energy; it refers to awareness beyond the ranges of the senses and reasoning abilities and to action that involves no known energy source.

So, according to the father of the field, parapsychology is "the branch of inquiry which deals with nonphysical personal operations or phenomena" (Rhine and Pratt, 1957, p. 7). At the same time, it is assumed, (a) parapsychological events/experiences are natural phenomena; (b) they are subject to natural laws; and (c) they may be investigated by methods of observation and experiment as in other natural sciences. The manifest paradox, the conflict between the two assertions—psychic phenomena are nonphysical and at the same time subject to natural laws—continues to fuel the controversy whether parapsychology is a science.

Parapsychological phenomena clearly constitute a distinct class of cases in which psychologically meaningful exchange of information between living organisms and their environment takes place. Such an exchange appears somehow to exceed the capacities of our sensory and motor systems, as they are presently understood. These experiences have one thing in common: they are marvels in that we know not how they occur and how we may explain them in terms of normal causes. Commonsense conceptions of cause-effect relationship between stimulus and response no longer appear to hold since the connecting links in the causal chain are missing. Thus, they represent a set of anomalous interactions. Beyond this, any assertion that they are nonphysical and yet subject to natural laws goes well beyond all available evidence. It is merely an assumption.

Such an assumption, however, has far reaching implications for parapsychological research. First, it espouses the notion that nature has a nonphysical component and that it can be studied by employing the same methods that are used to study the physical aspects of nature. These assumptions are not necessarily shared even by those involved in the study of these phenomena. One may accept that parapsychological phenomena are indeed nonphysical; but question if they could be studied by naturalistic methods of observation and experiment or vice versa. To bifurcate nature into physical and nonphysical is as radical a postulate as the mind-body divide in Cartesian dualism. If parapsychological phenomena are indeed nonphysical effects, as Rhine repeatedly asserted, how are they mediated to manifest as observable and measurable physical events? If parapsychological events are observable/measurable in terms of physical parameters, what makes them truly nonphysical phenomena? These are vexatious questions, and they have no easy answers.

Therefore, a more prudent and theory-neutral way, it would seem, is simply to treat them as anomalous phenomena; phenomena that are inexplicable within the framework of principles accepted by science in general. Such anomalies are regarded by some as *paranormal*. The British philosopher C.D. Broad (1953), for example, defined psychical research (the earlier name for parapsychology) as the "scientific investigation of ostensibly paranormal phenomena" (Broad, 1962, p. 3); i.e., phenomena that seem prima facie to conflict with one or more of the "basic limiting principles" (BLPs). For Broad, BLPs are a fundamental set of assumptions that "we unhesitatingly take for granted as the framework within which all our practical activities and our scientific theories are confined" (Broad, 1953, p. 7). Broad (1962) has stated that parapsychological phenomena conflict with the following four "basic limiting principles" of science: (a) a person cannot have knowledge of the thoughts and experiences of another person that is not based on normal sensory perception or inferences therefrom (this principle would be violated by telepathy); (b) a person cannot have knowledge of a future event that is not based on inference from past events (which would rule out precognition); (c) a person cannot directly modify by volition the state of motion of any object other than parts of his or her own body (which would rule out psychokinesis); and (d) upon the death of the physical body, a person's consciousness either ceases or is unable to manifest itself in any way to those still living (which is ostensibly violated by the evidence suggestive of the survival of human personality after death). According to Broad, parapsychology's task is "to investigate ostensibly paranormal phenomena, with a view to discovering whether they are or not genuinely paranormal phenomena" (Broad, 1962, p. 5).

Some parapsychologists have problems with linking parapsychology with the paranormal. H.J. Irwin, for example, writes in his popular textbook on parapsychology: "The common notion of parapsychology as the study of the paranormal is not embraced in this book. Rather, parapsychology is here defined as the study of experiences having the appearance of being in principle outside the realm of human capabilities as conceived by conventional scientists" (1999, pp. 3–4). It is difficult to see how Irwin's definition of parapsychology is different from Broad's in any significant way. What Broad regards as ostensibly paranormal implies no more than "the appearance of being in principle outside the realm of human capabilities as conceived by conventional scientists." If Broad's definition of parapsychology is negative, so is the one proposed by Irwin.

The real problem here is not definitional. Rather it is inherent in the very paradox of "naturalizing the supernatural." The basic limiting principles are derived from the assumptive base of science. Putative paranormal phenomena, if genuine, would at once demolish that base. Therefore, there is little room for conceptual maneuver or escape. If parapsychological phenomena are genuine and real, the current assumptions of science would be wrong. They need to be abandoned, suitably revised or qualified to acknowledge their limited application. If on the contrary the assumptive base is solid and sound to cover all areas and aspects of science, the ostensibly paranormal phenomena would have a normal explanation. They would then be considered spurious. So long as the evidence for the existence of parapsychological phenomena is non-conclusive, they may be referred to as ostensibly paranormal. For one who considers the evidence conclusive they are paranormal. For Rhine and many others involved in parapsychological research, some of the parapsychological phenomena like ESP are real because the evidence for their existence is compelling. Inasmuch as they are real, parapsychological phenomena are paranormal, which meant to Rhine that they are nonphysical. Non-physicality believed to be inherent in parapsychological phenomena does not negate the physical properties and characteristics of the universe. Rather, it points to another dimension of existence. In this view, physical science is not wrong, it is incomplete. Again, Rhine recognized the relativity of the terms "physical" and "nonphysical." By physical he meant the physics of his day.

The contrarian view is that there is error somewhere in the evidence cited, even though we may not know at present where the error lies. Research should aim at discovering the sources of error that give the appearance of paranormal to the phenomena that are in reality quite normal. The only reasonable alternative to the paranormal hypothesis in this view is the "error somewhere" hypothesis. If the parapsychological data are genuine and error free, the phenomena they refer to are not only real, but they are also paranormal in that they violate the basic limiting principles derived from the assumptive base of science. The parapsychological research methods are designed with the express purpose of excluding all normal explanations.

Irwin argues that "the task of the parapsychologist is not the study of negatively defined underlying paranormal factors, but rather it is deemed to entail a systematic exploration of various possible bases and characteristics of experiential studies." One could hardly have any quarrel with this statement when it is limited to the "experiential reports." If we go beyond them to well-designed and executed experimental studies, which by their very nature control for normal explanations, we have no choice but to choose between the paranormal hypothesis and the "error somewhere" hypothesis. Parapsychology over a century of effort has accumulated a large database. If the data lead to a conviction of the reality of the phenomena involved, the next step would be to explore the underlying paranormal factors. In the absence of such a conviction, it is entirely reasonable to look for possible errors in published data. Rhine believed in the veracity of the data and the genuineness of the phenomena. Therefore, he attempted to formulate a program of research to discover the underlying paranormal factors, which he assumed to stem from the nonphysical aspects of nature.

What is interesting here is that both Rhine and those who oppose the prima facie paranormality of parapsychological phenomena believe that scientific inquiry comprising of experiments and third-person observations would ultimately reveal the underlying factors, whether normal or paranormal, that explain the phenomena parapsychologists investigate. The expectation is justified that, if there is error somewhere, it would be identified sooner or later by further observations and experiments designed to discover them. However, it is not obvious that any of the paranormal aspects of parapsychological phenomena would be revealed by future experiments. The possibility exists that the experimental methods and third-person accounts so eminently suited to study physical sciences may be simply inadequate and inappropriate to investigate the paranormal/non-physical aspects of nature. It would seem that Rhine himself became increasingly aware of the possibility that the research methods he so meticulously developed and assiduously applied in his work might have a very limited value and might be inadequate to understand the true nature of the phenomena he was investigating. Therefore, in his later years he spoke of the need for developing what he called "psi methodologies" (Rhine, 1975b) that go beyond the physical methods he espoused earlier. Unfortunately, Rhine himself, so steeped in behaviorist methodology, was unclear about the new methodology needed for parapsychological research.

At this point, if we take the position advocated by the Parapsychological Association (PA), the U.S.–based international professional society of parapsychologists, as the official version, the understanding of what parapsychology stands for is clearly ambiguous. According to PA's preferred definition, parapsychology is the study of "apparent anomalies of behavior and experience that exist apart from currently known explanatory mechanisms that account for organism–environment and organism–organism information and influence flow" (Parapsychological Association, 1989, pp. 394–395). This definition is more a compromise for accommodating the diverse perceptions of the field rather than a forthright statement of what parapsychology is really about.

Parapsychology, Paranormal Psychology and Anomalistic Psychology

The implied ambiguity in the perception of parapsychology as a field of study has led to a proliferation of other terms such as paranormal psychology and anomalistic psychology, which also did not catch on as viable substitutes. Paranormal psychology and anomalistic psychology may be seen as the extreme ends of the belief continuum relating to psychological observations that do not readily fit into conventional conceptual categories in science. At one end is the belief that these observations are anomalous in the sense that we are currently ignorant of their causes, which, it is hoped, will be revealed eventually in a manner consistent with the basic assumptions we make in science. This is the position that anomalistic psychology takes. At the other end is the conviction that these phenomena by their very nature do not fit *in principle* with the basic assumptions that govern normal psychology and, therefore, call for a radically new set of assumptions. This is the posture that paranormal psychology takes. Parapsychology may be seen as occupying the middle ground espousing theoretical neutrality, leaving open the possibility that the phenomena it investigates might be just anomalies that would be shown in time to have natural explanations or that they might lead us to discover new principles and factors that are genuinely paranormal. It is possible then that some parapsychologists may be actually anomalists in as much as their research focuses essentially on discovering possible sources of error in experiments purporting to provide psi and finding convincing normal psychological explanations to alleged parapsychological phenomena. Following the above categorization, it is more appropriate to label them as anomalist psychologists rather than parapsychologists. In a similar vein, we can argue that those parapsychologists who believe that the phenomena they are investigating are genuinely paranormal may be labeled more appropriately as paranormal psychologists.

Parapsychology, as mentioned, makes a systematic study of psychic experiences and experimental data relating to them. It does not make any theoretical commitment that they are genuinely paranormal, therefore requiring a set of new assumptions and postulates that are not hitherto considered necessary to explain human interactions. In contrast, paranormal psychology investigates all types of human functioning that seem to require the postulation of a new set of principles and postulates distinct from those in mainstream science. It is broader than the study of psychic phenomena. The unitary sense of personal identity, the integration of the visual field, and even the bare fact of awareness itself may require the postulation of the existence of a mental realm separate from the physical brain, which is clearly inconsistent with the basic principles of current mainstream psychology. Paranormal psychology deals with all kinds of psychological phenomena, whether considered anomalous or normal, that require the postulation of principles and factors that are not conventionally accepted by behavioral scientists. Parapsychology, however, is concerned with cognitive anomalies, which at this time define its scope and substance. Under cognitive anomalies we include ESP as well as PK.

Paranormal psychology is broader in scope than psychology, whereas parapsychology is narrower. Genius, creativity, scientific intuition and similar phenomena may or may not involve parapsychological phenomena. Yet, if they should require the postulation of a mind separate from the brain as an explanatory principle, then they become legitimate subject matter of paranormal psychology. However, inasmuch as psychic phenomena appear to manifest characteristics that cannot be parsimoniously explained within the confines of sensory-motor processes, they become the central focus for paranormal psychology. Whereas psychology attempts to explain human nature without making the distinction between mind and body as two qualitatively different processes, paranormal psychology tends to involve dualistic assumptions.

Leonard Zusne, in his book *Anomalistic Psychology*, regards parapsychology as a part of anomalistic psychology, which includes among its topics the study of occult and other phenomena with which parapsychology is not concerned. Zusne (1982) mentions two kinds of anomalistic phenomena (1) "psychological phenomena that do not fit the current scientific world view" and (2) "paranormal phenomena of other kinds that at least in part can be explained in terms of known psychological phenomena." This distinction is not very helpful because the second category is hardly anomalous if the phenomena can be accounted for in naturalistic terms.

The distinction between parapsychology and anomalistic psychology Zusne makes is similar to the one made between parapsychology and paranormal psychology. Parapsychology, unlike paranormal psychology and anomalistic psychology, does not, as mentioned, make any theoretical commitment whether psi is genuinely paranormal phenomena. While paranormal psychology makes a priori assumption that if parapsychological phenomena are real, they are ipso facto paranormal. Anomalistic psychology assumes that there can be no paranormal phenomena and that all purported evidence for psychic phenomena would have natural explanations in terms of known principles and laws. The latter implies that phenomena that now appear anomalous are truly not anomalous. This leads the anomalistic psychologists to search for "normal" explanations such as cheating, loopholes in experimental conditions, errors in data analysis and other fallacies and foibles in parapsychological research. In short, anomalistic psychology is a convenient skeptical phrase adopted by psychologists who work within the framework of physical determinism to discredit anomalous phenomena that appear inconsistent with deterministic assumptions.

As mentioned, parapsychologists as a professional group are unwilling to commit themselves to view parapsychological phenomena as paranormal. However, it is not difficult to see that, if these phenomena are real and that the best of these experiments are artifact-free, they are indeed more than genuine anomalies, i.e., phenomena that at once question the assumptive base of science as understood now. Science, which accepts the reality of such phenomena as telepathy would be different indeed, calling for a completely different worldview. Unwilling to face up to this challenge, parapsychologists as well as their detractors are content with characterizing the occurrence of parapsychological events as anomalies, which would be ultimately incorporated into science either as a troublesome artifact or as genuine phenomena in a nonmechanistic universe.

As the battle goes on, we continue to see parapsychology as a theory-neutral discipline concerned with cognitive anomalies attempting to unearth empirical facts. If the battle is decisively won by anomalistic psychologists, then there will be no parapsychology, except as a remnant of history. Yet, paranormal psychology might persist, holding on to a theoretical position in search of supporting facts. If, however, anomalistic psychology loses in this context, it would seem paranormal psychology would gain enormously and parapsychology would become a part of paranormal psychology (or whatever name by which it might be known by then).

The mind-body problem is a perennial philosophical question, which has defied an empirical solution so far. Neither the extraordinary success of physical sciences nor the incisive, logical and linguistic analysis of the problem has helped to dissolve or eradicate it. Both commonsense and moral experience revolt against the thought that humans are merely biophysical machines and that their minds are identical with their brains. The orthodox scientific approach sees it as exceedingly unlikely that minds have independent existence and that they involve principles and processes not causally dependent on physical events. At the same time, scientific knowledge has not reached a stage where one can confidently assert that every mental event has a corresponding state in the brain. J.B. Rhine (1947) discussed the psychocentric and cerebrocentric viewpoints in his *Reach of the Mind* in a chapter titled "The Central Question about Man."

The assumption that there is a perfect correlation between one's experiences and the events in the brain and central nervous system has not been empirically established. Even if such a correlation is found to exist, it does not logically follow that one could be reduced to the other. Consequently the mind-body problem will persist. If, however, parapsychological phenomena are considered genuine and real, then, there would be a shift likely in favor of a dualistic position. Hence, some, like the Edinburgh psychologist John Beloff, have argued that parapsychology is the "ultimate battle ground on which the mind-body controversy must be fought out" (Beloff, 1962, p. 229). This statement was made two generations ago; but there does not seem to be a victor in sight. Normal science goes on as if there are no compelling behavioral anomalies. Parapsychologists continue to struggle to make a case for themselves with the huge database they have laboriously accumulated over a century of effort.

Conceptual Confusions and Consequent Controversies

Psychical researchers have used a variety of concepts to refer to the cognitive anomalies that constitute the subject matter of parapsychology. These concepts are often loaded with assumptions concerning the nature of the phenomena they denote, assumptions that go well beyond the available evidence. This state of affairs has led to some avoidable confusion and controversies. Setting aside the esoteric concepts in vogue before the advent of laboratory based investigations, we find "extrasensory perception" (ESP) as possibly the most widely used and known concept. J.B. Rhine titled his groundbreaking monograph *Extrasensory Perception*, first published in 1934, and ESP has since become a household word in the English speaking world. However, there are attempts during more recent years to replace it with other teens that are ostensibly less theory-loaded, such as anomalous cognition (May and Marwaha, 2014). I find them no less theory ridden. This book *Anomalous Cognition* has the subheading "Remote Viewing Research and Theory." Again, two of the projected volumes by May and Marwaha begin with the title *Extrasensory Perception*.

Extrasensory perception refers to awareness of objects and events shielded from the senses as well as direct awareness of others' thoughts in the absence of any sense mediated information. Rhine argued that in ESP we have awareness which is perceptual but not sensory. It is arguable, however, if one could have perceptual awareness devoid of sensory content. Nonsensory perception may be seen as a contradiction in terms because perception essentially involves processing of sensory inputs.

Those who saw the inherent contradiction in the concept of ESP called for a new term. For example, philosopher C.D. Broad (1953) preferred paranormal cognition to ESP. Several British psychical researchers like G.N.M. Tyrrell (1946a) also used the term paranormal cognition in their writings. Again, this term is not without its share of problems. First, it assumes that the so-called cognitive anomalies are indeed cognitions; and second, they are paranormal, which implies, as we have seen, a call for new postulates and principles, qualitatively different from those currently accepted by science in general.

Recognizing the need for theory-neutral terms, R.H. Thouless and Weisner introduced the term psi, represented by the Greek letter "Ψ." Psi is broader than ESP and includes anomalous physical effects attributed to the direct action of mind over matter. Thouless and Weisner (1947) write: "In order to avoid the misleading implications of such terms, we have preferred to adopt the symbol 'Ψ' which, to begin with, has no implications except that all that it is used to cover are supposed to be processes not essentially different from one another" (p. 179). Psi phenomena refer to telepathy, clairvoyance and precognition as well as the effects of mind over matter. Thouless and Weisner insist that all these are not different processes, but are essentially the same. Under psi they thus include ESP and psychokinesis (PK): PK is regarded as the motor aspect of psi, while ESP is its cognitive counterpart. Psi-gamma refers to the cognitive processes of psi, while psi-kappa refers to the motor processes of psi. The term "psi" proved to be less controversial. Rhine accepted it; and it is now used widely in parapsychological writings. However, psi did not replace ESP, which is still seen as a subcategory of psi. Suggested subcategories psi-gamma and psi-kappa are little used.

There are other concepts that are employed in place of ESP, but their use is more or less limited to specialized areas. For example, Russell Targ and Hal Puthoff (1977) gave currency to the term remote viewing. The use of this term is restricted by and large to a specific procedure for testing ESP. Robert Jahn and Brenda Dunne (1980), who carried out studies similar to those of Targ and Puthoff, term the phenomena remote perception rather than remote viewing.

Rhine's use of ESP includes telepathy, clairvoyance and precognition. Telepathy is nonsensory awareness of thoughts, feelings or activity of other beings. Clairvoyance refers to nonsensory awareness of objects or physical events. The term general extrasensory perception (GESP) refers to an ambiguous situation, which permits the possibility of ESP of thoughts (telepathy) as well as of objects (clairvoyance). ESP may be time displaced. When nonsensory awareness relates to a future thought or event, it is called precognition. It is retrocognition when the information relates to a past event.

Psychokinesis (PK) is defined as the direct influence of mind on a physical system that cannot be accounted for by the intervention of any known physical source of energy. In the early literature telekinesis was used to refer to such unexplainable physical effects. There are other esoteric terms such as teleportation and levitation which are believed to involve a kind of PK.

Myers (1903), who was among the first to use the term telepathy, defined it as "the communication of impressions of any kind from one mind to another, independently of the recognized channels of sense." This definition has become conventional and has met with general acceptance. However, the term telepathy is not immune to adverse criticism. Schiller for instance, argues that this definition of telepathy is essentially negativistic, as it tells us nothing about the nature of telepathy. He further points out that Myers' definition of telepathy fails to suggest the difference of relation between the well established fact of hyperaesthesia and telepathy. Antony Flew (1953), a logical positivist, also argues against the adequacy of the term telepathy. Firstly, it leads us to think that telepathy is a process analogous to the process of wireless transmission, an idea which has little favor among the investigators in this field. Secondly, this term has encouraged controversies as to whether success in a particular experiment is produced by telepathy or clairvoyance. These controversies made the term, he says, "inordinately tortuous and intricate."

Clairvoyance is usually defined as the perception of distant/remote objects/(events) without the aid of the recognized senses. The definition suggests that this faculty is an extension of vision. But clairvoyant perception is not necessarily visual, it may be tactual or auditory. Myers, seemingly aware of this difficulty coined another term teleaesthesia. Rhine (1934) criticizes this term on the ground that it assumes an unknown receptive system, a sense. Whatever unwarranted implications these terms may suggest and however foreign their applicable connotations may be to their actual meaning, telepathy and clairvoyance have come to stay with distinctive connotations.

There are, however, continuing controversies whether the outcome of a given parapsychological experiment is evidence of telepathy or clairvoyance, which suggests that this demarcation is somewhat porous. An interesting controversy ensued with the publication of an article entitled "Telepathy and Clairvoyance Reconsidered" by Rhine (1945a) in the *Journal of Parapsychology*. Rhine maintained that there is no adequate evidence for the occurrence of ESP if clairvoyance is excluded, while there is adequate evidence for the occurrence of ESP when telepathy is excluded. He argued in this article that pure clairvoyance had been established. He considered Tyrrell's experiments with an electrically operated ESP test machine as providing conclusive evidence for it. This apparatus, in his judgment, excludes any possibility of telepathy, since the recording and selection of targets are done mechanically without the conscious knowledge of the experimenter or the subject.

Since the publication of Rhine's article, Gertrude Schmeidler (1964) carried out computer based ESP tests considered to provide evidence for clairvoyance that cannot be attributed to any form of telepathy. Examining the evidence for pure telepathy, Rhine considers the experiments of Soal and Goldney as not providing sufficient evidence for precognitive telepathy. He says that the results of these experiments may be suggestive but not conclusive. The main reason for regarding them as evidence for precognitive telepathy, according Soal and Goldney, is that the success of the experiments varied with the agents. The experimenters claimed that their percipients can score successfully with particular agents only. Rhine says that this fact is not sufficient to show that precognitive telepathy is operating in these experiments in view of the findings of Schmeidler. Schmeidler showed that the belief in the occurrence of telepathy or clairvoyance has a great effect on the rate of scoring.

The subjects of Soal and Goldney, convinced of the reality of telepathy alone, could have inhibited the rate of scoring, when the conditions did not conform to their beliefs or preferences. But Soal claimed that the percipients did exactly the same way even when they are not aware of the persons who are acting as agents. Against this Rhine argues that since there is the possibility of the subjects' being aware of the agent through the faculty of ESP their experiment at best may suggest precognitive telepathy, but does not prove it. Rhine goes on to say that so far no experiments have been successfully carried out to prove pure telepathy or precognitive telepathy. He concludes: "As a matter of fact, I have the same degree of personal bias towards telepathy that most students of parapsychology seem to have. But this situation must be frankly faced: there is at the moment no adequately reliable case for telepathy" (Rhine, 1945a). It may be noted parenthetically that Soal's experiments have since been discarded.

Whately Carington (1946), commenting on Rhine's paper, argued that it is inherently impossible to distinguish between telepathy and clairvoyance. He says that all that we know is the ordered sequence of "cognized cognizables." If the cognitive process is effected by the associative mechanism involving another mind or minds, it is telepathy; and if it is effected not by any other mind, but directly, it is clairvoyance. So Carington believes that to discuss whether telepathy can be explained by clairvoyance or clairvoyance by telepathy is a waste of one's time. Telepathy and clairvoyance are not two rival hypotheses, but closely related modes of the same phenomena.

According to Thouless (1946), the whole confusion is due to the use of the terms telepathy, clairvoyance and precognitive telepathy, etc. It is better to discard these terms and regard these phenomena as the conditions under which psi cognitions occur. This, he contends, will give rise to a great simplification of the perplexing issues.

Tyrrell (1946a) and Hettinger (1946) deplored that Rhine did not take into consideration the valuable data of spontaneous cases. Hettinger argued that the qualitative experiments, which he had carried out, provide strong evidence for the occurrence of pure telepathy. Tyrrell also emphatically asserts that spontaneous cases of telepathy cannot be explained by clairvoyance. When the percipient reads out a record, running through several words with astounding accuracy, it is absurd to regard this as a manifestation of precognitive clairvoyance. If precognition of such a quality exists, he asks why do the mediums or the percipients not unfold the mystery of the future? He opines that card guessing is a very limited field of investigation. "Professor Rhine," writes Tyrrell (1946a), "has blinded himself to the facts by considering only card-guessing. He has actually been led by his self-imposed blindness to put forward a general hypothesis, which is contradicted by a large part of the evidence."

Elsewhere, Tyrrell (1947a) gives the following reasons to show that precognitive clairvoyance cannot explain the spontaneous, ostensible telepathy. If Rhine applies himself to explain cases of spontaneous telepathy by clairvoyance, precognition or retrocognition, he has to explain how the supposed clairvoyant faculty is guided to reach that object. Tyrrell thinks that only by invoking telepathy can we explain the process by which the clairvoyant faculty is directed. Numerous things of equal interest are simultaneously happening in different places; still, clairvoyant perception alone gives us the knowledge of the desired situation. How is this particular thing alone clairvoyantly perceived and not others? There must be a sort of *rapport*, and this *rapport* could be conveyed only by telepathy. Tyrrell alleges that Rhine fails to notice this, because he refused to recognize the evidence of spontaneous cases.

Concluding the discussion on Rhine's paper "Telepathy and Clairvoyance Reconsidered," Broad (1946) says that though Rhine's arguments have a logical possibility, the facts do not warrant such a view. He agrees with Rhine in saying that Tyrrell's experiments do not need telepathic conditions for significant success. But, he disagrees with Rhine as regards the Soal-Goldney experiments. He says that telepathic conditions were necessary for a significant success in Soal-Goldney experiments. Finally, assessing the significance of Rhine's paper, Broad suggests that the paper underlines a "praiseworthy desire to stimulate experimenters to devise experiments in which telepathic conditions are present and clairvoyant conditions completely absent, in order to find out whether paranormal cognition can then take place."

The curious thing is that all the participants in this discussion are inclined to agree on the fundamental issues. They believe that telepathy and clairvoyance hypotheses do not oppose each other and are not mutually exclusive. They agree that clairvoyance and telepathy are the conditions under which an unknown ability operates. The nature of this unknown ability is vague. The only problem that has perplexed them is whether such a faculty could operate if either of these conditions is totally absent. Rhine argues that it is proved that such a faculty operates when the telepathic conditions are totally absent, and it is not established that such a faculty operates when the clairvoyant conditions are completely absent. Hettinger (1946) says that our insight into the nature of these phenomena is not adequate and as such to exclude one in favor of the other is premature. Carington (1946) is of the view that the relevant experimental conditions do not admit of any distinction between telepathy and clairvoyance. Tyrrell (1946b), vehemently opposing Rhine, says that there is evidence to show that telepathy occurs even when the clairvoyant conditions are absent. It would seem that the difference of opinion is the result of their respective theoretical commitments and a solution to the muddle, as Thouless (1946) suggests, is the use of theory neutral concepts.

A similar controversy, but possibly of far greater significance, is that of whether ESP and PK are distinct abilities, as is often assumed. As in the case of telepathy and clairvoyance, a degree of overlap between ESP and PK is apparent when a given psi effect could be classified either as ESP or PK. This has led some to attempt to reduce one to the other, while some others proposed that ESP and PK constitute a psi-continuum. William Roll (1961) made a somewhat radical suggestion that ostensible cases of precognition might just be instances of PK. He argued that what is cognized as a precognitive event could in principle be a PK effect caused by the subject in a number of possible ways, including biasing target generation in precognitive trials by means of PK. Ed May and colleagues advocated for a contrary view. They argued (1995) in their decision augmentation theory (DAT) that PK effects like those obtained in micro–PK experiments involving random event generators may be instances of ESP. They suggest that the subject could scan for information about the target outcomes by means of ESP and do the things such as pressing the button to start a PK trial at the appropriate moment so that the generated targets match the subject's intention. In PK experiments, the DAT "suggests that rather than mind influencing some target system an array of precognition-mediated decisions by the experimenter and/or participant are made to mimic PK" (May 2015, p. 208). This view is not very different from the one suggested by L.E. Rhine. Spontaneous PK efforts she thought "could be the bearers of messages concerning events beyond the range of the senses" (1981, p. 84). However, some spontaneous cases of PK in her own collection defy that they are merely precognitive events. For example, if a clock suddenly stops for no normal reason, at the very moment of death of its owner, it is difficult to interpret it as a precognitive event.

Lance Storm and Michael Thalbourne (2000) raised some basic objections to the assumed ESP-PK dichotomy and argued in their theory of psychopraxia that psi is a single process and that the dichotomy is untenable. They review supporting evidence from 12 major meta-analyses, which, they contend, support the notion of a single psi process.

J.B. Rhine was led increasingly to the view that psi may be a unitary ability and the distinctions such as clairvoyance, telepathy, precognition and psychokinesis are convenient expressions. Rhine and Pratt wrote: "As the science of parapsychology has advanced, the basic similarity of the processes of telepathy and clairvoyance has become more and more apparent. It now seems doubtful whether there are two different processes after all" (1957, p. 9). As we have seen, it is even more doubtful now that the conceptually differentiated types are truly distinct. It would seem that these types may be seen as conditions under which psi manifests. For example, telepathy is psi awareness of thoughts and clairvoyance is that of objects. In other words, in one case the target is thought and in the other it is a physical object. In precognition, the target is in the future. Thus, telepathy, clairvoyance and precognition may be seen as target conditions rather than as distinct processes.

The same may be said about PK as well. The original assumption that ESP is the cognitive or sensory aspect of psi and PK the motor aspect makes little sense because psi is conceived to be extrasensory and extra-motor. The more sustainable difference between ESP and PK is the assumption that in case of ESP the information flow is from the target to the subject, whereas in PK it is from the subject to the target. However, all that we know about ESP indicates that it does not involve energy patterns emanating from the target object that are processed by the subject.

Rather it is the subject who reaches out to the object. In other words, what is active here is the subject. In fact, the choice of the word "target" to denote the object of psi awareness is meaningful, because the process is not seen as stimulus impinging on the subject. It would seem that ESP is *directed at* and not *evoked by* the target. It is instructive that available evidence suggests that the active person in telepathic communications is more likely the subject (percipient) and not the agent (target person) (Rhine, L.E., 1961). Moreover, in cases of time displaced ESP, like precognition, the target at the time of ESP occurrence is simply nonexistent.

Therefore, and also in view of the theory-neutral commitment of parapsychologists, the differentiation of psi into various forms or types has little justification. ESP and PK may refer to a single process or they may involve distinctive processes. At this point there is no decisive evidence in favor of one viewpoint as opposed to the other. In the present state of our relative theoretical ignorance, it is just as well to regard the different so-called psi types as anomalies of cognition that seem to occur under different conditions.

The Paradox of Naturalizing the Supernatural

The inherent normal–paranormal dichotomy that characterizes the field of parapsychology spills over into the methods designed and used to test the subjects for psi in the laboratory. As mentioned, it was J.B. Rhine who pioneered in systematically developing a variety of measures for testing psi. He designed tests to isolate the different types of psi. He described standardized procedures to administer them. He experimented with a variety of targets, but settled for a specially designed deck of cards known as ESP cards. He had designed tests for individual testing as well as group testing, even though most of his work was with individual subjects with forced-choice targets.

There are two assumptions that underline Rhine's research methods. First, it is the belief that science has answers to all questions. Rhine and Pratt (1957) wrote, "it should be possible for science to investigate any real phenomenon, any true operation in the universe" (p. 18). "The general principle to be followed is that anything in the universe man will ever know about creates effects; and through these effects it can be indirectly studied, even if the process itself is beyond the range of the senses and even beyond reach of the instruments that so greatly extend the range of the senses" (Rhine and Pratt, 1957, p. 18). Rhine was after objective methods and research that is done in "correctly describable fashion." Objective methods are of "prior importance" because the "sound status of the facts of parapsychology" depends on them. Therefore, in the process, Rhine thought, parapsychology developed research methodology that is more rigorous than that of other branches of science and has a wider range of safeguards against error than in any other field. Few parapsychologists disagree with Rhine on this.

The second assumption is that psi is nonphysical. It is extrasensory and extra-motor, which meant that psi-testing basically involves exclusion of all physical and sensory-motor factors. This is an exercise of naturalizing the supernatural. How can supernatural be naturalized? How can we measure the immeasurable? Whatever procedure one may adopt, the process of measurement is physical and the parameters of measurement are also physical. Here then is a gap between the inherent nature of the phenomena involved and their manifest forms one measures. This is the paradox of naturalizing the supernormal, a serious methodological challenge for those who, like Rhine, work within the paranormal/nonphysical paradigm and at the same time have a complete commitment to and faith in the methodology of natural science.

The neutral posture taken by the Parapsychological Association that psi is a mere anomaly, without imputing to it any nonphysical or paranormal characteristics, it is hoped, would permit the development of a methodology that will uncover facts, even if they were inconsistent with current notion of cognition and action. The methods of psi testing developed by Rhine and further refined by others might be quite suitable for testing the limitations of physical paradigm. They, however, might prove to be inadequate to reveal the nature of the paranormal or nonphysical phenomena. The physical methods would of course be eminently appropriate if psi is not paranormal, i.e., it is explainable within the physical paradigm. In this case it would be an artifact of some sort. If, however, psi is indeed paranormal, important concerns would arise about the legitimacy of currently used experimental methods.

As mentioned, parapsychological inquiry is inspired by the so-called psychic experiences reported across cultures since the beginnings of recorded history. These experiences are viewed as "seemingly impossible." Consequently their verifiability has always been a matter of argument and the establishment of their genuineness and validity has been a daunting task. Examining and understanding the context and the sources of error, including psychic fraud, and controlling for all possible alternatives to psi have consumed a major part of the methodological effort of psi researchers.

Moving from anecdotal reports of experiences, through authenticated case studies and field investigations and finally to well-controlled laboratory based on experimental investigations and the collection and analysis of reliable data, parapsychologists have traveled far from the colorful landscape of life experiences to arid statistical data that appear to deviate significantly from chance expectations and are therefore real but make little sense except to those who are trained to infer statistical meaning from them. In the process, if a less sophisticated observer wonders whether the obtained experimental data are of the same kind as the spontaneously occurring psychic events, his concerns may not be dismissed as impertinent.

This issue is not addressed with any degree of clarity or finality. Therefore, the last word on it is yet to be spoken. The experimental efforts to employ hidden targets or covert test procedures do not quite address this matter. Time and space-displaced psi tests depend essentially on similar statistical methods of evaluation. What we need are studies in real life situations and results in terms of real life events.

Methods of Study

Case Study Methods

There is, as we noted, more to parapsychology than testing subjects in the lab with ESP cards and other test materials. Some would consider the life experiences of people as constituting the bedrock of the science of psi. As mentioned earlier, spontaneously occurring psychic events and experiences were noted throughout recorded history. According to the Hindu epic *Mahābhārata*, at the time of the war between Pāṇḍavas and Kauravas, the Kaurava King Dhritarāstra, who was blind, is said to have secured the clairvoyant abilities (*divya dṛṣṭi*) of Sanjaya to learn instantly about the happenings in the battlefield. The German philosopher Immanuel Kant recounted the story he heard about Emanuel Swedenborg, a versatile scholar and mystic.

One way of studying the occurrence of psychic phenomena in real life is archival research to collect, analyze and assess cases like the above recorded in journals, newspaper articles and published biographies. Archival research is useful to give us a general description of psychic events reported in the past. The main drawback, however, is that only a very few of the naturally occurring psychic experiences get recorded. Also, the biases of those reporting or recording them pose a problem for proper interpretation.

Survey research is somewhat an improved method over archival research. It generally uses questionnaires to elicit information about psychic experiences as well as factors associated with them. Case collections may also employ media announcements and appeals to accumulate cases for analysis. The work at the Society for Psychical Research (SPR) established in London in 1882 was the first major systematic attempt to actually collect spontaneously manifesting psychic phenomena. SPR was able to collect through public appeals, many reports of spontaneous psychic experiences. These were published and discussed in some detail in a two-volume book *Phantasms of the Living* authored by Edmund Gurney, Fredrick Myers and Frank Podmore (1886). The SPR team took several steps to authenticate the cases in their collection by examining evidence. According to these investigators, their cases provide *prima facie* evidence for the existence of telepathy, mind to mind communication. These efforts might have reduced to some extent the problem of inaccurate reporting and faulty perceptions, but the possibilities of shared inaccuracies cannot be completely eliminated by corroborative testimony. Nor can we rule out entirely unrecognized extraneous factors responsible for the apparent psychic event. Also there is the problem of sampling. Reported cases of psi experience may be selective. It is possible that people differ in their dispositions to report certain experiences. Some may exaggerate, whereas some others may shun reporting for a variety of reasons. Thus any generalizations based on the reported cases may turn out to be inaccurate and biased.

These difficulties led towards the formulation of a somewhat different policy from the SPR exercise of collecting "authentic" cases. "If the case studies are taken as merely suggestive at best and in no sense relied upon for evidential value," wrote J.B. Rhine, "they can furnish new hypotheses for the research worker that he might otherwise never obtain from any other source" (1950, p. 164). It is in this spirit that his wife, Louisa E. Rhine, studied her vast collection of spontaneous cases. When large numbers of cases are analyzed, she believed, the emerging patterns are more likely to represent the actual aspects of the cases because they are less likely to be caused by individual whims, fancies and predispositions. These suggestive aspects may be put to appropriate experimental tests with necessary controls. They thus constitute the beginning point of research.

L.E. Rhine (1961) analyzed several thousand cases systematically and found that people appear to receive information in a non-sensory manner from another person's consciousness (telepathy), from a remote object or event (clairvoyance), and from an event that has not yet happened (precognition). Some of her cases involved puzzling physical effects (PK), such as inexplicable stopping of a watch at the exact time of its owner's sudden death and unexplained physical occurrences such as poltergeist phenomena. L.E. Rhine's collection of several thousand cases is now deposited in the Duke University archives.

Ian Stevenson (1970, 1974, 1977), who began his studies of reincarnation with archival research, moved quickly to collect cases and *interview* the respondents not only to ascertain the authenticity of the cases but also to learn more about the factors associated with reincarnation. He or his associates interviewed several people involved in the cases. The interview could be a valuable method to supplement the questionnaire data. Interviews may give more qualitative information not captured by questionnaires, which are designed to be relatively free from demand characteristics and to be readily available for statistical analysis.

Spontaneous cases generally are isolated one-time occurrences. There are some, however, that are recurrent such as poltergeist phenomena and haunted houses or cases of "possessed" or "reincarnated" persons. In poltergeist cases, unusual events like flying objects, moving things or explosive noises appear to occur in the presence of certain individuals, without any observable cause. Alan Gauld and A.D. Cornell (1979) collected and analyzed about 500 haunting and poltergeist cases. Other collections of poltergeist cases include those by William Barrett (1911), A.R.G. Owen (1964) and William Roll (1970). Cases of faith healing and miraculous cures (Leuret and Bon, 1957; West, 1957) may also be included among the recurring type. Andrew Nichols (2000) reported an interesting case of poltergeist where among other things a cup filled with water flew across the kitchen a distance of eight feet. One advantage of the recurring cases is that they permit the possibility of field investigations and, on rare occasion, enable the investigators to make observations and recording of actual events as they happen.

Field Investigations

Field investigations are an important advance over survey research. They help to overcome to some extent the uncertainties about the authenticity of the cases. Also they provide an opportunity to the investigators to be in the fortunate position of being present to make detailed observations of naturally recurring events and they may even affect specific manipulations to learn more about the events. However, recurrent paranormal events are somewhat rare. Often investigators arrive at the scene after the phenomena have ceased to manifest. Also, events of this sort attract significant media attention, which complicates research efforts to collect unbiased data.

Once researchers learn of a recurrent psi event and decide to investigate it, they need to collect the background information, check the antecedent incidents for possible fraud on the part of those involved, and assess the worthwhileness of the effort to investigate the case. While exposing fraud or demystifying an event is a worthy cause by itself, the main motivation of the parapsychologist is to identify and learn from a putative psi event. Therefore, if the background information overwhelmingly suggests fraud or nonparanormal conditions responsible for the purported event, the case is likely to be of little interest to parapsychologists.

One would think that field investigations would be favored by psi researchers, because psi may be captured here in their natural settings and real life situations. Also, in some instances, the phenomena appear very spectacular and attract a lot of attention. It should be relatively easy to fund researches that attract such attention. However, the contributions of field investigations to advance parapsychology are very modest indeed. Currently, very few parapsychologists are involved in field research. The reasons for this include (a) rarity of the cases, (b) difficulties in obtaining the cooperation of the people involved, (c) obstacles in the way of controlling the conditions to allow unambiguous observations, (d) problems in focusing and identifying the agency responsible for the events, and (e) notoriety and fraud associated with some of the well-publicized cases. Also field investigations call for specialized expertise and sophistication in magic and conjuring arts that is not part of the training of the laboratory oriented scientists who are accustomed to work in situations they have themselves set up rather than in surroundings over which they have little prior control.

Notwithstanding these problems, there has been some noteworthy work by a few determined people, such as William Roll, especially in the area of poltergeist phenomena, which are labeled by him as RSPK (the recurrent spontaneous psychokinesis). The study of the Miami poltergeist (Roll and Pratt, 1971) is a model investigation that exemplifies the complexity of factors that influence research in this area. One of the suggestions that comes out of Roll's RSPK research is that it may be associated with nervous system disturbances. Examining the records of 92 focal persons centrally involved in RSPK cases, Roll (1977) noted that many of them suffered from epileptic disturbances. About one fourth of them gave evidence of dissociative states or seizures. We find interesting data on this topic in Michael Persinger's neuro-scientific investigation of anomalous cognition (2015).

As Robert Morris (1982) remarks, "spontaneous case surveys have had relatively little impact upon modern researchers, beyond suggesting useful hypotheses" (p. 16). The same may be said about field investigations as well. However, the types of psi and their categorization as ESP and PK are suggested by reported cases of psi and field phenomena. Receptive psi experiences, whether they are telepathic, clairvoyant or precognitive, constitute ESP whereas expressive effects refer to PK. We learn from the available surveys that ESP experiences are more frequently reported than PK phenomena. ESP seems to manifest more predominantly as intuitions and dream experiences. Females are more likely to be the receivers (percipients) rather than agents (target persons) in ESP communications. The motivation for receiving a telepathic impression seems to rest more with the percipient than with the agent (L.E. Rhine, 1961).

Her analyses of spontaneous cases led L.E. Rhine to believe that psi is a two-stage process (L.E. Rhine, 1965). The first stage is a nonphysical process by which psi information is acquired at the unconscious level. The second stage involves the psychological processes of projecting unconscious information into awareness. Her analyses further revealed that there are essentially four different forms in which psi information manifests itself in our awareness, which she called, following Tyrrell, mediating vehicles. They are (a) realistic dreams, (b) unrealistic dreams, (c) hallucinations, and (d) intuitions. The realistic experiences are in pictorial form and occur mostly in dreams. On rare occasions, however, someone may see something in his or her "mind's eye" that is later found to correspond to an actual event. The unrealistic experiences contain imagery that is fictitious or symbolic, and they seldom occur in combination with realistic elements. Hallucinatory ESP experiences are vivid, sensory-like experiences and occur when one is awake. These are the least frequently observed. Unlike the other forms, intuitive experiences do not involve imagery. An intuitive experience is a hunch, a sudden "just knowing" feeling. The vehicles by which psi is mediated are thus *normal, ordinary,* and *familiar* forms of mental life. *ESP has no distinctive form of its own"* (L.E. Rhine, 1961, her emphasis). The processes by which the unconscious ESP information finds its way into overt behavior is understood by Rhine to be the same as in other psychodynamic functions.

Experimental Methods

Notwithstanding the importance of naturally occurring psi in real life situations, the bulk of parapsychological research is experimental and lab oriented. Experimental research as generally recognized has several advantages over studies of spontaneous case collections and field investigations. First, unlike case studies, laboratory phenomena are observed and studied under controlled conditions, which means that the laboratory environment can be precisely designed, created and controlled by the investigator to provide answers to specific questions of interest. The variables involved may be held constant or manipulated to observe their effects. The observations themselves may be recorded in a manner to ensure their objectivity and reliability. Second, in the context of psi research, which aims at studying seemingly impossible phenomena, laboratory research would allow the investigator to rule out with some confidence the possibility of sensory leakage of information from the target to the subject. The experiment can be designed to control and eliminate nonpsi explanations of significant results, including fraud on the part of the subjects. Third, the feasibility of manipulating the variables opens up possibilities to carry out process-oriented research. Fourth, laboratory data are quantifiable. They can be recorded, measured and analyzed more thoroughly and accurately than the data from case studies. Fifth, reports of laboratory experiments can give us all the relevant details of the experimental setup so that they can be repeated and improved upon by other researchers.

It is no surprise, therefore, that scientists investigating psychic phenomena wasted no time in embarking on laboratory based investigations ever since the SPR was started. The standardization of laboratory procedures and techniques began, however, as pointed out previously, with the work at Duke University by J.B. Rhine and associates. Rhine employed ESP cards in a variety of test procedures to test individuals for their ESP ability and to distinguish between different types of ESP, viz., telepathy, clairvoyance and precognition. He described in great detail the elaborate experimental precautions required to rule out sensory communication, recording errors and deception (see Rhine and Pratt, 1957).

As noted earlier, a variety of procedures were used to test for psi in different modes. These procedures fall into two categories labeled as free-response and forced-choice tests. The early methods were generally the free-response type in which the universe of target selection is unrestricted. The subject in free-response tests has unrestricted freedom to respond. In the forced-choice tests, such as those used by J.B. Rhine and his associates, the subject responds by choosing one of the possible prespecified alternatives, such as "star," among the possible five ESP symbols. The Rhineian experimental paradigm with its emphasis on controlled and quantifiable results overshadowed for almost half a century the free-response type of tests. However, with the development of suitable and sensitive statistical techniques to evaluate free-response data, there has been in more recent years a resurgence in the use of free-response tests; and the use of free-response targets has become more common now. Many experimenters today appear to regard free-response tests as capable of eliciting rich and more meaningful responses than the card experiments. Moreover, free-response experiments appear to mimic life situations and to be better suited for administering during naturally occurring states of the mind believed to be conducive to psi. For example, remote viewing experiments are modeled after such "psychic" practices as locating missing persons and "divining" hidden or lost objects. The 59th annual convention of the Parapsychological Association (2016) had the focal theme "Accessing the Exceptional, Experiencing the Extraordinary."

In recent years, parapsychology has grown by emphasizing elements not in focus earlier. *Parapsychology: A Handbook for the 21st Century*, edited by Etzel Cardeña, John Palmer and David Marcusson-Clavertz (2015), mentions (1) experimenter psi (the experimenter may paranormally influence the outcome); (2) non-intentional psi (psi may manifest without the specific intention of participants—Global Consciousness project, pre-sentimental effect, and retroactive psi influence on psychological tasks are examples); (3) the role of physical energies such as the earth's geomagnetic field as psi mediating vehicles; (4) greater interest in psychophysiological variables affecting psi (e.g., such phenomena as direct mental influence on living systems); and (5) new statistical procedures such as meta-analyses to evaluate results of parapsychological studies.

Remote Viewing

At Stanford Research Institute, two physicists Russell Targ and Harold Puthoff successfully carried out remote viewing ESP experiments, which use free-response test procedures. The remote viewing protocol simply consists of having an experimenter (the outbound experimenter) visit a randomly selected target site and then asking the subject, who is sensorially unaware of the location, to describe to a second experimenter the place which the outbound experimenter is visiting at the time. A judge later attempts to match the subject's description to predetermined pool of target sites. The results of the Targ-Puthoff experiments were published in their book *Mind Reach* (1977). A more technical version of it may be found in Puthoff & Targ (1976). Attempts to replicate Targ-Puthoff experiments include those by J. Bisaha & B.J. Dunne (1979), Schlitz and Gruber (1980), and Robert Jahn & Brenda Dunne (1987; 2003), Subbotsky & Ryan (2009), Bierman & Rabeyron (2013).

Several of the remote viewing experiments were severely criticized with some justification. D. Marks and R. Kammann (1978, 1980) criticized the Targ-Puthoff experiments on the ground that subjects' transcripts, which were used to match with the target locations, may have contained clues relating to the order of the trials. These clues could have been helpful to the judges in successfully matching the target locations with the subjects' descriptions. Targ and Puthoff attempted to counter this criticism by conducting new judging and fresh analysis after the presumed clues were edited out (Tart, Puthoff, and Targ, 1980). Marks and Scott (1986), however, were not satisfied with the adequacy of the editing, which did not really matter because the target sequence was also randomized. In the Bisaha-Dunne experiments the judges were provided with pictures of the target location. It is argued that the pictures may have contained cues as to weather and seasonal variations that might have provided for an artificial match of the target location and the transcript (Marks, 1986). Again, some experiments by Jahn and Dunne were criticized on the grounds of nonrandom target selection (Hansel, Utts, and Markwic, 1994), but this was disputed by Dobyns, Dunne, Jahn and Nelson (1994).

In the successful transcontinental remote viewing experiment conducted by Marilyn Schlitz and Elmar Gruber (1980) the subject was in Detroit, Michigan, while the experimenter visited sites in Rome, Italy. This experiment is also not completely free from possible artifacts. In this case, the judges had access to the impressions of the agent. Like the photographs in the experiments by Bisaha and Dunne, it is suggested that they may provide cues that could bias the judge's matching. Allowing for the possibility of such artifacts, (though they consider such a possibility quite remote), Schlitz and Gruber (1981) arranged for rejudging by new judges, without providing them the agents' impressions. The results of rejudging also showed statistically significant evidence for psi. Some critics are not satisfied. Ray Hyman (1986) argued that since Gruber, who acted as the agent, was associated with the translation of the subject's transcript into English for presentation to the judges he may have biased the translation so that the judge's matching would still be successful.

The remote viewing ESP experiments, as mentioned, were first designed and carried out by Targ and Puthoff at Stanford Research Institute. They were funded for several years by U.S. government agencies. Federal government support continued for this line of research at SRI International and later (1992–94) at Science Applications International Corporation (SAIC). Edwin May and associates at SAIC conducted several ESP studies, which they prefer to call anomalous cognition experiments. These experiments are somewhat procedurally different form the original remote viewing studies and are more like traditional ESP tests with distance intervening between the targets and the subject. For example, in the study by Lantz, Luke, and May (1994) there was no sender. The main finding of this study is that free-response ESP studies can be conducted successfully without a sender in clairvoyance type of experiments.

As a member of the panel to review the Federal Government's program in remote viewing and related areas, statistician Jessica Utts reviewed the relevant work within the broad framework of contemporary psi research. Utilizing eight methodological criteria, Utts found significant evidence for the existence of psi. Ray Hyman (1996) another member of the panel, also found little to criticize in the SAIC experiments. His main concern, however, was that in these experiments, the main investigator, Ed May, served as the judge. May, however, was completely blind to the targets when he performed the judging. Therefore, it is difficult to see how he could have biased the results. Hyman prefers, however, to withhold his judgment on the significance of these results as evidence for psi because, in his view, they may contain hidden biases and subtle errors that may come to surface in due course. Thus, it would seem, as Douglas Stokes (1998) pointed out, "Hyman and other critics are starting to absolve themselves of the need to point to possible flaws in an experiment when they fail to find any. It is now evidently sufficient merely to state that there may be undetected flaws" (p. 166). Richard Wiseman and Julie Milton (1998) pointed out some possible pathways for information leakage and weakness in the conduct of some of these experiments. May (1998), however, questioned the possible leakage hypothesis of Wiseman and Milton and argued that they simply ignored contradictory evidence in their criticism of the Lantz, Luke, and May (1994) experiments.

A recent review of remote viewing studies by Baptista, Derakhshani & Tressoldi looked into nine new studies completed since February 2014. It showed that there is no sign of decline in the significance of results. This is somewhat reassuring that the ESP effects of remote viewing experiments are genuine.

ESP in Dreams

According to some estimates (L.E. Rhine 1962), 65 percent of spontaneous psychic experiences occur in . A number of psychoanalysts have reported what appear to be paranormal dreams in a therapeutic setting (Devereux, 1953). Therefore, it is only natural to consider the dream state as psi-conducive. As pointed out by Van de Castle (1977), the earliest experimental effort to influence a dream in a paranormal manner was reported by H.M. Weserman in 1819.

With the advent of dream-monitoring techniques made possible by the discovery of such physiological correlates of the dream state as rapid eye movements (REMs), the opportunity came about to study ESP dreams in laboratory settings. Montague Ullman and associates were quick to avail themselves of it. The full account of a decade-long study of ESP and dreams at the Maimonides Medical Center in Brooklyn, New York, is to be found in the book by Ullman, Krippner & Vaughan (1973). Other publications by the group include Ullman, Krippner & Feldstein (1966), Krippner (1969), Ullman & Krippner (1970), Honorton, Krippner & Ullman (1971), Krippner *et al.* (1971), Krippner, Honorton & Ullman (1972), and Krippner, Honorton & Ullman (1973). Michael Persinger and Stanley Krippner (1989) reported that in the Maimonides dream studies, the 24-hour periods in which the most accurate telepathic dreams occurred had significantly quieter geometric activity than the days before or after, suggesting that geometric activity has something to do with the manifestation of ESP.

Among the attempts to replicate the Mainmonides dream studies is the one carried out by E. Belvedere and D. Foulkes (1971) at the University of Wyoming, which did not give significant ESP results. An early review of ESP and dreams is available in a chapter by Robert Van de Castle (1977) in Wolman's *Handbook of Parapsychology.*

After a careful review of the Maimonides research carried out by Ullman and colleagues and the attempted replications of it by others, Yale psychologist Irvin Child (2001) examines incisively the manner in which the Maimonides research is represented in books written by psychologists. Pointing out numerous distortions and misrepresentations of ESP research in psychology books, Child argues that "psychologists are ill served by the apparently scholarly books that seem to convey information about the dream experiments" (p. 178). In Child's view, the Maimonides dream-ESP experiments "clearly merit careful attention from psychologists who, for whatever reason, are interested in the question of ESP" (p. 177).

There were a number of studies on ESP in dreams following Maimonides research. These were reviewed by Sherwood and Roe in 2003 and by Storm *et al.* in 2010. The results continued to be promising relating dreams with ESP.

Methods for Testing PK

In the first PK experiments, as mentioned, J.B. Rhine used rolling dice as a method to test the influence of human intentions on biasing the dice to a desired face. After nine years of intensive experimentation with dice-throwing in laboratory tests, he and his associates satisfied themselves that their experiments made a definite case for PK. In the first experiment carried out by Louisa and J.B. Rhine (1943), the subjects concentrated on obtaining "high dice" when a pair of common dice were thrown by hand or released by a semi-mechanical method. If the faces of the two dice totaled eight or above, the trial was a hit. Twelve throws of the pair completed one run, and the subject was expected to obtain an average of five hits per run. Trickery in throwing the dice was eliminated by the introduction of mechanical throwing. One significant finding of these tests was decline in scores from run to run. Among those subjects who did three or more runs in a sequence, the average scores for the first, second and last runs were 6.09, 5.15, and 5.05, showing a steady decline. Since the same dice were used in all three runs, it is difficult to maintain that the faulty dice could have produced the deviation. If the extra-chance scores in the first runs were attributable to faulty dice, it is logical to expect similar results in the last runs also. In the later experiments, more effective controls against faulty dice were introduced by using all the faces of the dice equally or randomly as targets.

Position effects have been a source of sound evidence in early PK experiments. In fact, they provide more conclusive evidence than any one single experiment conducted by Rhine and associates. It was found while re-examining the earlier PK data that the subjects seemed to succeed at the beginning of the test better than at the end and that the scoring tended to decline to the right on the page on which the trials and targets were recorded successively. In order to check on the decline tendencies involved here, Rhine and Betty M. Humphrey (1944) divided each of the record sheets into four sections with one vertical and one horizontal division. As expected, the upper left and lower right quarters showed consistent and significant differences in scoring trends. The first report by Rhine & Humphrey (1944) on the quarter distributions of the page contained an analysis of 18 available series of PK experiments. Rhine and Humphrey found with remarkable consistency from series to series that the highest scores were found in the upper left quarter and the lowest in the bottom right quarter. The combined results were found to be highly significant. Further studies of the PK data (Humphrey & Rhine 1945; Rhine 1945b; Rhine & Humphrey 1945) confirmed these effect patterns in the quarter distributions on the page. The point of interest here is that these effects were not expected when the data were collected. This rules out the possibility of unintentional errors or other known artifacts as responsible for the significant results.

Significant PK results with dice were obtained by parapsychologists working independently to replicate Duke experiments. L.A. Dale (1946) worked with 54 college students in New York. In this experiment, four commercial dice were shaken in a dice cup and thrown into the open mouth of a chute, three and one-half feet long. The dice rolled down through baffles and came to rest in the dice box. Each of the subjects was asked to throw four runs for each dice face as the target, with each run consisting of six throws. The subjects were divided into six groups of nine. The first group began throwing with face one, the second group with face two, and so on. Both the experimenter and the subject kept a complete record of all trials. The results provide significant evidence for PK. Dale also found that most of the deviation was concentrated in the top half of the first run.

In an experiment that mechanized throwing of dice and photographed the fall and faces of the dice, McConnell, Snowden and Powell (1955) again observed significant declines in PK scores, confirming Rhine's original findings.

A variant of Rhine's PK tests with dice are the placement studies by W.E. Cox (1954) in USA and H. Forwald (1961) in Sweden. In these tests, target objects, such as dice and balls, were released down a slide while the subjects attempted to influence mentally the movement of the objects to the desired side or location.

More recently a variety of new avenues and techniques have been explored such as random event generators movement of objects ambient energy, and biological systems (Palmer, 2015).

PK on Living Systems

Attempts to mentally heal sick people through such practices as prayers, laying-on of hands and other procedures are pervasive across cultures from time immemorial (Ehrenwald, 1976). Some of these practices appear to be in vogue in some societies even now (Inglis, 1977). It is a legitimate question whether PK is behind the success of some of these practices. If it can be shown that human intentions, expressed in whatever form, are shown to have observable influence on living systems, whether human, animal or plant, then we would be closer to finding a scientific explanation to many of the reported miraculous cures and remedies. There are indeed numerous experimental reports suggestive of the effects of human intentions on living systems such as plants, animals and humans.

As Schmeidler (1982) pointed out, most of experimental PK research with plants is aimed at facilitating or impeding the growth of plants by mental influence. Among the successful attempts to influence plant growth (including germination) includes those reported by Bernard Grad (1967), J.L. Hickman (1979) and C. Nicholas (1977). There are equally numerous studies reporting null results (Lenington, 1979; Pauli, 1973; and Munson, 1979). A positive enhancement effect was replicated by Roney-Dougal and Solfvin (2002) in a field study involving a healer who attempted to enhance the growth and health of lettuce seeds. Studies were also conducted with bacteria (Rauscher and Rubik, 1980), fungus (Barry, 1968; Haraldsson and Thorsteinsson, 1973) and enzymes (Edge, 1980; Smith 1968, 1972).

Among the studies with animals, the better known ones are by Bernard Grad (1977) and Watkins and Watkins (1971). With the healer Estabany as the subject, Grad attempted to study if the healer could slow down the development of goiter among the experimental group of mice compared to the control groups, the only difference between the two groups being that the experimental group is treated by Estabany by (laying-on of hands) touching the cage in which the mice were housed. The results showed significantly slower growth of goiter among the treated mice. In another study (Grad *et al.*, 1961) the same healer attempted to heal surgical wounds in laboratory mice. It is reported that the group of mice treated by the healer showed smaller wounds when measurements are taken after fifteen and sixteen days than the nontreated control group.

Bengston and Krinsley (2000) reported complete remission in laboratory mice afflicted with terminal cancer after treatment by "laying of hands" by an experimenter (and not a healer), who learned the technique from a healer. The authors conclude that the effect is reproducible and predictable. The method of "laying on of hands," they contend, stimulates immune response and the mice retain the immunity even after cancer remission.

Watkins and Watkins (1971) developed a procedure whereby the subjects attempted to arouse a randomly chosen mouse (from a pair of anaesthetized ones), to a wakeful state. They reported significantly shorter times for the experimental mice compared to those in the controlled group. In other words, the mice in the experimental group assisted by the healer, who had no physical contact with them, resuscitated significantly faster than their controls.

Among the mental healing studies with humans, notable are those by Krieger (1986). In three series of experiments, in which the experimental and control subjects were drawn randomly from the patients, she measured hemoglobin before and after the treatment by a mental healer. The healer in this case is again Estabany, who previously worked with Grad. It is reported that the post-test hemoglobin values of the subjects treated by the healer are significantly higher than those of the controls. These studies are unfortunately not methodologically rigorous because those measuring the post-hemoglobin values were not blind to the condition. Therefore, their measurements could have been biased by their knowledge whether the subject is in the experimental or the control group.

The most important studies with human systems are those by William Braud and associates. Braud (1979) reported highly significant results showing that one could use PK to influence the galvanic skin response of humans and the rate of hemolysis of human blood. Meta-analyses of all published papers on PK influence on human systems (involving the phenomenon of the feeling of being stared at) by Stefan Schmidt *et al.* (2004) showed a significant effect.

A later investigation of psychokinesis on living systems is "the Love Study" by Dean Radin *et al.* (2006), which recorded significant psychokinetic effects on the electro-dermal activity (skin conductance) of subjects. More recently Vieten, Radin, Schlitz & Delorme (2013) reported that a spiritual master was able to influence heart rate of the subjects by psychic means.

Micro-PK

A major methodological advance in PK research was with the introduction of random event generators (REG) by Helmut Schmidt in the 1970s. The subject in these tests attempts to bias a Random Event Generator (REG). REG consists of a radioactive (or electronic noise) source connected to a counter and a visual display. The counter spins with high speed until it is stopped by a signal emitted from the source. It is well known that the interval between consecutive emissions of particles is theoretically random. This means that it is impossible to predict reliably when the spin stops. The display is the target to focus on; and it is also the feedback source. The task of the subject is to mentally influence the system so that the REG output is biased in the desired direction. The REG can be connected to a computer so that the trials and their outcomes are recorded automatically. Also, the display the subject focuses on can be of different kinds to suit subject motivation and other factors. Schmidt used colored lights, a lamp switched on or off, a swing pendulum and so on. Robert Jahn *et al.* (1977) used even more colorful and interesting displays such as polystyrene spheres shooting down through a five-chute array and competing scenes appearing on the computer screen.

The studies with REGs are known as micro-PK experiments. Unlike macro-PK where effects are gross and observable, the micro-PK effects can only be inferred from statistical analysis of the data. Several hundred micro-PK experiments with REGs were reported. The evidence shows that subjects are able to bias the REGs to a statistically significant degree (Nelson and Radin, 1988; Steinkamp, Boller and Bösch, 2002). In a review article, Mario Varvoglis and Peter Bancel (2016) believe that the overall evidence for micro-PK is quite strong (2015); but they argue that micro-PK is not widely distributed, but exceptional.

PK with Prerecorded Targets

The most puzzling of the PK experiments are those conducted first by Helmut Schmidt (1976) with prerecorded targets. In these experiments the subject was asked to influence targets, unobserved by any one, that had been recorded and kept in a computer file. The prerecorded targets were randomly assigned to the high-aim and low-aim conditions. The subject's task was to attempt to influence retroactively the targets in the desired direction. In other words, the effort flows backward in time, if we believe in the linearity of time. Schmidt reported results suggesting that PK could work backward in time. In an experiment carried out with extraordinary precautions to exclude experimenter's incompetence, negligence, and even fraud, Schmidt, Morris and Rudolph (1986) found significant evidence for PK with prerecorded targets. It is difficult to explain significant PK results with prerecorded targets by any commonsensical or conventional explanations. It cannot be clairvoyance because the subject's task was not of perceiving but influencing the target system. We may speculate that the PK effect in this case is truly a noncausal in that the subject's PK could reach back in time and influence the targets when they were generated. Alternatively, as Schmidt argues, the events the subject had attempted to influence in those trials were not physically determined (real) until they were observed. In either case, commonsense physics stands upside down when confronted with these results. Even parapsychologists do not find it easy to digest these results. J.B. Rhine himself resisted and withheld his approval until the accumulated data were too massive to ignore. Perhaps, at some level of our being, time and space do not exist or simply are irrelevant.

Process-Oriented Methods

As the concept ESP suggests, Rhine modeled the phenomena after perception; but perception that does not involve sensory processes. ESP is conceived as an information processing ability. In the ESP situation, there are three interrelated elements, the stimulus (called target), the subject (sometimes referred to as percipient) and the process manipulated by the experimental conditions. Experimental studies of ESP have these three different angles, even though they are often interrelated. They constitute the variables to be studies to understand the psi process.

Obviously, the subject is the most important angle of the psi triangle. A large number of studies were conducted to learn about subjects who do better on ESP tests than others. Investigators attempted to understand the personality characteristics, attitudes and values of successful psi subjects as distinguished from less successful ones. The effects of age, sex, health and intelligence of subjects on their ESP scores were tested. Also, the physiological and mental states believed to be psi conducive were a major focus of research interest. In all these studies the researchers make the assumption that the source of ESP is the subject. In other words, it is the ability of the subject that is being tested—an ability that could correlate with the personality and other subject-related factors.

Parapsychologists have also attempted to manipulate target variables to test if they could influence the subject's ESP performance. The variables include the physical and psychological factors associated with targets, the spatial and temporal location of the targets, their complexity and content categories. The third set of variables relates to the process and experimental conditions and generally involves the test environment and procedures. The objective is to learn about the factors in the testing situation that are maximally conducive for the subject to manifest psi. The areas of concern here include group vs. individual testing, intentional vs. nonintentional psi tasks, restricted vs. free-choice responses, cognitive and affective responses, verbal and somatic responses and so on. Surprisingly, however, the experimenter, the one who prepares, administers and evaluates the test, turned out to be an equally important variable that is hardest to crack, as we will see in a later chapter. The importance of the experimenter as a crucial variable has important methodological ramifications. The question whether the experimenter is merely a facilitator of psi or whether he or she is the source of psi has been a difficult and frustrating concern of parapsychologists.

Parapsychologists have developed a methodology and a set of standards that are based on certain assumptions, which, with few notable exceptions, most experimental parapsychologists seem to share. The assumptions are (a) that psi is an ability like perception, (b) that it functions independently of our sensory-motor systems, (c) that it manifests even when the subject is shielded from all other modalities of subject-target interaction, and (d) that it can be detected and measured as distinct from and independent of other modalities. To the extent that we succeeded in obtaining laboratory evidence for the existence of psi by pursuing methods presumed to exclude all other modalities of subject-target interaction, the above assumptions are indeed supported. But there are other factors which make us wonder whether a re-examination of these assumptions and the experimental methods based on them may be in order now. First, there is the continuing controversy over whether all the alternate modalities of subject-target interaction are indeed excluded as claimed. Second, the low level of psi in terms of its effect size in laboratory tests and the notorious unreliability of results have been constant impediments to a proper understanding of psi and its place in the order of things. Third, psi, as it manifests in real-life situations, does not seem to be congruent with the assumptions mentioned above. All these observations point to the possibility that our testing procedures themselves may be psi inhibitory and that they may mask or filter out psi to the point of effectively reducing it to a trickle that cannot be ignored. They may also indicate the need for looking at alternate models that promise stronger effects.

Is Parapsychology a Science?

Parapsychology as a scientific attempt to study psychic phenomena represents a methodological revolution that is best characterized by William McDougall as the "naturalization of the supernatural." Behind this revolution is a commitment to the following assumptions: (1) Psi or psychic phenomena are objective phenomena that are observable and measurable. (2). Therefore, the methods of observation and experiment as practiced in those areas of inquiry which are known as sciences and are believed to provide credible results can be applied to study these phenomena. (3) And whatever may be the outcome of this endeavor, it will enrich our understanding and advance our knowledge. The purpose of the Society for Psychical Research since its establishment in 1882, therefore, has been to examine those real or supposed faculties "without prejudice or prepossession and in a scientific spirit." This unreserved commitment to objectivity and science in exploring psychic abilities for a period of over one hundred years has not resulted in a general acceptance of the field as a legitimate scientific discipline.

Many of us at one time or another have wondered why this is so. It would be absurd to suggest that parapsychology has no subject matter and that consequently mere adherence to scientific method is insufficient to make it a science. Events purported to be psychic are experienced by a majority of the population (Greenley & McCready, 1975). McClenon (1994) in his survey of experiences of ESP and contact with the dead found no cultural differences among those who report such experiences. Ross and Joshi (1992) found in this survey that paranormal experiences have no pathological base. An overwhelming majority of scientists and college professors surveyed believe that investigation of ESP is a legitimate scientific undertaking (Evans, 1973; Wagner and Monnet, 1979). This is quite a contrast with the generally assumed belief that science does not consider the field of parapsychology a legitimate scientific discipline. This is an interesting anomaly, an examination of which could be instructive to philosophers and sociologists concerned with the nature and practice of science and to parapsychologists still struggling to gain the scientific acceptance so essential for the financial and institutional support to continue their work.

Legitimacy in Science—Is It a Question of Method?

If the essential aspect of science is its method, then an examination of its methods should settle the question of whether a given area of study is a legitimate science. Indeed, the belief in the existence of a uniform method underlying the practice of science in various disciplines was quite popular for a long time among those writing and reflecting on the nature of science. Perhaps the most widely known and influential statement of this viewpoint is by Karl Pearson in his *Grammar of Science*, first published in 1892.

According to Pearson, science consists of "classification of facts and the formation of absolute judgments" that are independent of the idiosyncrasies of the individual entertaining those judgments. The essence of science, according to Pearson, is its method and not the facts; and this method is the same in all its branches. To quote Pearson: "The unity of all sciences consists alone in its method, not in its material" (p. 15). The essential features of the scientific method are: "(a) Careful and accurate classification of facts and observation of their correlation and sequence; (b) the discovery of scientific laws by aid of the creative imagination; (c) self criticism and the final touchstone of equal validity for all normally constituted minds" (p. 45).

Today few would subscribe to the notion that there is a single, objective scientific method by the pursuit of which we will be led indubitably closer to "truth." It has been pointed out that all attempts to precisely characterize the scientific method have so far failed to be convincing. Feyerabend (1975), for instance, has shown how even "the most advanced and sophisticated methodology" of science, such as the one described by Lakatos, is inadequate in that there always exists a possibility that a research program that was once condemned as degenerative may be revived. Science as practiced by such celebrities as Galileo is more ad hoc, and less methodical than is generally presumed. Any description of the so-called scientific method can be shown to have been violated by at least one major advance in science. Therefore, Feyerabend concludes: "There is only *one* principle that can be defended under *all* circumstances and in *all* stages of human development. It is the principle: anything goes" (p. 14).

It is not only the anarchistic philosophers of science who have questioned the existence of the objective scientific method. James Conant, for example, writes: "There is no such thing as the scientific method. If there were, surely an examination of the history of physics, chemistry, and experimental biology would reveal it.... Yet, a careful examination of these subjects fails to reveal any *one* method by means of which the masters in these fields broke new ground" (1951, p. 45).

Thus it is difficult to argue for the existence of *the one* scientific method. This does not, however, necessarily invalidate the view that regards science as method. Contemporary defense of this view can be found in Brown (1979). We therefore find some, like Truzzi (1980), who hold that investigation of psi is legitimate even if psi is not. I am not sure that it follows necessarily from this that parapsychology is legitimate, as Truzzi seems to assume. To make such an assertion we need to assume a philosophy of science which is itself subject to severe problems. Let us examine briefly some of the more dominant conceptions of science.

What Is the Thing Called Science?

"Science," whatever it may mean, has had a profound influence on our lives, on our beliefs and actions. We think we know what we mean when we call someone a scientist and something scientific. All this, of course, does not necessarily imply that we all agree on what science really is. Nor is it the case that everyone would agree that science is *the* gateway to "truth." The views of philosophers of science vary all the way from reification of science to its caricature and condemnation and from an absolute faith in the ultimacy of science as the only means of ascertaining facts and of advancing knowledge to the view that science is yet another ideology which has no special intrinsic certitude.

Whether or not the current high status enjoyed by science is justified on logical grounds, notwithstanding those that deny climate change and anti-science advocates which are increasing in numbers, it would be well to remember in the context of seeking scientific legitimacy for parapsychology that parapsychology is a party to the pyramiding of values that places science at the apex. Parapsychologists want to be recognized as scientists because it is good and honorable to be so recognized as long as they are in the knowledge business. Therefore, I have very little sympathy for those who are bothered by the methodological "scientism" in the field. A return to hermetic contemplation may give one a more satisfying picture of psi, but such will not constitute a scientific endeavor.

It is widely believed that science is objective, that scientific knowledge is reliable and proven to be true and that personal opinion and speculation have no place in it. Closest to this commonsense view is the inductivist conception of science. Science, according to this view, starts with observations. Unprejudiced observations enable us to make statements about the world that are true or probably true. We are led from observation to generalized statements through the process of induction. It has been pointed out, however, that such a view is logically untenable. Inductive reasoning involves a leap from what is observed to what is not observed. There is no logical necessity that a conclusion reached by inductive reasoning is true even if the premises of inductive inferences are true. For example, one could conclude after making a large number of observations of swans in several parts of the world that swans are white. From this it does not logically follow that the next swan you observe will be white. David Hume (1939) showed over two hundred years ago that the attempt to establish the logical validity of induction is patently circular. He argued that "what is possible can never be demonstrated to be false."

One way of solving this problem is to give up the inductive method of science altogether. This is what Popper (1959) and his followers, who emphasized "falsification" instead of "verification," attempted to do. They concede that there is no logical necessity for scientific generalizations to be true. Science, according to them, is a set of hypotheses, hypotheses that are *falsifiable*. By *falsifiable* is meant the logical possibility of making an observation or set of observations that is inconsistent with a hypothesis. While no amount of witnessing white swans is logically sufficient to justify the conclusion that all swans are white, just one observation of a nonwhite swan is sufficient to falsify the statement that all swans are white. Singular statements of fact such as "this crow is black," however numerous, are insufficient to logically establish the truth of a universal statement such as "all crows are black."

Science, according to falsificationists, begins with problems. Problems lead to hypotheses. Hypotheses are subjected to test with an intent to falsify. Some will be falsified quickly, others may prove more successful. However, the process of falsification continues indefinitely. The theories that have withstood tests of falsification are not necessarily true, but are superior to those that have failed. Science is an unending process of rejecting false hypotheses. The scientific worth of a theory is proportional to its degree of falsifiability. A theory that is clear and precise is more falsifiable than the one which is vague and ambiguous. Falsificationists much prefer "an attempt to solve an interesting problem by a bold conjecture, *even* (*and especially*) if it soon turns out to be false, to any recital of irrelevant truisms" (Popper, 1969, p. 231, emphasis in the original).

A conjecture is bold if it is judged to be easily falsifiable. But such a judgment presupposes background knowledge. If, on the basis of available knowledge, a conjecture is unlikely to be proven, then its falsification is hardly an advance, but its confirmation, however, might constitute a major breakthrough. On the other hand, the falsification of a cautious hypothesis might be very significant whereas its confirmation would be quite trivial.

It may be seen historically that a presumed falsification of a hypothesis did not always amount to its rejection. It is pointed out, for example, that "Newton's gravitational theory was falsified by observations of the moon's orbit" (Chalmers, 1978). Bohr successfully persevered with his theory of the atom despite its early falsification (Lakatos, 1974). Chalmers (1978) illustrates the inadequacies of inductive as well as falsificationist accounts of science with reference to the Copernican revolution. At the time of the publication of Copernican theory in 1543, there were more things against it than in its favor. Without the development of the telescope and the new mechanics that eventually replaced Aristotle's it would have been impossible to defend Copernican theory against those that it sought to replace. As Chalmers points out: "New concepts of force and inertia did not come about as a result of careful observation and experiment. Nor did they come about through the falsification of bold conjectures and the continual replacement of one bold conjecture by another. Early formulations of the new theory, involving imperfectly formulated novel conceptions, were persevered with and developed in spite of apparent falsifications" (p. 71).

The valiant attempts by Lakatos (1974) to improve on Popper with his emphasis on progressive research programs as opposed to degenerative programs is beset with similar problems. There are real difficulties in deciding whether one research program is better than the other. Again, programs that appeared to be degenerating at one time were revived at a later date and found to be fruitful. So we have Feyerabend describing Lakatos's methodology as "a memorial to happier times when it was still thought possible to run a complex and often catastrophic business like science by following a few simple 'rational rules'" (1974, p. 215).

Kuhn's (1970) notion of scientific paradigms is well known among parapsychologists who seem to feel encouraged that parapsychology is heralding a new paradigm (McConnell, 1968). What is important in Kuhn's characterization of the paradigms is that there are no easy criteria that determine the superiority of one paradigm over another. Inasmuch as rival paradigms subscribe to different metaphysical assumptions, no logically compelling demonstration of the superiority of one over the other is possible.

The reasons for switching paradigms are more psychological and sociological than logical. Therefore, the arguments between those subscribing to rival paradigms are usually aimed at being psychologically persuasive rather than logically compelling.

From the foregoing it should be fairly obvious that it would be somewhat naïve to assume (1) that scientific inquiry is so objective that we can specify certain criteria that define genuine science and (2) that the generalizations of science are arrived at by truly objective observation. Our observations themselves are to a degree subjective. Scientific inquiry does not grow in a vacuum. It is carried out against the background of a culture with certain belief systems. These beliefs suggest problems as well as their probable resolutions. No science can claim absolute independence over its environment. To quote Schrödinger (1966): "The engaging of one's interest in a certain subject and in certain directions must necessarily be influenced by the environment, or what may be called the cultural milieu or the spirit of the age in which one lives. In all branches of our civilization there is one general world outlook dominant and there are numerous lines of activity which are attractive because they are the fashion of the age, whether in politics or in art or in science" (p. 64).

The "internationality of science" or its apparent universal character is not an argument in favor of the objectivity of science. We have a similar consensus in international sports. It does not follow from it that these are the only possible ones. To quote Schrödinger again: "In science we are acquainted only with a certain bulk of experimental results which is infinitesimally small compared with the results that might have been obtained from other experiments.... It would, generally speaking, be a vain endeavor on the part of some scientist to strain his imaginative vision toward initiating a line of research hitherto not thought of" (p. 63).

Feyerabend (1980) put this somewhat differently, but more forcefully. The apparent universality in science, he argued, is due to "objectivization of the subjective" which enables the scientists to "transform their own personal or group idiosyncracies into 'objective' criteria of excellence" (p. 53).

If science is a fashion, as Schrödinger acknowledged, its pursuit is a passion. We find a convincing exponent of this view in Michael Polanyi (1958). Polanyi distinguished between three kinds of passion: First, is the intellectual passion, which affirms the scientific value of certain facts; then, the heuristic passion, which provides the impetus for originality and creativity; and finally, the persuasive passion which is behind most controversies in science. "I certainly affirm," writes Polanyi, "that passion and controversy moved by passion, must continue in science and that a comprehensive revision of our philosophy of science is needed to give due weight to this essential aspect of scientific truth" (p. 103).

There are thus severe difficulties in characterizing science as this or that. Yet, the situation is not as hopeless as some anarchistic philosophers would picture it. There are some basic assumptions on which most of us who call ourselves scientists can agree. We would agree, I think, that there is a world out there which is real and relatively independent of us. That world can be known through observation and experiment. Despite certain subjective characteristics of experience, most of us experience the outside world in similar ways. While the principle of induction and the notion of the uniformity of nature may not be logically compelling, they seem to work pretty well in practice. Our problems in understanding science at least in part are due to our failure to appreciate its complexity. Science is a complex activity carried on against a certain background by men and women of flesh and blood. Therefore, proper understanding is possible only when we consider the business called science in the light of the beliefs and behavior of those engaged in that trade.

It seems to me that science is a complex milieu consisting of scientists and their thoughts, actions and passions. Thought is composed of a scientist's background knowledge which suggests problems and possible solutions. Action is the method which prescribes how questions should be posed and treated and how to verify initial assumptions in relation to the questions raised. Passion is that which is involved in a scientist's mode of discourse and his interpretations of the results. It is what colors his statements and meanings which he relates to truth and falsity. These three elements—thought, action and passion—blend in any given scientific enterprise to give us a mix called science. Inasmuch as the proportions of these vary from area to area, from inquiry to inquiry we have sciences of various shades and persuasions. However, from all accounts there is little reason to believe that parapsychology is not a science. It is not the same as saying that it has received acceptance as a legitimate science.

3

Accumulating Evidence

Why Is Parapsychology a Controversial Subject?

Before one goes any further into the advances in psi research, one question needs to be addressed: Why is it that parapsychology continues to be a controversial subject in the Western academic community despite the massive data accumulated over a long period of time? It is a matter that relates to the nature of evidence in its conceptual and methodological dimensions, especially when controversial claims are made and when anomalous phenomena are the subject of study. So some discussion on the matter of evidence in parapsychology in some detail may be in order.

Since the establishment of the Society for Psychical Research in London in 1882, a vast amount of data has accumulated and many parapsychologists are convinced that a clear case has been made for the existence of cognitive anomalies. In fact, nearly 75 years ago, parapsychologists (Thouless, 1943) made a deliberate choice to move on from merely accumulating more evidence to prove the existence of psi to the collection of data that would throw light on the nature of psi; that is, to shift from proof-based research to process-oriented research. As described in the previous chapter, some progress has been made in this direction. However, this has not helped enough to integrate psi research into academic psychology or gain for it a greater measure of acceptance in the mainstream science. Beyond the confines of parapsychological community, there is no general consensus on the matter of evidence for the existence of psi. By and large the scientific establishment has ignored thus far the parapsychological claims; and parapsychologists themselves continue to be more concerned with the *proof* and with convincing the skeptics rather than with the *process* of psi, notwithstanding the general claim of carrying out process-oriented studies. The reason for this is the continuing and relentless criticism of psi research by the skeptical community and the desire of the parapsychologists to convince those in the mainstream. This has been an uphill task and has led to "reinventing the wheel" by way of making new claims of evidence and even giving new names only to invite fresh criticism. The case of remote viewing research is a revealing example.

I happen to think that the best of criticism, constructive and consequential, is what followed Rhine's early experiments. Before the end of 1933, Rhine identified five outstanding subjects and his monograph *Extrasensory Perception* made a strong case for the existence of psi. Understandably the scientific community reacted with caution. There was a spate of criticism, advancing 35 critical arguments in 56 published reports. Several of these criticisms are specific and have to do with data collection and analysis. These criticisms and Rhine's response to them were reviewed in the book *Extrasensory Perception After Sixty Years* (Pratt *et al.*, 1940).

One line of criticism has to do with the experimental conditions. An essential requirement for an acceptable ESP experiment was that data should be collected under conditions that provide no reasonable opportunity for sensory leakage of information or inferential knowledge of the targets. Skinner (1937), Wolfle (1938), and J.L. Kennedy (1938), among others, pointed out that under certain lighting conditions the commercially produced ESP cards could be read through their reverse sides. Rhine's response was that the original experiments were conducted with hand-printed ESP cards that were free from such defects. In his more formal experiments, Rhine used screens and distance, which prevented the subjects from obtaining any visual cues from the cards. Kennedy (1938), Kellogg (1936), and Leuba (1938) argued that an increase in the experimental rigor of ESP research had resulted in a corresponding decline in ESP results suggesting that extra-chance ESP scores were possibly due to loose conditions in earlier experiments. Rhine responded by pointing out that the Pearce-Pratt series of experiments, which is the most rigorously controlled of all, gave highly significant results (Rhine *et al.*, 1940).

Another line of criticism is related to data analysis. Willoughby (1935), Kellogg (1936), Heinlein and Heinlein (1938), Herr (1938), and Lemmon (1939) criticized various features of the statistical analysis used by Rhine and his colleagues. In particular, the criticism focused on Rhine's assumption that the binomial theorem is applicable to "closed decks," decks in which the number of times each type of card appears is not free to vary. The statistical debate essentially ceased in 1937, when Burton Camp, president of the Institute of Mathematical Statistics, issued a statement that Rhine's "statistical analysis is essentially valid. If the Rhine investigation is to be fairly attacked it must be on other than mathematical grounds" (Camp, 1937). Further discussion of the statistical issues of psi experiments may be found in Burdick & Kelly (1977) and Tressoldi & Utts (2015).

Rhine's research was not of course without any blemish. His experiments were not of course perfect. They had not conclusively eliminated every alternative explanation, even though his Pearce-Pratt series comes very close to it. This study is as well controlled as any in behavioral research. In hindsight, one could suggest improvements in the experimental conditions of almost any experiment. However, for his time, Rhine's best experiments were ahead of others in behavioral sciences. The experimental precautions he took, including two-experimenter controls and double-blind procedures, were rare in other disciplines at that time. Nonetheless, much of the early criticism of Rhine's experiments was helpful in progressively raising the standards of ESP research and reducing the possibility of experimental errors and artifacts.

In a paper entitled "The Scientific Credibility of ESP" psychologists Samuel Moss and Donald Butler (1978) offered several criticisms of experimental parapsychology. These criticisms broadly reflect the skeptical mindset to psi research at that time among psychologists. Moss and Butler reject the case for ESP on six grounds. (1) The test procedures are so inadequately reported and the experimental designs are so informal that the evidence generated by parapsychological experiments cannot be regarded as establishing the existence of ESP. (2) Replication by a qualified non-sympathetic observer is essential before results should be accepted, and no such replication has been successfully carried out in parapsychology. (3) In order to believe in ESP we must discover at least one lawful relationship involving ESP, and there are no supposed "ESP laws" that cannot be accounted for more parsimoniously by existing psychological laws. (4) ESP is not in harmony with established laws; and therefore it must be rejected. (5) We do not encounter ESP in the marketplace; therefore, it must be spurious. (6) There is no need to have an open mind on the question of ESP if the evidence has not yet established it.

I have argued elsewhere (Rao, 1979) (1) that the reporting style and experimental design of good experiments in parapsychology are just as good as any in any of the behavioral sciences. (2) Replicability cannot be a primary criterion for demarcating the genuine and the spurious in every controversial area. (However, as we will discuss in the next chapter, parapsychological findings have, in a significant sense, been replicated.) (3) Failure to find lawful relationships does not logically negate the existence of a phenomenon; however, there is sufficient evidence in ESP data to suggest lawful relationships. (4) Lack of perceived harmony with the "established laws" does not warrant the rejection of evidence. (5) The "marketplace" test is irrelevant to the question of the existence of a phenomenon even if it fails; but the belief in and application of psi is fairly widespread across cultures. (6) The evidence for the ESP in any conventional sense is strong enough to compel an unbiased observer to take it seriously.

With all this going for psi research, why then is the skepticism? What more needs to be done to make the case for psi more convincing and acceptable to science?

One of the vocal critics of psi research who consider that the null hypothesis is not rejected by parapsychological data is James E. Alcock. Alcock attempts to locate psi in the human belief system, the fallibility of judgment and the frailties of individuals who tend to "infer causality when none exists" and "maintain erroneous beliefs even in the face of evidence to the contrary" (1981). He argues, following Hansel, that parapsychologists hold certain beliefs and are searching for data to support them, and that there are no credible data in search of explanation (Alcock, 1981). Thus according to Alcock (1985) parapsychology is a "spiritual science" and parapsychologists are in "search for the soul" (Alcock, 1987).

In a more recent appraisal of parapsychological claims, Alcock (2003) reaffirms, "I continue to believe that parapsychology is, at bottom, motivated by belief in search of data, rather than data in search of explanation. It is the belief in a larger view of human personality and existence than is accorded to human beings by modern science that keeps parapsychology engaged in their search. Because of this belief, parapsychologists, never really give the null hypothesis a chance" (p. 49). Alcock may well be right that psi researchers are in search of "a larger view of human personality and existence" to find a viable explanation for their data. He is utterly unconvincing, however, in suggesting that the experimental data of parapsychology do not reject the null hypothesis.

Alcock (2003) has put forward twelve reasons for skepticism about the existence of psi. The first is that parapsychology lacks "definition of subject matter." On the face of it, this sounds too simplistic and somewhat naïve. What has the definition of the field to do with the existence of the phenomena? Scientists researching a bunch of phenomena may not agree on the definition of the field. Does it imply the nonexistence of the phenomena they are investigating? Again, there may be no agreed on definition of intelligence among psychologists. May we on that score reject intelligence as a sensible concept?

Alcock quotes extensively from some of the website statements of the Parapsychological Association, the Society for Psychical Research and the American Society for Psychical Research and correctly points out "that there is a great variety of opinion as to what constitutes the essential and appropriate subject matter of parapsychology" (Alcock, 2003, p. 32). From this he goes on to conclude, incorrectly in my opinion: "This all reflects the fact that to the extent that parapsychology constitutes a 'field' of research, it is a field without a core knowledge base, a core set of constructs, a core set of methodologies, and a core set of accepted and demonstrable phenomena *that all parapsychologists accept*" (*ibid.*, emphasis added). There is no doubt that glaring differences among parapsychologists exist as to what constitutes the best evidence. One may also acknowledge that there are significant deficiencies in our understanding of psi. However, these are insufficient to reject the field as such in the manner Alcock does.

Let us take the case of psychology, Alcock's own discipline. There is no one set of constructs, methods or theories that all psychologists would accept. In fact psychology can boast of not a single overarching theory that psychologists of all persuasions working in different areas could accept. Psychology has bits of theories but no one single theory that is universally accepted. The very fact that there are so many systems and schools attests to this. However, the existence of these systems and schools does not vitiate psychology as a discipline worthy of scientific investigation. As the history of psychology shows, the definition of psychology, after its emergence as an academic discipline, has changed continuously and sometimes drastically. Once it was a science of consciousness, then of behavior. Even now it is difficult to find a definition that *all* psychologists would accept. Parapsychologists have indeed differences among themselves as psychologists do. But to conclude from this that they do not agree on what constitutes the field is far from truth.

Most psi researchers (the professionals in the field) would have little difficulty in agreeing on the subject matter. It was the great contribution of J.B. Rhine to have given the field "a shared language, methods and problems." Different emphases either on methods or phenomena studied in a given discipline would not, however, necessarily invalidate that discipline as a scientific enterprise. One psychologist may value real life experiences more than laboratory results. Some psychologists may work with the assumption that the brain holds the key for understanding human cognition and conduct whereas some others may focus on socialization, values or culture.

The basic fallacy in Alcock's reasoning is that he compares controversial areas with conventional subjects and asks that we judge the former with the standards of mature sciences. To reject psi because it is conceptualized differently in different cultures or because it is investigated by different methods by different investigators or because one parapsychologist finds one experiment more convincing or one line of research more promising and productive, whereas another picks a different experiment or another area, is logically unwarranted and factually misleading.

Informed skepticism has a place in science. If the best of parapsychological research is among the best in behavioral research from the standpoint of design and data collection, part of the credit should go to the critics who did their best to find all possible loopholes and artifacts. Occasionally, however, one wonders whether they did not go beyond the limits of rational discourse. G.R. Price (1955) once attributed significant psi results that were not otherwise explainable to "a few people with the desire and the ability artfully to produce false evidence for the supernatural," a statement he has since retracted (Price, 1972).

The same journal, which published the article and the retraction by Price has among others published another critical article by Diaconis who describes himself as both a statistician and a magician. Diaconis unhesitatingly embraces a strategy that is common among critics. He attempts to set up straw men to knock them down. He raises pseudo-problems or problems parapsychologists have since long recognized and solved. We will discuss at some length the critique of Diaconis as an illustration of the skeptics' attempts to explain away parapsychological data.

Diaconis states unambiguously that "modern parapsychological research is important." He acknowledges that Feller's criticism of the statistics used by J.B. Rhine and his co-workers was wrong and concedes that many parapsychologists are statistically sophisticated. He even credits the parapsychological community with solving "numerous statistical riddles in its own literature." Yet, in the same breath, he accuses parapsychologists of violating elementary statistical assumptions. He writes as though parapsychologists are unaware of the statistical problems related to feedback and multiple analyses. The fact of the matter is that these problems have been discussed in the parapsychological literature, and procedures for correcting for artifacts arising from them are well known to most parapsychologists.

"A common problem in the evaluation of ESP experiments," Diaconis states, "is the uncertainty about what outcomes are to be judged as indicative of ESP" (p. 131). On the face of it, this statement is tantamount to saying that parapsychologists do not know how to conduct experiments; they only make ad hoc observations. Obviously, this is not what he means. He seems to say that parapsychological experiments are so loose-ended that it is difficult to make any sense of the evidence. This is simply not the case. As we have repeatedly asserted, any serious review of recent experimental research would reveal that investigators in this field are as methodologically sophisticated as in any behavioral science. Diaconis thus displays a lack of understanding of the way parapsychological experiments are carried out.

The first required reading for any student of parapsychology is *Parapsychology: Frontier Science of the Mind* by Rhine and Pratt (1957).This book makes a clear distinction between exploratory research methods and methods of verification. A critic who does not grasp this distinction between exploratory and confirmatory studies has simply not done his homework and cannot talk meaningfully about parapsychological experiments. It is suggested in the book that a pilot experiment be carried out before undertaking any elaborately designed project because "the many uncontrolled variables....are especially likely to cause trouble in investigations with so elusive a capacity as psi" (p. 26). The triviality of Diaconis's criticism becomes obvious if one looks at the two statistical requirements stated for many years on the inside back cover of the *Journal of Parapsychology,* a leading journal in the field:

1. The precise statistical formulation of the hypothesis (or hypotheses) being tested in a research report should be concisely stated and listed in advance of the presentation of the results. It is recommended that the type of statistical test(s) that are planned be given along with the hypothesis.
2. Any statistical analysis not previously stated as preplanned should be accompanied by a brief statement of the motivation or circumstances leading to that analysis, and the probability value should be in close enough proximity to this statement that its association is obvious.

The criticisms of psi experiments by Diaconis are not applicable to much of serious research in the field; and where they are applicable, they have already been discussed in the parapsychology literature itself. Let us consider briefly his remarks regarding the experiments with the special subject, B.D., carried out at the Institute for Parapsychology by Ed Kelly and associates.

His criticism of the Kelly and Kanthamani experiments (Kanthamani & Kelly, 1974a, 1974b; Kelly & Kanthamani, 1972) is twofold. It concerns

(a) informal design, and (b) subject cheating. The evidence for these criticisms is not obtained either by an examination of the actual experiments or of their reports in professional journals, but from his own observations of B.D.'s informal performance in another place and setting by Diaconis.

What Diaconis refers to as uncontrolled experiments were, in fact, informal presentations by B.D. to groups of people at Harvard. They can in no sense be construed as experiments. It is difficult to see how observations made during such informal presentations could be cited to invalidate the results obtained under a different set of experimental conditions which he does not even attempt to criticize.

Again, the implied accusation that in the experiments reported by Kelly and Kanthamani, the significance of the results are at least in part due to "exploiting multiple end points" had no basis in fact. Diaconis refers only to a part of the first report of Kelly & Kanthamani (1972). They present results that could not have been obtained by following the methods Diaconis describes. In the second report to which Diaconis refers (Kanthamani & Kelly, 1974a) the subject B.D. obtained three times more the number of exact hits than expected by chance. Such a score gives a z score of 12; which requires an inconceivably large number of multiple end points. The fact is that neither the subject nor the experimenter was allowed such multiple ends.

The second criticism is subject cheating. Diaconis (1978) accuses B.D. of having employed sleight-of-hand tricks in the Harvard presentations that he had witnessed. Among the observations he makes are (a) "I saw him glance at the bottom card of the deck he was shuffling" and (b) "B.D. *secretly* [italics added] counted the number of cards between the card he had seen and the selected card" (p. 132). To publicly accuse someone of cheating, I would think that we should have something more evidential than "I saw him glance at the bottom card." The critic cannot use one set of standards for evaluating evidence for psi and another set for convincing himself that there was fraud in the experiment. Would Diaconis be convinced that B.D. has ESP if someone with similar training and background as Diaconis testified that he did not see B.D. use sleight of hand when he obtained significant psi scoring? If one of my colleagues, who was also a professional magician, had told me that his broken watch was paranormally mended by Geller and that he saw Girard paranormally bend an aluminum rod, it would not convince me that they are genuine psychic feats; we need to have something more than informal observation. We need data; and we need to know the conditions under which the data were obtained so that we can reach sound conclusions. In support of his accusation, Diaconis should provide more objective evidence than he had. It would have been a simple matter if the subject's movements were monitored through video recording, if they had any reason to believe that B.D. would use such sleight-of-hand tricks. Again, one would ask what evidence Diaconis had for concluding that B.D. "secretly counted."

Apart from the ad hoc hypotheses and post hoc surmises he makes, the shallowness of Diaconis's criticism becomes obvious when one looks into the actual experimental set-up and realizes that none of these hypothetical tricks are appropriate for explaining the results obtained in the Kelly-Kanthamani experiments with B.D. The fact of the matter is that this report also presents significant results obtained with Schmidt's four-button machine and with a dice machine which leave no scope for the sleight of hand tricks. Kelly & Kanthamani (1972, p. 188) specifically state that B.D.'s card trials in their exploratory research cannot be considered as scientific evidence for ESP. Their subsequent research (Kanthamani & Kelly, 1974a, 1974b) was aimed at confirming under controlled conditions the suggestions that came out of the exploratory work. To dismiss the results of controlled studies on the basis of speculative inferences drawn from ad hoc observations made at informal "performances" is just another indication of the Humean prejudice against those phenomena that do not seem to fit into the current corpus of science. People's prior beliefs often prejudice their judgment.

Diaconis was not of course the last critic of psi research. In a sense, his criticism was somewhat dated; but the general tenor and even substance of skepticism have not varied in any significant manner over the years. Hansel's book ran into several editions with similar arguments, unmindful of several refutations by psi researchers. Therefore, it serves little purpose to discuss other skeptics since Diaconis.

The "Conclusive" Experiment

Critics of psi research often call for a conclusive experiment, by which they mean an experiment that controls for all conceivable errors, incompetence and fraud by the subject and the experimenter(s). The rationale for this demand is provided by a statement attributed to Phillip Abelson (1978), editor of *Science.* He is quoted in the *U.S. News and World Report* as saying, "extraordinary claims require extraordinary evidence." A corollary to this is that it is impossible to prove the existence of a phenomenon conceived a priori to be impossible. Inasmuch as one assumes that the strength of evidence required to establish the existence of a phenomenon is directly proportional to its perceived nonexistence, if one accords a priori zero-probability for the existence of a phenomenon, no amount of evidence is sufficient to establish that phenomenon.

Those who demand a "foolproof" experiment that would control for all conceivable kinds of error have argued that if a claim is made for the existence of a phenomenon that conflicts with "established laws," it is much more parsimonious to assume error or even fraud on the part of the claimant than it is to assume the reality of that phenomenon (Hansel, 1966; Price, 1955). This argument is often identified with David Hume's (1825) maxim that "no testimony is sufficient to establish a miracle, unless the testimony be of such a kind, that its falsehood would be more miraculous than the fact which it endeavors to establish" (p. 115). Hume's maxim is a metaphysical statement, and it is inappropriate to use it when one speaks of empirical evidence. Moreover, his definition of a miracle as a universally nonexistent event is self-contradictory inasmuch as any claimed evidence in support of a miracle is also evidence against the universality of its nonexistence (Rao, 1981). As Saint Augustine remarked, "Miracles occur in contradiction not to nature, but to what is known to us of nature." It should also be kept in mind that Hume might not have regarded psi phenomena as miraculous or as anything more than extraordinary events.

As we (Rao and Palmer, 1987) have argued elsewhere, the call for a totally "foolproof" study assumes that at a given time one can identify all possible sources of error and how to control against them. Such a methodological stance is comparable to the epistemological position which assumes that one can determine for all time to come what is and is not possible. This is obviously an untenable position. Again, the demand for experimental controls against experimenter fraud is unique to discussions of evidence for what are perceived to be extraordinary claims. Pushed to its extreme, the hypothesis of experimenter fraud becomes nonfalsifiable, in that it is impossible to be certain that fraud is completely eliminated in any given experiment.

If one assumes that ESP is *impossible* and fraud is *possible*, however improbable it may be, then no amount of experimental evidence would be sufficient to establish the existence of psi. The concept of a "conclusive" experiment, totally free of any possible error or fraud and immune to all skeptical doubt, is thus a practical impossibility in the empirical domain. In reality, evidence in science is a matter of degree; the fact that one can concoct alternative explanations of a finding does not automatically render that finding evidentially worthless. Evidentiality must be assessed on a continuum and in relation to the plausibility of and the empirical support for the competing hypotheses. These considerations demand that a "conclusive" experiment be defined more modestly as one in which it is highly *improbable* that the result is artifactual. In *this* sense, we think a case can be made for more than one "conclusive" experiment in parapsychology. As an example, I refer to the experiments conducted by Helmut Schmidt. In a target article published in *Behavioral and Brain Sciences* we (Rao and Palmer, 1987) discussed Schmidt's experiments at some length. We draw freely from it in this section.

Schmidt's REG Experiments

Helmut Schmidt's (1969a; 1969b) experiments may be cited as an example of probabilistically conclusive evidence for psi. Although they are somewhat dated, Helmut Schmidt's experiments with random event generator (REG) are important for several reasons. (a) They represent one of the major experimental paradigms in contemporary parapsychology. (b) They are regarded by most parapsychologists as providing good evidence for psi. (c) They have been subjected to detailed scrutiny by critics. In no sense, it may be construed, that these are the only good experiments the field has to offer. For the reasons stated above, there can be no crucial experiment or definitive experimental program on which the case for psi does or could rest exclusively.

At the time of conducting these experiments, Helmut Schmidt was a physicist at Boeing Scientific Research Laboratories. The studies were designed to test the possibility of ESP and were carried out with the help of a specially built machine that was designed to rule out all artifacts arising from recording errors, sensory cues, and subject cheating known at the time. The safety features of the Schmidt machine are actually superior to those of the VERITAC machine used earlier by Smith and his colleagues to test for ESP (Smith *et al.*, 1963). Parapsychology's most articulate critic C.E.M. Hansel (1966) had praised VERITAC as "admirably designed" and had suggested that it could be "standardized for testing subjects for extrasensory perception" (p. 172).

The Schmidt machine randomly selected targets with equal probability and recorded both the target selections and the subject's responses. The subject's task was to guess which of the four lamps would light and to press the corresponding button if he was aiming for high scores (or to avoid that button if aiming for low scores). As Schmidt (1969b) described it:

> During a test, the subject sits in front of a small panel with four pushbuttons and four corresponding colored lamps. Each of the pushbuttons simultaneously activates a recorder switch and a trigger switch. The recorder switch serves to register which of the buttons has been pressed. The four trigger switches are connected in parallel such that pressing any one of the buttons closes a circuit, in turn triggering the random lighting of one of the four lamps. The system is designed so that on repeated pressing of the buttons the lamps light up in random sequence, i.e., each lamp lights with the same average frequency, and no correlation was found between successively lit lamps or between the buttons pushed and the lamps lit [p. 101].

A sophisticated electronic random event generator that used a radioactive source, strontium 90, produced random lighting of the lamps following the subject's response. The subject's task is to cause by his intention to bias the random event generator in the desired direction. A complete account of the hardware design and methods of statistical evaluation of the data was provided by Schmidt (1970b). The REG was extensively tested in control trials and found not to deviate significantly from chance. The procedure of recording in Schmidt's own words is as follows:

> The sequence of buttons pressed and lamps lit is recorded automatically on paper punch tape. In the research reported here, the two types of test (trying for a high or low number of hits) were recorded in different codes, such that the evaluating computer could distinguish between them. The number of trials made and hits obtained were displayed to the subject by electromechanical reset-counters. These numbers were also registered by nonreset counters, and the readings of all counters were regularly recorded by hand. This record agreed with the results obtained from the paper tape. The equipment was fraud proof, so that one could, in principle, let the subjects work alone. This was done, however, only in a small part of the tests with subject OC in the first experiment and did not increase the scores. In all other tests the writer was present in the same room with the subject [Schmidt, 1969b, p. 103].

Schmidt's first report was based on two experiments. The subjects in this study were preselected on the basis of their performance in the preliminary tests. In the first experiment, there were three subjects. All of them attempted to obtain high scores. Together they did 63,066 trials and scored 16,458 hits, which was 691.5 more than mean chance expectation (MCE). The probability that such a result occurred by chance is smaller than 2×10^9.

In the second experiment, two subjects from the first series and one new subject participated. One subject aimed for high scores and another for low scores. The third aimed high in some trials and low in others. The total number of trials was 20,000. Of these, 10,672 were high-aim trials and 9,328 were low-aim. The combined deviation of hits in the desired direction was 401 greater than MCE, which has an associated probability smaller than 10^{10}.

In the third experiment, Schmidt (1969a) tested six subjects, including two who had participated in the trials just described. The experiment was designed to test primarily for clairvoyance; the targets were digits from a random number table further shuffled by a congruential generator and recorded on paper punch tape. The subjects completed a total of 7,091 high-aim trials and 7,909 low-aim trials, for a grand total of 15,000. The combined deviation of hits in the desired direction was +260 ($p = 0.3 \times 10^6$).

Criticisms of Schmidt's Random Event Generator Experiments

Hansel (1980) discussed the "weaknesses" in Schmidt's experiments under three headings: (1) experimental design, (2) unsatisfactory features of the machine, and (3) inability to confirm the findings. He criticized the experimental design (1a) for its failure to specify in advance the "exact numbers and types of trials to be undertaken by each subject," (1b) for its introduction of high-aim and low-aim conditions, and (1c) for its lack of control of the experimenter.

Strictly speaking, criticism (a) relating to experimental design is not relevant to the main purpose of the experiment, which was not intended to determine whether a given subject had ESP, but to learn whether the experiment as a whole provided evidence for ESP. It is true, however, that in Schmidt's first experiment the number of total trials was not specified precisely in advance. The high level of statistical significance obtained, however, renders the possibility that this factor of optional stopping could account for the results extremely unlikely. And, as Hansel acknowledges, this problem was corrected in the later experiments.

Criticism (b) is not substantiated. Noting that high-aim scores gave a positive deviation and low-aim scores a negative deviation, Hansel argued, "The fact that when positive and negative deviations are combined (maintaining their sign) they invariably give a purely chance score suggests that sampling from a common distribution may have taken place" (p. 230). In the first place, this argument fails to account for Experiment I, which involved only the high-aim condition and gave results that were just as significant as in the other experiments. Second, it is not clear how Hansel's criticism could account for the results, since the high and low conditions were assigned in advance and recorded automatically on paper punch tape in *different codes*. It would seem, in fact, that the introduction of high/low conditions has a certain additional merit in that one condition could be considered as a control for the other, as well as for machine bias. It is of interest that in discussing a different Schmidt experiment, Hansel (1981) himself criticized Schmidt for not having a control condition and recommended the introduction of a condition in which "the subject would not be 'willing' the light to move, or *he would aim at moving the light in the opposite direction*" (p. 32, emphasis added).

Hansel went on to contend that two different machines, one for high aim and the other for low aim, should have been used. But would not such a procedure have been criticized on the grounds that any obtained difference between the scores could have been due to the opposite bias of the two machines?

Criticism (c) is valid if by "control of the experimenter" Hansel meant control against experimenter fraud. It would have been entirely possible for Schmidt to fake the results if he had wished to. In the extreme case, for example, the whole experimental report could simply have been fabricated. We cannot conceive, however, how a nonintentional error on the part of the experimenter could have artifactually produced the significant results.

Hansel's criticism (2) of the machine itself overlaps criticism (1b) above and as explained it is without merit.

The final reason given by Hansel for his rejection of Schmidt's results was that they have not been confirmed. But this again is erroneous. Hansel made no mention of several experimental reports already in the literature that did in fact claim to confirm Schmidt's results; he instead referred only to the 1963 report of Smith *et al.*, which gave null results when VERITAC was used to test for ESP. But even this comparison is problematic. First, the machines, experimental procedures and manipulation of the psychological conditions differed markedly between the two studies. Second, Schmidt's subjects were carefully screened through pretesting procedures, whereas those who participated in the VERITAC experiment were not.

In a more recent publication, Hansel (1981) proposed a scenario that permits the *possibility* of trickery without providing any evidence that fraud had indeed occurred. Referring to one of Schmidt's PK experiments (Schmidt, 1970a), he claimed that the subject could have shorted "either the +1 or the −1 input in the display panel to the earth line according to whether he wished to produce a high or a low score" (p. 30), which would account for the significant results. This argument seems fallacious. Because the REG and electronic counters were sealed in a metal box and the REG outputs were completely buffered, there was no way the subject could have tampered with the apparatus in the way Hansel suggests. Second, the data were independently recorded on punch tape. Had the subject shorted the tape machine, the total number of punches would have differed from the 128 specified for each run. Inspection, of the tapes revealed no such discrepancies (Schmidt, personal communication).

Hansel went on to argue that the experimenter himself could easily have affected the punched record. This is debatable, but the possibility that Schmidt could have faked his data *somehow* has already been acknowledged and answered. Some years later, Schmidt published a PK experiment designed to rule out the possibility of his (or his two co-experimenters') falsifying the data without collaboration from at least one of the others (Schmidt *et al.*, 1986). Briefly, Schmidt, located at his lab in San Antonio, Texas, prepared lists of paired six-digit random numbers, called seed numbers, which were to be used to generate sequences of quasi random binary digits by means of a complex mathematical algorithm known only to Schmidt. These seed numbers were mailed to the private address of Professor Luther Rudolph (L.R.) of Syracuse University. Robert Morris (R.M.) of the same university independently obtained a list of random target directions (high and low), one for each binary sequence, by using his laboratory's own REG. R.M. and L.R. exchanged their copies of the target-direction sequences and the seed numbers and then made the former available to Schmidt.

For the test proper, the subject in San Antonio entered the seed numbers into a computer. The computer then derived the binary sequences, which in turn governed the display on a computer screen of a pendulum swinging with random amplitude. The subject's task was to will the pendulum to swing with larger amplitude on high-aim trials and with smaller amplitude on low-aim trials. At the end of the run, which lasted for about a minute, the display showed the average swing over the run; thus the subject was given feedback about his rate of success.

Schmidt *et al.* (1986) reported significant results in support of their hypothesis. The combined z for all the ten sessions was 2.71 ($p < .005$). Because (a) the seed numbers for the binary sequences and (b) the target directions were independently derived by Schmidt and Morris, respectively, we know of no way Schmidt or Morris alone could have artifactually obtained the results. Such security procedures involving experimenters working independently in two different laboratories are seldom used in scientific research; but it is understandable that Schmidt felt that the validity of his results should not be based ultimately on his honesty alone. Of course, the possibility of fraud is still not eliminated completely. Even if we grant that Schmidt alone could not have faked the results, it remains possible, though less probable, that Schmidt and Morris, or Morris and Rudolph, could have conspired to produce them spuriously.

Hansel's criticisms of Schmidt's experiments are routinely taken as valid by most writers skeptical of psi (e.g., Alcock, 1981). One of the few critics of psi who questioned the basic premises of Hansel's reasoning on this point is Hyman (1981). "There is no such thing as an experiment immune from trickery," says Hyman. "Even if one assembles all the world's magicians and scientists and puts them to the task of designing a fraud-proof experiment, it cannot be done" (p. 39). Hyman, however, agrees with Hansel that Schmidt's PK experiments "do not provide an adequate case for the existence of psi" (p. 34). His reasons are twofold: (1) "Experience shows that the most promising research programs in parapsychology will most likely be passé within a generation or two" (p. 37); and (2) although Schmidt's randomization tests control against "long-term, or even temporary" machine bias, they do not "control against possible short-run biases in the generator output" (p. 38). He suggested, as did Hansel, that matched experimental and control sequences would have been a superior procedure.

The first point is not really a substantive criticism but merely counsels patience. The same thing can be said of research in many areas of psychology. Moreover, "passé" does not necessarily mean "discredited," and much of the older research in parapsychology has withstood criticism rather well. After decades, Schmidt's results do seem plausible to many investigators in the field. The second point, as Hyman himself recognizes, "does not automatically provide an alternative explanation for how Schmidt obtained his results" (p. 38). Schmidt, who was aware of such a possibility, notes that "many more randomness tests were done than published to satisfy my own questions about the possibility of temporary random generator malfunctions" (Schmidt, 1981, p. 41). Also, it is difficult to see how such malfunctions could account for subjects' ability to anticipate the timing and direction of the hypothesized short-run biases in Schmidt's early PK research, which used a high-aim, low-aim protocol (Schmidt, 1970a). Finally, in some of Schmidt's later work, direct comparisons *were* made between experimental and control sequences (e.g., Schmidt, 1976).

Fraud Proof Results

It is understandable and in fact necessary that the findings of parapsychology, which challenge some basic assumptions of the prevailing paradigm in science, are given a close and critical scrutiny before they are finally accepted. However, rational rejection of psi should be based on scientific examination of evidence rather than a priori assumptions, just as scientific acceptance of psi should not be predicated on any personal convictions or belief systems. As we have seen, parapsychology has had its share of severe scrutiny by its critics. First, there was the question of sensory cues, then of methodology, and then of the statistical treatment of the data. When the experimental conditions and controls in some of the important psi experiments were so tight and the evidence too strong to reject and the critics could find no alternative to psi, they shifted their focus to the "error somewhere" hypothesis. The simpler version of the fraud hypothesis is that the experimenter or a collaborator had cheated. For example, George Price (1955), in one of the prestigious science journals, characterized successful psi researchers as "a few people with the desire and ability to produce false evidence for the supernatural." Echoing the Scottish philosopher David Hume, Price argued that the hypothesis that the experimenters or their subjects fraudulently produced these results was more probable than the hypothesis that psi exists. Some years later Price (1972) withdrew his accusations and apologized through the columns of the same journal that first published his criticism.

This did not end the controversy. Price's arguments were picked up by others who began looking for possible places where fraud could have occurred. Foremost among them was the British psychologist C.E.M. Hansel. His criticism of Schmidt's experiments was referred to earlier. While agreeing that he could not categorically prove trickery to be responsible for the results, Hansel (1966) argued that "so long as the possibility [of trickery] is present, the experiments cannot be regarded as satisfying the aims of their originators or as supplying conclusive evidence for ESP" (p. 241). Others (Medhurst and Scott, 1974) went further and used their ingenuity to search for evidence of fraud in some of the published experiments.

It should not be surprising if evidence suggestive of experimenter fraud is uncovered in some cases. In fact, it is no secret that experimenter unreliability has been a concern of psi researchers. J.B. Rhine (1974) spoke of it in a forthright manner even before the Levy affair, which raised questions about the integrity of results in his own backyard. An accusation of fraud against an individual is quite in order if there is evidence indicative of it. No field of human activity, and this includes science, is completely immune to the possibility of fraud, as history has made painfully aware. However, what seems to be unique and unprecedented is the accusation of fraud against the whole field. It is not difficult to see how antecedently improbable it is that a large group of scientists should conspire to conjure up and publish fraudulent results. What would be the motive to do so in a situation where involvement in psi research more often brings disapproval and disrepute than reward? Accusation of fraud on the grounds of a priori improbability of the phenomena is generally detested as imprudent and distasteful in scientific discussions. However, all the same, such accusations do find their way into print when it comes to parapsychology.

To be accused of fraud is an occupational risk in this field, so it seems, and the wise researcher would do well to impose on himself protective guards by such action as reporting his findings precisely, keeping complete records for posterity and making them publicly available and involving others in his research so as to share responsibility.

How do we obtain any evidence which is intrinsically fraud-proof? After the manner of the Cartesian axiom, *cogito ergo sum*, we can say one can doubt another's honesty but not one's own. If X does a psi experiment under rigorously controlled conditions and obtains significant results, he has found for himself fraud-proof evidence, because he knows that he did not cheat. But this personal conviction, however profound and objective it may be for him, will not satisfy the criterion of being fraud-proof for the community of scientists. Are there any experimental data in psi research that contain evidence for psi but are immune to the hypothesis of fraud?

Long ago, I was struck by the following line of J.B. Rhine (1975) in the "comments" section of the *Journal of Parapsychology:* "I had based my own judgment of the psi research findings," he wrote, "most of all on these incidental blocks of data (like those showing psi-missing, diagonal declines, and other position effects)" (p. 41). This led me to go back to Rhine's earlier writings and to reread, for example, in *The Reach of the Mind* (1947) his assessment of the position effects as constituting a superior type of objective evidence for psi. He wrote as follows: "Around 1940 we came upon the first of what might lightly be called fingerprint evidence—effects left unconsciously in the records, but capable of being observed and analyzed by anyone, once their presence was pointed out. This finding was something new and surprisingly concrete in the way of evidence for ESP." "The new evidence," continued Rhine, "comes from the same old records, yet is independent, too. It was an incidental effect of ESP, discovered not by the original experimenter but by later investigators. It thus transcends all the common counter explanations of ESP" (p. 169).

What is most interesting about the effects referred to is the fact that they were found in the data of investigators who were not expecting them and often did not even notice them. The later discovery of such effects by others reasonably rules out the hypothesis of fraud on the part of the investigator. While the relentless search for evidence of fraud may reveal the unreliability of some reported results and thus cast doubt on others, we may find in these incidental effects evidence for psi independent of experimenter artifacts.

The Case of Position Effects

It would seem that position effects, like declines in ESP scores, have occurred almost from the beginning of serious scientific psi research in academic settings. The results of Estabrooks (1927) are a revealing example. In four series of card experiments conducted between October 21, 1925, and May 18, 1926, at the Harvard Psychological Laboratory, Estabrooks found evidence of ESP in terms of a gross deviation from chance expectation. He noticed a decline in the performance of his subjects from the first 10 to the last 10 of their 20-trial runs and reported the results for the two halves separately, even though he made no attempt to evaluate the decline effect. A subsequent analysis by J.B. Rhine showed that there was significant difference in the subjects' rate of scoring between the two halves of the run. What is interesting is that in Series I there was a rest pause after the first 10 trails. There was no such rest period in Series II and III, and the decline was the least in Series I. Even more interesting was Series IV where distance was introduced between the agent and the subject, making sensory cues less likely.

Estabrooks describes the results of this series as "wholly negative." But the truth of the matter is that on calls of suits the subjects obtained 130 hits where 160 are expected. The deviation of −30 is significant beyond the 1 percent level, thus giving evidence for psi-missing. Also, the decline from the first half of the run to the second is statistically significant. This is not all. Series I and Series IV were carried out on the same subjects (for the most part) and in the same session, with the only difference in the test conditions being that in Series IV the distance factor was introduced. The agent was moved from room 10 to room 11 of Emerson Hall. This is a condition, as we can easily see now, that permits differential response, the tendency to score positively in one condition and negatively on the other when the subject participates in an experiment that has two conditions. I analyzed the results of Series I and IV to test for the differential effect and found very strong evidence. For calls on card suit, the subjects obtained a positive deviation of 31 hits in 560 trials in Series I and a negative deviation of 30 in Series IV. There is a highly significant difference between these scores ($x2 = 16.07$, $1\,df$; $p < .001$). The difference in the rate of scoring is significant even if we take the color instead of the suit as the target ($x2 = 13.05$, $1\,df$; $p < .001$). It is also plausible to interpret the difference in the rate of scoring between the two series in terms of decline because the subjects were tested in the distance condition after they were first tested in the same room.

While declines in scores were noticed by Richet (1923) and Jephson (1929) among others, it was J.B. Rhine who first suspected any lawfulness in them. In his first book, *Extrasensory Perception* (1934), he graphically presented the chronological declines in the scores of Linzmayer and Stuart, and the U-curves in the data of Pearce, Stuart, Cooper and Linzmayer. He also reported inverted U curves in the data of Ownbey and the striking declines in the runs of 50 or more trials found in the data of Frick and Linzmayer. The following passage from *Extrasensory Perception* reveals the thinking at that time about these effects:

> The unquestionable order shown by these curves reveals the factor that has become habitual for Pearce, varying regularly from call to call, giving the same general pattern with each cross-section group of 5 calls. What factor varies thus regularly, habitually? We would not expect ability to vary; cognitive and perceptual abilities are not known to vary thus. We look rather to the conative side, to variation in effort, again in the form of attention, since this is a factor we would naturally expect to find varying. Why attention should vary in just this pattern cannot be said. Some rhythm of the mind, some odd habit, perhaps originating in counting habits, or some earlier experience with the number 5 may be responsible. More force of conation is put into call No. 2 than in the others. And, as Dr. McDougall would say, more striving in perception would mean increased attention. There are, then, curves of attention pattern peculiar to this percipient for these conditions [Rhine, 1934, p. 183].

Extrasensory Perception After Sixty Years (Pratt *et al.*, 1940), which summarized all experimental research prior to 1940, does not add much except to make a note of the declines and U curves as pointed out in the 1934 monograph. It was only in 1941 that we have the first report of systematic effort to study the position effects represented by the observed U curves. The paper, entitled "Terminal Salience in ESP Performance," dealt with the Duke work on terminal salience in terms of the salience ratio and reported significant evidence that the subjects were more successful on the first and the fifth trials when runs of 25 trials were broken into five segments of five trials each. It is interesting that the evidence is stronger in the interrupted runs where the run sequence is "broken into five segments of five rails each by interposing cards in the deck containing drawings, numbers, or letters" (p. 181). The report also noted: "Salience ratios of all similar work by other experimenters, for which the essential data are available, have been computed. The results show terminal salience wherever the conditions would warrant expectation of it; otherwise they either show none or at most a trace" (p. 181).

This kind of "backward verification" of a finding, in an important sense, counters the fraud hypothesis and provides "fingerprint evidence" and throws new light on the question of experimenter artifacts. There are quite a few such analyses, especially in the PK area. What is needed, perhaps, is a systematic and comprehensive presentation with a focus on this evidence. The results of selected published reports which satisfy predetermined criteria might be examined to see whether the expected effects occurred. If they did, even when the experimenter himself was not aware of them, and if this happened across experimenters, we would come close to falsifying the fraud hypothesis.

The U curves and the salience ratios as incidental effects have since occurred in too many studies to be reviewed here. Interestingly enough, these effects have sometimes occurred in data which otherwise have given no evidence of psi. For example, the transoceanic ESP experiment by Rhine and Humphrey (1942) in which the subject, Karlo Marchesi in Zagreb, Yugoslavia, attempted to guess the sequence of cards in decks located in the Parapsychology Laboratory in Durham. The overall ESP results of this experiment did not significantly differ from chance. But when the results were reanalyzed, it was found that the covariation of salience ratios for the segment and the run gave $p < .0002$. In another experiment, an interesting U curve was observed in the data of tests carried out by Marchesi himself with cards located nearby. Even though the experimental conditions in this study were less than satisfactory, the observed U curve enhances the credibility of data in this experiment.

Betty Humphrey (1943) carried out a series of ESP experiments at Earlham College between 1938 and 1940 with the objective of discovering possible relations between ESP on the one hand and intelligence and personality ratings on the other. These tests were carried out before the publication of Rhine's paper on terminal salience. Analyzed for position effects in 1942, the data gave significant evidence of a covariation of the salience ratios for the segment and the run. There was also a significant decline between the first and the last 12 trials of the run. The covariation of salience ratios for the segment and the run seems to be a kind of reliability measure indicating a consistent patterning of subjects' responses in relation to the target position on the record sheet. Referring to her study, Humphrey wrote: "This is the fifth report using the salience statistic and it is the fifth instance of a significant and positive SSR-RSR covariation" (p. 17).

The position effects found in Schmeidler's sheep-goat data also suggest the improbability of experimenter or other such artifacts. Schmeidler (1944) reanalyzed her data of earlier sheep-goat experiments for position effects and found the familiar U curve in the pooled data of her two groups. Humphrey and Rhine (1944a) analyzed Schmeidler's data and found significant segment and run salience ratios as well as a significant covariation between them for the pooled data. Neither the ratios nor their covariation are significant for either of the groups separately. As Humphrey and Rhine (1944a) observed, "The point of principal interest is that although neither group of subjects produces significant salience ratios when the results of each group are taken separately, *both types of SR are significant* when the deviations of the two groups of subjects are pooled" (p. 125). It may safely be assumed that Schmeidler was not looking for these effects at the time of the experiment. Otherwise, she would have analyzed her data for these effects when she first prepared her reports. It is also interesting to note that the effects are found in the pooled data and not in the data of either group separately. So, if the difference in the scores of believers and disbelievers is artifactual in any sense, one should expect mirror images between the curves for sheep and goats. That this is not the case provides independent evidence for psi in this experiment.

With such a start and a number of subsequent confirmations, one would have thought that finally we had a dependable measure to track down the evasive ESP. Alas! Like several other promising leads, the covariation of salience ratios as a measure of psi fell into disuse and we hardly find any reference to it during the past 70 or more years. Again, how can one explain this state of affairs? It would not be conceivable that such a useful measure in the quest for a dependable psi effect could simply have been ignored. Nor is there any reason to believe that there is anything wrong with the covariance statistics employed. It is frustrating to me to think that this may be a consequence of changing fashions in psi inquiry. J.B. Rhine, in a private discussion, gave the following among possible reasons why this statistic fell into disuse: World War II dried up active research at Duke around the years from 1941 to 1946; major attention was diverted to the PK work and its publication beginning in 1943: new people coming into the field often had little acquaintance with the history of parapsychology and therefore overlooked this particular statistical device; and as time went on, the members of the Parapsychology Laboratory themselves were anxious to progress to other areas, such as the animal work, the classroom studies and the case collection. The research methodology and test procedures have changed. So the promising effects were lost in the process.

Whether or not these peculiar and unexpected distributions of hits in the data provide fraud-proof evidence of psi, the study of these "fingerprints"—position effects and such—is important for yet another good reason. They constitute virtually the only available tool that enables us to gain insight into the source of psi in an experiment and the relative roles of the experimenter and his subjects. As J.B. Rhine (1975) pointed out, the question of who is responsible for a given psi effect, whether it is the experimenter, the subject, or a judge (when one is involved), is often left unresolved in a number of experimental reports. This has become quite complicated with the widespread use of procedures to test for nonintentional psi. Thus, these effects, in addition to constituting what might conceivably be fraud-proof evidence of psi, promise a veritable gold mine for process-oriented research. From them the research workers in this area may hope to find evidence of a certain lawfulness in an otherwise evasive and capricious phenomenon. They may hope to discover similarities and differences between psi and other cognitive processes. More importantly, they may find in these effects the necessary identifying marks which will enable us to trace the true source of an observed effect. This in turn could help us to understand such puzzling phenomena as experimenter effects. The best payoff would be the development of typical parapsychological methods, as Rhine hoped.

It would be foolhardy to assume that the position effects, such as the declines, would convince the skeptics either of the lawfulness or reality of psi. On the contrary, critics have recklessly castigated psi research by pointing to these effects as post hoc and arbitrary labels to account for negative results. Alcock (2003), for example, referring to quarter declines in PK data writes: "While such an 'effect' always struck skeptical observers as somewhat convenient and arbitrary, it was touted as again suggesting some strange property of psi." He goes on to assert: "Note that none of these so-called effects [position effects] are anything other than arbitrary, post-hoc labels attached to unexpected negative outcomes. The employ-ment of arbitrary post hoc constructs to explain away failures and incon-sistencies in the data is a serious problem where one considers the scientific status of parapsychology" (Alcock, 2003, p. 39).

To an uninformed reader unfamiliar with the parapsychological lit-erature, the above admonition of Alcock appears to be a convincing refu-tation of psi claims. The truth of the matter, however, is different. Alcock is wrong in what he says and what he implies. The effects described were not arbitrary as contended by Alcock; rather, they were consistent across a number of studies. If they were post hoc, they were so in the best possible use of post hoc analysis in that they rule out the possibility of experimenter bias in cases where the experimenter did not expect and look for these effects. Again, it is naïve to think that these effects are peculiar to para-psychology. Parallel results are frequent, for example, in memory research. Salience and declines are commonly observed in the results of numerous ability testing situations. Also, it is misleading to imply that these effects are invented to explain away the failures. In many (not all) cases, the data contained significant evidence for psi independent of the presence of these effects. The effects themselves were shown to indicate some kind of law-fulness of the phenomena. We have argued that these effects, found post hoc in the data of experimenters not expecting them, is some kind of insurance against the hypothesis of experimenter bias.

The target article we (Rao and Palmer, 1987) published in the main-stream journal *Behavioral and Brain Sciences* is accompanied by nearly 50 peer commentaries. Commentators included well-known critics like James Alcock, Marco Bunge, Martin Gardner, C.E.M. Hansel, Ray Hyman, John Kihlstrom and Marcello Truzzi. Among parapsychologists are John Beloff, Stephen Braude, Stanley Krippner, Roger Nelson and Dean Radin, Rex Stanford and Charles Tart. There are of course others well known outside the field of parapsychology such as Yale psychologist Irvin Child, British psychologist H.J. Eysenck, philosopher Antony Flew, Nobel Lau-reate physicist Brian Josephson, and sociologist of science Trevor Pinch. The commentaries contain no surprises. Parapsychologists agreed that a good case has been made for psi and that much of the criticism has little validity and relevance in the light of the carefully weighted evidence. The critics are, however, equally firm in their assertion that psi research is methodologically flawed and the claims for the existence of different forms of psi are unsupported by valid data.

James Alcock presented the case from the skeptical perspective. His criticism of parapsychology is two-pronged. First, he attacked the motivation of parapsychologists. Second, he found fault with research that in his opinion is methodologically weak and flawed and lacks replication and consistency. Alcock characterized parapsychological inquiry as a "search for the soul." He went on to say that parapsychologists, who assert the existence of psi, are motivated by their concern for the soul and their covert commitment to a dualist metaphysics. He asserted that "parapsychological inquiry reflects the attempts to establish the reality of a nonmaterial aspect of human existence, rather than a search for anomalous phenomena" (Alcock, 1987, p. 553). Interestingly, Alcock ignores the fact that our article carefully argues against these unwarranted assumptions of critics.

Referring to the articles by Rao and Palmer (1987) and Alcock (1987), another skeptical commentator wrote: "Most of what is said here has been said before. What is perhaps surprising (especially to those of us who are inclined to doubt that there is anything unusual going on in the "psi" experiments) is that Alcock is not able to make a stronger case and that Rao and Palmer are as reasonable as they are" (Sanders, 1987, p. 607). Alcock is criticized by several commentators, including some skeptics, for his attempts to discredit psi research by suggesting that the proponents of psi champion a nonmaterial (nonnatural) causation of the phenomena. Alcock is obviously on the wrong track when it came to scientific parapsychology, as the thrust of psi research is essentially an attempt to naturalize the paranormal.

Parapsychologists, whatever their personal metaphysical preferences, are committed to treat psi as cognitive/communication anomalies in search of an explanation. As Sanders points out: "Alcock uses the terms in such a way that *either* the phenomena in question are 'paranormal' (i.e., to be explained in a way that transcends the normal parameters of explanation) *or* they are 'based on error and self-delusion.' This rules out, *a priori,* the possibility of *natural* phenomena which, although as yet inadequately documented, are really there and explainable in natural ways" (1987, p. 607, emphasis in the original).

Again, William Woodward (1987) suggests that Alcock is making a category mistake by attacking parapsychology for its dualist overtones. He asks, "Since when is 'mind-body dualism' a criterion by which to censure a scientific theory? And with what right is 'materialistic monism' a *desideratum* of good science? Are not monism and dualism metaphysical positions allowable to any scientific claim?" (pp. 617–618).

In response to the criticisms such as the above, Alcock somewhat toned down his original argument, and wrote that the term "search for the soul" is a metaphor and that "mind body dualism" is a label for the notion that mind can act independently of the body. Alcock now says that he does not consider that "the large majority of parapsychologists are trying to demonstrate the existence of disembodied 'souls' as such." However, he contends "there is an implicit search for something that lies outside the scientific worldview as we know it today..." (p. 627). He reiterates, "my view is that parapsychology reflects a worldview that opposes the predominant materialistic worldview of contemporary science" (p. 628).

When I first read Alcock's critique, I felt that his uncompromising prejudice and ad hominem arguments lacked logical conviction, and did little to promote healthy skepticism. Also, there was not much in his critique or other commentaries that suggested any crippling design defects, methodological flaws, or statistical fallacies in the research cited in Rao and Palmer that required us to revise our view that a strong case for cognitive anomalies is made by the existing evidence. However, on rereading more recently Alcock's *Behavioral Brain Sciences* articles, I have become a little more sympathetic and see some sense in his approach.

First, in his reply, Alcock makes a meaningful distinction between parapsychology and parapsychologists. Parapsychology in his view claims to study paranormal phenomena that, if genuine, could act independently of the physical constraints such as the body and the senses. He concedes, however, that parapsychologists are not necessarily committed to this view inasmuch as they regard psi as an anomaly that could eventually fit into the scientific paradigm. In other words, parapsychological phenomena, if real, warrant the assumption of primacy of mind/consciousness.

Alcock may be right on two counts. Psi may indeed imply independence of mind/consciousness from physical constraints. Also, it may be the case that science, as we understand it today, can tell us little about phenomena that are not understood within the known physical parameters. In other words, the scientific method, as we use it now, may be inappropriate to investigate psi.

Alcock would be wrong, however, if he infers from the presumed primacy of mind/consciousness implied by psi phenomena that psi is unreal and that the data accumulated in support of the phenomena are spurious. The real question is whether parapsychology has methods to investigate psi and learn of its nature if it were a manifestation of mind/consciousness conceived as a fundamental principle. Can the research efforts that are underway, in principle, take us beyond the current "anomalistic phase" to reveal the nature of psi? To put it somewhat crudely, how can we study "nonphysical" phenomena by physical methods? Thus it is the inherent paradox of naturalizing the supernatural that Alcock may have attempted to highlight by his colorful phrases.

Now, one may raise the question whether parapsychologists and the skeptical community of nonbelievers in psi share the same worldview and evaluative norms for evidence as implied by the mainstream science. If they do, the discussions and exchanges of the sort that took place in Alcock's and a few other forums would have settled the matter of evidence for psi to a large extent. There are fairly shared criteria for assessing scientific evidence; but they get distorted by the assumptions one makes. This possibility is not peculiar for parapsychological discussions. As William Woodward (1987) points out, even in the so-called hard sciences, during moments of controversy, it is possible to find experimental evidence that is compelling to some scientists but contested by others. Studies of these controversies have shown that the interpretation of experimental evidence is rarely straightforward and that experiments are always embedded within a network of assumptions—some theoretical and some related to the practical contingencies of experimentation. The outcomes of experiments can always be contested by challenging one or more of the many assumptions upon which those outcomes rely. Subsequent experiments to test the assumptions called into question may not resolve the issue because they too rest on a further network of assumptions.

The appearance of sharing the same worldview is promoted by psi researchers who attempt to minimize the revolutionary implications of psi and seek to adopt methods, models and procedures of conventional science. The opposite strategy is adopted by the critics of parapsychology such as Alcock who exaggerate the potential of psi to break away from the working paradigm in science. Parapsychologists, as Pinch suggests, want to look like other scientists; their critics wish to paint them in different colors. Neither have succeeded in an appreciable measure. Consequently, the controversy continues with no victor in sight.

That the debate about evidence continues inconclusively has thus more to do with the assumptions we make and the a priori probability accorded to psi than with the perceived flaws in research. Much of the methodological criticism leveled against parapsychological experiments would simply be ignored in many areas of mainstream science. Critics are rarely specific about the conditions psi experiments should satisfy (Pinch, 1987). Therefore, mere accumulation of more evidence is unlikely to take us any further. Crucial, critical or conclusive experiment in parapsychology is a mirage. We must look for progress from other perspectives such as replication and application of psi. The extent to which psi experiments are replicated and applied, their criticism would be muted to that degree.

4

Problems of Replication
and Application

Whereas a call for a conclusive and completely error-proof experiment seems to be somewhat misconceived, the emphasis on the need for replication, especially when controversial empirical claims are made, is well founded. If parapsychological phenomena are not replicable, though genuine, they would hardly excite any scientific interest. Isolated findings and unique events ordinarily hold little interest to scientists, unless they lead to or are capable of leading to some kind of general laws. ESP as a laboratory effect must be repeatedly observed with reasonable ease in order that it can be studied and understood as a natural phenomenon. Also, the necessity of a foolproof experiment recedes into the background as the phenomenon becomes increasingly replicable. Further, not-repeatable phenomena would have little possibility for application.

"If there is one common and basic feature of experimental science," wrote Moss & Butler (1978), "it is the possibility of the reproduction of findings by independent investigators" (p. 1067). One would hardly disagree with this statement in principle. But they go on to say: "Replication by a qualified nonsympathetic observer is the only valid guard against results which may have been contaminated by conscious or subconscious bias" (p. 1068). This statement cannot be accepted for at least two reasons. First, there are valid procedures for shielding the experimental results from being contaminated by the experimenter's preconceptions and bias. All good psi experiments involve double-blind procedures which are designed to control against experimenter or subject bias. Second, the argument that a skeptical experimenter is the only person whose replication of an ESP experiment is valid is untenable on several grounds:

(a) A skeptical experimenter may be just as strongly biased against ESP as the believer may be in the opposite direction. By the same argument, the skeptic's findings, when null or negative, would carry no greater credibility than the positive findings of the believer. (b) The nature of psi may indeed be such that a negatively motivated experimenter would interfere with its occurrence. This possibility is not unique to parapsychological phenomena. For example, certain experimenters do not, for a good reason, obtain Rosenthal's experimenter expectancy effects (Rosenthal, 1976). (c) When a skeptic obtains significant psi results, he would cease to be a skeptic. Since he is now a "believer," his positive results, by this logic, would not be expected to carry any weight with other skeptics. (d) Finally there is no guarantee that a person who is skeptical of psi would employ the correct experimental procedures, would draw only legitimate inferences or would be honest.

Parapsychologists like their critics have stressed the importance of replication, even though they seem to disagree as to what constitutes a replication. At one extreme, there are those who believe that parapsychological phenomena have been replicated over and over again (Radin, 1997); and at the other extreme there are those who dismiss the whole field on the ground that the only test for the reality of a phenomenon is that it be reproduced by anyone wishing to verify its existence (Alcock, 2003). This situation is a consequence of the fact that Radin and Alcock mean different things by replication.

There are two significant senses in which the term *replication* is used while discussing parapsychological experiments. It is used in the sense of replication on demand. Replication as a criterion for distinguishing the genuine and the spurious in science makes the assumption that "to *be* is to be replicable." As an existential criterion, replication may be understood as producibility of a phenomenon on demand. This is replication in a strong sense.

Some consider replication, not in a strictly "either-or" fashion, but as a continuum that may involve several gradations. This is *statistical* or weak replication, which refers to the fact that in a given number of experiments, an effect occurs more often than one has reason to expect by chance. Again, replication is used to answer two different sorts of questions. First, it is used as a test to ascertain the existence of psi. In this use it raises reality questions and seeks to answer whether psi is genuine or spurious. In the second use replication addresses the frequency question, i.e., how frequently is a given phenomenon reported to have been observed or expected to be observed?

Statistical replication is of two sorts, the predictive and the postdictive. The postdictive replication is a judgment based on a retrospective assessment of all the attempted observations of an effect which may or may not have predictive validity. A predictive replication, on the other hand, involves a successful or credible predictive assertion of the frequency of the occurrence of a given effect.

Postdictive findings are of course relevant for making predictions. In fact, their greatest value lies when they lead to predictive findings. But it does not logically follow, however, that a postdictive finding is invalid if it fails to prove predictive, because in some areas of study the fact of making a prediction may itself be a contaminating variable. Psi may operate in such self-obscuring ways as to render the postdictive analysis devoid of any predictive value. If this is the case, psi researchers need to actively reconsider their methodology.

Jessica Utts (2015), writing on what constitutes replication in parapsychology, refers to different meanings of replication in scientific literature and their relevance to parapsychology. Replication does not simply mean finding a repeatable experiment. Such is bound to be an elusive goal, because in experiments involving human subjects it is almost impossible to replicate the original conditions. In psi research it is especially so because the experimenter's beliefs enter into the manifestation of psi. Complicating the matter there is widespread evidence in the literature for experimental psi effects. Utts argues that "there is no such thing as an exact methodological replication in studies using human participants" (2015, p. 181). What is possible, however, is what she calls statistical replication. Statistical replication in her view refers to several numerical measures. They include consistent hit patters, consistent correlations, consistent effect sizes and consistent relationships. Utts agrees that p-values by themselves do not define replication. "Erroneous attempts to define replication by using p-values have misled researchers across many disciplines for many years" (2015, p. 191).

The notion that "to exist is to be replicable" is of course logically untenable. As Michael Scriven (1962) pointed out, such a notion "is based on a simple misunderstanding of the requirements of scientific experiments. We cannot repeat the study of the eclipse that was made three years ago.... Repeatability is not a requirement unless the claim made is of a very strong kind" (p. 97). The evidence for psi comes from spontaneous case reports as well as laboratory results. The issue of replication for the purpose of attesting their reality is clearly irrelevant when dealing with spontaneous happenings. However, replication has a legitimate place when we consider experimental results.

Even for Karl Popper, who insists on inter-subjective testability, repeated observation is not essential for believing in a phenomenon. Popper credits Kant as perhaps the first to realize that the objectivity of scientific statements requires that they be inter-subjectively testable. As Popper (1959) puts it: "Only by such repetitions can we convince ourselves that we are not dealing with a mere isolated 'coincidence,' but with events which on account of their regularity and reproducibility, are in principle inter-subjectively testable" (p. 45). To the question how often an effect has to be actually reproduced in order to be a "reproducible effect," Popper's answer is: "In some cases *not even once.* If I assert that there is a family of white ravens in the New York zoo, then I assert something which can be tested *in principle.* If somebody wishes to test it and is informed, upon arrival, that the family has died, or that it has never been heard of, it is left to him to accept or reject my falsifying basic statement. As a rule, he will have means for forming an opinion by examining witnesses, documents, etc.; that is to say, by appealing to other inter-subjectively testable and reproducible facts" (p. 87n). It is clear from this that even for Popper replication does not necessarily involve repeated observation beyond the possibility of inter-subjective validation.

Harry Collins (1978) argued that "in controversial areas replicability does not work as a demarcation criterion for the genuine and the spurious, but rather, replicability is a notion that is attributed to what are considered genuine phenomena" (p. 19). As Collins points out, replication is a social process and there is sometimes room for disagreeing on whether a finding is replicated. If a student in a chemistry laboratory does not obtain the results he or she is supposed to, we do not question the veracity of previous results but conclude that the student did not do the experiment properly. This is so because we have already accepted the original result as an established fact. In a case where we have not accepted the results of a study as genuine, we are more likely to interpret a failure to replicate as a refutation of the original claim rather than question our own ability to carry out an exact replication of the original study. Thus, our interpretation of the result of a replication attempt depends strongly on our prior notions about the credibility of the original finding.

The crucial point is that a basic condition for a replication is that it be an *exact copy* of the original. But the notion of exact copy is itself problematic inasmuch as some of the knowledge involved may be "tacit" and not subject to clear articulation, more like acquiring a skill than communicating a formula. Collins (1978) illustrates this point by referring to seven attempts to build a certain type of laser after the details of inventing this device were made public in 1970. As he puts it: "Where scientists tried to build a laser based on written information, or information provided by third parties who were not themselves replicators, they failed. Furthermore, even prolonged personal contact was not necessarily sufficient. Some scientists could not succeed in building a TEA laser and eventually abandoned the project in spite of their good access to the sources of help" (p. 9).

So, then, the possibility that tacit knowledge may be required to replicate a finding successfully leaves open the question whether a replication attempt is an exact copy of the original. The proponents of the original finding could argue, when the replication fails, that it is not an *exact copy,* while the opponents may insist that it is. Thus, the whole issue of the replicability of a phenomenon, it would seem, boils down to an exercise in persuasion.

It may be argued that the distinction between *absolute* (strong) and *statistical* (weak) replication is not indeed that basic and that the latter is simply imperfect replication. A real phenomenon is something that is *in principle* repeatable. If a phenomenon occurred once, it will occur again, provided the same set of circumstances arise. If one had perfect understanding of the critical variables, he could invariably predict its occurrence; if he had control over those variables he could produce the phenomenon on demand.

The above argument also has severe problems. First, the notion of perfect duplication of conditions is an absurdity. No two experiments can be exactly alike if for no other reason than that each must occur at two separate points in time. Understanding of crucial variables is helpful and necessary for replicating a phenomenon. But lack of such an understanding is the beginning point of all inquiry. The goal of scientific investigation is to achieve such an understanding. Therefore, it is inappropriate to suggest that a phenomenon is spurious because it has not been replicated. What is spurious may be one's claimed understanding of that phenomenon.

Even if we can thus separate the issue of existence from replication, we will still find the question of replication an important one for parapsychology. Replication may be seen as a frequency index: what are the possibilities of psi occurring in a given experimental context. Such information would help one to make informed decisions whether to commit to researching in such an area. Psi may be real, but it will have little consequence for a researcher if the prospect of obtaining it in one's laboratory is dismal or remote.

Are Psi Phenomena Replicable?

Now, let us turn to an examination of the extent to which psi phenomena are replicated or replicable. No one in the field, I think, would argue that psi phenomena are replicated in the strong sense. But most would hold that the phenomena have been observed repeatedly in the past. One could hardly expect fifty years of unbroken investigation of any phenomena if they were not repeatedly observed. In another sense, too, parapsychological phenomena seem to have been replicated. A review by Charles Honorton (1977) forty years ago shows that of the 16 psi studies involving meditation, nine gave evidence of psi beyond the conventional 5 percent significance level. There were 42 studies using hypnosis, and 22 of them gave significant evidence of psi. Ten out of 13 studies involving induced relaxation, and eight out of 16 involving ganzfeld stimulation gave significant results supportive of psi hypotheses. Thus Honorton has made a strong case for the replicability of psi effects as early as in 1977. Since then a number of other reviews yielded results that provide strong evidence of the reality of certain effects in psi research.

Of the 19 reported series of experiments bearing on EEG alpha activity and ESP scores, 15 contained significant effects of one sort or another. Only four showed no effect. Nine of the 15 significant studies had at least one effect that might be reasonably assumed to have been predicted (Rao, 1979). Palmer's (1971) review of sheep-goat studies has shown that in 13 of the 17 experiments that employed standard methods of analysis, the sheep (who believe in the possibility of ESP) obtained better scores than the goats (who do not believe). Six of these 13 achieved statistical significance. None of those which gave opposite results were significant. Carl Sargent (1981) reviewed English-language reports on the relationship between ESP and extroversion and reported that significant confirmations of a positive relationship occur at more than six times the chance error. Honorton, Ferrari & Bem (1998) published a meta-analysis of ESP and extroversion studies and a new confirmation.

Apart from these general reviews and counts of successful experiments in a given area, there have been systematic meta-analyses of a number of parapsychological effects. As Mullen and Rosenthal (1985) explain, meta-analysis is "a method of statistical analysis wherein the units of analysis are the results of independent studies, rather than the responses of individual subjects" (p. 2). It is generally believed that meta-analysis "provides a much more accurate assessment of a body of research than the traditional descriptive and narrative literature review" (Radin, 1997, p. 54).

Dean Radin (1997) gave cumulative results of psi experiments in different areas with impressive overall effects. In dream-telepathy studies, for example, the hit rate of all the 450 experimental sessions carried out between 1966 and 1973 is 63 percent when the chance expected rate is

50 percent. This is an extremely improbable result were it attributed to chance (odds of 75,000,000 to 1). Julie Milton (1993) published a meta-analysis of all the free-response ESP experiments conducted without any alteration of ordinary state of consciousness, such as dreaming and hypnosis. The data came from 55 published reports involving 35 investigators and 1158 subjects. The overall observed effect is highly significant (odds of 10,000,000 to 1 against chance). Milton concludes that the result cannot be explained away by selective reporting of successful results. A meta-analysis of Tony Lawrence (1993) of sheep-goat effect investigated by 37 different investigators and published in 73 reports involving about 4500 subjects shows that people who believe in the possibility of psi tend to obtain higher ESP scores then the nonbelievers. Lawrence reported that neither the file-drawer problem (selective reporting of successful experiments) nor the experimental quality of the studies can explain away the statistical significance of the sheep-goat studies.

Charles Honorton and Diane Ferrari (1989) published a meta-analysis of all the forced-choice precognition experiments conducted between 1935 and 1987. The cumulative results of 309 studies have a p value of 10. The analysis showed that it did not seem reasonable that either selective reporting or quality of the studies is related to the significance of the results. There are a number of other meta-analyses. (For a more recent list of reviews and meta-analysis of parapsychological results see Kelly *et al.*, 2007; Cardeña, Palmer & Marcusson-Clavertz, 2015.)

Replication of REG Experiments

We have referred earlier to the work of Helmut Schmidt using REGs in micro PK tests. These experiments follow a long series of experiments by J.B. Rhine and others on the effect of human intention on dice in motion. Dean Radin (1997) summarized the results of 69 PK experiments with dice and concluded that there was "highly significant evidence for mind-matter interaction... the effects were constant across different measures of experimenter quality; and the selective reporting 'file-drawer' required a twenty-to-one ratio of unretrieved, non-significant studies for each observed study. Thus chance, quality, and selective reporting could not explain away the results" (pp. 137–138).

Schmidt, as we have seen, pioneered in micro PK experiments using REGs. During the past four decades, literally hundreds of experimental reports on micro PK have appeared. Nelson and Radin (1989) conducted a survey and meta-analysis of all REG (also referred to as RNG) experiments done until 1987. Their survey gave 152 references and uncovered 832 studies, 597 of which are experimental and 235 control series. The overall PK results are highly significant (trillion to one odds against chance). Nelson and Radin analyzed the results to see if the significance of the REG PK results are related to the experimental quality of the studies. One of the criticisms of the meta-analysis is that by grouping together experiments of uneven quality, we compromise on the quality of experiments and that studies involving poor experimental controls and possibility of errors may be the ones responsible for the overall significance. Therefore, one aspect of meta-analysis is to check if the quality of experimental conditions is related to the experimental outcome. If, for example, there is a significant negative correlation between the quality of experimental controls and PK results, then it is likely that the results are not genuine PK, but spurious artifacts. To test this possibility Nelson and Radin developed a set of 16 quality criteria and rated each experiment on the basis of them. They found the observed hit rates (effect size) were not related to the experimental quality of the studies. Further, they estimated that over 50,000 unreported insignificant experiments would be required to reduce the overall significance of the results to chance levels.

Further confirmation of the replicability of REG PK results comes from an analysis of the large database provided by the Princeton Engineering Anomalies Research (PEAR) laboratories headed by Robert Jahn. The PEAR Lab had 284 studies in 1989. By 1996 this number grew to 1,262, which means that nearly 1000 more experiments were added since the publication Nelson-Radin meta-analysis of REG PK experiments. According to an analysis by York Dobyns (1996), the results of the new experiments provide evidence for close replication of the results reported by Nelson and Dean in their meta-analysis. Further, there are also later meta-analyses by Radin, Nelson, Dobyns & Houtkooper (2006a, 2006b). Thus, a case has been made for predictive replicability of REG PK results, even though there is some evidence for decrease in the effect size across Princeton experiments.

Ganzfeld and ESP

A second major research paradigm in which the replication rate over a relatively large number of studies has been systematically evaluated concerns ESP in the Ganzfeld. Since the publication of the first Ganzfeld experiment in parapsychology in 1974, significant ESP results in the Ganzfeld were reported replicated by Terry & Honorton (1976), Braud *et al.* (1975), and Sargent (1980), among others. According to a count adopted both by parapsychologist Honorton (1985) and critic Ray Hyman (1985), there were by then 42 published ESP experiments that used the ganzfeld procedure. After correcting for multiple analyses, if any, Honorton concluded that 19 of the experiments (45 percent) gave significant evidence for psi at or beyond the 5 percent level. Moreover, 26 of the 36 studies for which the direction of the effect could be clearly determined (72 percent) gave deviations in the positive direction, as compared to the 50 percent expected by chance. Hyman (1985) dissented, concluding that the "rate of 'successful' replication is probably very close to what should be expected by chance given the various options for multiple testing exhibited in the data base" (p. 25).

Responding to Hyman's critique Charles Honorton pointed out examples of inconsistent or inappropriate assignment of flaw ratings in Hyman's analysis. He then presented his own meta-analysis that eliminated multiple analyses and other problems mentioned by Hyman and argued that neither selective reporting nor alleged procedural flaws account for significant psi effects reported in the ESP-ganzfeld studies.

Subsequently, Hyman & Honorton (1986) issued a "joint communiqué" on the psi Ganzfeld debate. In it they agree that the overall significance of the effect cannot be reasonably explained away by such considerations as selective reporting or multiple analyses. They disagree, however, on the degree to which the effect constitutes evidence for psi, because of remaining differences over the impact of alleged flaws. More important, however, are the recommendations they make for conducting future experiments in this area.

Interestingly, Cornell psychologist Daryl Bem and Honorton (1994) published subsequently a report of their ESP-ganzfeld experiments in the mainstream psychology journal *Psychological Bulletin*, which essentially incorporated the secure and stringent procedures recommended by Hyman and Honorton in their joint communiqué for ESP ganzfeld experiments. This study, consisting of 11 experiments, utilized computer control of the experimental protocol. The new setup with all the necessary controls, called autoganzfeld, gave results that strongly support the existence of a psi effect in the data. Thus the new study replicates the ESP ganzfeld effect meeting the "stringent standards" requirement as recommended by Hyman and Honorton in their joint communiqué.

Julie Milton and Richard Wiseman (1999) published a follow-up meta-analysis of 30 more ganzfeld–ESP studies conducted between 1983 and 1997. Their analysis did not provide significant cumulative evidence for the ganzfeld effect. Bem, Palmer & Broughton (2001) further updated the ESP ganzfeld database by adding ten more studies published after 1997 and not included in the meta-analysis by Milton and Wiseman. When these 10 additional studies are included, the meta-analysis yields a mean effect size that is again statistically significant, though smaller than the one observed in the earlier studies. Bem *et al.* (2001) in the above mentioned study updated the database of ganzfeld–ESP and reported that studies which followed standard ganzfeld procedures yield comparable significant effect sizes. They also noted, however, that some of the experiments included in the new database appeared to deviate significantly from the standard protocol of the ganzfeld experiment. Therefore, they arranged for three independent raters unfamiliar with the studies involved to rate the degree to which each of the 40 studies in the new database deviated from the standard protocol. As expected, they found that "the effect size achieved by a replication is significantly correlated with the degree to which it adhered to the standard protocol." They point out: "Standard replications yield significant effect sizes comparable to those obtained in the past." As it stands now, they report, we have a broad range of replications covering a long period, involving over 90 experiments by a wide range of investigators. They show a fairly robust effect comparable across studies that adhere to the standard ganzfeld protocol.

Palmer (2003) in a comprehensive review of the debate of ESP in the ganzfeld observed that the "first conclusion is that the aggregate database does provide evidence for a genuine psi effect. However, heterogeneity of results across experiments indicates that the phenomena [are] not easily replicable. The second conclusion is that conventional alternative explanations offered for the observed results tend to be conceivable, but even critics sometimes agree that they are implausible" (p. 51).

The proportions of statistically significant studies in the two areas we have reviewed are not trivial, and they compare favorably with comparable examples from psychology, such as the placebo effect (Moerman, 1981) and the experimenter expectancy effect (Rosenthal & Rubin, 1978). The latter authors, for example, reviewed evidence on the experimenter expectancy effect in eight types of experiments. The median replication rate was 39 percent. Except for one highly replicable topic (animal learning: 73 percent), the percentages ranged from 22 to 44 percent, which is very similar to what we find in parapsychology.

More recently, Storm *et al.* (2010) did a meta-analysis of 30 ganzfeld-ESP studies carried out between 1997 to 2008 and found that the ganzfeld procedure continues to be a useful method for obtaining psi more consistently in the laboratory.

Replication of ESP Extroversion-ESP Experiments

For more than half a century, extroversion-introversion as one of the most widely explored dimensions of personality in relation to ESP. We have already referred to the review of the English-language reports bearing on the extroversion-ESP hypothesis published until 1980 by Sargent (1981) and significant evidence for replication of ESP-extroversion experiments.

Honorton, Ferrari and Bem (1998) reported a comprehensive meta-analysis of 60 independent studies of ESP-extroversion relationship involving 2,963 subjects. The overall weighted mean correlation for all the studies is significant, suggesting that extraverted subjects tend to obtain higher ESP scores than introverted subjects. They point out, however, that, when the order of presentation of the ESP test in relation to the personality test is taken into consideration, only the free-response studies and not those involving forced-choice tests show significant overall correlation between extroversion and ESP scores. When the personality tests were administered first and the subjects did not have any knowledge of their ESP scores before they took the personality test, the results of forced-choice ESP tests showed no significant correlation with extroversion scores. Only the free-response scores are correlated significantly with personality scores across experiments. This observation leads them to conclude that the significant correlations observed in forced-choice studies may be an artifact of the subjects' knowledge of their ESP scores. The report also contains the results of a new confirmation of ESP/extroversion relationship in a free-response study.

John Palmer and James Carpenter (1998) question the conclusion of Honorton, Ferrari, and Bem (1998) that the extroversion/ESP relationship is limited only to free-response studies. They point out that (a) personality scales are not generally susceptible to situational biases and that (b) additional analyses show that the extroversion-ESP relationship for forced-choice tests is a genuine psi effect. Extroversion-ESP studies used in the meta-analysis include both group testing and individual testing for ESP. Most of the free-response studies employed individual testing whereas many of the forced-choice studies were done in groups. This is more likely to be the confounding variable rather than testing by forced-choice or free-response methods.

Palmer and Carpenter show that a significant relationship between ESP and extroversion score is present in the data of individual tests and not in the group test data. When group testing studies are removed from the analysis, the extroversion–ESP relationship is found to be of comparable magnitude for forced-choice and free-response ESP tests. Palmer and Carpenter refer also to Experiment C of the Kanthamani & Rao (1973a, 1973b) study in which the subjects did not have knowledge of their ESP scores at the time they took the personality test. Moreover, a study by Krishna & Rao (1991) showed that feedback of ESP scores did not bias the responses of the subjects to a personality questionnaire, as the hypothesis of Honorton *et al.* assumes. As mentioned before, a report on a meta-analysis of ESP-extraversion studies and a new confirmation was published by Honorton, Ferrari & Bem in 1998. Among the more recent studies of ESP and extraversion is the one by Parra & Villanueva (2003).

Broughton (2004) reported a study where he found no significant relationship between psi scores and extraversion measured by MBTI. If openness to experience is considered as an aspect of extraversion, there are studies that found significant relationship between psi scores and openness to experience (Hitchman, Roe, & Sherwood, 2012).

Some Criticisms of Meta-Analyses

A number of objections can be raised to the kind of procedures used in obtaining these replication rates, objections similar to those that have been raised in discussing experimenter expectancy effects (Barber, 1969, 1973). Some of the shortcomings of meta-analysis include their inability to determine the true effect size involved (Baptista, Derakhshani, & Tressoldi, 2015).

Comparability of Studies: One objection to such analyses is that the studies included are often not directly comparable. This objection has merit, but only to a point. We should not insist, for example, that all experiments be strict replications of one another. So long as they constitute conceptual replications, methodological differences can often be treated as random variables that actually serve to increase the generality of any conclusions that might be drawn from the analysis. On the other hand, it is usually desirable that the outcomes of the studies be represented by, or reduced to, some common metric. One of Hyman's (1985) criticisms of the ganzfeld database, for example, was that the studies used divergent and sometimes multiple measures of the dependent variable, and that the primary measure was sometimes not specified in advance. In response to this objection, Honorton (1985) computed a new analysis, using as a single, uniform z-scores measure representing the proportion of trials in the experiment in which the subject correctly picked out the target during the judging (i.e., direct hits). This was the measure used in the original ganzfeld experiment by Honorton & Harper (1974), and it was the measure most frequently reported in the database as a whole. Sufficient information for this analysis was provided for 28 of the 42 experiments in the database of the first meta-analysis. These experiments came from ten different laboratories. Twenty-three of the 28 experiments (82 percent) yielded positive z-scores, 12 of which were individually significant at the .05 level on a one-tailed test. The cumulative z-score for all 28 studies, computed by the Stouffer method (Rosenthal, 1984), was 6.60 ($p < 10$).

Publication Bias: A second criticism concerns whether these analyses possibly suffer from biased selection and the so-called publication artifact; that is, nonsignificant results may systematically go unreported, and therefore the sample of studies may not reflect the true state of affairs. This is called the 'file-drawer effect" which assumes that studies with insignificant psi results go systematically unreported. This argument works both ways. One could say that investigators predisposed to disbelieve in psi tend, to suppress their findings if they are suggestive of psi. Close scrutiny of the field suggests that publication bias cannot explain away the significant number of replications in parapsychology. It was indicated earlier how many unreported nonsignificant studies would be required to reduce the results to chance levels. Parapsychologists are sensitive to the possible impact of unreported negative results, more so than most other scientists. The Parapsychological Association (PA) has advocated a policy of publishing the results of all methodologically sound experiments, irrespective of outcome. Since 1976, this policy has been reflected in the publications of all the journals affiliated with the PA.

This policy, however, cannot guarantee that researchers will submit negative findings for publication. Fortunately, thanks to a technique developed by Rosenthal (1979), it is possible to estimate the number of unpublished and nonsignificant experiments that would be necessary to reduce an entire database to nonsignificance. Honorton (1985), for example, used Rosenthal's technique to estimate that 423 nonsignificant ganzfeld studies would be needed to reduce the direct-hit studies in this database to a nonsignificant level. Given the complex and time-consuming nature of the ganzfeld procedure, it is unreasonable to suppose that so many experiments exist in the "file drawer." As noted earlier, Hyman now agrees that selective reporting cannot account for the aggregate findings in the ganzfeld database (Hyman and Honorton, 1986).

Finally, there are some areas in parapsychology where we can be reasonably certain we have access to all the experiments done. One such area concerns the relationship between ESP performance and the ratings obtained on the Defense Mechanism Test (DMT) developed in Sweden by Ulf Kragh and associates (Kragh and Smith, 1970). Because the administration and scoring of this test requires specialized training available only to a few individuals, it has been possible for Martin Johnson of the University of Utrecht, the leading authority on the DMT and a man very sensitive to the issue of publication bias, to keep track of the number of relevant experiments conducted by qualified persons. In all ten of these studies, the less defensive subjects scored higher on the ESP test. In seven of them, this effect was significant at the .05 level, one-tailed (Johnson and Haraldsson, 1984).

There are more recent critics who harped on the publication bias argument to account for significant psi results attested by a number of meta-analysis, for example, Bösch *et al.* (2006). They conclude that publication bias "appears to be the easiest and most encompassing explanation of the significant findings of the reported meta-analysis. Radin *et al.* (2006b) rebutted the criticism by pointing out because the model assumed by Bösch *et al.* leaves about half of the heterogeneity unaccounted.

Controls and Flaws: A third line of criticism relates to experimental controls. As pointed out earlier, it is argued, for example, that the replication of an experimental result by other experimenters "does not assure that experimental artifacts were not responsible for the results in the replication as well as in the original experiment" (Alcock, 1981, p. 134).

It is true, of course, that the replication of an effect implies nothing directly about its cause. But it is also a basic premise of experimental science that replication reduces the probability of *some* other alternative explanations, particularly those related to the honesty or competence of individual experimenters. As Alcock (1981) himself states in another context, "It is not enough for a researcher to report his observations with regard to a phenomenon; he could be mistaken, or even dishonest. But if other people, using his methodology, can independently produce the same results, it is much more likely that error and dishonesty are not responsible for them" (p. 133).

A more specific set of criticisms has been offered by Hyman (1985) with reference to the Ganzfeld-ESP database. He concluded that the case for replication in this area is unconvincing because of the presence of methodological flaws such as potential sensory cues (e.g., including the target handled by the sender in the set given to the subject for judging), suboptimal randomization of targets (e.g., hand-shuffling), and multiple statistical analyses of the data. Honorton (1985) replied that Hyman made several unsupported assumptions in his analysis and interpretation of the ganzfeld-ESP data, and, in particular, that he often did not assign flaws properly with respect to his own criteria. Honorton presented his own analyses, arguing that the replication rate is not significantly influenced by the presence or absence of potential flaws in these studies. Although continuing to disagree on the seriousness of the "flaws," the reviewers have agreed that "the present data base does not support any firm conclusion about the relationship between 'flaws' and study outcome" (Hyman and Honorton, 1986).

"Disbelievers" as Replicators: Several critics of psi research (Alcock, 1981; Kurtz, 1981; Moss and Butler, 1978) have argued that the replication work must be done by investigators who are unsympathetic to psi, a category that would exclude most (but not all) parapsychologists.

It should be pointed out that it is not a common practice in other sciences to disqualify positive results from experiments conducted by researchers who are favorably disposed to the hypothesis they are testing. The personal beliefs of researchers are rarely reported and may often be difficult to determine reliably. However, if such a standard could be applied retrospectively to published research in psychology, it is likely that there would not be much left. The fact that parapsychologists are singled out for this treatment is symptomatic of the often ad hominem nature of the psi controversy. By the same token it may be argued that negative results from "disbelievers" in psi be rejected on this basis.

Although it is reasonable to assume that experimenters who obtained strong positive results in the first few psi experiments they conducted were converted to a "belief" in psi by these results (if they were not "believers" already), we have far too few data to draw any conclusions about the distribution of attitudes of investigators at the time they undertook their first psi experiments. Thus we really do not know how many "disbelievers" have obtained positive psi results. Even if it happens to be the case that only believers obtain positive results, it is not sufficient justification to question their positive results. We independently know that in psi research, belief is a significant variable.

Limitations: Having noted above some of the skeptical comments on and the response to the use of meta-analysis in ganzfeld-ESP research, we may note that meta-analysis is essentially meant as a post-hoc analysis of the data and therefore entails its associated limitations. J.E. Kennedy (2004; 2006), who has expertise in parapsychological research and also familiarity in recent medical research, argues persuasively that meta-analysis is a poor substitute for a good experiment. He quotes from a research methodology book in the field of oncology:

> Our inclusion of [meta-analysis] in a chapter on exploratory analyses is an indication of our belief that the importance of meta-analysis lies mainly in exploration, not confirmation. In settling therapeutic issues, a meta-analysis is a poor substitute for one large well-conducted trial. In particular, the expectation that a meta-analysis will be done does not justify designing studies that are too small to detect realistic differences with adequate power [Green, Benedetti, & Crowley, 2003, p. 231].

Kennedy suggests that the meta-analysis should be followed by large well-designed experiments using power analysis, whose results may be considered as confirmatory. He further points out that there are no such well designed studies to confirm the exploratory findings of meta-analyses in parapsychology. Referring to the ganzfeld-ESP database, which is arguably the best in psi research, Kennedy points out that a well-designed confirmatory study with a sample size of at least 192 would be required to confirm the positive findings of the ganzfeld-ESP experiments and that he knows of no such study.

Kennedy (2006) makes another important point. Normally there should be positive correlation between effect size and sample size. As stated by Egger *et al.* (1997), a negative correlation between the two is indicative of some kind of a bias involved in the meta-analysis. It is the case that in parapsychological research we often do not find a positive correlation between effect size and sample size. In fact there is some evidence that effect size and sample size are negatively correlated in PK studies with RNGs (Bösch, Steinkamp & Boller, 2006). In psi research, the decline of effect sizes is all too common, leading researchers to frequently change their strategies often resulting in reinventing the wheel. All this makes Kennedy wonder whether indeed "psi conforms to the properties of standard statistical research" (2006, p. 411).

If we assume that in some ways current statistical modeling is inappropriate for parapsychological research, does it follow that the cognitive anomalies of the kind discussed above are simply artifacts arising from inappropriate use of statistics and experimental methods? The present author does not believe so. Kennedy (1994; 1995) himself called attention to the goal-seeking dimension of psi and argued that the "hypothesis of goal-oriented psi experimenter effects is logically consistent ... and now has strong empirical support that the outcomes of psi experiments are typically unrelated to sample size" (Kennedy, 2006, p. 412).

Concluding Comments

For many psi researchers there is reasonable evidence that psi phenomena are replicated in a statistical sense. However, this view is not uniformly shared, as seen from Kennedy's incisive comments. While the massive empirical database clearly rejects the null hypothesis and suggests the existence of an anomaly in the data, it is not obvious what the observed replications really mean. Therefore, it seems premature to conclude that parapsychologists are now in a position to take up the critics' challenge and say that, if one carries out a psi experiment following a set of procedures, a certain number of times he will probably obtain significant evidence of psi. For those of us who are in the field long enough, greater caution appears to be in order.

A relevant discussion of this issue is found in a controversy relating to a "distribution" problem as posed by Greenwood and Greville (1979a), the two statisticians long associated with the quantification of parapsychological data. While affirming that the statistical methods employed to establish the existence of psi are generally valid, they caution that several of the statistical tests used to establish relationships between psi and other variables "are unwarranted since no statistical or probability distribution is known to exist involving psi scores." The implication is that if psi exists but is too capricious to permit any regularity as measured by our statistical tests, then we may not expect to understand its nature by following the test methods we have used since midcentury. Whether or not the position of Greenwood and Greville is logically and mathematically justifiable, there appears to be a general agreement that our methods of statistical evaluation are appropriate only if psi phenomena are *known* to have a statistical model or at least are *assumed* to have one whose nature is not yet known.

Greenwood and Greville (1979b) agree that "it is not necessary to know the nature of the distribution but merely the fact that there is one." In other words, our methods of studying psi assume that there is a measure of orderliness and regularity in its occurrence, even if such a regularity is not presently established; and if the phenomena inherently have no regularity, then all our attempts to understand them following these methods have been in vain. This leads us to the distinction made above between predictive and postdictive replication. What we have in parapsychology is postdictive replication, and we need to have more data in support of predictive replication.

There is an important distinction between two kinds of generalizations made from the data bearing on the question of replication. The conclusion that certain parapsychological effects had in the past a replication rate of 50 percent arrived at by a thorough review of all the previous experiments, does not necessarily warrant the assertion that these effects have a .5 probability of being replicated. The relevant distinction is between what may be called *summary* probability statements and *predictive* probability assertions. Summary probability is the probability derived by a complete enumeration of all the relevant events. Such a probability may or may not have predictive validity. Predictive probability, on the other hand, involves an inductive leap and refers to the past as well as future events. We should be in a position to say not only that 50 percent of the previously conducted micro-PK effects were significant but that we also expect to obtain 50 percent replication in all future micro-PK experiments. The former merely suggests a trend, whereas the latter assertion makes an assumption of regularity of occurrence whose validity can be established, not by the enumeration of past events, but by a verification of the predicted future occurrences. Thus, one has little difficulty in believing that the micro-PK experiments have, in the past, an excellent rate of replication. One can even be encouraged to assume a certain amount of regularity in the occurrence of micro-PK effects. But such an assumption needs further validation by a series of planned studies.

Available evidence warrants the assertion that some of the findings in parapsychology are replicated to a statistically significant degree. It does not follow, however that psi effects can be reproduced on demand. Also, replicability in the "predictive" sense has not been established. The "weak" replication in a statistical sense, evidenced by a number of meta-analyses, is unlikely to be any more convincing to the skeptical community than the experiments cited for evidence of psi. The reasons are the same, even though the arguments vary. Statistical evidence of the sort reported by psi researchers does not simply meet the evidential criterion of skeptics who accord near zero a priori probability for the existence of psi.

The distinction between predictive and postdictive replication is crucial in parapsychology. As already mentioned, it may throw light on the so-called self-obscuring aspects of psi, which some critics may consider no more than ad hoc justification for failure to replicate. There are a couple of more specific reasons for the nonpredictability of replications. These include the possibility of declines across experiments as well as experimenter effects. The case of DMT-ESP studies illustrates both these possibilities. The database of DMT-ESP studies is the one least likely contaminated by selective reporting, publication bias and the "file-drawer" problem. Therefore, what is to be found in that area may be more typical of psi then in other areas.

The 1978 review of the experiments by Haraldsson (1978) involving DMT-ESP relationship and the subsequent review by Johnson and Haraldsson (1984) confirm significant replicability of DMT-ESP results. Perceptual defensiveness as measured by the Defense Mechanism Test (DMT) developed by Ulf Kragh in Sweden correlated across experiments significantly with ESP scores. The low-defensive subjects tended to obtain higher ESP scores than high-defensive subjects. A meta-analysis of six experiments (the first five published experiments and one unpublished experiment) gave highly significant results with an effect size of .318. Haraldsson conducted ten DMT-ESP experiments at the University of Iceland between 1977 and 1991 (Haraldsson and Houtkooper, 1992). Again the correlation between DMT and ESP scores is significant. The average effect size observed in these experiments is .121, which is considerably smaller than the effect size obtained in the previous studies. Here is then a clear case of decline in the effect size, notwithstanding the overall significance of the results. Again, as Haraldsson and Houtkooper (1995) report in the 10 Icelandic experiments conducted over a period of 14 years there is a chronological decline in the DMT-ESP correlation from a high of .3888 in the first experiment to .0756 in the last. It is interesting to note that in the other six U.S. and Dutch experiments the correlation coefficients declined from a high of .1079 in the first experiment to the low of −.019 in the sixth.

Subsequently, Haraldsson *et al.* (2002) published a report comprising the data of a German DMT-ESP experiment carried out in 1995. The correlation between ESP scores and DMT ratings is virtually nil. The authors conclude that the present experiment and the more detailed analysis of the previous DMT-ESP experiments it engendered suggest that the explanation of the DMT-ESP correlation may be explained by either a parapsychological experimenter effect or a specific ability of Martin Johnson to interact with the participants' ESP to produce the correlation or a nonformalized ability to derive from the DMT protocols ratings which correlate with ESP performance. In any case, a person-specific ability to produce the DMT-ESP correlation appears to be certain. This means that, despite an interesting rationale and an underpinning by highly significant combined evidence in favor of its reality, the DMT-ESP correlation cannot be regarded as one of parapsychology's reproducible findings.

Some parapsychologists like Honorton (1993) have complained that psi researchers have a tendency to look at their research in isolation and fail to look at the magnitude of the effect size of parapsychological findings in relation to adjacent areas. Making a distinction between effect size and inference level, Honorton refers to the study of the effect of aspirin on heart attack rates among healthy, male physicians. To quote him:

> The study involved some 22,000 physicians. It was terminated prematurely because the investigators believed that it would be unethical not to stop at the point where it was quite implicit that aspirin had a highly significant effect on the prevention of heart attacks. Now this was widely publicized in both the popular and the scientific media as representing virtually an absolute proof of the efficacy of aspirin in the prevention of heart attacks. When you calculate the effect size associated with that finding in the way that we calculate effect size in parapsychology, you find that the effect size is about .28, which is exactly the effect size in the meta-analysis of the ganzfeld work. Indeed it is still a small effect, but that calculates to roughly about a quarter of a standard deviation on the average. While we need to do everything we possibly can to increase the magnitude of our effect sizes we also need to be aware of the fact that these are competitive with what is being produced in many other areas of the social sciences that have had much longer periods and more resources to deal with their problems than we have had. I would suggest that the problem is not really one of getting larger effect sizes as it is getting more consistent effect sizes of the magnitude that we are currently getting [Honorton, 1993, pp. 19–20].

Now, as Honorton admits, the problem is one of consistency and the lack of predictive validation of the rate of replication. How can this matter be remedied? Obviously, what is required is a greater understanding of the nature of psi, especially those aspects that seem to constrain and complicate the manifestation of psi. These include (a) psi-missing, the phenomenon related to the negative occurrence of psi, i.e., the tendency to miss the target when attempting to hit, (b) the decline effect and (c) the psi experimenter effect, the often observed tendency that some experimenters appear to obtain significant psi results with greater frequency and facility than others. Another avenue is applied psi research. ESP results may be questioned and ignored when the discussion is at the theoretical level. But when their practical utility is seen, even if the effect sizes are small, psi phenomena would hold the attention of those who help make decisions on funding and promotion of research. Clearly this was the case with the aspirin study and the beneficial effects of aspirin on preventing heart attacks.

The Matter of Application

References to "psychic" applications abound in antiquity. The alleged practices of psi in such endeavors as divining, scrying, healing, and black magic still exist in many of the nonliterate societies. For example, Melanesian islanders believe in and practice a force called *mana*, which is defined as "a kind of material fluid devoid of personal intelligence ... in which the intentions of men and spirits can be incorporated so that they can fulfill their aims." *Yoga Sutras* of Patañjali refers to a variety of paranormal abilities. Five hundred years before Christ, Chinese generals were reported to have used *chi* (psychic force) to work on the minds of enemies to adversely influence them. Practicing shamans, psychics and claims of spiritual healing are found even now in many societies. There are thus good reasons to believe that psi enters, acknowledged or unacknowledged, in a variety of human activities.

Notwithstanding the age-old belief in psi practice and the claims of psychics all over the world, psi researchers in the past have evinced little interest in studying the practical applications of psi. This was so despite the fact that, as philosopher F.C.S. Schiller pointed out long ago, such applications are important for establishing a widespread conviction in the reality of psi. In 1945 J.B. Rhine raised the question: "Can any practical use be made of these parapsychical abilities?" "The answer," he wrote, "has invariably had to be, 'NO.' No practical use can be made of them with our present state of knowledge. They are not reliable enough." Parapsychology's pioneers were motivated more by psi's implications for discovering "a true philosophy by which men can live better and more happily" than the possibility of applying it for achieving our common needs.

Have we made sufficient progress since 1945 to warrant a more optimistic response? Is psi reliable enough now to render its applications feasible? Important strides have been made during the past half of a century that give a reasonable hope for replicating psi in our experimental laboratories, even though no claim of producing the phenomena on demand can be made with justification. We are, however, still mystified by the enigma of psi's elusiveness and annoyed by the low signal and high noise in psi retrieval. Hence ethical questions continue to haunt when researchers seriously contemplate writing a grant application for applied psi research. It seems to me that the matter of highest priority in this context is a reasonable demonstration that at least some psi effects are replicable in a predictive sense. If it is the case that psi effects are weak but predictably replicable, we would then be led into developing techniques and strategies designed to filter out noise and optimize the signal. Multiple calling and other redundancy techniques suggest themselves as possible methodological approaches for quality enhancement in psi detection.

Now, as we have seen, psi results do not seem to engender the conviction that they are predictably replicable. Do we, then, need to shelve the question of application until the replication issue is favorably settled? Not necessarily so. First of all, whether or not there is valid justification for such practices, psychic practices for utilitarian purposes continue to exist in many societies. Systematic studies of these are necessary and important not only for determining the scope, range, and validity of these practices in the context of applying psi, but also for understanding the nature of psi itself. These field studies in a sense show that there is no hard line that separates applied and pure research in parapsychology.

Again, there are areas where judicious application of psi is not unwarranted. These involve low risk and high reward cases. For example, an oil executive who is unable to choose between four different sites for drilling on the basis of available geophysical information may seek the help of a psychic, and the parapsychologists need have no ethical worries as long as they make no false promises. In any case, applied psi research may be seen as an important avenue for making inroads into main stream science. It may be recalled that R.H. Thouless (1960) suggested a threefold strategy to overcome the skepticism: (a) that we create a pool of successful subjects who would be available to skeptical scientists to work with, (b) that we encourage replication of successful results, and (c) that we get psi to work by employing such techniques as repeated guessing.

Efforts along the above lines were made in various measures. The strategy of pooling outstanding subjects for testing by skeptical experimenters is the one least practiced, for obvious reasons. Such subjects are hard to come by and, when they do appear, understandably the priorities shift in favor of those experimenters already in the field and fortunate enough to have discovered them. Also, the interests of the subjects themselves cannot be overlooked. All these factors point to the intrinsic difficulties of providing star subjects to skeptical experimenters. A notable exception in this connection, however, is the work with Pavel Stepanek (PS). Milan Ryzl, who discovered and trained PS, took the extraordinary step of inviting interested researchers from various parts of the world to work with him. Many of them were able to observe firsthand the successful performances of PS with binary psi targets (Pratt, 1973). But then the results of work with PS carried no more credibility with the skeptics than other significant studies in the field (Hansel, 1980; Gardner, 1989). More recent cases include Mathew Manning investigated by Braud *et al.* (1979), Alex Tanous by Osis & McCormick (1980), and poltergeist mediums by William Roll *et al.* (2012).

Field Studies of Applied Psi

As mentioned, applications of psi, whether genuine or spurious, are not uncommon in many societies. There is evidence to suggest that psi is used in several settings, including medical, business and intelligence gathering, warranting careful field studies of psi application.

Intelligence Gathering and Military Applications: If ESP and PK are genuine phenomena, the scope for their application is limitless. ESP could be used, for example, in intelligence gathering and spying and PK to jam an enemy's communication systems and cause the malfunction of sensitive equipment and so on. These possibilities are not lost sight off by the major military powers. There are reasons to believe that the global powers during the Cold War period had programs to use psi for military purposes and did in fact support some psi research. For example, there is evidence that the Central Intelligence Agency of the U.S. government supported secretly a series of programs over a period of some 23 years under the code name Star Gate.

The infamous *Nautilus* story carried by the French press in 1959 is a case in point. *Nautilus* was an American atomic submarine. It was prominently reported in the French media that the U.S. Navy was using ESP aboard the *Nautilus* with headlines such as "Has the American military mastered the secret of mind power" and "Will ESP be a deciding factor in future warfare?" The *Nautilus* story is probably a fiction. However, it had enormous impact on laymen as well as scientists who read those headlines. For example, the *Nautilus* news provoked the distinguished Russian physiologist L.L. Vasiliev. He said at a meeting of Soviet scientists in 1960:

> We carried out extensive and, until now, completely unreported investigation on ESP under the Stalin regime! ... Today the American Navy is testing telepathy on their atomic submarines. Soviet science conducted a great many successful telepathy tests over a quarter of a century ago: It's urgent that we throw off our prejudices. We must again plunge into the exploration of this vital field [quoted from Ostrander & Schroder, 1970, p. 6].

There are anecdotal accounts that some British army personnel had in secret psychic family members involved in their military successes

(Radin, 1997). General George Patton of the U.S. Army is credited with sixth sense (Mishlove, 1993). There are two books on American psychic spying–one by J. Schnabel (1997) and another by J. McMoneagle (1993). The latter in his *Mind Trek* describes the test that was carried out at the instance of the U.S. National Security Council in which correct information relating to secret construction of a submarine in Northern Russia is reported to have been psychically obtained.

Information declassified a few years ago reveals that some agencies of the U.S. government, notably CIA, has supported research in remote viewing for a number of years. Government sponsored psi research began in 1971 at the prestigious Stanford Research Institute (SRI), later at SRI International. This research program was continued until 1989. Again, during the following year the support of the U.S. government was extended to Science Applications International Corporation (SAIC) under the direction of Edwin May who had earlier directed the program at SRI International. This is the Star Gate program mentioned above.

One of the experts commissioned for CIA to evaluate the government program on psi research, Jessica Utts (2001) of the University of California at Davis concluded her assessment thus:

> I believe that it would be wasteful of valuable resources to continue to look for proof. No one who has examined all of the data across laboratories, taken as a collective whole, has been able to suggest methodological or statistical problems to explain the ever-increasing and consistent results to date. Resources should be directed to the pertinent questions about how this ability works. I am confident that the questions are no more elusive than any other questions in science dealing with small to medium sized effects, and that if appropriate resources are targeted to appropriate questions, we can have answers within the next decade [Utts, 2001, p. 133].

Intuition in Business: Many successful business persons are credited with intuitive ability to foresee future and take unexpected decisions. For example, Norma Bowles and Fran Hynds (1978) quote Alexander Poniatoff, founder of Amplex Corporation, as saying, "In the past I would not admit to any one, especially business people, why my decisions sometimes were contrary to any logical judgment. But now that I have become aware of others who follow intuition, I don't mind talking about it" (p. 114). Similarly, William Keeler, former chairman of Phillips Petroleum, says of intuition, "There are too many incidents that can't be explained merely as coincidences. I had successes in unchartered areas. My strong feelings towards things were accurate when I would let myself go... Oil fields are found on hunches, through precognitive dreams, and by people who didn't know anything about geology" (Bowles and Hynds, 1978, p. 114). At a personal meeting in 1983, Indira Gandhi told me, while she was the prime minister of India, that when she wanted something to happen, she concentrated on it and several times unexpected things happened as she concentrated.

Jeffrey Mishlove (1993) in his *Roots of Consciousness* recounts the tests conducted by the *St. Louis Business Journal*. In these tests the performance of a psychic was compared with that of eighteen professional stock brokers over a period of six months. It is reported that the psychic outperformed the stock brokers. Also, the stocks picked by the psychic went up by *17* percent when the Dow Jones Industrial Average fell *8* percent during that period.

The role of "hunches" and intuition in business was the subject of a book entitled *Executive ESP* by Douglas Dean and John Mihalasky of the Newark College of Engineering. Dean and Mihalasky (1974) report significant correlations of business success with the ESP scores of business executives. In one study, they found dynamic (successful) business managers obtained higher precognition scores than nondynamic managers in 16 of the 20 groups they tested. In another study two groups of presidents of business companies were administered precognition tests. A comparison of precognition scores of the presidents with the profit records of their companies showed that the more successful presidents obtained higher scores on precognition tests.

Like the hunches of successful business persons, it is said that some of the seminal ideas of great scientists are an outcome of intuition. Dean Radin (1997) refers to the finding of Buckminister Fuller who examined the diaries of great scientists and inventors. It is reported that "their diaries declared spontaneously that the most important item in connection with their great discovery of a principle that nobody else had been able to discover, was intuition" (Radin 1997, p. 200). Thus it would seem that intuition might play a useful role not only in decision making but also in new discoveries.

Psi and the Healing Arts: Medical applications of psi are widespread, and they have been in vogue from antiquity. The practices may take different forms in different societies, but the core content appears to be the same, whether we are dealing with shamans, psychic or spiritual healers or witchdoctors. The application of psi in the area of health has two broad lines, paralleling the two basic forms of psi. One involves use of ESP-like ability to diagnose disease. The other is the PK-like ability to cure disease psychically. There is abundant anecdotal and some scientific evidence to suggest that psi may be involved in some of these unorthodox and nonconventional practices of diagnosis and healing. In this context one may also keep in mind that psi, because of its bidirectional nature, could also have negative outcomes. If healing is considered a positive manifestation of psi, then psi can also negatively influence the healing process—an analog of psi-missing. Indeed studies of PK on living systems (Braud, 1979) clearly suggest the possibility of both positive and negative effects of psi on healing. In the Indian tradition, Yoga which deals extensively with supernormal abilities (*siddhis*) emphasizes the ethical aspects of psychic abilities, which again seems to recognize the adverse consequences of using psi.

Edgar Cayce was perhaps the most celebrated "psychic diagnostician" in the United States. Cayce (1877–1945) was a professional photographer and had no medical background or training. It is said that he developed his ability when he attempted to treat his own throat problems (Cayce, 1969; Bro, 1989). During a period extending over forty years, he saw literally thousands of patients, attempting to diagnose and even suggest remedies. In each case, Cayce would enter into a self-induced trance-like state. He would then be given the patient's name and address. Cayce would proceed to give his diagnosis and suggest a course of treatment. A stenographer would record Cayce's statements, which were usually sent to the patient or physician. The suggested treatments are often unorthodox, involving psychological suggestions, herb and food remedies, and sometimes specific chiropractic manipulations. It should be mentioned that the patient was not required to be physically present. All that was needed was the patient's name and address. It is believed that Cayce would "telepathically tune in on the patient's mind and body" and learn about the affliction.

Inspired by Edgar Cayce's work, Shafica Karagulla, a trained physician, carried out field studies of psychic diagnosis, which she prefers to call "higher sense perception." In her book *Breakthrough to Creativity,* Karagulla (1967) gives a number of examples of psychic diagnosis based on her field studies. The procedure involves asking a reputed psychic diagnostician to diagnose a patient selected by Karagulla at random among patients in a hospital. Neither Karagulla nor the diagnostician would have any knowledge of the patient's condition. Then Karagulla would check the medical records of the patient and compare them with the psychic diagnostician's assessment. Karagulla reports some strikingly accurate diagnoses by the psychic.

It is said that numerous nurses in conventional settings use "therapeutic touch," a psychic healing technique (Quinn, 1984). Dolores Krieger (1986) who reported earlier that a healer could influence hemoglobin levels in blood by laying-on-of-hands had worked with a number of nurses in the U.S. to promote therapeutic touch as a healing technique.

Epidemiological research in the area of religiosity and a variety of health conditions suggests significant relationship between religious practices and human health (Koenig, McCullough & Larson, 2001). In a series of studies, Koenig and colleagues looked into various aspects of the relationship between religious activity and health outcomes. They examined the effect of religious involvement on mortality, which showed a significant association between private religious activity such as prayer and longer survival in certain population groups (Helm, Hays, Flint, Koenig & Blazer 2000). They also found significantly less anxiety disorders among the people who attended religious services regularly (Koenig, Ford, George, Blazer & Meador, 1993) and an inverse relation between religious coping and scores on depression scales (Koenig, Cohen, Blazer, Pieper, Meador, Shelp, Goli & DiPasquale, 1992). Several studies with different groups ranging from terminally ill (Reed, 1986, 1987) to healthy adults (Mattlin *et al.*, 1990) suggest that a significant majority of people report that they use religion as a coping mechanism to deal with health problems and other stressful situations. As Koenig, McCullough & Larson (2001) observe, among the 16 studies that have examined possible relationship between religious involvement and blood pressure, 14 report lower blood pressure among the more religious. Steffen, Hinderliter, Blumenthal and Sherwood (2001) reported that among African Americans, religious coping is associated with reduced blood pressure.

Goldbourt *et al.* (1993) reported that in a 23 year follow-up study, the risk of death from coronary artery disease (CAD) was 20 percent lower among the most orthodox Jews than the less orthodox or nonbelievers. In their study of religious struggle as a predictor of mortality among medically ill elderly patients, Pargament, Koenig, Tarakeshwar and Hahn (2001) found that the patients who experience religious struggle in comparison to those who religiously cope with their illness are at a greater risk of death. In a six-year follow-up study of 3968 older adults, they observed, those who attended religious services at least once a week appeared to have a survival advantage over those who attended services less frequently. This effect of religious activity on survival, they contend, is equivalent to that of nonsmoking vs. smoking on mortality (Koenig *et al.*, 1999).

There are several significant studies that explored the relationship between religiosity and a variety of health conditions. In about 150 studies on alcohol and drug abuse and religious involvement, most of the studies "suggest less substance and drug abuse and more successful rehabilitation among the more religious" (Koenig, McCullough and Larson, 2001). Also, numerous studies investigated the effect of religion on mental health, delinquency, depression, heart disease, immune system dysfunction, cancer, and physical disability. (For a comprehensive early review of research in these areas, *see* Koenig, McCullough and Larson, 2001).

Surveys of literature and meta-analysis of published research seem to confirm the claims of individual researchers linking religious practices with better health outcomes. For example, in a systematic and comprehensive review, Townsend, Kladder, Ayele & Mulligan (2002) assessed the impact of religion on health outcomes. They reviewed all experiments involving randomized controlled trials published between 1996 and 1999 that assessed the relationship between religious practices and measurable health variables. The review revealed that "religious involvement and spirituality are associated with better health outcomes, including greater longevity, coping skills, and health related quality of life and less anxiety." In a meta-analytic review of 29 independent samples McCullough *et al.* (2000) reported that religious involvement has a strong positive influence upon increased survival ($p < .001$).

If religious involvement does have beneficial health outcomes, as many of the published reports in the West seem to suggest, then we may ask: How does this relationship work? What is its modus operandi, and the nature of the process that underlies the presumed effect? What is the channel? Who is the source? These important, though often tricky, questions have no easy answers. The favored explanation is a secular one. Religious beliefs and practices may have psychological effects, which in turn bring about somatic changes. If indeed religious beliefs and activities help to reduce anxiety, stress and depression, they could also help to shield their negative effects on general health and well-being.

As Koenig, Larson & Larson (2001) surmise, when people become physically ill, many rely heavily on religious beliefs and practices to relieve stress, retain a sense of control, and maintain hope and a sense of meaning and purpose in life. It is suggested that religion (a) acts as a social support system, (b) reduces the sense of loss of control and helplessness, (c) provides a cognitive framework that reduces suffering and enhances self-esteem, (d) gives confidence that one, with the help of God, could influence the health condition, and (e) creates a mindset that enables the patient to relax and allow the body to heal itself. Again, the values engendered by religious involvement such as love, compassion, charity, benevolence and altruism may help to successfully cope with debilitating anxiety, stress and depression.

All these may be true. Yet, there are issues that go beyond these explanations. For example, if the observed effects of distant intercessory prayer on the health of patients, who did not even know that someone was praying for them, are genuine, as they are claimed to be, the above secular explanations become somewhat inadequate. We need more than a healthy mindset on the part of the patient to recover from illness because someone, unknown to him, had prayed for his recovery. There may be more to religion than being a social and psychological support system. Let us therefore consider briefly the case of remote intercessory prayer and its ramifications for future research in the area that explores the effects of religious activities on health and well-being.

The Case of Distant (Remote) Intercessory Prayer: Michael Miovic (2004) in his book refers to two well documented cases of spiritual healing by a Russian healer Nicolai Levashov reported by Koopman and Blasband (2002). In one case, a baby girl was completely healed from gioblastoma multiforme (GBM), considered the most aggressive form of brain cancer and believed to be incurable and ultimately fatal. In another case, the same healer is reported to have successfully cured a boy who was diagnosed with testicular absence at the age of one month. At the age of 11, serial tests of free testosterone showed near absence of any hormone production. Then, in 1999, Levashov began distant healing on the boy. By August of 2000, testosterone reached near normal levels. By 2002, doctors reviewing the case "acknowledged that functional testicles had appeared in a genetic male who had presented well past the age at which testicles can develop" (Miovic, 2004, p. 129).

A number of studies gave positive evidence linking intercessory prayer with beneficial health outcomes. Intercessory prayer involves praying for others' benefit. In some of these studies, the patients did not know that someone was praying for them. Yet, their condition seemed to have improved compared to the control group of patients who did not have the benefit of someone praying for them. In a double blind study involving 393 coronary care patients, Randolph Byrd (1988) divided his subjects into two randomized groups. One group is the intercessory prayer group and the other is the control group. Neither the physicians attending on them nor the patients themselves knew which patients were being prayed for. Also, those who actually offered prayers did not know the patients for whose recovery they were praying. Results showed that the patients in the intercessory prayer group experienced significantly fewer episodes of congestive heart failures ($p < .05$) and fewer cardiac arrests ($p < .05$), received fewer antibiotics ($p < .005$) and required less respirator support and medication ($p < .0001$). Byrd's (1988) study was criticized for multiple analyses and "methodological and factor" by Chibnall *et al.* (2001). However, J.E. Kennedy on reevaluating the data concluded that "the results for two of the outcome measures are significant at the .05 level even after conservatively correcting for 29 multiple analyses" (2002, p. 181). W.S. Harris *et al.* (1999) conducted a double blind study of distant intercessory prayer with 990 patients in the cardiac care unit. In this study with randomized controlled trials, it was observed that the experimental group (the prayed-for patients) recovered better than the control group of patients. The results are statistically significant, even after correction for multiple analyses.

In a meta-analysis of published studies, Mueller, Plevak & Rummans (2001) found that randomized controlled trials had shown a significant positive effect between intercessory prayer and recovery from coronary disease. They observed that addressing the spiritual needs of the patient may enhance recovery from illness.

Based on later meta-analysis of 14 studies, Masters, Spielmans & Goodson (2006) concluded that "There is no scientifically discernable effect for IP [intercessory prayer] as assessed in controlled studies. Given that the IP literature lacks a theoretical or theological base and has failed to produce significant findings in controlled trials, we recommend that further resources not be allocated to this line of research."

Impressed with the extensive publications in the area, Chibnall, Jeral & Cerullo (2001) toiled for a couple of years to do a methodologically sophisticated and conceptually unambiguous study to test the influence of distant intercessory prayer on health. They found themselves unable to proceed beyond a critical review of the published reports. Their paper "Experiments on Distant Intercessory Prayer: God, Science, and the Lesson of Messiah" turned out to be more a debunking exercise rather than a constructive contribution. They conclude that this area of research is simply unproductive. They argue among other things that the notion of intervention by supernatural beings does not simply meet the basic testability and explanatory requirements of science. They write: "Science does not deny God, miracles, and the like, it merely neglects them.... Science cannot actualize spirituality, so why do we ask this of it?" (p. 2535). This paper became quite influential among health professionals in the West for the reason that its rationale is quite consistent with their mindset that makes a clear separation between science and spirituality, between what is believed to be natural as distinguished from the supernatural, which is considered ex-hypothesis, beyond the scope of science. Such separation of the natural and the supernatural engenders among scientists the fear of trespassing into the sacred, which, it would seem, is one of the powerful reasons behind the efforts to fault researches in this and similar areas.

One might think, however, that the argument that the research efforts in the religion-health area do not meet the testability requirements of science is unconvincing. In addition, there is no intrinsic reason to bring in God or supernatural beings as the source of observed effects of distant intercessory prayer on health. Breslin and Lewis (2008) have identified ways in which prayer may promote health. According to them: "(a) prayer may improve health because of the placebo effect; (b) individuals who pray may also engage in health-related behavior; (c) prayer may help by diverting attention from health problems; (d) prayer may promote health through supernatural intervention by God; (e) prayer may activate latent energies, such as chi, which have not been empirically verified, but which nevertheless may be beneficial to health; and (f) prayer may result in a unity of consciousness which facilitates the transmission of healing between individuals." Also, as Kennedy (2002) argued, an alternative to god's intervention through prayer is the psi from the people involved in the study that is responsible for the observed effect. Paranormal healing is an age old healing method; and psi may well be the medium involved in the healing process. Indeed it is an eminently testable hypothesis.

Consider, for example, the wealth of studies that show similar effects of the influence of direct mental influence on remote biological systems. There is a large empirical database accumulated over the years by William Braud and associates that provides strong evidence suggestive of the possibility of influencing the physiology of a remotely situated person by sheer mental intention of another person. Braud and Schlitz (1991) review eight separate experiments in which the subjects attempted to influence remote biological systems by simply wishing such a change. The crucial difference between prayer and such wishing is that no supernatural being is invoked in the wish phenomenon, unlike in the prayer, which is generally directed at seeking the help of God to grant the wish. The results of the experiments by Braud and associates show that a subject by mental intention alone could influence in the desired direction (a) the autonomic nervous system activity of a remotely situated person, (b) the muscular tremor and ideomotor reactions, (c) mental imagery of another person, and (d) the rate of hemolysis of human red blood cells in vitro. There is no reference in these studies to supernatural beings or non-testable entities. As Braud points out, based on the overall statistical results, the distant mental influence effects are relatively reliable and robust. The magnitude of the effects is not trivial and is comparable to self-regulation effects. The ability to mentally influence is apparently widely distributed. Thus, these experiments not only show the feasibility of scientifically studying such phenomena as healing through distant intercessory prayer, but they suggest also that the source of the effect may be a living person and not necessarily a supernatural entity like God.

It would seem that attributing to people the ability to bring about miraculous nonconventional cures elevates them to a divine level because traditionally such abilities are attributed to gods and the so-called godmen. Such belief and faith in the healing ability of the person may be an important element in the healing process. Without having a further understanding the conditions that enable one to heal, it is difficult to determine what precisely is the role of the notion of god in situations of healing like the above.

Therefore, it would appear possible to do field studies to test the possibility of applying psychic abilities to influence health outcomes. Braud's work was largely ignored because it was confined to laboratory studies that produced no more than small effects. If, however, his studies were conducted in the context of healing with real patients, even small beneficial outcomes would have generated a significant public interest, which would have added further impetus to this line of research. It follows then that applied psi research is not only warranted, but it may be necessary to bring parapsychology into the main stream.

Further, recent research on the effects of intercessory prayer on human health seems to yield results not unlike the results in psi research. For example, an extensive study by Benson *et al.* (2006) involving six U.S. hospitals and 600 patients undergoing coronary bypass graft (CABG) surgery. In this study, the patients were randomly assigned to one of three groups. In Group 1, the patients were informed that they may or may not be prayed for, but they were prayed for. In Group 2 like Group 1, the patients were also uncertain whether they would be prayed for. However, they were not prayed for. In Group 3, the patients were told that they would be prayed for and they did indeed receive intercessory prayer. We can clearly see that Group 3 is the target group where the intercessory prayer effort is most likely to be present.

The results of the study were analyzed in terms of uncomplicated recovery after surgery. The most striking finding is that 63 percent of the patients in Group 3 as per the interim analysis had a complication after surgery compared to 51 percent in Groups 1 and 2. The difference is statistically significant ($p = .003$). The final analysis also showed similar results. In Group 3, 59 percent of the patients had complications after surgery compared to 52 percent in Group 1. The difference between the two groups is statistically significant. Other secondary analysis also showed that "patients in Group 3 were consistently more likely to have a complication than those in Group 1 across the planned sub-group analyses." Notwithstanding the above significant differences between groups, Benson et al. conclude: "Intercessory prayer itself had no effect on complication-free recovery from CABG, but certainty of receiving intercessory prayer was associated with a higher incidence of complications."

Krucoff, Crater & Lee (2006) critique the design of the Benson et al. (2006) study on the following grounds: (a) the use of just a few prayer groups may have affected the actual prayers performed, (b) the reason for use of a certainty vs. uncertainty model instead of a double-blind method have been left unexplored by the authors, (c) the certainty/uncertainty design could have provided insight into the placebo effect, which was also not explored, (d) the authors have not discussed the significant results that indicated a worsening of the condition, beyond explaining them as a chance finding. Krucoff et al. comment, "If the results had shown benefit rather than harm, would we have read the investigators' conclusion that this effect 'may have been a chance finding,' with absolutely no other comments, insight, or even speculation?" Krucoff et al. further state that "the study results appears to reflect more the cultural bias that healing prayer could only seriously be explored for effectiveness, not for safety issues. Culturally, 'harm' resulting from prayer is generally ascribed to overtly 'negative' prayer, such as hateful prayer, voodoo, spells, or other black magic. Positively intended intercessory prayer is considered a priori to be only capable of doing good, if it does anything at all."

Benson et al. (2006) as well as Krucoff et al. (2006) miss one point that is familiar to psi researchers; psi may have positive or negative effects. There is a great deal of evidence for psi-missing, a tendency of the subject to consistently miss the target, resulting in a significant negative deviation. What we have here in the study of Benson et al. is psi-missing in Group 3, which is the worsening of the condition of patients following intercessory prayers. Also the design of the experiment and the experimental conditions appear to be quite similar to those known to be associated with psi-missing. It would seem therefore that the key relevant ingredient in intercessory prayer that may have an effect on patients' health may be psi on the part of one or more persons involved in the study rather than god or the prayer per se.

Normal-Paranormal Mix

If there are indeed genuine psi effects in the above mentioned field practices, are there any lessons the researchers can learn from them? One striking contrast between the field practices and the laboratory explorations of psi is that, in the field, the normal and paranormal go in tandem. No attempt is made to exclude the normal sources of information. The dowser visits the site and examines the landscape. Business executives driven by intuition do not shut their eyes to the generally available information. They appear to build on it. No scientific discoveries are made by people who have no scientific background. The crystal gazers, practitioners of automatic writing, palm readers and a host of other types of psychic practitioners appear to need a sensory medium to generate relevant imagery from a nonsensory (intuitive) source of input. In fact, Rex Stanford's PMIR model of psi presupposes this possibility. It would seem, therefore, that the concern to separate the normal and the paranormal and to control the former to test psychic field practices may be disingenuous and counterproductive. What may be more appropriate is the development of methods that incorporate the inclusion rather than exclusion of normal channels of information in our experimental designs.

Parapsychologists are of course concerned with the problem of demonstrating the reality of psi as distinct from other modalities. Being distinct, however, does not necessarily imply that psi is independent of and can function without the aid of other modalities of our normal cognition and action. What if psi functions, as Gardner Murphy (1961/1970) suspected, in juxtaposition or in coalescence with other modalities including the sensory? What if the normal and the paranormal blend and function in fusion reinforcing each other rather than in isolation and independently of each other? What if the sensory and other normal processes are needed to sustain, guide, channel, trigger, or focus on the paranormal? And what if psi merely supplements rather than supplants the sensory and motor functions? If we give any credence to these possibilities, we would be in a totally new ball park, playing a different game with a completely new set of rules.

Gardner Murphy (1961/1970) referred to special cases in which the normal may call upon the paranormal for aid and the two kinds of functions may be blended. "The faint sights and sounds may offer a matrix upon which paranormal information may be grafted.... We may be able to see what will happen when normal and paranormal occur in juxtaposition or in *coalescence* or *reinforcement,* one of another" (p. 278). This point was discussed at length as long ago as J.H. Rush (1964) in his monograph *New Directions in Parapsychological Research* and they by Sudhakar & P.V.K. Rao (1986). Sonali Marwaha & Edwin May (2015) also discuss this issue. One is tempted to argue that it is precisely this way that psi functions generally and not merely in very special cases. Psi as it manifests in human experience may not occur in a vacuum. It occurs, to use Stanford's phrase, in disposed systems. Disposed systems are not merely those "with a need, wish, or want of some kind." There may be systems that creatively link the normal and the paranormal. The normal may be the fuse that ignites the paranormal or simply the base on which the paranormal is mounted. ESP may be more like creativity in problem solving than perception of hidden phenomena. It does not merely interpret what is given, it builds on it. If so, what could be more important in parapsychology than studying the conditions under which the normal and the paranormal interact? How can we study such interactions if we are bound by a methodology which basically attempts to exclude the normal so that the paranormal can be observed? Our obsessive concern to isolate psi from other human functions has provided minimal opportunity for psi to manifest. Either psi is inherently evasive and therefore unreplicable and uncontrollable or it is essentially masked and passes mostly unrecognized in our lives as well as in our laboratories. If the latter is the case, as some of us have begun to suspect, the current research strategies appear to be largely inadequate and probably irrelevant to the task of obtaining psi in a measure that is hard to ignore.

What parapsychologists are pleading for is not just one more turn in the shifting scenes and changing fashions in psi testing as seen over the years—as we moved, for example, from using restricted response materials to free response targets, from testing unselected subjects to preselected subjects, from group testing to individual testing, and so on. It is more radical than that. There appears to be a need for new testing procedures in which the subject is provided with sensory as well as extrasensory information with the objective of discovering whether the sensory awareness somehow helps to expand the extrasensory and whether the normal tends to enhance the paranormal. A new strategy is needed to study normal-paranormal interaction which, if successful, would yield results that could not be ignored, because they would be too striking and significant in their import. In other words, what is needed now is predictive replicability, which the field does not seem to have. A new strategy may effectively achieve this.

Anomalous results with low effect size and high rate of inconsistency can and will be ignored, however stringent the controls may be and whatever precautions one may take to avoid error and deception. Again, such results render process-oriented research very difficult indeed, as is evident from the history of the field. But a tangible and consistent effect, even when obtained under conditions that may not have the best of controls, could be very valuable in understanding the phenomenon—an understanding that would lead to greater control and more progressive research programs. Controls become irrelevant when the demonstrated effects are of practical value. Suppose we are investigating the dowsing capabilities of subject or the ability to forecast weather. If subjects are able to locate water, oil, or whatever they are divining when the geophysicists employing the state-of-the-art technology fail, or if they predict weather better than professional meteorologists do, who cares whether they had available to them geological data about the terrain or the weather patterns of the region? With the low level information that is mediated through ESP is it reasonable at all to expect the dowser to outperform the geologist without the geological information?

It is possible of course to test one's dowsing abilities by *excluding* all relevant information from the subject, as we have done in the past, so that when he does make a correct identification we may say that he was able to do so by ESP or some paranormal ability. We could also test his ability by *providing* all the available information and see whether he could do any better in identifying the correct location than others who have the same information and no less professional skill in making use of that information. Psi researchers have been doing mostly the former with less success. The suggestion is that they do the latter as well and see if there would be greater success. In the past, what was done is testing the *exclusion* hypothesis. It is time to test the *fusion* hypothesis, namely, that psi functions in unison with other abilities, building and adding on the information that normally becomes accessible.

The basis for our confidence in the fusion hypothesis is the conviction that psi plays a significant role in many of our successful activities. The business intuitions of successful corporate executives and the creative genius of outstanding scientists and inventors may involve a healthy mix of normal and paranormal inputs. Consider, for instance, the case of scientific discovery. As mentioned in Chapter 2 there are usually two ways in which hypotheses occur to scientific thinkers—one involving step by step observations of phenomena that lead to generalizations, theories and laws, and the other incorporating intuitive insights gained entirely independent of observations. Ramanujan, for example, is credited with resolving several mathematical paradoxes with such intuitive insights.

There are several instances in Ramanujan's life that suggest a psi source for his mathematical genius (Rao, 1972). In the case of many other scientific discoveries a case can also be made for the operation of psi, even though it is manifestly less spectacular, being shadowed in most cases by the scholarly and logical synthesis of purported discovery with empirically derived data and rational argument. Intuition appears to be an important but hidden vehicle for scientific discovery and technological invention. An examination of the diaries of great scientists reveals that "the most important item in connection with their great discovery of a principle that nobody else had been able to discover, was intuition" (Harman & Rheingold, 1984).

A strong case can be made for studying psi in life situations where the normal and the paranormal appear to operate co-existently. Such a model is also readily amenable for conducting applied psi research. It is neither premature nor unethical to conduct applied psi research at the present juncture, as long as we are cautious in our conclusions and do not espouse more optimism than what is warranted by the data. In fact, applied research appears to be the need of the day.

The implications of this model for laboratory psi research may appear to be more tenuous inasmuch as laboratory research is usually tied to controls, and controls in psi tests essentially involve excluding the normal. Arguments in favor of studying the fusion hypothesis may be misinterpreted as justifying loose conditions and incompetence and even chicanery in psi research. Are we justifying the view that the mediums may be allowed to cheat so that they can produce some psi effects? Are we pleading for loose experimental conditions where subjects may successfully perform a psi task by using normal means? The answer is clearly "No." What, however, appears reasonable is that we set up experimental conditions that permit the interaction of the normal and paranormal with the expectation that a stronger effect may be registered when the two work together. Obviously we need to bring creativity and freshness to bear on the development of new research strategies and evaluation procedures to test the suggested model. What is interesting, however, is that we have long had already available to us test procedures that we can adapt with ease to test the fusion hypothesis at different levels of complexity.

Kreitler & Kreitler (1972) carried out a series of important experiments to determine whether ESP could influence subliminal perception. In one series, for example, the subjects, who were completely unaware of the ESP component of the experiment, attempted to identify subliminally projected alphabets. Unknown to the subject, during half of the trials an agent in another room concentrated on the target alphabet and attempted to "transmit" it to the subject. The procedure of target presentation was such that each target was presented to the subject twice, once with the agent "transmitting" and another time without the agent. The Kreitlers reported that the subjects correctly identified significantly more letters when the agent was "transmitting" them than when he was not. In 102 cases, the letters which were incorrectly identified with no senders in the subliminal perception test were correctly identified with the sender. In the opposite case, i.e., when the subliminal targets were correctly identified without a sender, in only 76 trials were they correctly identified without the sender. Without ESP in the sender condition, the numbers of correct identifications are expected to be equal in both conditions. However, the significant difference in the hits in the two conditions, suggests that the agent looking at the targets has an effect on the subliminal perception scores of the subject.

The above result is of some interest because it does support the Kreitlers' hypothesis of telepathic influence on subliminal perception. But the total number of correct identifications in the two conditions do not differ significantly from each other. The total number of hits with an agent transmitting is 286 as against 260 hits obtained without the agent.

Such a comparison, as the Kreitlers recognized, would not be very appropriate in the present case. Their reasoning was that "this method is based on raw numbers inflated through the inclusion of 184 correct identifications common in the two conditions" (p. 12). But there is a more compelling reason against such a comparison. At best, a significant difference between the two is indicative more of the relative success of SP (subliminal perception) target identification under GESP and clairvoyance conditions rather than a true comparison of SP and SP plus ESP conditions. We may recall how Coover (1917) mistook GESP and clairvoyance conditions as telepathy and control conditions, respectively, and erroneously concluded that there was no ESP in the data.

Interestingly, the Kreitlers tested their subjects in the same session to determine their subliminal thresholds and found that they averaged 3.34 hits per 12 trials, which gives a success rate of 27.83 percent. In comparison, the percentage of correct identification in the experimental trials under both the conditions combined is 39 percent. The difference between the baseline hit rate and the hit rate in the experimental trials is thus highly significant. The authors very casually dismiss such a comparison as "based on the false assumption of comparing observations with fictional rather than empirical values" (p. 12). Such a dismissal seems unwarranted unless the experimenter was not careful enough while testing subjects in that condition, or the slides used in experimental trials were different in crucial respects from those used in the preliminary trials. There is nothing in the report to suggest either of these was in fact the case. Therefore, greater attention should be paid to the highly significant difference between the success rate in baseline and experimental trials than the Kreitlers did.

While one can conjecture a number of possible artifacts for increased correct identifications in the experimental trials in this study, the view of the Kreitlers that we are comparing any fictional values here is unwarranted. Surely neither of the values is fictional. Both are empirical values and if there are any other variables such as learning or adaptation to the experimental set-up that are conceivably relevant to enhanced scoring in the experimental trials, they could be identified and controlled. But the true comparison would be the one in which the baseline scoring rate is compared to scoring in the ESP plus subliminal condition and not between the telepathy and clairvoyance conditions.

The above line of research, in my view, is important and deserves to be explored further. If these results are any indication, we can expect a stronger effect when an opportunity exists for psi to enhance or build on sensory information. The above experimental paradigm can be adapted to memory-ESP studies, ESP-examination studies and numerous others that link normal psychological abilities with ESP. For example, in a memory-ESP study, the subject may be asked to recall paired associates which he has learned under conditions when his learning is reinforced with ESP. These scores may be compared to baseline scores obtained without ESP reinforcement. Reinforcing may be effected by presenting the correct response words as ESP targets concealed in sealed envelopes or by other procedures such as the use of agents. We may compare the memory scores in both the conditions with the expectation that the scores obtained in the ESP-reinforced condition would be higher than the baseline memory scores obtained without ESP reinforcement.

We may anticipate one line of criticism to the above design. How can we really control ESP in the baseline condition? Even in simple recall tasks when they learned information is not available, the subject may obtain the information through ESP. Therefore, there can be no true baseline score. Such an argument has some merit and it is logically irrefutable. But in practice it can be ignored, for good reasons. First, psychological tests including tests for recall seem to work pretty well in practice. This is either because subjects in such situations do not use their ESP or because the

ESP use is so randomly distributed in the population that it makes little difference except as random noise which can be ignored. Second, while testing for ESP, we make some basic assumptions, the most important one being that the subject's volition is somehow relevant and that the act of participating in a psi test triggers psi. This does not necessarily rule out the possibility of psi manifesting in a nonintentional way, but in laboratory tests the subject's performance is, by assumption, linked to intentions of the subject or those of someone else who is connected with the experiment.

At this point, one may not ignore the apparent differences between spontaneous psi and laboratory psi. In spontaneous cases, it just happens that someone has an experience that warrants paranormal explanation. The person, as far as one can tell, is not seeking the experience and in no sense has any control over it. In laboratory psi, the situation is somewhat different. Where we are testing for intentional psi, the subject is presumed to exercise his psi. Even in experimental studies of so-called nonintentional psi, there is someone in the experimental situation, the experimenter, the agent, or other persons associated with the experiment, whose intentions are presumed to relate to the experimental outcome.

Are these differences really so crucial that we need to postulate two different kinds of psi? Or is it possible that, at a higher level of organization, these are integrated and that we can speak of an essential unity between them? The analogy of dreaming may be relevant to a discussion of these issues. Dreaming, like psi, is an experience that spontaneously occurs to people. No doubt it is nearly universal and more pervasive, regular and predictable than psi. But all the same it is an experience over which one ordinarily makes no claims of control. Yet, there is evidence that the contents of dreams can be manipulated by a variety of means, which suggests that we have a measure of control over what we dream about. Similarly, what is happening in the laboratory tests of psi is that an attempt with varying degrees of success is made to gain volitional control of psi. Therefore, instructing subjects to use their ESP, placing them in or creating for them a psi-conducive situation, or attempting to influence the outcome psychically are legitimate and meaningful manipulations by the experimenter. The resultant scores in comparison to the baseline (control) scores may be regarded as a function of the strength of the manipulation. Thus the transition from ESP in life to ESP in lab is no more different in crucial respects than the one from at-home dreams to dreams induced in a laboratory.

The second proposal relates to free-response material and is probably a more direct test of the assumptions we made about psi manifestation. We consider presenting to the subject some aspects or parts of the targets subliminally or at supraliminal levels during ESP orientation with the expectation that those aspects or parts of the targets that were not presented to the subject at all will also find a place in the subject's mentation. For example, after the necessary ganzfeld preparation, we could provide carefully selected auditory subliminal cues representing certain aspects of the target while the subject reports what is going on in his or her mind. Or alternatively we could mix these subliminal cues with the "white noise" during the Ganzfeld preparation. If the hypothesis has any validity, we would expect that the mentation of the subject would be a lot richer and that ESP would be seen in the manifestation of the other aspects of the targets than were sensorially unavailable to the subject and were not logically inferable from them. The subliminal cues provide the matrix on which information mediated by psi may be grafted, resulting in a sufficiently strong and replicable effect. Of course, there will be new problems in judging and quantifying the data of this sort, but surely they would not be insurmountable. Unless we are missing something here, there do not seem to be any serious methodological pitfalls that would give us spurious data, which we might mistake for psi. In any case, the lesson we learn from field studies of psi application is that psi may manifest more reliably when subjects are not constrained by control of normal channels of information.

5

Process-Oriented Research

We can say with some confidence that psi research has gone well beyond accumulating evidence for the existence of ESP and PK. There have been many studies attempting to demonstrate various forms of psi. A variety of test procedures are developed and a vast amount of data is now available. Even though there continues to be skepticism about the reality of psi phenomena, there is evidence that lawful regularities exist between psi and other psychological and physical variables. There are indeed some significant process oriented research yielding interesting results. We review in this chapter some of the major findings that attempt to relate psi to other variables. We limit ourselves, however, to the original studies and their early confirmation without referring to the more recent research unless it warrants its mention in the light of new developments.

Complexity of Psi Task: Space and Time Variables

Quite early in his experimental investigations, J.B. Rhine found that the distance between the subject and the target in ESP experiments made no significant difference in the success rate of his subjects (Rhine, 1934). Similarly, Russian physiologist L.L. Vasiliev (1963) reported that he was able to hypnotize his subject telepathically during randomly determined periods of time from a distance of about 1,700 kilometers. He found also that his attempts to shield any possible electromagnetic wave transmission between the hypnotist and the subject by placing them in separate Farady cages did not diminish the success rate of the telepathic induction of hypnosis. Marilyn Schlitz & Elmar Gruber (1980) successfully carried out transcontinental remote viewing experiments in which the subject, totally unaware of it sensorially, attempted to describe a randomly selected location in another continent being visited by an experimenter. Robert Jahn

& Brenda Dunne (1987) at the Princeton Engineering Anomalies Research Laboratory also carried out remote viewing experiments involving long distances. The cumulative results of their 334 remote viewing trials are highly significant. These and other successful long distance ESP experiments suggest that ESP may be unconstrained by space variables. More recently, the Global Consciousness Project of Roger Nelson (2015) provides support to the hypothesis that space and time are not constraining factors for psi functioning. Joseph McMoneagle (2015) discusses extensively the evidence for precognition in studies of applied remote viewing. Precognition obviously overcomes the constraint of time.

There is also experimental evidence to support the precognition hypothesis. As in spontaneous cases in which people have reported their experiences of having information about future events apparently without any other means of knowing them, experimental studies have also shown that it is possible to have information about a target that does not exist now but will come into being at a time in the future. For example, it was found in some remote viewing experiments that the subjects were able to successfully describe the location where the experimenter will be at a pre-determined future time (Jahn, 1982). Earlier, J.B. Rhine (1938) had reported significant results suggesting that his subjects were able to guess correctly the target order in a deck of ESP cards randomized after the subjects made their calls. In a survey of forced-choice precognition experiments published between 1935 and 1987, Honorton & Ferrari (1989) found 309 studies involving over 50,000 subjects and 62 different experiments. A meta-analysis of this large database shows a highly significant effect suggesting that subjects were able to guess future targets. In another meta-analysis of forced-choice experiments comparing clairvoyance, and precognition, F. Steinkamp, J. Milton & R.L. Morris (1998) found no significant difference in the success rate in precognition and clairvoyance studies, and that the cumulative overall effect is significant in both clairvoyance and precognition studies. As John Palmer (2015) persuasively argues, it is practically impossible to separate in any given situation precognition, clairvoyance or telepathy as *the* source of psi. The distinctions made among these concepts is more an ontological one than a practical matter. Richard Corry (2015) discusses at length ESP and the possibility of precognition.

Another significant aspect of psi appears to be the relative ineffectiveness of task complexity in constraining it. Rex Stanford (1977) and Kennedy (1978) have reviewed the relevant literature and concluded that the efficiency of the PK function is not reduced by an increase in the complexity of the target system. The question arises, why is it that the complexity of task does not appear to be a constraining variable? There is significant evidence to suggest that psi is goal-directed and does not always follow the usual steps involved in information processing. Kennedy (1978; 1979) reviewed the relevant literature and concluded that the majority-vote studies support the validity of the goal-directed concept of psi. This seems to be the case with PK as well as ESP studies. If it is the case that ESP in a given instance gives only partial information, repeated attempts to guess an ESP target should help to accumulate more information, enhance the signal and be more reliable.

This thinking is behind the experiments that involved redundancy and repeated calling. In other words, the success rate in ESP tasks should be greater when subjects make multiple calls and take the majority decision as the appropriate call than when they make a single call. There is no evidence in the literature to suggest that it is the case. Results of redundancy or multiple calling tests do not seem to favor the hypothesis of signal enhancement. Rather, as Kennedy asserts, the majority-vote experiments "provide quite consistent support for the goal-oriented psi hypothesis" (1979, p. 304).

Consider, for example, the experimental study of Schmidt (1974) in which he compared the outcomes of majority-vote trials and single-event trials to test the signal enhancement and the goal-directed hypotheses. In this PK experiment the subject's task was to influence by PK one of the two lights to come on by pushing an appropriate button. Which of the two lights would come on was determined in a random manner. The subject's PK is believed to bias the randomness in the desired direction. The experiment was so designed that in about one half of the trials the decision for the lights was determined by a single event of the random event generator whereas in the other half it was determined by the majority outcome of 100 events. The experimental design controlled for other known variables by mixing the two types of trials randomly and by keeping the subject and the experimenter blind to the condition. Schmidt found the scoring rate to be approximately the same between the two conditions with no significant difference between them. Thus it would seem that the evidence is against the signal enhancement model and in favor of goal-directed nature of psi, as Kennedy argues. I have not seen since a more plausible hypothesis than the goal-orientedness of psi.

Thus, psi, which is believed to involve no sensory mediation, is also not bound by the physical properties of the items of information constrained as is the case with the variables of space and time. There is nothing to indicate from the research results available to date that any energy patterns emanating from the target objects reach the subject in ESP tests. It would seem that somehow the subject has access to information under conditions that simply do not permit any known physical energy transmission from the target. Such a possibility raises serious questions about the subject-object distinctions in cognitive processes and the representational theory of knowledge in general.

For example, if it is the case that a subject (S) in a telepathy experiment is able to know what an agent (A) is thinking at a particular time, what then is the cause of S's knowledge? One would normally assume that the cause of S's knowledge is the act of A's thinking. We know, however, that A's act of thinking cannot cause telepathy in S, because not only are we unable to discover any causal sequences connecting A's act of thinking and S's extrasensory knowledge of his thoughts, but we also know that S could do the same thing if A were not actually thinking at that time but were to do so at some time in the future.

It would seem that C.G. Jung had a better insight into this problem than his critics when he described ESP in terms of synchronicity or acausal relationships (Jung & Pauli, 1955). Similarly, Polanyi's (1958) concept of tacit knowing appears to be more appropriate than conventional perceptual models to conceptualize paranormal awareness. Tacit knowing, according to Polanyi, consists in the "capacity of attending from one thing to another"—that is, from a *proximal* term to the *distal* term. The perceptual process, for example, consists in the tacit integration of perceptual clues into feelings. The way we see an object is mainly determined by our awareness of certain events inside our bodies, which are not observable in themselves. In a perceptual process, then, we are attending from the internal processes to the qualities of things outside.

Now, if the tacit integration or structuring of perceptual clues that results in meaningful experiences is fundamental for perceptual knowledge, there is then no good sense in which we can say that the perceptual experiences are produced primarily by the action of material things on our senses. While the perceptual clues may be necessary, on occasion, to have veridical perceptions, they may not be sufficient. It is important to note that the clues of the steps involved in tacit knowing need not be identifiable and in some instances may not even be discernible. As Polanyi (1964) puts it, "Tacit knowing will tend to reach conclusions in ignorance of the steps involved."

Likewise, ESP seems to involve a sort of tacit knowing in ignorance of the clues involved. In an ESP experience we are not merely ignorant of the clues involved, but the clues themselves do not appear to have any sensory basis. It is more like the stage-I processing speculated by L.E. Rhine, which is believed to be unlike other cognitive processes. At this stage, the individual psyche appears to resemble a microcosm, potentially capable of acquiring all the information in the cosmos. "ESP," as L.E. Rhine (1967) puts it, "is not limited by inherent unavailability, but by the person, the individual himself, through whose psychological structure it must be filtered into consciousness" (p. 264).

Subliminal Perception and ESP

There are interesting similarities between ESP and subliminal perception (SP) that encourage us to consider them as two species of covert awareness. In fact, a number of researchers were sufficiently impressed by these similarities to undertake research relating SP and ESP (Kreitler & Kreitler, 1973; Rao & Rao, 1982). The French philosopher Henri Bergson (1921) pointed out the relevance of implicit awareness to psychical research. J.B. Rhine (1977) also observed: "It is here in the common unconscious function of both sensorimotor and extrasensorimotor (or psi) character, that parapsychology comes closest to psychology." He added that it would therefore "be advisable to keep our attention on all the psychological research on unconscious mental activities, watching for similarities and differences" (p. 171).

Norman Dixon (1979), a well known researcher in the area of SP, identified several areas of contact between subliminal perception and parapsychology. He pointed out that a number of variables, such as motivation, memory, altered states of consciousness (e.g., relaxation and dreams), right-hemispheric modes of functioning, etc., have similar influence on both SP and ESP. Gertrude Schmeidler (1971) also remarked that "whatever psychological laws apply to the processing of ambiguous sensory material will apply also to the processing of ESP information" (p. 137). Another psi researcher, Charles Honorton (1976), wrote: "Both subliminal and psi influences are facilitated by internal-attention states, both are subject to subtle experimenter effects and situational factors, and both involve the transformation and mediation of stimulus influence through ongoing mentation processes" (pp. 215–216).

So far, however, the results of the experimental studies of ESP and SP have not been clear-cut. Stanford (1974a), in analyzing the data of an experiment by Eisenbud (1965), found a significant positive correlation between SP and ESP scores. Rao & Puri (1978), however, reported a significant negative correlation. But in a study by Rao and Rao (1982), a significantly positive correlation was found to exist between the SP and ESP scores of subjects who practiced transcendental meditation immediately before the testing. The possibility of interaction between ESP and SP is explored in a series of investigations by Kreitler & Kreitler (1972, 1973, 1974a, 1974b) and by Lübke & Rohr (1975).

Stuart Wilson (2002) conducted a study to test for ESP using an experimental paradigm of "false recognition effect" in subliminal perception research, now more commonly designated as perception without awareness. A number of studies have shown that if a word in an old/new recognition test is preceded by a biasing stimulus exposed subliminally (50 ms), the subjects tend to classify the "new" word in the category as "old." In the Wilson experiment when the biasing stimulus was an ESP target, substituted for a subliminal exposure, no false familiarity effect was found. No attempt was made, however, to correlate the scores of subjects in the subliminal and ESP parts of the experiment. James Carpenter's (2015) *First Sight Theory* postulates that psi is basically a subliminal process and is ubiquitous in life, underlies all thinking and is implicitly present in every thought. He sights as an example his own study (Carpenter, 2012). He further interprets the presentiment studies of Dean Radin (1997; 2004) as supportive of his contention.

Influence of Beliefs and Attitudes on ESP Scores

In her well known studies, Gertrude Schmeidler asked her subjects if they believed ESP to be possible under the conditions of the experiment. On the basis of their replies, she labeled them as "sheep" (those who believed in the possibility of ESP) and "goats" (those who rejected such a possibility). She found that sheep generally tended to obtain more hits than goats. The sheep-goat effect, as it is now known, is one of the more widely researched topics in parapsychology. Her first report was published in the July 1943 issue of *The Journal of the American Society for Psychical Research*. A comprehensive account of sheep-goat experiments is available in the book by Schmeidler & McConnell (1958). One of the strong independent confirmations of the sheep-goat effect may be found in the report of Bhadra (1966), who worked in the Psychology Department of S.V. University in India. John Palmer's (1971, 1972) review of sheep-goat studies shows that, of the 17 experiments that used standard methods and analyses, the sheep obtained better scores in 13 of the experiments, with six of these achieving statistical significance. Also suggestive is the fact that the results in none of the four experiments giving results in the opposite direction are significant.

As Palmer (1978) points out, the effect of belief on ESP scoring is more complex than it appears. In contrast with Schmeidler's sheep-goat classification, which was based on the subject's belief or disbelief that ESP would occur specifically in the testing situation, some other investigators classified their subjects on the basis of their belief in ESP in the abstract. The latter classification generally tended to be less successful in separating the sheep and the goats in terms of significant differences in their ESP scores. Results further suggest that the sheep-goat effect may interact with other variables. Again, manipulation of belief and expectancy factors seems to produce predictable effects (Lovitts, 1981; Taddonio, 1976). A meta-analysis of sheep-goat studies by Tony Lawrence (1993) also provides strong evidence in support of the hypothesis that believers in the possibility of the existence of psi tend to obtain higher scores in ESP tests than the disbelievers.

Inspired by the work of Dutch parapsychologist J.G. Van Busschbach (1958, 1955, 1956, 1959, 1961), American researchers Margaret Anderson and Rhea White carried out a series of experiments with children. They used a clairvoyance technique for group testing and attempted to explore interpersonal dynamics between the experimenters, who administered the test, and the subjects. Anderson & White (1956, 1957, 1958) reported results suggesting a significant relation between teacher-pupil attitudes and the clairvoyance scores of the pupil subjects. In these studies, the teachers gave the tests to their students. The attitudes of pupils to their teachers and those of teachers to their pupils were ascertained by means of questionnaires. Anderson & White found that significantly positive scores were associated with a positive attitude on the part of the teacher towards the students and negative scoring was associated with a negative attitude. When the teacher and pupil attitudes were combined, it was found that mutually positive attitudes on the part of both teacher and pupils were associated with highly significant positive results while mutually negative attitudes were linked with significant negative results.

Deguisne (1959) repeated the Anderson-White experiment and obtained results which were in the same direction. The ESP scores of the subjects who had favorable attitudes towards their teachers were significantly higher than those of the students who expressed unfavorable attitudes. The subjects in the Anderson-White experiments and in the experiment of Deguisne were high school students. In another study by

Goldstone (1959) with grade school pupils as subjects, no significant results were obtained. Rilling, Pettijohn and Adams (1961) reported an experiment in which the mutually opposite attitudes of teachers and students gave positive significant results, suggesting that there may be still other variables involved in the subject-experimenter relationship. Two other attempts to repeat the Anderson & White findings, by Rilling & associates (1961; 1962), failed. A repetition by White & Angstadt (1961) also failed to give significant results.

However, a review of all published experiments with high school students bearing on teacher-pupil attitudes by White & Angstadt (1965) showed that the total results for all the experiments were quite significant even though only one third of these experiments gave significant results in line with the original experiment by Anderson and White. This was so because for the most part the experimental results were in the same direction and because the scores in the original A-W experiments were so high that they still maintain their significance.

It is reasonable to assume that the failures in some experiments to repeat the A-W findings may be due to other variables in the personality of the teachers. The study by White & Angstadt (1965), in which the teachers showed a marginally significant consistency in obtaining results as related to the teacher-pupil attitudes in two separate experiments, clearly suggests this. In this experiment, the teachers who obtained results in line with the A-W hypothesis during the first year tended to get similar results during the second year and the teachers who obtained opposite results from Anderson & White during the first year tended to do the same the following year.

The results of these studies are interesting because they point to an important dimension of the experimenter-subject relationship. It is likely that mutually agreeable relationships and favorable attitudes between the teacher and the pupils help to create the experimental context necessary for the successful manifestation of psi and that a contrary situation favors psi-missing.

ESP and Personality Variables

In the search for the characteristics associated with hitting and missing in psi tests, researchers have also explored the subjects' moods (Humphrey, 1964a, 1964b; McMahan, 1946; Nielsen, 1956), interests (Stuart, 1946), and a variety of personality measures. Neuroticism, defined as a tendency "toward maladaptive behavior caused either by anxiety or by defense mechanisms against anxiety" (Palmer, 1978), is an area that has received considerable attention. Parapsychologists have used inventories such as Taylor's Manifest Anxiety Scale (Freeman & Nielsen, 1964; Honorton, 1965; Rao, 1965) and Cattell's 16PF or the HSPQ (Kanthamani & Rao, 1973a; Kramer & Terry, 1973) as measures of anxiety/neuroticism and have attempted to correlate these scores with ESP scores. After listing a large number of these studies, Palmer (1978) observed that "there is a clear trend" for subjects with relatively good emotional adjustment to score better on ESP tests than their counterparts.

Extensive research in personality-ESP area was carried out at Andhra University by H. Kanthamani (Kanthamani & Rao 1973a; 1973b) in India and by Betty Humphrey (1951) and Gertrude Schmeidler (Schmeidler & McConnell, 1958) in the U.S. The results provide a strong case for a positive relation between extroversion and ESP scores of subjects. In all the four experiments of Kanthamani, for example, the extraverts obtained higher ESP scores than the introverts, and in three of them the differences are statistically significant. The ESP tests in Kanthamani's experiments were forced-choice type with ESP symbols as targets. The personality factors were measured by Cattell's HSPQ. It may be mentioned that in the fourth experiment (Experiment C), Kanthamani (the main investigator) did not administer the ESP tests. She administered the personality test before the subjects took the ESP tests administered by another experimenter. Consequently, the subjects had no knowledge of their ESP scores at the time they took the personality test. The difference in the ESP scores obtained by extraverts and introverts is significant in this experiment as well.

Using the scores from the Defense Mechanism Test (DMT), we may recall, Ulf Kragh and his associates (Kragh & Smith, 1970), Johnson & Kanthamani (1967) found, as one would expect, a negative relationship between the scores on the projective test, the DMT and ESP scores. During the first ten years of research in this area, as Haraldsson (1978) points out, there were seven series of experiments, all but one of which gave statistically significant results in support of a negative relationship. Considering the specialized training required to administer and score the DMT, training that only a few in parapsychology have had, one can be reasonably confident that Haraldsson's review covered all the studies up to that time. DMTESP studies thus seem to show a fairly stable, replicable effect, suggesting that less defensive subjects tend to obtain better ESP scores. Other reviews of DMT-ESP studies by Johnson and Haraldsson (1984) and Haraldsson and Houtkooper (1995), also show their significant replicability, even though there appears to be a gradual decline in the success rate over time. A more recent attempt to replicate the DMT-ESP relationship in an experiment conducted in Germany failed, however, to confirm the previous findings (Haraldsson *et al.*, 2002). This has led the experimenters to conclude that these results throw "serious doubts on the prospect of replicability of the DMT-ESP correlations in future experiments" (p. 249).

Psi in Animals

That some animals may possess extraordinary psi abilities is suggested by numerous anecdotes of psi-trailing cases in which pets apparently have traveled long distances to find their masters. An excellent review of these cases is found in Rhine and Feather (1957). ESP on the part of animals is designated as "anpsi."

Karlis Osis (1952) and Osis & Foster (1953), among others, have systematically studied anpsi. Other anpsi experiments of considerable interest are those carried out by P. Duval & E. Montredon (1968a, 1968b), S.A. Schouten (1972), and R.L. Morris (1978). Although W.J. Levy reported the most extensive series of experiments with animal subjects, his work has been completely discredited on the grounds of possible tampering with the data (Rhine, 1974). Robert Morris (1970), James Davis (1979) and Sheldrake (2015) have published very useful reviews of anpsi literature. There is significant evidence of psi in these studies. However, these experiments by and large do not rule out the possibility that psi on the part of the experimenter or someone else associated with the experiment might be responsible for the observed effect. The possibility of psi experimenter effect looms large in this area. The inability to control for this has been an important impediment to further anpsi research.

Psychophysiological Studies of Psi

Psychophysiological measures are used in psi research in three different ways. One way is to use them as indicators of a psi conducive state. Another is to use physiological responses as indicators of psi response. The third is to use physiological responses as targets to be influenced by PK. In the first category we have studies correlating select physiological indices such as monitoring EEG of successful subjects with successful psi performance. The second and third categories include among others the so-called presentiment and direct mental action with living systems (DMILS) and remote staring studies.

Psi Conducive Physiological States: Biofeedback studies in the 1960s and 1970s have raised the hope that a number of internal responses that are normally considered to be beyond the range of voluntary control can be brought under such control. By receiving instant information about heart rate, blood pressure, muscle tension, brain activity, and the like, human subjects, as well as some animals, learn to regulate these internal responses (Miller *et al.*, 1974). Joe Kamiya (1969) and Barbara Brown (1970), among others, have successfully trained subjects to regulate their own brain wave patterns through biofeedback. Kamiya's subjects, when trained to produce high levels of alpha activity, reported feelings of relaxation and passivity. Also, studies of yogins (Anand, Chhina & Singh, 1961) and Zen meditators (Kasamatsu & Hirai, 1969) have shown that yogic and meditative states produce EEG patterns characterized by alpha abundance. Traditionally the yogins are credited with psychic abilities, and there is experimental evidence to suggest that relaxation as well as meditation facilitates ESP manifestation (Honorton, 1977; Rao *et al.*; 1978; and White, 1964). It is, therefore, reasonable to suppose that there may be a positive relation between alpha activity of the brain and ESP scores. If such a relation should exist, the ability to self-regulate brain wave activity opens up the possibility of achieving greater predictability, if not control, of ESP performance.

Alexander *et al.* (1998) collected from a previously successful (gifted) subject Sean Harribance EEG and SPECT ("single-photon emission computerized tomography") data when he was engaged in three different types of psi tasks. They report that "alpha was dominant bilaterally in the paraoccipital region, with alpha power being strongest in the right parietal lobe at electrode placement p4. A lack of alpha activity was seen in the frontal and temporal lobes" (p. 103). The authors speculate that the parietal cortex is activated when the subject was engaged in the psi task to facilitate "visual search attention via the posterior attention network."

Among the EEG-ESP studies of interest are those by Honorton (1969); Stanford & Stanford (1969); Honorton, Davidson & Bindler (1971); Stanford (1971); Morris, Roll, Klein & Wheeler (1972); Stanford & Stevenson (1972); Stanford & Palmer (1973) and Rao & Feola (1979). Even though the results of these studies are not uniformly significant, the bulk of the evidence is suggestive of a positive relationship between ESP and alpha activity. A review of the earlier work on the physiological correlates of psi is found in Beloff (1974). More recent studies relating to brain activity and psi include Alexander, Persinger, Roll & Webster (1998), Radin (2004b), Wackermann, Seiter, Keibel & Walach (2003) and Ambach (2008).

Physiological Measures as Psi Responses: There have been a number of attempts to use physiological indices as indicators of psi. S. Figar (1959) and Douglas Dean (1962), among several others, utilized plethysmographic recordings as ESP indicators. Soji Otani (1965) and K. Tenny (1962) employed skin resistance measures to monitor psi. William Braud and others (1990) examined autonomic detection of the phenomenon of "being stared at" using electrodermal response. In the category of studies that use physiological indicators to monitor psi in the subjects are those that attempt to study what has now come to be known as "presentiment."

Presentiment in parapsychological research refers to psi-mediated anticipatory response, which is measured by autonomic changes that may take place consequent to subject's nonconscious awareness of the target information even before the target was presented. For instance, a subject subliminally exposed to a threatening stimulus picture or word may not be able to consciously perceive or recognize the word. However, there may be detectable bodily changes in the subject following the presentation of the threatening stimulus. It would be interesting to see, therefore, if similar physiological changes would occur when the stimulus word is presented as a psi task. This is what the studies by Figar (1959), Dean (1962) and Otani (1955) attempted to do. The presentiment studies go a step further and raise the question whether such detectable physiological changes occur systematically even before the stimulus was present as an anticipatory orienting response. In other words, do the subjects respond unconsciously to future events, a response that can be objectively measured by changes in the autonomic nervous system?

A number of studies provided significant evidence for presentiment. An early investigation of presentiment was reported by Vassy (1979). Dean Radin reported results in support of a presentiment hypothesis followed by a confirmation study by Bierman & Radin (1997). In a confirmatory series of experiments with 31 subjects Radin monitored the heart rate, blood volume in fingertips, and skin resistance before, during and after the presentation of a randomly chosen picture. Some of these pictures arouse emotions and some are neutral or calm. Radin reported that the combined physiological measures indicated that the subjects differentially responded to emotional and calm pictures with the expected orienting reflex. Examining the data of three previously published nonparapsychological studies, Dick Bierman (2000) found significant differences in the baseline physiological measurements of subjects preceding randomized emotional versus calm stimuli. In another study, Bierman and Scholte (2002) examined the neural substrates of anticipation, utilizing functional magnetic resonance imaging. The stimulus pictures were 48 emotional and neutral pictures presented randomly. Bierman and Scholte report significantly larger anticipatory activation in the subjects when they experienced emotional stimuli preceding emotional stimuli compared to neutral stimuli. A meta-analysis of 37 experiments involving presentiment by Patrijio Tressoldi (2011) yielded a combined affect size with associated Cohen's d of 0.26, which compares well with similar studies in behavioral sciences.

Norman Don, Bruce McDonough and Charles Warren have attempted to study event-related potentials (ERPs) as indicators of psi. ERPs are minute fluctuations in the voltage of EEG recordings from the scalp following sensory stimulation. In one study with Malcolm Bessent the psychic, Warren, McDonough & Don (1992a) recorded ERPs elicited by target and nontarget stimuli in forced-choice ESP tests. They observed that P100, a positive spike at about 100ms after the onset of the stimulus, and NSW (a negative slow wave 400–500ms after the stimulus is applied) were significantly larger in response to target stimuli than to nontarget stimuli. In an attempted replication of the above with the same subject (Warren, McDonough & Don, 1992b), the P100 effect did not occur, but there was evidence of the NSW effect. In a later study, Don, McDonough & Warren (1998) attempted to test the NSW effect at the 400–500ms range as well as at the 150–400ms range. The subjects in this study were unselected volunteers. The results confirmed the NSW effect in the 150–400ms range. For the NSW at 400–500ms range the results fell short of significance (p=0.085). The authors interpreted the results as evidence of unconscious psi.

Physiological States as Psi Targets: Experiments to test for PK on living systems were carried out with plants, animals and humans as subjects. In experiments with humans, researchers employing the healing paradigm attempted to study if PK could be utilized to influence the physiological states such as those measured by GSR. The leading researcher in this area was William Braud. He called the psychokinetic influence on human physiology allobiofeedback. Typically in these experiments the physiological activity of a person (e.g., the GSR) is monitored and the subject who is physically isolated from that person receives the feedback of the relevant physiological activity in the former. The subject at randomly determined periods attempts to influence the GSR of the target person, while watching the polygraph tracing of that activity, with the intention either to relax or activate the subject. In the first study Braud reported statistically significant differences in the GSR amplitude measures in the attempted "relaxed" and "activation" conditions. This observed effect of greater GSR activity during activating periods than during the relaxing periods is confirmed in a second experiment. Braud and his colleagues later conducted several experiments exploring PK effects on living systems (Braud & Schlitz 1983, 1991).

Akin to the above Bio-PK studies are remote staring studies, also initiated by Braud (Braud, Shafer & Andrews, 1993a, 1993b), which use electrodermal activity (GSR) in the target persons to measure the PK effects.

Braud's Bio-PK work was replicated under the new term "direct mental influence on living systems" (DMILS) by researchers at the University of Edinburgh (Delanoy & Morris 1998–1999) and by Radin, Taylor & Braud (1995). An overview of the DMILS/remote staring studies by Schlitz and Braud (1997) shows that 14 out of 30 studies provide significant evidence for these effects. Stefan Schmidt and Harald Walach (2000) published an important critic of DMILS (as well as remote staring) studies on the grounds that these studies did not incorporate the state-of-the-art methodology in monitoring and measuring the electrodermal activity (EDA). Therefore, they conclude, all DMILS/remote staring studies may contain artifacts or may not have found existing effects because they do not use the appropriate technology" (p. 157).

Schmidt *et al.* (2002) reported meta-analysis of DMILS and remote staring studies separately. Among the 40 DMILS experiments they examined, they found strong negative correlation between effects size and methodological quality. Using sensitivity analyses and weighing effect sizes for sample size and methodological quality, they found a small but highly significant ($p=.001$) mean effect size ($d=0.11$). However, analysis of the seven studies with the highest methodological standard showed a much smaller and nonsignificant effect size ($d=.05$). The remote staring data of 15 experiments are found to be homogenous. The meta-analysis yielded a mean effect size of $d=0.13$ ($p=.01$). The authors also report a significant decline of the effect size over time. Thus, the overall obtained effect sizes are much smaller than in the previous analyses. As Schmidt *et al.* (2002) point out: "For the DMILS meta-analysis, it has to be assumed that some of the effects reported earlier are due to artifacts and shortcomings."

Memory and ESP

There are a number of interesting similarities between ESP and some cognitive processes, such as memory. Memory, like ESP experience, involves representations of objects and events with which the organism is not directly in sensory contact. We know something about the way memory representations are stored in the brain and retrieved, as well as their biochemical and physiological bases. However, our knowledge of ESP does not provide any evidence that psi representations have a cortical basis. Further, much of our memory material, unlike ESP, is accessible for introspective analysis. These important differences notwithstanding, memory and ESP seem to have a good deal in common as psychological processes, and the understanding of one may aid the understanding of the other. Therefore, it is not surprising that, from the time of F.W.H. Myers (1915/1903) to that of J.B. Rhine, a role for memory in ESP was anticipated. J.B. Rhine wrote in *Extrasensory Perception* (1973/34): "It [ESP] is simple cognition ... but it uses memory, visual or other imagination ... in its functioning" (p. 191).

Herman Ebbinghaus (1964/1885), who pioneered quantitative studies of memory, wondered, as have most experimental psychologists since, how to control "the bewildering mass of causal conditions which, insofar as they are of mental nature, almost completely elude our control, and which, moreover, are subject to endless and incessant change." The challenge for him was how to "measure numerically the mental processes which flit by so quickly and which on introspection are so hard to analyze" (p. 7–8). He attempted to solve the problem by inventing nonsense syllables for use in memory tests, which the subject may learn and recall under controlled conditions, a tradition which is strikingly similar to the one heralded by early ESP testers who used forced-choice card-guessing methods.

Considerable similarity is also found in the topics for research chosen for study by memory researchers and parapsychologists. Just as memory researchers are concerned with the effect on recall of differences in the material to be remembered, so are parapsychologists concerned with the effect of target differences on subjects' ESP scores. Individual differences are as extensively investigated in studies of memory as they are in studies of psi. The search for states favorable to improved ESP scoring bears similarity to the research into the conditions for optimal memory. Whereas the classical card-guessing tests are like the methods used by Ebbinghaus and those who followed him, the open-ended, free-response studies of psi remind us of the Bartlett (1932) tradition in memory research. Again, the position effects, such as the tendency to score higher on the first and the last trials of a test run, the differential effect, and psi-missing seem to have their analogs in memory—e.g., U curves in serial learning, retroactive inhibition, and parapraxes. If both memory and ESP involve information-processing mechanisms, as some hold, memory psychologists and parapsychologists may find common points of theoretical interest. For example, the "retrieved it" model of William James (1890/1952) or its later development in Underwood's (1969) notion of retrieval and discrimination attributes may be applied to the ESP process for a better understanding of the nature of psi. Also, some of the concepts found in memory literature such as short-term and long-term memory, episodic and semantic memory, and productive and reproductive memory may be relevant not only in suggesting new lines of ESP research but also in clarifying some of the questions already raised. The memory psychologist also has much to gain by reflecting on such concepts as psi-missing and the methodological advances parapsychology has made in recent years.

The first significant attempt to relate memory scores with ESP scores was made by Sara Feather (1967). In two series of preliminary tests the subject was first shown a list of ESP symbols or digits for 15 or 20 seconds, then was given a card-calling ESP test, and finally was asked to recall the symbols or numbers seen initially. The results showed that the subjects whose recall was better also performed better in the ESP test than did those whose recall was poorer. In a confirmatory experiment consisting of three series, she again obtained significant positive correlations between memory and ESP scores. Other studies that explored the memory-ESP relation include those by Stanford (1970, 1973), Kanthamani & Rao (1974), Rao, Morrison & Davis (1977), and Rao, Morrison, Davis & Freeman (1977). More recently, Rock, Storm, Harris & Friedman (2013) reported that psi performance correlated negatively with memory.

Geomagnetic Activity and Psi

In recent years, a number of studies have attempted to explore the relationship between the occurrence of psi and geomagnetic activity in the atmosphere. Investigators reported significant positive correlations between the frequency of spontaneous ESP experiences and quiet geomagnetic activity (Persinger, 1985; 1989), and between successful psi tests and low levels of geomagnetic activity at the time the tests were conducted (Berger and

Persinger, 1991; Persinger and Krippner, 1989). These correlations are interpreted as evidence in support of the ELF hypothesis. The ELF hypothesis assumes that extremely low frequency (ELF) waves are involved in psi communication and that ESP is a primitive communication system, consisting of electromagnetic field effects which may function more effectively during periods of less turbulent geomagnetic activity (Becker, 1992).

However, some other investigators (Haraldsson and Gissurarson, 1987; Nelson and Dunne, 1986) did not observe a similar effect of geomagnetic activity on psi performance. Attempting to replicate the effect on a large database, James Spottiswoode carried out a metaanalysis of 1468 free-response ESP trials gathered from 21 studies, and found no significant correlation between ESP scores and the geomagnetic activity. This has led him to look for other physical variables modulating the effect. Spottiswoode examined 2,483 free-response trials and found a relationship between the effect size and the Local Sidereal Time (LST) at the ESP trial place. He observed that those trials that occurred within 1 hour of 13.5 hour LST showed a large 380 percent increase in the effect size (Spottiswoode, 1997a) in ESP test results.

In the next study Spottiswoode (1997b) looked at the ESP-geomagnetic fluctuations in conjunction with LST. He observed that the negative correlation between ESP scores and geomagnetic index held good within a limited region of local sidereal times and is absent in the data outside this range. The range is 4h of LST. The maximum effect size is seen to occur at 13.3h. Spottiswoode concludes from these results that ESP "effect size is strongly dependent upon the LST of the subject and in the limited region of LST ... and the effect size is modulated by some component of solar activity" (p. 11).

In a study by Houtkooper, Schienle, Stark and Vaitil (1998), a negative correlation between ESP performance and "sferics" activity was found. Sferics are Very Low Frequency (VLF) electromagnetic impulses, which are generated by lightening discharges. It is known that sferics have biological effects on humans. Positive correlations are reported between natural sferics rates and epileptic seizures and myocardial infractions. Also elevated sferics activity is known to be associated with reduced performance levels on tasks involving reaction time and concentration. Thus there is some reason and evidence in favor of the influence of atmospheric factors on ESP scoring rate, even though the carrier of this effect is yet to be identified.

A more recent study on the relationship between ESP and geomagnetic activity by Roney-Dougal, Adrian Ryan & David Luke (2014) found that the subjects with the highest temporal lobe questionnaire scores showed the strongest correlation of psi with geomagnetic activity.

"Global Consciousness" Project

The Princeton Engineering Anomalies Research group with Roger Nelson as the principal investigator launched an interesting project to study the effects of group mind (global consciousness) rather than individual subjects on random event generators. This study is in some respects paradigmatically different from other laboratory oriented PK studies. First, the PK task in these studies is nonintentional and there is no subject or set of designated subjects to whom the observed effects would be attributed as the source. In other words, the experimental paradigm ignores or sidesteps the source of psi issue—who is the source of the effect—by considering the entire population as the general source. Second, the measurement of the effects is not limited to a single system, but is distributed globally. Thus the dirigibility issue is also side-stepped. Dirigibility refers to the guidance mechanism that enables an ability like ESP to focus on a particular target. For example, there are these questions that need answers: what is the mechanism that guides a subject's ESP to a specific target (e.g., ESP card) among the several potential targets (the deck of ESP cards)? How is it that a subject's PK influences the designated random event generator (REG) and not others? Third, it is assumed that space is not a constraining variable, but that time is. In other words the PK effect is assumed to be spatially nonlocal but temporally specific and local.

As Nelson (2001) reports, the Global Consciousness Project (GCP) was a worldwide effort involving "more than two dozen researchers." A network of REGs is setup in various parts of the globe and their outputs are continuously monitored. Special purpose software collects data from these connected REGs and sends them over the internet to a dedicated server for storage and analysis. The central idea is that when "deeply engaging events," such as the occurrence of a great tragedy shared worldwide, take place, the people's collective consciousness reacts. And this reaction would have effects in terms of measurable nonrandom activity on the REGs that are poised for measuring such effects across the globe. In other words, the experimental hypothesis is that there would be nonrandom REG activity during periods of "widely shared experiences of deeply engaging events" such as the funeral of Princes Diana.

Nelson and associates began the formal "Field REG" experiments in 1993 and soon reported significant effects (Nelson et al., 1996; 1998). They were conceptually replicated by Radin et al. (1996) and Bierman (1996). Nelson (2001) in a detailed description of the project and the results obtained to January 2000, reports that the examination of all the 43 formally specified events shows significant support to the hypothesis (*p* <.001). The mean of the REG output during the identified events differs significantly from chance expectation. The most striking appearance of the effect (*p* = *.00066)* occurred during the U.S. embassy bombings in Nairobi and Tanzania on 7 August 1998. Nelson concludes "that by our simple measures there is robust evidence for anomalous departures of the data from expectation ... the most likely source and the most consistent correlate of the apparent effects is the relatively high coherence of wide-spread attention during events with a strong global focus" (p. 266).

Psi and Sensory Noise Reduction

ESP is considered by some to be "an ancient and primitive form of perception" (Eysenck, 1967). Therefore, it is suggested that conditions of high cortical arousal may inhibit ESP, whereas a state of relaxation and reduced sensory input may facilitate its occurrence. British psychologist H.J. Eysenck (1967) surveyed a large number of studies that have bearing on this. Pointing out that introverts are habitually in a state of greater cortical arousal than extraverts, Eysenck hypothesized that extraverts would do better in ESP tests than introverts. Indeed, as we have noted earlier, there is much evidence in support of this hypothesis.

There are several studies which shed direct light on the hypothesis of ESP facilitation via sensory noise reduction. There is substantial evidence to suggest that the occurrence of ESP may be enhanced by procedures that result in the reduction of meaningful sensory stimuli and proprioceptive input to the organism. In fact many of the traditional psychic development techniques such as yoga appear to employ sensory noise reduction procedures. So do a variety of relaxation exercises and altered states of consciousness. Psi researchers have explored some of them.

Relaxation and ESP

Several subjects who have done well on psi tests have claimed that they did their best when they were physically relaxed and their minds were in a "blank" state. Mary Sinclair, whom her husband, novelist Upton Sinclair, found to be an outstanding ESP subject, gave the following advice: "You first give yourself a 'suggestion' to the effect that you will relax your mind and your body, making the body insensitive and the mind a blank" (Sinclair, 1930, p. 180). Rhea White (1964), who reviewed the early literature on this topic, also concluded that attempts "to still the body and mind" are common among the techniques used by successful subjects.

The most extensive work in this area was carried out by William Braud and associates. Lendell Braud and William Braud carried out two experiments to explore the relationship between ESP and relaxation. In the first experiment, there were 16 subjects; and the subjects self-rated their degree of relaxation. Braud & Braud (1974) report that those who performed well in the ESP tests rated themselves as more relaxed than the poor psi performers. The second experiment consisted of 20 volunteer subjects who were assigned randomly to "relaxation" or "tension" conditions. Those in the relaxation condition went through a taped, progressive-relaxation procedure (an adaptation of Jacobson's) before taking an ESP test, which was to guess the picture being "transmitted" by an agent in another room. The subjects in the other group were given taped, tension-inducing instructions before they did the same ESP test. Each subject's level of relaxation was assessed through electro-myographic recordings. The EMG results showed, as expected, a significant decrease in the EMG activity among the subjects in the "relaxation" group and a significant increase among those in the "tension" group. As predicted, the ESP scores of the subjects in the relaxation group were significantly higher than those of the subjects in the tension group.

Other reports of interest are Braud & Braud (1973), Braud (1975), and Altom & Braud (1976). Confirmation of Braud's results may be found in Stanford & Mayer (1974). Honorton's (1977) summary of studies on relaxation and psi shows a 77 percent success rate. Ten of the 13 studies involving induced relaxation achieved statistical significance at the 5 percent level in support of psi.

Psi in Hypnotic States

The idea that the hypnotic state may be psi-conducive is as old as scientific parapsychology. A French physician, E. Azam, observed that one of his patients in a hypnotic state responded to an unspoken thought. Pierre Janet was reportedly successful in inducing a somnambulistic trance state 16 out of 20 times by mere mental suggestion (Podmore, 1894). Eleanor Sidgwick (Sidgwick *et al.*, 1889), at the Society for Psychical Research in England, experimented with hypnotized subjects by using two digit numbers and colors as targets. The Russian physiologist Vasiliev (1963) was highly successful in inducing hypnotic trance by telepathy from a distance. Within the card-calling paradigm, the first ESP experiment with hypnosis was reported by J.J. Grela (1945).

Jarl Fahler (1957) carried out some related experiments in Finland, which gave significant results when the subjects were under hypnosis. Important work in the area of hypnosis and psi was also reported by L. Casler (1962, 1964). Casler went a step further than Fahler by giving explicit suggestions to the subjects for improvements in their ESP scoring. Milan Ryzl (Ryzl & Ryzlova, 1962) claimed that he trained the outstanding subject Pavel Stepanek with the help of hypnosis. Charles Honorton's (1977) review lists 42 psi studies using hypnosis, 22 of which gave significant evidence of psi.

Another review and meta-analysis of the experimental studies of ESP and hypnosis was published by Ephraim Schechter (1984). His analysis confirms the hypotheses that subjects tend to obtain higher ESP scores in the hypnotic state than in a controlled waking state. That the hypnotic state is psi-conducive fits well with the observation that people who report spontaneous psychic experiences tend to have dissociative tendencies (Pekala, Kumar & Marcano, 1995). Hypnotic susceptibility, like psychological absorption, is a dimension of dissociative processes.

A more recent meta-analysis of ESP studies involving hypnosis and contrasting conditions is reported by Rex Stanford & Adam Stein (1994). Included in the analysis are 25 studies by 12 chief investigators. Claiming that their attempt was to extend and refine Schechter's work, Stanford and Stein also report cumulative ESP test scores significant for hypnosis. They, however, caution that we may not draw any substantive conclusions from the current database, because the difference in ESP scores between hypnosis and contrast conditions is significant only when the comparison condition preceded hypnosis. They point out also that there is significant psi-missing in the contrasting condition. Del Prete and Tressoldi (2005) report that hypnotic induction resulted in significant psi scoring. This was confirmed in a replication study (Tressoldi & Del Prete, 2007).

Meditation and ESP

The practice of yoga, it is said, enables one to develop psychic abilities. In the third century before Christ, Patañjali wrote a treatise on Raja Yoga (Woods, 1927) detailing the processes and procedures involved and the varieties of supernormal abilities one may obtain by practicing this discipline. Meditation is the most important feature of yoga. It is pointed out that the practice of intensely focusing attention on a single object and following this by meditation enables the practitioner to hold his focus for an extended period of time, which results in a standstill state of the mind (*samadhi*). The *samadhi* state is the one in which psychic abilities are believed to manifest. Unfortunately, there are very few systematic studies of yogins to test for their psi, even though there is a vast amount of anecdotal material concerning their extraordinary psychic claims. However, several exploratory studies in which some kind of meditation procedure was used seem to suggest a positive relationship between meditation and ESP.

We carried out a series of experiments at Andhra University in India to explore the possibility of enhancing one's psi abilities through the practice of yoga (Rao, Dukhan & Rao, 1978). In this study, 59 subjects who had various degrees of proficiency in meditation took ESP tests before and immediately after they had meditated for half an hour or more. The ESP tests involved matching cards with ESP symbols and guessing concealed pictures. Both the tests yielded results that showed that the subjects obtained significantly better ESP scores in the post-meditation sessions than in the pre-meditation sessions. Other meditation psi studies include those by Schmeidler (1970), Osis and Bokert (1971), and Schmidt and Pantas (1972). Honorton (1977) reports a survey that shows 9 out of 16 experimental series involving meditation to have given significant psi results. Since Honorton's review there are several other studies of relating to meditation and psi (Rao & Puri, 1978; Palmer, Khamashta & Israelson, 1979; Roll *et al.*, 1979; Roll & Zill, 1981; Harding & Thalbourne, 1981; Nash, 1982; Rao & Rao, 1982; Braud & Boston, 1986). During more recent work, we find significant psi results in six experiments by those who practiced meditation. These include studies by Radin (2008), Radin *et al.* (2012), Mason, Patterson & Radin (2007), and Nelson, Jahn, Dunne & Dobyns (1998) and Braud (1990).

ESP in the Ganzfeld

Finally, a number of well-designed experimental studies looked at the effects of reduced external stimulation on subject's ESP scoring by utilizing the ganzfeld technique. Ganzfeld is a homogeneous visual field produced, for instance, by taping two halves of a ping-pong ball over the eyes and focusing on them a uniform red light from about two feet. The subject may also be given "white" noise through attached earphones. After being in the Ganzfeld for about one half hour, subjects typically report being immersed in a sea of light. Some subjects report a total "black out" and complete absence of visual experience. Continuous uniform and unpatterned stimulation in the ganzfeld, it is believed, produces a state that, in the absence of meaningful external stimulation, enhances the possibility of attention to internal states, which in turn facilitates the detection of ESP signals.

In a typical Ganzfeld-ESP experiment, the subject, while in the ganzfeld for about 30 minutes, is asked to report whatever is going on in his or her mind at that time. The subject's mentation is monitored and recorded by an experimenter in another room via a microphone link. A second experimenter or an independent sender, acting as an agent, located in a different room isolated from the subject and the experimenter monitoring the subject, looks at a picture for about 15 minutes, attempting to "transmit" it to the subject in the ganzfeld. At the end of the Ganzfeld period, the monitoring experimenter gives the subject four pictures with a request to rank them 1 through 4 on the basis of their correspondence to the subject's mental images and impressions during the ganzfeld. The monitoring experimenter of course does not have any knowledge as to which one of the four pictures is the one looked at by the agent. After all the four pictures are ranked, the subject is shown the target picture. The rank the subject gives to the picture provides the score for a statistical analysis for matching the degree of subject's mentation with the target. Sometimes, the ranking is done by a judge in addition to or in place of the subject.

Honorton & Harper (1974) reported one of the first ganzfeld-ESP experiments, which provided evidence that the subject's mentation during the ganzfeld matched significantly with the target pictures that she was attempting to guess. About the same time William Braud (Braud, Wood & Braud 1975) independently carried out ESP tests in the ganzfeld. Between 1974 and 2004 there were in all 88 published ganzfeld-ESP experiments which have a combined hit rate of 32 percent against the chance expectation of 25 percent, which is a highly improbable result with odds running into 29 quintillion (Radin, 2006), it seemed that psi in ganzfeld is a highly replicable effect. However, at the joint conference of the Society for Psychical Research and the Parapsychological Association held at Cambridge University during August 1982, psychologist Ray Hyman made a presentation raising serious questions about the replicability of the ganzfeld psi experiment. Subsequently a comprehensive critical appraisal of ganzfeld–ESP experiments was published in the *Journal of Parapsychology* (Hyman, 1985). In this paper, Hyman (1) challenged the claimed success rate of replication, (2) argued that possible flaws involving inadequate randomization and insufficient documentation vitiate experiments reporting significant psi effects, and (3) concluded that the ganzfeld-ESP database is "too weak to support any assertions about the existence of psi."

The previous chapter discussed in some detail the controversy and the debate. As noted, Honorton noted inconsistencies in Hyman's analysis and argued that neither selective reporting nor alleged procedural flaws account for significant psi effects reported in the ESP-ganzfeld studies.

The exchanges between Honorton and Hyman, the subsequent publication of auto-ganzfeld-ESP studies by Bem & Honorton (1994) and the meta-analyses that followed strongly support the existence of a psi effect in the ganzfeld data. Also correlational studies have shown more psi when the subjects reported that ganzfeld stimulation produced an altered state of consciousness in them.

The results from ESP studies involving meditation, relaxation, hypnosis and ganzfeld thus meaningfully converge to suggest that a reduction of ongoing sensorimotor activity may facilitate the manifestation of ESP in laboratory tests. Whatever may be the mechanism involved in ESP, it is reasonable to assume that ESP is a weak signal that must compete for the information processing resources of the organism. In this process, any reduction of ongoing sensory activity should improve the chances of detecting and registering the ESP signal.

6

The Problem of Psi-Missing

The low replicability rate of ESP experiments and the manifest elusiveness of psi are likely due to a lack of understanding of the relevant but yet not identified variables that influence and inhibit the manifestation of psi in experimental situations. What is most frustrating to the investigating scientists in this area, however, are the three known special features that render psi less predictable. One of them is the often observed declines and reverses in scoring noted earlier. The second is the possibility that psi may have a negative aspect and manifest in a reverse direction, opposite to the goals sought and the targets aimed at. This is technically called psi-missing. The role of the experimenter in eliciting psi from the subjects tested, the so-called psi experimenter effect, is the third. Even though similar phenomena are occasionally observed in other human sciences, the critics of psi harp on them to discredit parapsychology. Therefore, it is of utmost importance to understand these aspects of psi not only to answer criticisms but also to gain a better handle for a greater replicability and control of the phenomena. We have already discussed the matter of declines earlier. We now turn to psi-missing and the experimenter effects in this and the following chapter.

Psi-Missing

Psi-missing is the tendency to miss the target when attempting to hit. Systematic studies of psi-missing are a late comer in psi research, but the phenomenon of psi-missing was encountered quite early in experimental parapsychology. For example, in Series IV of the 1927 experiment of Estabrooks (1961) at Harvard University, in which the variable of distance was introduced, as pointed out earlier, the subjects averaged 4.06 hits per run of 25 trials, where mean chance expectation (MCE) is 5.00. The negative deviation in this series is statistically significant, suggesting that the subjects tended to miss the targets more often than expected by chance. Rhine (1952) himself found that some of his outstanding subjects like Linzmayer and Pearce produced strong negative deviations from chance expectations when they were inadvertently kept over time, and also when they were exposed to not so pleasant experimental conditions. As L.E. Rhine (1965) noted, the early investigator considered psi-missing as "a kind of nemesis which could catch up with an ESP experimenter and trip him unawares" (p. 263).

The elusiveness of psi is legendary. The non-replicability of results is the main reason offered by skeptics for denying scientific legitimacy to psi research (Alcock, 1981, 1987, 2003; Kurtz, 1981). Even those favorable toward parapsychology have expressed despair on occasion (James, 1911; Pratt, 1974) and wondered whether this department of nature is destined to remain a mystery to science. Therefore, an understanding of the factors that contribute to the elusiveness of psi would be an important step forward. In that spirit William Braud (1984) attempted to identify a number of factors that seem to serve a "self-obscuring" function, as he called it, that masks psi. Psi-missing is possibly one of the main "self-obscuring" aspects of psi.

Psi-missing is no doubt quite frustrating to the parapsychologist seeking to gain control over ESP, but the discovery of psi-missing is itself a blessing in disguise. The knowledge that some subjects may miss a target when they are in fact trying to hit exactly it, along with the fortunate development of a methodology that takes the theoretical mean as the point of separating hitting and missing, have enabled parapsychologists to take advantage of this phenomenon in understanding the type of person who is likely to be the misser and the kind of conditions that may cause psi-missing. It would seem that a clear insight into psi-missing opens up possibilities for gaining greater replicability and eventual control over the apparently elusive psi ability.

What are the situations in which psi-missing is likely to occur? We have a fund of information on this point. The psi-missing situations encountered so far may be broadly classified into five categories. Schmeidler's (Schmeidler and McConnell, 1958) relentless and extensive studies and their widespread confirmation around the world (Bhadra and Parthasarathy, 1965; Musso, 1965) have shown that psi-missing is likely to occur when the subjects hold negative attitude towards psi. There have also been studies which indicate that the negative attitudes of the experimenter may cause psi-missing. Sharp and Clark (1937) observed that on one occasion, when an experimenter who was "definitely" skeptical about ESP was testing, the subjects gave a significantly negative deviation.

There are two explanations for such negative scores. Since subjects who hold negative attitudes are likely to be negatively motivated, it is likely that their efforts are misdirected, with the result that, when they are asked to guess the target correctly, their subconscious negative motivation leads them to do the opposite. Another possibility is that the subject's conscious desire to obtain more hits and the belief that it is not possible may create a dissonant situation that reverses the scoring trend. The skeptical experimenter is likely to affect the subject adversely in the interpersonal exchange, which may result either in negative motivation or a clash of attitudes.

The second factor, in addition to subjects' attitudes that seem to be associated with psi-missing, relates to certain moods and personality factors of the subjects. Experimental studies have been reported in which the withdrawn (Shields, 1962), the extrapunitive (Schmeidler, 1954), the ego-involved (Eilbert and Schmeidler, 1950), and the introverted (Honorton, Ferrari, and Bem 1998; Humphrey, 1951; Kanthamani and Rao, 1972) subjects tended to obtain negative deviations. No one knows for certain what factors determine psi-missing in these situations. It is unlikely that the personality of the subject as such has anything to do with it. It may simply be the way some subjects react to certain experimenters and test conditions. It would seem that the experimental conditions in psi tests are generally those in which the well-adjusted and the outgoing subjects are more likely to be at home than their counterparts.

The conflict-generating situations are the third kind that are known to contribute to psi-missing. Conflict may be intellectual or moral. A revealing case illustrative of intellectual conflict was reported by Rhine (1941). He tested for precognition a group of adults and a group of children and found that the adults gave a significantly negative deviation, while the children obtained an equally significant positive deviation. In cases where children did better than adults in precognition tests, Rhine suggested that the likely perception of the impossibility of precognition on purely rational grounds might have caused an intellectual conflict with the adults, whereas for the children there could have been no such conflict.

The fourth circumstance that seems to precipitate psi-missing is frustration. The situations in which the checking is delayed and the subjects do not have the feedback they expect and also those in which complicated tests beyond the comprehension of the subject are employed may be regarded as frustrating. And these situations are known to produce psi-missing (Rhine, 1958). Incentives, novelty and game-like situations that are found to facilitate psi are perhaps some of the devices that do not let frustration set in easily (Woodruff and Murphy, 1943).

Finally, differential situations are known to cause psi-missing. It has been frequently observed that when the subjects are presented with two contrasting conditions, such as two sets of targets, they tend to respond differentially to them (Rao, 1962, 1963, 1964; Carpenter, 1977). This tendency to hit and miss at the same time is called the differential effect.

While the first four situations in which psi-missing seems to occur can be interpreted at the psychological level, the fifth one seems to require something more than a simple psychological explanation. In the first place, the evidence is not strongly suggestive that subjects score positively on "preferred" targets. Even if we agree that preferred scoring on one set of targets is motivated because they are agreeable, novel or challenging, it is difficult to maintain that the subjects are negatively motivated to score low on the other set. Why does the subject who scores positively on target words printed in Telugu miss on English words? It is not reasonable to suppose that the experimenter somehow exerts differential influence on the subjects since in a number of studies the experimenter was not aware, for example, whether the subject was guessing the English or Telugu targets at a particular time, unless one assumes psi experimenter effects. Nor can it be said that a particular set is favored while the other is disfavored by the subject, because no such differential attitude towards the targets is generally observed.

The case of consistent missing also seems to favor a hypothesis other than simple negative motivation. In the case of consistent missing the subject shows a tendency to mistake a given target symbol consistently for another. While the work of Cadoret and Pratt (1950) definitely suggests the possibility of consistent missing, the experiments of Ryzl and Pratt (1963a, 1963b) with Pavel Stepanek (P.S.) in Czechoslovakia have given us further insight into this problem.

In an experiment with P.S. involving repeated calling of the same card, the target cards (green on one side and white on the other) were sealed in black envelopes. These envelopes were again randomly inserted into opaque outer covers. It is reported that neither the subject nor the experimenters had sensory clues at any time as to which side of the card was uppermost. It was found that P.S. was significantly consistent in calling certain cards green or white without any apparent clue to what his previous calls on the cards were. This consistency was not limited to the cards identified correctly but was also found in cases where the subject was calling the wrong color. The results of the experiments gave highly significant evidence for both consistent hitting and consistent missing, thereby suggesting some peculiar uniqueness about these individual target cards.

Ryzl and Pratt also observed that certain cards seemed to be good channels for psi operation. The subject's ESP seemed to "focus" better on certain cards than others. This did not mean that the subject continued permanently to hit on cards previously found to be psi-hitting targets or miss on the previously psi-missing ones. In one series, for example, a certain card was found to be a good psi-hitting card. The subject obtained 165 hits out of 250 trials on this card (p < 10). In another series, however, the same card was found to be a significant psi-missing target, suggesting that the positive and negative scores were not determined by the card alone.

The "focusing" of psi did not seem to be directed always to the cards. When the inner envelopes in which the target cards were enclosed were interchanged between "good" (previously successful) and "bad" (previously unsuccessful) ones, some of the "bad" cards, which happened to be in "good" envelopes, proved to be "good" targets, thus suggesting, according to the experimenters, "some sharing" of focusing between the cards and the inner envelopes.

The results of P.S. in these experiments seem to provide evidence for Rhine's (1952) cognitive error hypothesis of psi-missing. The subject could respond in these experiments either to the color of the target directly or to the identifying mark on the envelope in order to make a consistent call. If he were responding to the color itself, it is logical to assume that he would be either successful or unsuccessful in his task. But the fact that the subject was consistently successful on some while consistently missing some others raises the question whether he was responding to the identifying number and then associating this number with either green or white. If his association was correct, he would get psi-hitting on the card; if it was wrong, his calls would indicate psi-missing. Thus, if there is the possibility of a two-stage operation of psi, a chance error in one stage could produce consistent missing.

It must be mentioned, however, that even the cognitive error hypothesis does not explain the "focusing phenomena" and we need a further explanation for the uniqueness of the card insofar as it is either successful or unsuccessful in a given series. There were some criticisms of the experiments with P.S. that assumed some kind of sensory cues that the subject might have had from the target cards or the envelopes in which they were enclosed. Martin Gardner (1989) published an extensive critical review of these experiments. I find Gardner's arguments essentially unconvincing. Milan Ryzl (1990) provides a succinct rebuttal of Gardner's main argument and other reasons for discounting the latter's criticism of the experiments with P.S.

In two of his articles, Rhine (1952; 1969) discussed at length the question of psi-missing, described the different situations in which psi-missing is likely to occur, and suggested two hypotheses to account for it. He identified three main categories of conditions favoring the occurrence of psi-missing and considered all these three types as primarily psychological. Under the first category, he included psi-missing associated with position effects. Declines of scoring in ESP tests, as we have noted, are not uncommon. What is important, however, is the fact that in several cases decline was not from a high score to a chance score, but from a high score to a low score. The declined score often tended to be significantly below the MCE, suggesting the occurrence of psi-missing at one end. Even in cases of observed U-curves, the scores in the middle segments tend to be below the expected mean to a statistically significant degree, suggesting psi-missing in those trials.

Rhine also noted that psi-missing occurred under conditions of stress. As an example he cited the experiments of Rao, Kanthamani and Sailaja (1968). In this study, when the applicants who were awaiting important interviews were dragged in to take an ESP test without any notice, they tended to psi-miss.

In the third category, Rhine included psi-missing that occurs in one condition when a subject is tested under two conditions. This is what is referred to as the differential effect. When a subject in an ESP test is confronted with two features in a somewhat comparative way, the subject generally tends to score above chance on one and below on the other. Rhine cites the example of the precognition experiment by Sanders (1962) in which subjects indicated their preference between two methods of response—calling and writing—and obtained positive scores with preferred method and negative scores in the nonpreferred condition.

In his 1952 paper, Rhine suggested negative motivation and systematic cognitive error as possible explanations for psi-missing. The cognitive error hypothesis may perhaps explain the cases in which one finds consistent missing such as those reported and discussed by Cadoret and Pratt (1950) and Timm (1969). A review of consistent missing literature by Kennedy (1979) did not reveal that such missing is consistently related to the direct-hit scoring rate. In fact, in the two sets of psi-missing data available to him, Kennedy found that consistent missing did not appear to be the dominant factor contributing to psi-missing. The negative motivation hypothesis is obviously more appropriate in cases like those of the goats, the nonbelievers in psi, who tend to obtain negative deviations. One could also speculate that in cases where the subjects experience frustration or conflict, as suggested previously, their motivation to succeed in the test may take a negative turn. As Humphrey and Pratt (1941) noted, "if the social situation were one of the effective factors in producing the negative scores, it seems likely that the modus operandi would have been unconscious negative motivation rather than cognitive poor aim" (p. 289).

It is possible that psi-missing is perhaps more basic to the psi process than the cognitive error and negative motivation hypotheses suggest and that psi-missing may be nature's defense mechanism which has led to a general disuse of psi. If psi brings information that is as often wrong as it is correct, then such information becomes unreliable and, therefore, we as a species are less likely to exercise psi and depend on it for our interactions with the environment. There is reason to think, therefore, that psi-missing in general may indicate a truly parapsychological response pattern, a "self-obscuring" defense mechanism. Consequently an understanding of the dynamics of psi-missing might prove invaluable in the quest for the eventual control of psi. It would seem from what we know of psi in general and psi-missing in particular that psi is bi-directional and that, if there are any parapsychological principles, they are more likely to be discovered on the bi-directional hypothesis (Rao, 1965). In fact, James Carpenter's (2015) *First Sight Theory* has this in the background. Actually, Rex Stanford (2015) points out that the bidirectionality of psi is a corollary of Carpenter's *First Sight Model and Theory.*

Psi-missing appears to be ubiquitous in parapsychological studies. It appears to manifest in a number of contexts. There are a number of studies, among them by Bem (2011), Savva, Child & Smith (2004), Parker & Sjödén (2011), Cardeña, Marcusson-Clavertz & Wasmuth (2009), and Robinson (2011) that provide significant evidence for psi-missing.

The Differential Effect (DE) and the Bimodal Response Pattern

The differential effect (DE) is a consequence of the commonly observed tendency for a subject in a psi test involving two experimental conditions to score differentially—i.e., in opposite directions. As pointed out, subjects appear to score in modally opposite ways when tested in two contrasting conditions or test circumstances, which include two different kinds of targets, response modes and other experimental conditions. Carpenter (1977) discussed some of the conceptual issues involved in studies of this sort.

The differential effect which I first called the preferential effect is of special research interest to me. I have carried out a number of studies exploring it; and attempted to suitable explanation to what seem to me ubiquitous phenomena in parapsychology. What follows is more a summary of my work rather than a over all review of the literature.

Pointing out that the concept of the differential effect "has been construed rather loosely" (p. 207), Carpenter distinguished among three senses in which it had been used. First, there are those cases in which "the same subjects are tested in two different circumstances, and the different circumstances tend to elicit performances which are modally opposite for each subject" (p. 207). The example he gives is the study by Stuart, Humphrey, Smith, and McMahan (1947) in which a significant number of subjects were found to reverse their scoring directions when asked to respond by calling ESP targets instead of writing them and by producing free response drawings. There was positive scoring in cases where there was psi-missing. The second type involves those cases in which the subject, when repeatedly tested in two different tasks or conditions, tends to score significantly positive on one task and significantly negative on the other. Carpenter gives the example of the self-testing study of Thouless (1949). This example seems to be somewhat inappropriate because it included *three* and not *two* experimental conditions. Traditionally the differential effect is referred to only in these experimental situations in which there are two contrasting conditions and no more.

The third major type distinguished by Carpenter is one like the second type in all respects except that the deviation in the hitting or missing condition is not statistically significant by itself but the difference between them is. Carpenter suggests that we designate only the first type as the differential effect and call the other two preferential effects.

While the distinctions Carpenter makes are helpful in clarifying some of the conceptual problems in this area, they themselves are not devoid of difficulties. First of all, there is no basic or intrinsic reason for making these distinctions. Whether the observed deviation in one condition is statistically significant by itself does not seem to be an important factor. Statistical significance in several cases depends not only on the magnitude of the effect but also on the size of the sample. Also, the method of statistical analysis employed for testing the differential effect may have a bearing on some of the assumptions we make concerning it, but it is, at this stage, an inappropriate basis for distinguishing between the types of the differential effect. Therefore, what is important now is that we make explicit the assumptions underlying the usage of this concept and seek empirical support for them.

The two essential conditions that characterize an experimental situation to study the differential effect are: (a) there should be *two* circumstances or conditions in which the subject responds and (b) the *same* subject should be tested in both the conditions. It is not necessary for the accumulated score in one or both of the conditions to be statistically significant. A statistically significant difference in the scores obtained under the two conditions is, however, a *necessary* condition for considering the results as evidence for the DE. A statistically significant difference is not a *sufficient* condition because a significant, over-all difference between two scoring rates when both of them are in the same direction (negative or positive) is no evidence of differential response. Therefore, a result is referred to as evidence of the DE only when (a) the two scores are in opposite directions and (b) the difference between them is statistically significant. The term "differential scoring" may be used to refer to the fact that the two scores are in opposite directions, without regard to the significance of their difference. Ideally, differential scoring should show a mirror image of psi scores under the two conditions of the test.

Patterns of Differential Scoring

The differential response seems to occur in both ESP and PK tests and under various contrasting conditions. In Skibinsky's (1950) experiments, in which family names and ESP symbols were used as targets, the subject tended to score positively on symbols and negatively on names. In a study by Hallett (1952), the subjects guessed target positions as well as target symbols and obtained positive scores on position and negative scores on symbol. He found the difference between the two to be highly significant. Chauvin (1961), using normal and very tiny microfilmed symbols as targets, found that positive scoring was associated with normal symbols and negative scoring with small, microfilmed symbols. Freeman (1962) reported that 11 out of his 12 subjects responded differentially to emotionally-toned objects and ESP symbols.

There is also evidence that the differential effect occurs between agents (T-persons) in telepathy tests. In the GESP experiments of Stuart (1946), and later of Rice and Townsend (1962), the subjects obtained significantly positive scores when the agents were related persons and significantly negative scores when the T-persons were unrelated. Casper (1952) also reported a significant difference in the subjects' scores when they were working with the T-persons they liked most and with those they liked least, even though the direction was reversed. White and Angstadt (1961) also found evidence for the differential effect between T-persons.

A differential response was observed first in a PK experiment by Nicol and Carington (1947). In a series of PK experiments conducted by Nicol it was found that the subjects tended to obtain positive scores on high-value faces of the targets, 4, 5 and 6, and a negative deviation on low faces, 1, 2 and 3. The difference between the scores of high faces and low faces was statistically significant.

The editors of the *Journal of Parapsychology* (1948) commented that this effect, which they designated as "target preference in PK data," was independently discovered by Pratt in the U.S. and by Whately Carington in England. But it would seem that the effect observed by Pratt was somewhat different from the one reported by Carington. Pratt (1947) found highly significant patterns of hit distribution occurred in the data of a major PK subject when she was using the three higher faces of the dice as targets, but not when the three lower faces were the targets. This suggested that the subject's psi response was limited to the higher faces alone and that she did not influence the dice when the lower faces were the targets. But in the Carington study, it is likely that the subjects influenced the dice with their psi ability no matter what the target face was, even though their influence was positive on high-value faces and negative on low value faces of the dice.

The differential effect in PK has been noted by several other investigators since Carington. Forwald observed it on two occasions. In one study (1955), he used cubes made of two different materials and tried to influence only one kind, not the other, to fall on a specified area of a dice table. He found that there was a statistically significant difference in the results of the dice which he intended to influence and those which he did not. In another study (1957), he released smooth cubes and rough cubes simultaneously on his placement PK apparatus and tried to influence them to fall on a specified area. He observed that, while he was successful in influencing the rough cubes to fall in the specified area, the smooth cubes fell in a direction opposite to the one intended by him. This effect was most marked during the first throws, which gave a statistically significant difference between the results of the rough and smooth cubes.

Attempting to test the relative influence of placement PK on marbles and dice, Cox (1954) found that his subjects scored positively on marbles and negatively on dice. The difference between the number of hits on marbles and dice is statistically significant.

There is some evidence that the DE may result when two different experimental conditions are used in close association to test a subject. For example, when Sanders (1962) asked his subjects to state their preference for calling or writing their targets, the group as a whole scored positively on the preferred method and negatively on the nonpreferred method. The difference between the two was significant. Casper (1952) reported that his subjects scored positively in a BT test and negatively in a GESP test with the most liked agents. The difference was significant at the .02 level. In a long-distance experiment by Osis and Pienaar (1956) the subject made his calls at ten-second intervals between trials (slow rate) and at five-second intervals (rapid rate). The subject obtained significantly positive scores at the slow rate and significantly negative ones at the rapid rate. In an experiment by Freeman (1962) the subjects alternately carried out precognition and clairvoyance runs and obtained positive scores on precognition targets and negative scores on clairvoyance targets.

There is some evidence that a differential response occurs between the subject's states of mind just as it does between sets of targets. In one of my experiments (Rao, 1964), the subject SH obtained 82 hits in 20 runs before she was put into a "relaxed" state by hypnotic suggestion, and 113 hits in 20 runs after she relaxed. The difference between the two scores is significant at the .02 level. A repetition of this experiment with two other subjects also gave significant differences in scoring between the two conditions, but in the opposite direction. There is also evidence for the occurrence of the DE in a two-task situation (Rao, 1964). When a language ESP test was alternated with a test involving ESP symbols and masks, the subject who obtained a positive deviation on one task tended to obtain a negative deviation on the other and *vice versa.* Stuart, Humphrey, Smith and McMahan (1947) observed earlier that 42 of their 63 subjects reversed their scoring trends when participating in two different test procedures, one involving ESP cards and the other involving drawings.

The lawfulness of the differential response is evidenced not only by the frequency of its occurrence, but also by the way it seems to reflect the general characteristics of psi. We know, for example, that the position of the target in psi tests is found to be significantly relevant to the subject's performance. Evidence for the salience effect and U-curves—the tendency to obtain more hits during the beginning and the end segments of the run—was reported by Rhine (1935, p. 123), Pegram (1937), Gibson (1937), and Sharp and Clark (1937) among others. Interestingly, inverted U-curves are found in experiments yielding negative results, again suggesting the bi-dimensionality of psi.

In the Pegram experiment, for example, it was found that in those series in which the subject was aiming to get positive scores (high-aim) more correct calls occurred in the first and last segments of the run, while more incorrect calls occurred in the first and last segments in the low-aim tests in which the subject was trying to get as few hits as possible. Thus, the high-aim tests gave the U-curve, whereas the low-aim tests provided an inverted U-curve.

There is evidence for the mirror image of curves in the differential response situations in which the hit distribution under one condition would also appear to be the reverse of the distribution under the other condition. Thus, the plotting of hits on a graph separately for each of the two conditions seems to provide curves that are mirror images of each other. Anderson and Gregory (1959) reported an experiment consisting of clairvoyance and precognition conditions with a class of public-school students. When the hit distributions in terms of five-segment runs were represented in a graph separately for the clairvoyance and precognition experiments, the two curves were found to be mirror images.

In one of my experiments with "choice" and ESP cards (1962), a comparison of the curves for the choice and ESP scores in the serial order of the runs suggested a mirror pattern. Those runs in which the subjects scored the highest number of hits on *choice cards* were attended by runs with the lowest number of hits on *ESP cards*. In an unpublished study by me, almost perfect mirror images were obtained when the run scores for the six runs in each session before and after relaxation were compared in a graph. This experiment gave significant evidence for the occurrence of a differential response between the pre- and post-relaxed states of the two subjects.

In the beginning, it seemed that the differential response is related to the subject's preference for one condition relative to the other. I therefore called it the preferential effect. However, it soon became clear that the differential response might occur even when no such preference exists on the part of the subject. In fact, in some cases the direction of scoring was not consistent with the subject's preference. Therefore, it appeared more reasonable to call it the "differential effect" rather than "preferential effect." It follows that the effect is more than psychological, perhaps more basic to psi itself rather than the subject.

In connection with the differential response, a number of questions arise. These remain tempting areas for prospective researchers. First, is it necessary for the subject to be aware of the differential situation in order that she may respond differentially? Second, does the time lag between the presentation of one set of targets and the other make any difference to the occurrence of the differential response? Third, does the differential response manifest itself when there are more than two conditions, such as the comparison of three or more experimental techniques? Fourth, are there any areas in which differential response is more likely to occur than in others? Does the conscious preference of the subject for one condition have any effect on the direction of scoring? Finally, is it possible that comparisons of experimental and control conditions provide an occasion for the manifestation of the differential effect?

Since the time I first attempted to discuss the issues relating to the DE in 1965, we have accumulated considerable amount of information on it. During 1984, my associates and I had gathered all the experimental reports available to us in the English language at the time in an attempt to accumulate a complete database of the differential effect studies. H. Kanthamani, P.V. Krishna Rao, Anjum Khilji, and Shanti Krishna collaborated with me in collecting, classifying, checking and cross-checking the items included in the database. We were also helped by comments from John Palmer and Jim Kennedy.

In that 1984 effort we limited ourselves to ESP studies that had bearing on the differential effect. We attempted to make the database as comprehensive as possible through 1983 and include all the papers published in English since the establishment of the *Journal of Parapsychology* in 1937. In some cases we had to depend on abstracts and reports that did not provide all the information that we needed. Again, in a wider context, almost every comparison of an experimental and control condition may be construed to be a differential situation. Therefore, we needed to focus on a few clear-cut areas and not extend into unwieldy aspects of these studies. We took care to ensure that the studies listed did not suffer from any bias of selection by checking the studies independently by more than one person. In case of disagreement between them the study was reviewed by the group and a consensus decision was taken. In most cases the selection and scoring were clear-cut.

Quantitative Summary of the Review

Table 1 gives in a summary form the number of differential effect studies under various categories and their outcomes during the period under review. These studies fall into two broad categories, dual target and dual test conditions—one involving target variables and the other relating to test conditions. The latter may be further divided into two groups, those utilizing different tests and those involving different modes of subjects' responses. There are 73 studies in the category of dual target condition. The subjects in these tests attempted to guess two different sets of targets such as words in two languages. In 46 of them (63 percent) there is differential scoring, i.e., the scores are in the opposite direction for the two conditions, when you expect such a scoring in about one half of them. The probability of 46 studies showing differential scoring in a total of 73 such studies is *<.05*. In 20 of these 46 studies, the difference between the scores obtained under the two conditions is highly significant. The associated *p*-value with such an outcome is very, very small indeed.

In the area of dual test conditions, where the subjects participated in two different ESP tests such as clairvoyance and GESP there are 58 studies, and differential scoring was observed in 34 (58 percent) of them. The associated *p* is *>.05*. However, 19, or 33 percent, of these studies give significant evidence for the differential effect. Again, this is an extremely improbable result on the basis of the chance hypothesis. When the studies in this area are divided into contrasting test techniques and modes of response, we find that the occurrence of differential response was more frequent when the experimental conditions consisted of two response modes, such as writing or calling the responses, rather than two test techniques such as comparing free-response and forced-choice tests. In fact the differential response was observed in only 46 percent of the latter cases when one expects such a response 50 percent of the time just by chance.

TABLE 1: SUMMARY OF DIFFERENTIAL EFFECT STUDIES

Area	Total Studies	Differential Scoring			Significant Studies		
Between Targets	n	n	%	p	n	%	p
	73	46	63	<.05	20	27	<<.001
Between Test Conditions	58	34	58	ns	19	33	<<.001
Test Techniques	39	18	46	ns	8	20	<<.002
Modes of Response	19	16	84	<.005	11	57	<<.001
Grand Total	131	80	61	<.01	40	30	<<.001
Complex Variables	88	63	72	<<.001	28	53	<<.001
		All p values are two-tailed					

The database contains a total of 131 cases in which there exists a possibility for comparing two experimental conditions and for the differential scoring to occur. On the basis of chance hypothesis we expect one half of them to show differential scoring. Actually 80 (61 percent) of them have shown differential scoring. Such a distribution has a probability value of smaller than .01. Again, we expect 6.5 of the results (5 percent) to achieve statistical significance by chance at the .05 level. In fact 40 (30 percent) of the studies are significant at or beyond 5 percent level. The probability of such a distribution occurring by chance is very, very small. Thus, the database provides strong statistical evidence in support of the DE hypothesis across a large number of studies.

The above mentioned studies involve clear-cut direct comparisons of scores in two contrasting conditions. There are, however, other studies which involved complex variables in differential situations. In them there are additional variables, which further divide the data into subgroups. One example of a study with complex interacting variable is the one reported by Rex Stanford (1972), which consisted of two experiments. The subjects in this study were administered ESP tests under two conditions— (1) the "augury" condition, in which the subjects' guesses were determined by throwing dice, and the verbal calling condition. The additional variable is suggestibility. The subjects were divided into high suggestible and low suggestible groups. Stanford reported that his low-suggestible subjects scored *positively* in the "augury" condition and negatively in the verbal-calling condition. The high-suggestible subjects did the opposite and scored negatively in the "augury" condition and positively in the verbal-calling condition. The pooled results of the two experiments showed that the differences in the means of high- and low-suggestible groups of subjects are independently significant for both the conditions.

The 1984 database had 88 items involving complex variables like the above. Out of these 63 (72 percent) showed a bimodal response pattern. This again provides strong statistical evidence for differential scoring. Of the 88 experimental series 28, or 53 percent, gave statistically significant evidence for the DE. The probability of obtaining such a result by chance is again extremely small.

Differential Scoring in Experimental and Control Conditions

Some psychologists have criticized parapsychological experiments on the ground that several of the classic experiments in the field did not have non-psi control conditions (Boring, 1966; Calkins, 1980). Even parapsychologists like John Palmer (1982), who argued that such control conditions are not required in those experiments which are merely intended for demonstrating the existence of psi, have conceded that "such control conditions are necessary in research where the objective is to establish a causal relationship between psi and some external variable. For example, if I wanted to establish that hypnosis facilitates success at card guessing in an ESP test, I would need to demonstrate that ESP scores were significantly higher with hypnosis than under identical conditions without hypnosis" (Palmer, 1982, p. 13).

It is difficult to disagree with this argument on purely methodological grounds. If, however, the DE is as pervasive in psi test results as it seems to be, the setting up of control and experimental conditions using the within-subject design will automatically provide a differential situation, which leads the subjects to score positively on one condition and negatively on the other. If such were really the case, one would hardly be justified in attributing the superior scoring in one condition entirely to the variable that is manipulated. In fact, similar difficulties of interpretation have been expressed well in the past by psi researchers involved in process-oriented research (Rao, Dukhan, and Rao, 1978; Rao and Puri, 1978; Sailaja and Rao, 1973). Rex Stanford (1977), among others, pleaded for not using within-subject design, partly because of the possibility of the differential effect occurring in such a situation.

The possibility of the DE occurring in studies presumably involving the comparison of experimental and control conditions is clearly implied in the studies reviewed above. However, is there any direct evidence from the studies involving experimental and control conditions to support the occurrence of the DE? Since a comprehensive review of all the experiments bearing on this question would be far too extensive to be undertaken here, I have selected the studies that employed within-subject designs to investigate the effect of hypnosis on ESP scoring. The reason for selecting the area of hypnosis is that it has been extensively investigated with a solid database, lending a fairly strong support for a relationship between hypnosis and ESP (Schechter, 1984). The more recent studies which found hypnosis as a psi conducive procedure include Del Prete & Tressoldi (2005) and Tressoldi & Del Prete (2007).

Data are available for 20 series of experiments involving within-subject comparison of hypnosis and waking conditions. In 15 (75 percent) of these studies, the subjects scored positively in one condition and negatively in the other. The difference in scoring is significant in nine (45 percent) of them. Thus we find strong evidence suggesting, on the one hand, an hypnosis–ESP relationship, and on the other, the DE. In 12 of the 15 cases showing bimodal response, the average scores are positive in hypnotic condition and negative in the waking condition. Thus there is a consistency of direction, which may be attributed to the variable of hypnosis. Again, in some of these studies, such as the one by Fahler and Cadoret (1958), the significant difference between the hypnosis and waking conditions is almost entirely the result of significant positive scoring in the hypnosis condition.

In six of the nine significant differences in the ESP scores obtained in hypnotic and waking states, the scores obtained in the hypnotic condition are independently significant. These results thus clearly favor the interpretation that hypnosis is a psi conducive variable. At the same time, we may note that in 15 out of 20 cases the scores in the waking condition are in the negative direction when we expect about 10 by chance. This clearly favors the DE hypothesis.

The tendency to score positively in the hypnosis condition is accompanied by a tendency to obtain negative scores in the control condition. It would seem therefore, that in hypnosis–ESP studies the facilitative influence of hypnosis is enhanced to some extent by the presence of the DE. Thus it would seem that on theoretical as well as empirical grounds it might be necessary to control for the differential effect in studies that involve the comparison of experimental and control conditions. The obvious way of doing it is to avoid within-subject designs as far as possible in process oriented psi research.

Some Aspects of the Differential Effect

Assuming, then, that there is sufficient evidence in support of the DE hypothesis, one may ask if there are any variables that may enhance or inhibit the manifestation of this effect. The database allows us to examine (1) whether subjects' awareness of the existence of the two conditions is necessary for the DE to occur, (2) whether any preference on the part of the subject for one condition over another is related to the DE, and (3) whether the presentation of the targets in a mixed fashion (i.e., in random order) is better than the presentation of first one set and then the other. To answer these questions we analyzed the pool of 131 items in the areas of dual targets and double test conditions. Since the studies involving complex variables raise additional methodological problems in their analysis, they were not included in this exercise.

Subject's Awareness: In the 1984 database (see Table 2), there are 104 cases in which the subjects were aware of the two conditions and 25 studies in which they were not aware. We have no information in two other studies.

TABLE 2: SOME ASPECTS OF THE DIFFERENTIAL EFFECT

Total Studies			Differential Scoring			Significant DE		
Variable		n	n	%	p	n	%	p
Subject Awareness	Aware	104	65	62.5%	<.05	32	31%	<.001
	Unaware	25	15	60%	n.s.	7	28%	<.001
Preference Factor	Preference	32	25	78%	<.05	16	50%	<.001
	No Preference	99	55	55.6%	n.s.	23	23.2%	<.001
Target Contrast	Mixed	54	34	(63%)	n.s.	12	22%	<.001
	Separate	18	11	(61%)	n.s.	8	44%	<.001

In 65 of the 104 cases in which the subject was aware, there was differential scoring (62.5 percent). Thirty-two, or 31 percent, of them are significant at or beyond the 5 percent level. In those studies in which the subject is unaware of the existence of the dual nature of the conditions, differential scoring is seen in 15 (60 percent) of the cases. Seven (28 percent) of them are statistically significant. The difference between the "aware" and "unaware" groups of studies is not significant. Thus, it would appear that the subject need not be aware of the existence of the dual nature of the conditions for the differential scoring to occur.

The "Preference" Factor: In some of the DE studies reviewed in preparing the 1984 database, it is apparent that the subjects would possibly have a preference for one condition over the other. For example, in a study by Johnson (1969) pleasant and unpleasant words were used as targets. We can reasonably assume that the subjects would have a preference for pleasant words. Similarly, in studies where the subjects were asked to respond at their "tempo" and "non-tempo" rates, we may presume that the subjects' preference would be for tempo rates. On the contrary, we cannot make an assumption that the subjects would prefer "mask" cards to ESP cards or Telugu words to English words without explicitly asking the subjects about their preference.

In the review of past studies there are 32 cases in which we can presume that the subjects are likely to have had a preference for one condition over the other. In 25 (78 percent) of these, there is differential scoring which is significant in 16 (50 percent) of them. In 99 of the studies where no such presumption can be made, there is differential scoring in 55 and in 23 of them it is statistically significant. A 2 × 2 chi square test of significance for the number of significant studies in the two groups (those in which we can presume subjects' preference and the rest of the studies) gives a chi square of 7.06 (1 df) which is significant ($p < .01$). A similar analysis of the proportion of cases which showed differential scoring in both the groups gives a chi square of 4.28 (1 df $p < .05$). Thus it would appear that the differential effect is more likely to occur in cases where the conditions are such that the subjects are likely to prefer one condition over the other.

Further, in 15 of the 16 significant cases, the direction of scoring favored the condition for which there seemed to be a preference. The opposite happened in only one case (Rao, 1963). Thus the preference factor not only seems to precipitate the differential effect, but may also determine the direction of scoring.

"Mixed" and "Separate" Targets: It seemed to the present author from informal observations that the greater the contrast between the conditions, the greater would be the possibility of differential scoring. One way of helping to focus on the contrast between the two target sets is to mix them up and present them in the same run. This is the procedure I employed in a number of experiments. In the dual-target studies, there are 54 cases in which the two sets of targets were mixed. They were presented separately in 18 cases. No information is available in one case. Differential scoring occurred in 34 (63 percent) of the mixed target cases and 11 (61 percent) of the separate target cases. Thus, there does not seem to be any difference in the occurrence of differential scoring between mixed and separate targets. However, when we consider the proportion of significant number of studies in the two groups, separate presentation of target sets appears to yield more significant outcomes. In the mixed target group only 22 percent (12) of the cases are significant, whereas 44 percent (8) of the cases are significant in the separate target group. Therefore my hunch favoring the mixed target condition is not supported by the data.

In constructing the 1984 database, we also compared the cases in which the subject was tested on both the conditions in one session, such as the study by Casper (1951) in which the subjects were administered GESP and clairvoyance tests in the same session, with those in which the tests were administered in two separate sessions, such as the study by McMahan and Rhine (1947) where the clairvoyance test was administered in one session and the precognition test in another session. There are 48 cases in which the subjects were administered the tests involving both the conditions in the same session. Twenty-seven (56 percent) of them showed differential scoring and in 16 (33 percent) the difference is statistically significant. There are only eight cases in which the subjects were given the tests in separate sessions. Five of them showed differential scoring and two of them are significant. Obviously the number of cases involving tests in separate sessions are too few to draw any conclusion. But, if the trend is typical, whether the tests are administered in the same session or in two different sessions does not appear to make much difference to the outcome of the DE studies.

Dual vs. Multiple Targets: The differential response experiments considered so far are limited to the studies that involved only two conditions. It is an interesting but as yet unresolved question as to what happens when there are more than two conditions or tasks. There are no systematic studies even now (2017) to answer these questions. There are, however, several ESP experiments in which the subjects performed on multiple tasks. Interestingly, the tendency in these experiments appears to be one in which the subjects show a unimodal rather than a bimodal response pattern.

In the experiment by Woodruff and George (1937) there were six different target conditions and the subjects scored positively in all six conditions. Gibson (1937) compared three calling and three matching procedures and obtained positive scoring on all the six. Pratt and Woodruff (1939) studied the effect of the size of various symbols. In one series consisting of 45 subjects they compared *three* sizes and in another series with 32 subjects they compared *four* sizes. Total deviation in each of these conditions was positive. Humphrey and Pratt (1941) compared five ESP test procedures. The ESP scores showed negative deviations in four conditions and positive deviation with one procedure.

Van de Castle (1953) reported results in which his single subject responded to five different target sets; she obtained positive deviation on four and negative deviation on one set. Van Busschbach (1956) also compared three target conditions in three different series of experiments. In the Amsterdam series the scores were positive on all three. In the Utrecht and North Carolina series they were positive on two and negative on the third. Alcock and Quartermain (1959) tested 101 subjects with (a) when they responded to a sequence of targets without a break in between (DT method) and (b) when there was a break between responses (BT method) procedures. The total scores showed negative deviations on all the three conditions. Roll (1972) compared three target conditions and obtained positive scoring on all three. Winkleman (1981) tested subjects in five different conditions. The scoring was positive on all of them. Similarly Blackmore (1981) tested subjects in five different conditions. In one series, the scoring was negative in all the conditions. In another series it was negative in three, positive in one, and at chance on the other.

From this review of scoring patterns in multiple task situations that involved more than two conditions, it is clear that, for whatever reason, the subjects seem to show a tendency to score in the same direction and not switch their responses between positive and negative modes. In other words, there is no evidence of the DE of the kind we find in dual task situations in tests involving more than two conditions.

In order to statistically test this observation we performed a simple sign test. Taking the direction of scoring in the first condition (as recorded in the report) to predict scores in other conditions, we counted the number of cases in which the scoring is in the expected direction or otherwise. We found that the scoring is in the expected direction in 86 cases and in the opposite direction in 30 cases. The probability of such a distribution occurring by chance is much smaller than .001. It would seem therefore that the differential effect is generally an outcome of the dual task situation and that multiple conditions seem to favor unimodal response.

How to Explain the Differential Effect?

From the review above of the differential effect there can be little doubt that DE is a fairly robust parapsychological effect. There are far too many significant studies in this area to question its genuineness. Our research efforts have been generally expended in understanding whether an individual, assuming that he or she has ESP, is likely to be a positive-scoring or negative-scoring subject under the given circumstances. Insofar as they are successful in separating the hitters and missers, many of the attitude questionnaires, personality studies and like tools enable us to anticipate which of the outlets is likely to have the opening.

The motivational studies in which such devices as reward, challenge, novelty and competition are used are similar to the measures one would take to increase the "pressure" in the pump. The effect of drugs, such as alcohol, and even the use of hypnosis, may similarly enhance the "pressure" without necessarily providing a better control.

Let us take, for example, the case of hypnosis. Grela (1945), Fahler (1957), and Casler (1962; 1964) found significant positive scoring to be associated with hypnosis. The meta-analyses of hypnosis–ESP studies we referred to clearly suggest also that hypnosis is an independently effective variable to enhance psi in the positive direction. However, Rhine (1946) reported that his subjects who were scoring well above MCE before hypnosis dropped way below in the post-hypnotic test period. This was contrary to the suggestions he gave to the subjects. He concluded: "The important finding, and one that stands out fairly clearly, is that there was an effect. The hypnosis did something, even though in four out of six cases it was a reversal of the intended effect" (Rhine, 1946, p. 138). A similar result was also reported by Nash and Durkin (1959) who gave two of their subject's 300 trials each in the waking state with single digits as targets, and an equal number of trials under hypnosis with positive suggestion. The subjects obtained a positive deviation when they were working in the waking state and a negative deviation under hypnosis.

Thus it is apparent that psi is manifested in the positive as well as negative direction during hypnotic states. In order to understand and control psi, we need an insight into the factors that enhance the ability and guide its direction. For this reason, though short and exploratory, and now more than fifty years old, Honorton's (1964; 1966) studies, in which the subjects were first predicted to be positive or negative scorers on the basis of an interest inventory and then, while hypnotized, were told to demonstrate a high degree of psi ability without regard to direction, presents an idea which can be developed and pursued with profit. Also, there is need to develop special strategies: first, to channel psi in a manner consistent with its bi-directionality, and second, to investigate whether there are any means by which we can study the operation of the outlets themselves—how to open and close them.

If we assume that the exercise of psi is like inflating a hard rubber balloon with an air pump having outlets in opposite directions, then we could successfully inflate the balloon to the desired pressure only if we could close or attach another balloon to the opposite outlet. Something similar to this may happen when a subject is successful. It would seem that, at least in the case of those individuals in whom the outlets are not completely uncontrolled, we need devices which will provide for the simultaneous operation of both outlets.

The frequency of the occurrence of differential response reported in the literature suggests that it may well be that device. My own efforts in experimental parapsychology were directed mainly towards this problem of providing simultaneous outlets for psi-hitting and psi-missing. Others were on this trail as well. As noted, the possibility of differential response was suggested in some of the early experimental reports, and also some announcements of its discovery were made many years ago, even though not much was done to approach this problem systematically until the 1960s. Referring to our analogy, one might say that what we need is a way to control the valves at the outlets of the air pump. In order to control an ability whose characteristic feature is a perpetual oscillation between hitting and missing, we would do well to study such disciplines as yoga, which seem to be primarily directed toward the control of the mind. It may be in the very nature of the mind to drift and shift unless it is made steady by deliberate training and effort.

It should be kept in mind that the DE studies reviewed here are restricted to ESP studies alone. There is also evidence that differential scoring occurs in PK tests as well, when subjects are tested under contrasting conditions. As mentioned earlier, the 1947 PK experiment by Nicol and Carington was among the earliest to record significant evidence for the DE. In this experiment subjects showed a significant tendency to obtain positive scores on high-value faces and negative scores on low-value faces of the target dice. Again, W.E. Cox (1954) reported that in his placement PK experiment the subjects scored positively on marbles and negatively on dice as targets. The difference in the number of hits between marbles and dice is statistically significant. Therefore, any discussion of a theory to explain differential scoring should take into account the fact of its occurrence in PK tests also.

Given that there is also strong evidence in favor of psi-mediated experimenter effect (Kennedy and Taddonio, 1976; and see the next chapter) the possibility exists that the differential effect is an outcome of the experimenter effect. In many psi tests involving two experimental conditions the experimenter is looking for a significant difference in scores between the two conditions. Inasmuch as the significance of the result in a study of the experimental effect is a function of departure from chance-expected scores in opposite directions for the two conditions, the experimenter's goal is subserved by the observance of modally opposite trends in the scoring of the subjects in the two conditions. Thus, it may be that the DE is simply a kind of psi experimenter effect. If such were the case, we must expect that even when independent groups of subjects are tested by an experimenter, they would also show differential scoring.

For example, if one group of subjects are tested with one set of targets and another group with another set, we should expect one group to score positively and the other negatively, when the intention of the experimenter is one of testing the statistical significance by the difference in the scores of the two groups. It would be worthwhile to review such studies in the literature to see whether differential scoring of the kind observed in the DE studies is also present in them. Further, a review of the literature to see whether experimenter expectations are related to differential scoring would be of interest. The indications are that there may indeed be a positive relationship.

As pointed out earlier, L.E. Rhine's studies of target-size difference gave no evidence of differential scoring. It is reasonable to assume that she was not expecting a difference. Similarly, the failure to find differential responses in some of the experiments involving dual-aspect targets may be attributed to experimenter's interest (also subject's) in obtaining overall hitting rather than differential scoring. Again, the fact that the differential effect is seen more frequently in experiments where we can presume preference for one condition over the other than in experiments where no such preference can be presumed is consistent with the experimenter or subject expectancy hypothesis.

As we have noted, the DE appears to manifest more frequently when the subject is likely to have preference for one condition over the other. Does the same hold for the experimenter's preference as well? Does the differential effect manifest with the same frequency and magnitude when the experimenter carries out the experiment with the DE in mind? In other words, are there any meaningful differences between post hoc observation of the DE and its expected occurrence? While the results seem to indicate that the DE is rather widespread across experimenters, it would be worthwhile to see if there are any idiosyncratic patterns associated with certain experimenters.

As James Kennedy (private communication) in his comments on our analyses of the DE studies pointed out, the perception of contrasting conditions of the experiment either by the subject or the experimenter may be psychological rather than physical. In a given experimental situation, the subject or the experimenter could in principle contrive any number of distinctions including targets and responses. For example, targets may be sorted into preferred and nonpreferred. Even when a subject is participating in a standard ESP test with ESP cards, she or he may have a preference for some symbols and not for others. This may create a differential situation for the subject. Therefore, there may be any number of differential situations that go undetected. Carpenter (2012) explicity suggests that how the bidirectionality of psi manifests—when psi is positive *and* when it manifests in a negative manner—is among the significant questions that need to be yet addressed and answered.

What we have done so far is merely scratch the surface of the DE. We need to make more analyses and make the database more up-to-date and inclusive. Again, as Kennedy suggests, Stanford's response bias may be a type of DE, since there is generally a tendency to miss the frequently made responses. The fact that in cases where there are more than two conditions the subjects tend to manifest unimodal rather than bimodal response patterns may be important, in that it suggests that the psychological rather than the physical conditions may be more relevant to DE studies. Further analyses of the DE should keep this in perspective.

Finally, the concept of the differential effect may need further refinements. Carpenter's (1967) three-fold distinction is helpful in some ways, but it falls short of providing the necessary clarifications. At the conceptual level, there does not seem to be any need for the score in at least one of the two conditions to be statistically significant as a necessary condition for the DE. A significant difference between the scores obtained under the two conditions is sufficient to justify designating it as the differential effect. However, the possibility exists that the observed effect is entirely due to psi in one condition. The performance in the other is entirely fortuitous. This is what one expects when an outcome of the experimental condition is compared to that of the control condition. In such a case it does not seem appropriate to call the significant difference in the scoring of the two conditions as an instance of the differential effect.

We may properly distinguish between three levels of the DE. The first category involves the instances where not only the scoring is in opposite directions, but is significantly so in each of the conditions. In the second category are those in which the scores are in opposite directions in the two conditions, not significant in either condition but the difference between the two is significant. The third category includes those cases of differential scoring in which the scores in one of the two conditions is not only significantly different from the scores in the other but they are also significantly different from chance expectation. Whereas the first two categories may be called strong and weak differential effects, the third would seem to be somewhat ambiguous and unclear. We may need further statistical refinements that take the effect sizes in both conditions as a measure of the DE.

Also, we need to keep in mind that differential scoring in the two conditions may be due to a subject's positive attitude towards one condition and negative attitude towards the other. In such cases it would be clearly inappropriate to label differential scoring as the differential effect. For example, as in Rhine's precognition experiment (Rhine, 1938a), the subjects to whom precognition appeared to be impossible tended to psi-miss. Similarly, as we noted, situations causing frustration and subjects with negative attitudes (goats) tend to give rise to psi-missing. If the two conditions in which a subject is tested are such that one is conducive to hitting and the other to missing we may reasonably expect differential scoring in the experiment, whether we test the same subjects or independent groups of subjects. However, such differential scoring cannot be taken as evidence of the differential effect.

While the studies bearing on the DE are extensive, the attempts to understand it are sparse. My personal inclination is to think that bi-directionality is a typical characteristic of psi. The differential response, which shifts the mode of psi response between hitting and missing in a rather capricious manner, is perhaps a built-in defense mechanism which may have led to a progressive disuse of psi. If psi gives wrong information as often as it gives correct information without the subject's knowing which is the case at a given time, then psi naturally becomes an unreliable and often misleading instrument. Inasmuch as the DE thus serves a "self-obscuring" function, it is necessary to bring this tendency under control in order to make any reliable use of psi.

Psi, as mentioned, appears bidirectional. Bi-directionality implies that psi may take a hitting or missing direction. To return to the metaphor that it is like an air pump with two openings in the opposite directions: Experience tells us that in psi, the opening and closing of the valves at these outlets is seldom under the conscious control of the individual; the ultimate control of psi would be analogous to the voluntary opening and closing of these outlets. In some individuals the valve on one side may be operational to a greater degree than the one on the other side. So we have psi-hitters or psi-missers, depending on the side of the valve which is operational. In some individuals, both the valves may remain closed or open without any voluntary control. In either case, psi is unlikely to be put to any use. So, then, we have subjects who are outstanding because they obtain consistently high or low scores, and subjects who do not show any ESP, either because this ability is absent in them or because it oscillates between hitting and missing so unpredictably that it cannot be easily detected.

Further reflection on theoretical implications of DE studies suggests that the DE may be a very basic and intrinsic feature of psi, analogous to the behavior of elementary particles as in the Einstein, Podolsky, and Rosen (EPR) paradox. It may be recalled that when two initially united particles, such as protons, in a state with zero spin, are allowed to separate, the spins of the two separated protons on any axis will have opposite signs. If one is observed to spin in positive direction, the other spins in the negative direction. Without going into the quantum complications of non-locality and the role of an act of observation on the collapse of the state vector, we may note that the two particles are not as distinct and separate as they appear. Rather they are united at some level. Zero spin in psi data is indicated by their insignificant deviation from chance expectation. When the data of an experiment (a basic unit like a proton in a state of zero spin) is split into two units on some variable (axis) under study, the two parts would register opposite signs as in hitting and missing. On the basis of this postulate, it might be possible to develop a mathematical formalism to predict the occurrence of the DE in psi experiments. A prerequisite for such formalism is definitional clarity as to what constitutes an experiment and a more precise understanding of the units of measurement in the analysis of data in psi experiments.

7

The Experimenter Effect

In contrast to research in physical sciences and to a degree in the biological sciences as well, the experimenter is an important factor in human sciences. In psychological studies the occurrence of experimenter expectancy effects (Rosenthal, 1966; Rosenthal and Rubin, 1978) is widely acknowledged. It has been observed from the early days of scientific research into psi that the experimenter is a relevant variable. It is now a well known fact that a few researchers are more successful than others in obtaining significant psi scores. As we have noted, this is sometimes construed by the critics as a weakness in psi research. A strong case can be made, however, that experimenter effects observed in parapsychological research are genuine psi effects and not artifactual outcomes of experimenter incompetence or unreliability. The main problem with parapsychological experimenter effects is that their range and modus operandi are still unclear. This is hardly surprising, because the nature of psi itself is little understood.

The experimenter effect in parapsychology is arguably the effect most detested by psi researchers themselves. It is detested because (a) it stands in the way of wider replication of psi effects and (b) it gives a ready handle to critics to debunk parapsychological research as an artifact of incompetence of a few investigators (Hansel, 1966; 1980, Alcock, 1981; 2003). At the same time, it is potentially the most important aspect of psi (Palmer, 1997). Without a proper understanding of the role of the experimenter, psi research is unlikely to advance much further than merely accumulating more data favoring the existence of cognitive anomalies, which could be ignored as unconvincing by those with a strong skeptical mindset. The resolution of the riddle of the experimenter effect is necessary not simply to counter the skeptical argument of incompetence in psi research but also to deal with the problem of replication. Further, it may hold the key for unlocking the doors as it were to enter the sanctum of psi and gain a better understanding and necessary insights into possible ways of applying it for enhancing human potential.

Such a realization of the importance of the experimenter in psi research is not a recent revelation. Fifty years ago, when I reviewed the results of psi research available at that time (Rao, 1966), I wrote that "the role of the experimenter in psi tests is extremely delicate and very important" (p. 85). However, at that time I was more inclined to attribute the experimenter effect to normal psychological variables rather than regard it as an intrinsic psi effect. The developments in this area since the publication of my book *Experimental Parapsychology* (Rao, 1966) have shown that the experimenter effect is a genuine psi effect, which goes far beyond normal and conventional psychological explanations such as the experimenter expectancy effects explored by Robert Rosenthal and others. Its occurrence is no less puzzling than psi itself.

There appear to be three distinct phases in the development of interest is studying experimenter effects in parapsychology. The first phase involves the appreciation of the important role the experimenter plays in psi tests. The second is the phase of review and recognition of the experimenter effect as a genuine psi effect. The third is the current phase of puzzlement and bewilderment at the intractability of the obviously pervasive effect.

The Early Phase

When I first wrote about experimenter effects (Rao, 1966), it seemed that the experimenter's angle was the least explored of all, despite clear recognition of the fact that the role of the experimenter in psi tests is extremely delicate and very important. I felt that this was also an aspect of parapsychological research that was little understood and appreciated by its critics, who often made unreasonable demands for the repeatability of the experimental results as the criterion for their acceptance. Repeatability is a good thing worthy of relentless pursuit. But failure to repeat an experiment does not invalidate the experiment itself; it only makes the findings less valuable in a practical sense.

In contrast to the situation in the physical sciences, the experimenter is an important variable in the studies of human nature. His attitude and skills in handling his subjects assume increasing importance with the complex character of the behavior under study. To the degree that eliciting a response is dependent on the skills and personality of the experimenter, the response loses its apparent objectivity and becomes less repeatable. However, the response itself may not be considered any less real. The chemist who discovers a new element can expect instant verification by every other investigator who cares to do so, while the psychotherapist who successfully treats a patient by a new and radically different method cannot be so certain that others in his profession will be able to succeed by using the same method. This difficulty exacts a costly toll in parapsychological studies, and possibly is the main reason why ESP experiments are not more frequently repeated.

We have known for a long time that some experimenters were more successful than others in finding psi in their test results, and that some experimenters were successful with certain subjects but not with others. While everything in the literature has tended to suggest that successful experimentation in parapsychology called for certain special skills which are not easily acquired or retained, not many systematic studies were conducted to discover what factors in fact make a good experimenter.

In an experiment reported by Sharp & Clark (1937) in the very first volume of the *Journal of Parapsychology,* it was observed that during the fifth, sixth, and seventh weeks of' the first experimental period, when Sharp's wife was critically ill and the experimenter much disturbed, the subject's rate of scoring fell below mean chance expectation. During the first four weeks, when there was no illness, and the last week, when Mrs. Sharp recovered, a total of 1,235 runs were done which gave a positive deviation of +231. This result gives a significant z score of 3.28. During the disturbed weeks, however, there was an insignificant deviation of -31 in 2,092 runs. While these results indicate a possible connection between the drop in the rate of scoring and the experimenter's disturbed state of mind, one cannot rule out the possibility that chronological decline and beginning-and-end salience or some other variable might have been responsible for the poor scoring during the fifth, sixth, and seventh weeks.

Sharp & Clark also reported further evidence suggesting that some experimenters "may be unable to secure positive results," while others "are better able to secure good results" (1937, p. 142). For example, in a total of 79 runs four subjects obtained an average of 4.30 hits per run of 25 trials (MCE=5) when Myers was the experimenter; and the same subjects averaged 5.38 hits per run in a total of 61 runs in which Sharp was the experimenter. One of these subjects reportedly "stated privately that Myers distracted her to such a point that she was unable to think of what she was doing. While conducting the tests, Myers kept swinging his watch chain and talked about extracurricular activities. He manifested little interest in the work at hand" (Sharp & Clark 1937, p. 136). Although these observations are interesting and perhaps instructive, the results of this study cannot be regarded as conclusive, not only because the experiment lacks adequate controls against other possible explanations, but also because a subject's reports after a test is completed are often unreliable. It is a common observation that subjects tend to complain when learning about their poor results and are often in a jubilant mood when their scores are high.

MacFarland (1938) published a study in which he tried to compare the relative success of a previously successful and an unsuccessful experiment by asking each of his five subjects to respond with a single call to separate target decks prepared by the two experimenters. According to the reported results, the previously successful experimenter obtained highly significant results; while the previously unsuccessful experimenter obtained results close to chance, thus suggesting that the subjects had shown discrimination between the experimenters.

After examining MacFarland's record sheets, Kennedy (1939) suggested that the extra-chance results of this experiment could be explained by the hypothesis of inversion errors in recording the cards. He also found a number of recording errors which, he thought, would explain most of the deviation. Stuart (1940) replying to Kennedy's criticism, concluded that in the part of the work where the DT technique was used, the errors were simple observational errors which did not invalidate the results; whereas in the GESP part of the work the errors might have been motivational, but they did not account for the observed deviation. He further pointed out that the hypothesis of inversion errors is "wholly unsubstantiated."

J.G. Pratt & Margaret Price (1938) reported that in independent experimental studies under comparable conditions, one of them obtained highly significant results while the other got only chance results. So they jointly conducted another experiment to discover whether they could produce different results by handling the subjects differently. The experiment was divided into two parts. In the first part, some subjects were handled in what the experimenters thought a "favorable" manner and others in an "unfavorable" manner. The results of this part of the data were not significant. In the second part, the previously successful experimenter, M.M. Price, "handled the subjects in a manner which was natural to her" as the second experimenter recorded the results. The second part gave significant results with an average score of 5.53 hits per run which is similar to the average in her first experiment while she was working alone. Whether or not this experiment "goes far to establish an effect of the experimenter-subject relationship on the results of tests for ESP" as the report states, it is clear that certain experimenters do seem to obtain significant results while others do not. Also, the failure of the first part to produce the predicted difference between the scores obtained under conditions of "favorable" and "unfavorable" handling forewarns us of the difficulties inherent in defining and determining any precise measures of experimental handling. It also suggests that this aspect of the experimenter's task is more an art than an easily acquired scientific skill.

Osis & Dean (1964) reported an experiment in which one of them acted as the experimenter following a 40-minute lecture. When the data were divided according to experimenters, it was found that the subjects scored positively (p= .03) when Osis was the experimenter and that Dean's subjects obtained a negative deviation. The difference between the scores of the two experimenters was significant at the 2 percent level. Osis and Dean conclude: "Personality and motivational factors would seem to need consideration in experimenters as well as in subjects" (p. 180).

In an interesting early experiment by West & Fisk (1953), each of the 20 subjects responded to 32 sealed decks of cards containing 12 clock cards (each of the cards was printed like the face of a clock). The subjects recorded their calls on the sheets provided by pointing out what they guessed was the hour depicted by the card inside the envelope. Half of these packs were prepared by Fisk and the other half by West. The subjects did not know that half of these packs were made by West; and even if they had known, they could not have recognized which deck was prepared by whom, since the decks were arranged in a random order. All the target decks were sent to the subjects by Fisk; and, as far as the subjects knew, Fisk was the only experimenter. The total results of this experiment were statistically significant. On further analysis, it was found that the results relating to the decks prepared by West gave only chance results and the significance of the experiment as a whole was entirely due to the highly significant scoring on the decks prepared by Fisk.

This experiment is important for various reasons. First, it is perhaps the first published report in which the effects of two experimenters were systematically compared, even though their relative roles as experimenters were somewhat different. The subjects knew what Fisk's association with the test was, but not West's. Second, the results show that the subjects can discriminate between the targets prepared by two experimenters even when they do not know the involvement of the second experimenter. Thus the results suggest a genuine parapsychological effect rather than a psychological effect. Third, the most outstanding subject in this experiment, S.M. (who also gave outstanding scores in a previous ESP experiment), gave significantly positive results on West's targets as well. This suggests that probably a good subject may be successful with any experimenter.

There is some evidence that the attitude of the experimenter towards ESP, like the attitude of the subject, may be related to the subject's scoring. In their experiment with college students, Rilling, Adams & Pettijohn (1962) found that subjects with a professor who believed in ESP acting as the experimenter obtained an average of 5.23 hits per run, whereas other subjects working with two skeptical professors scored at a below-chance average. It was not reported, however, whether these differences in the rate of scoring were significant.

As we have noted in another context, in the experiments reported by Anderson and White (1956; 1957; 1958), a significant relation between teacher-pupil attitudes and the clairvoyance scores of the pupil subjects was found. In these studies, we may recall, the teachers administered the tests to their student subjects. By means of questionnaires, the attitudes of pupils to their teachers and those of teachers to their pupils were ascertained. Anderson and White found that significantly positive scores were associated with a positive attitude on the part of the teacher towards the students and negative scoring was associated with a negative attitude. When the teacher and pupil attitudes were combined, it was found that mutually positive attitudes on the part of both teacher and pupils were associated with highly significant positive results and mutually negative attitudes with significant negative results.

The results of these studies were extremely interesting because they pointed to an important dimension of experimenter-subject relationship. It is likely that mutually agreeable relationships and favorable attitudes between the teacher and the pupils help to create the experimental complex necessary for the successful manifestation of psi and that, in a contrary situation, conditions favor psi-missing.

C.B. Nash (1960) reported a study on the effect of subject-experimenter attitudes on clairvoyance scores. Each of his nine students in a parapsychology course acted as experimenters in two sessions and as subjects in other sessions. While one student acted as the experimenter, the other eight participated as subjects. The positive and negative attitudes were determined by having every subject and the experimenter list at every session four of the other eight students whom he preferred as members of his class. Nash found that a negative attitude was associated with negative scoring and a positive attitude with positive scoring. The difference between the scores when the attitudes were mutually positive and when they were mutually negative were also significant.

The importance of the experimenter and his skills to elicit psi were recognized long ago and have been emphasized by the pioneers of experimental parapsychology. The textbook *Parapsychology: Frontier Science of the Mind*, by Rhine & Pratt (1957), states that "the experimenter himself can be a limiting factor in the test situation" (p. 132). Rhine & Pratt seem to consider that the ability to elicit psi in an experimental situation is a personal gift and something that is not easily learned. They went as far as saying that the experimenter "had better find out by preliminary tests of himself *as experimenter.* The only rule to follow is that of the old motto: 'Pretty is as pretty does.' A psi experimenter is one who, under conditions that insure he is not fooling himself, can get results. All others should do something they *can* do well" (Rhine & Pratt, 1957, p. 132).

Rhine & Pratt, however, did not indicate that the successful psi experimenter needed to have special psychic skills. Rather they were inclined to believe that it is the psychological conditions that they create and inspire that are responsible for the experimental outcomes. This was made amply clear in that first compendium of experimental parapsychology, *Extrasensory Perception After Sixty Years*, which laid stress on the experimenter's interest, enthusiasm and skills to motivate the subject to perform well in the tests. As Pratt *et al.* (1940) put it: "All the skills and methods that can be devised by the experimenter for conveying encouragement, inspiring confidence, implanting a realization of the importance of the tests, and arousing and maintaining an ambition to perform well in the tests will be decidedly to the point" (p. 341). Rhine (1938b), while emphasizing the importance of the experimenter's motivation to succeed, reminiscences thus: "As one looks back to his own days of most productive work with psi tests, he recalls a sense of adventure, of suspense, of concentration on the problem that one can acquire only through a very genuine and quite profound personal interest in knowing what the experiment will reveal" (p. 74).

The enthusiasm to search for a suitable experimenter for psi testing was not limited to Rhine and his associates at Duke University. A prominent psychologist of the time and a keen and sympathetic observer of parapsychological research, Gardner Murphy (1949) was equally clear in his emphasis on the role of the experimenter in successful psi tests. Noting the "glowing intensity" and the "rugged force" with which Rhine had inspired his coworkers and driven some of his subjects "to get extrasensory phenomena," "the intensity of Mrs. Dale's devotion" and the "brilliant personality" of Whately Carington, who were also successful psi experimenters, Murphy (1949) wrote: "I doubt, whether we can go on with the tradition that an experimenter—any experimenter—undertakes to test a subject—any subject—with a standard method—any standard method—ESP or PK. If an experimenter in the abstract tests a subject in the abstract with a method in the abstract, experience shows that we can be pretty certain that we shall have nothing to show for our pains" (p. 14). Murphy suspected that the personality of the experimenter that combines "flexibility and terrific determination" is important for successful psi testing. "From all I have seen of these elusive phenomena over thirty years," Murphy (1948) wrote, "I'm convinced that they come to certain people and not to others largely because of deep-seated personality factors in those investigating them and that the searchlight should be turned for a while directly upon the investigator" (p. 18).

Referring to the successful experimental psi research of David Kahn, J.G. Pratt (1953) again emphasized the personality and motivation of the experimenter. Also, Gertrude Schmeidler & R.A. McConnell (1958) felt that the subject-experimenter relationship is important in that it engenders a mood in the subject which is related to subject's performance in psi tests.

I concluded my earlier review of the role of experimenter in parapsychological research with the following observation, which summarizes the state of experimenter effects in parapsychology at the end of the early phase:

> On the basis of our somewhat limited knowledge of the role of the experimenter in psi tests, it may perhaps be said that the first and foremost condition for success is that the experimenter must be acceptable to the subject. The precise aspects that make the experimenter acceptable have not yet been experimentally established. The experimenter's personality, his attitudes towards psi in general and the subject in particular, his mannerisms, his mood, his enthusiasm, his perceptiveness, the clarity with which he presents his test, the confidence he instills into his subject, and a host of other factors are likely to make up the psychological complex that accounts for his success or failure [Rao, 1966, p. 91].

The Second Phase of Noting the Effect

In the half-century since I made the above assessment in 1965, a lot of things have happened. First, more studies have provided further data bearing on the role of the experimenter. Second, a strong case has been made for non-intentional psi—that ESP and PK effects may manifest without the subject consciously intending them. Third, the PMIR model proposed by Rex Stanford (1974a, 1974b) appeared to provide some theoretical ground for expecting the experimenter effects. Finally, the experimenter effect seemed to go far beyond the special psychological skills of the experimenters. Against this background, there appeared influential reviews by Kennedy & Taddanio (1976) and White (1976a, 1976b, 1977). These reviews brought into focus the magnitude of the problem, the range and scope of the experimenter effects in parapsychology and their implications to psi research.

More Evidence of the Experimenter Influence

Since 1965, there have been other studies which provided further evidence for the experimenter effect in parapsychology. A few of them have explicitly attempted to explore the experimenter effects. Kanthamani (1965a), attempting to replicate language ESP experiments, obtained results opposite to those obtained by me. However, when she attempted in a follow-up study to present the tests in a method more closely resembling my method, Kanthamani (1965b) obtained similar results. It appeared, then, that the experimenter differences were probably due to the instructions and the manner of presenting the test to the subject rather than the personality or attitudes of the experimenters.

C.B. Nash (1968) carried out a series of tests to determine the effect of experimenters' attitudes on subjects' scores. Nash reported a significant negative correlation between the run score averages of subjects rated as "liked" and "disliked" by the experimenter. In the data of an experiment reported by Feather and Brier (1968), Kennedy and Taddanio (1976) found significant differences between the "other checker" data of Feather and Brier. Differential results between experimenters were reported also by Rao & Sailaja (1973).

Honorton and Barksdale (1972) reported results of a PK study in which the two acted as experimenters. The experiment attempted to explore group PK effort under conditions of muscular tension and relaxation. In one series, Honorton tested the effect of six subjects intending to influence a random number generator (RNG) and found a significant PK effect in the muscle tension condition. In another series, Barksdale tested a group of ten as they attempted to influence the RNG in the same manner as Honorton's subjects. There was no evidence of PK in Barksdale's data. The interesting part of this study is that in the third series Honorton himself participated as a subject and attempted to influence the RNG, which he successfully did with a highly significant outcome (p <. 0005). This result gives an important twist to the interpretation of the results in PK experiments regarding the true source of the PK effect. It seems entirely reasonable to assume that indeed Honorton was the source of PK in the first series when he was not the subject but an experimenter. Honorton & Barksdale (1972) concede, "If the PK hypothesis has to be taken seriously, it would appear that traditional boundaries between S[ubject]s and experimenters cannot easily be maintained" (p. 213).

The experimenter effect assumes that the experimenter may influence the experimental outcome by some means, known or unknown. Therefore, the first order of business in attempting to understand the experimenter effect is to test if the experimenters do in fact succeed in biasing the experimental outcomes in any consistent manner. If they do, what are the likely factors involved? Martin Johnson and his colleagues attempted to investigate these issues in a series of experiments. In one study Johnson (1971) explored the possibility of influencing the ESP scores of his subjects by the way he treated them. Johnson administered ESP tests to his subjects in two parts. The ESP test consisted of the subject choosing the envelopes containing the questions that would be asked in the examination. Obviously, the subject who has advance access to this information normally or paranormally would have an advantage in preparing better for the test. Half of the envelopes contained a blank paper and thus gave no information to the subjects. The other half contained one of the questions that they would have to answer in the exam. In other words, the subjects who chose the envelope with the question (presumably by using ESP) would have the advantage of preparing the answer to that question in advance of the exam. Johnson had a positive mind set for this part of the test and hoped that the subjects would succeed in picking the envelopes containing the questions to an extra-chance degree.

In the second half of the experiment, which was conducted two days after the actual examination, an identical test was administered with the experimenter expecting a negative score. The subjects were given the test abruptly with no notice and were treated in a rude and inconsiderate manner. Johnson reported a significant difference in the rate of scoring between the first and second parts of the experiment. In the first part, as expected, the subjects obtained significantly positive scores. In the second part, however, they scored at chance.

In an extension of this study (Johnson & Johannesson, 1972), the experimenter, Johannesson in this case, differentially treated the two groups of subjects. In the expected positive group the subjects were tested in a friendly and warm comfort of the experimenter's home. They were given suggestions for relaxation; refreshments were served and music was played. The subject in the negative group were not provided with refreshments, music or suggestions for relaxation. They were tested in an "unpleasant" room with the experimenter dealing with them in an authoritarian and abrupt manner. There were other variables distinguishing the expected positive and negative groups such as offer of rewards to the positive group and not to the other. The results showed that the expected positive group obtained insignificant negative scores. However, the expected negative group scored significantly below chance (p < .0002).

Honorton, Ramsey & Cabibbo (1975) carried out an experimental study to test the hypothesis that the way the experimenter interacts with the subjects has an effect on their ESP scores. They administered ESP tests to two groups of subjects. With one group, the experimenter acted in a friendly casual and supportive way; and the subjects in this group obtained significant positive scores. The other group, with which the experimenter interacted in an abrupt, formal and unfriendly manner, showed psi-missing.

Adrian Parker (1975) carried out an experiment designed to test the effect of experimenter expectancy on the ESP scores of subjects. There were six experimenters. Three of them "with a strong prior bias toward belief in ESP" and three with a strong bias toward disbelief. The results showed significant difference between the ESP scores of subjects tested by the two groups of experimenters. The subjects tested by the experimenters with bias toward belief in ESP tended to obtain more hits than those tested by experimenters with bias toward disbelief.

Judith Taddonio (1976) reported results which also suggest that the expectations of the experimenter could influence the subject's ESP scoring. In this study consisting of a pilot and a confirmatory series, Taddonio had six experimenters who administered in an identical manner a clairvoyance type of ESP test to groups of subjects. The only difference was that three of them were told that they were using a test that was proven to be "very conducive to psi" while the other three experimenters were informed that the ESP test they were administering was "very inhibitory to psi and that subjects tended to psi-miss consistently on it" (p. 46). The results of the confirmatory series were highly significant. The experimenters with positive expectancy obtained results indicating psi-hitting (positive scoring, $p < .001$), whereas the experimenters with negative expectancy obtained equally significant psi-missing scores ($p < .001$). The results of this study provide interesting parallels to those reported by Rosenthal (1976) in his studies of experimenter expectancy effects in psychology. Broughton, Millar, Beloff & Wilson (1977) investigated the psi component in experimenter effects and Broughton reviewed research and raised the question whether subjects are really necessary in psi experiments since the experimenter appears to be the most important factor (Broughton, 1978). The review of literature by Adrian Parker and Brian Millar (2014) provides a strong case for successful experiments using their own psi to produce positive results. They suggest that experimenter psi may be seen as having far-reaching implications for both psychology and parapsychology.

Non-Intentional Psi

The studies reviewed above provide further experimental evidence that the ESP performance of the subject is subject to significant influence by the experimenter. This is hardly surprising because (a) similar effects are observed in many areas of psychology and (b) psi is so elusive and known to be affected by very subtle influences. What is somewhat surprising, however, is that the influence appears to be non-intentional and sometimes experimenter-specific and relevant more to the goals of the experimenter than those of the subjects. The experimental paradigm of psi generally assumes that the subject is the *source* of psi and that his *intention* to succeed in a psi task, such as attempting to identify a hidden symbol, is a necessary condition for ESP to occur. The latter assumption, however, is not suggested by spontaneous psychic experiences, which seem to occur without the subject's specifically intending or seeking them.

Rex Stanford (1974a; 1974b) published an important review of experiments in which subjects appear to be successful in responding psychically to non-target information and even when they do not know that they are participating in a psi test. He also proposed a theory of psi that assumes the possibility of non-intentional psi. In his review, Stanford found evidence for three types of non-intended psi effects. In the first category he includes experiments in which the subject psychically responds to aspects of the test that are motivationally important to him, even though information about them is not sensorially available to him.

For example, in one of his experiments, Johnson (1971) carried out a group precognition test in which the subjects attempted to guess numbers one through five. Unknown to the subjects, Johnson associated the target numbers with words that had pleasant or unpleasant association to the subjects based on the information gathered by the experimenter from the subjects earlier. The subjects did not know that Johnson was going to use the information in the manner he did. Johnson also had a control group of trials which had targets with no such association, pleasant or unpleasant. Note that the pleasant and unpleasant word association to the targets built into the experiment was not known to the subjects. Johnson found significant difference in the rate of ESP scoring between positively associated and negatively associated targets as expected. On the set of control targets with no association in the mind of the experimenter the ESP scores were at chance level. In other words, it would seem from this study that the subjects responded to aspects of targets not known to them sensorially but which are of interest to them. This is really not surprising in the sense that the subjects in ESP tests are always believed to respond to the targets to which they have no sensory access. What is of interest here is that the ESP subject does not have to know about the experimental hypothesis or the details and the goals of the test, which are presumably available for his ESP like the ESP target itself. There are a number of other studies in this category which employed similar procedures for biasing a subject's ESP by manipulations, unknown to the subject, based on the subject's likes and dislikes. These include studies by Carpenter (1971) and Johnson & Nordbeck (1972).

The second category of non-intentional psi effects in Stanford's classification is similar to the first except that the subject in this case responds to "the wishes, intentions, moods, etc., of the *experimenter*" and not that of his own. For example, in the experiment of West & Fisk (1953) referred to earlier, the ESP subjects responded successfully to Fisk and not to West. Fisk and West (1958) reported another experiment, a PK experiment in which the target was displayed by the experimenter at a remote location. The subject in order to succeed had to know the target by ESP and then use her PK to exert the desired influence on the PK target. As far as the subject knew, Fisk was the experimenter. Unknown to the subject, Fisk and West alternated in displaying the target faces. Fisk of course did not know what the targets were when West was displaying the targets and vice versa. The results showed that the subject was successful in that part of the experiment when Fisk displayed the targets. In the other half of the data where West was the displayer the results were at chance. In a series of experiments carried out by Osis & Carlson (1972), there is some evidence that subjects were responding to the mood of Carlson, a co-experimenter unknown to the subjects.

The third category in Stanford's classification includes studies in which the subjects did not know that they were participating in an ESP test. The best example in this category is a series of three experiments conducted by Johnson (1973). In these experiments, the ESP test was disguised as an academic examination. In the first two experiments, the subjects were college students who were taking a psychology examination with eight questions. The sheets on which the subjects had to write their answers were attached to the front and back of an envelope. The envelope contained answers to four randomly selected questions. The subjects did not know this; and as far as they were concerned they were taking a psychology examination. The results of both the experiments showed a significant difference between the scores on questions which had answers concealed in the envelopes and the scores on questions which did not have the answers in corresponding envelopes. The subjects scored higher on questions that had, unknown to them, answers concealed in the envelope.

In the third experiment, one half of the envelopes contained information which is relevant to the questions but *incorrect.* The envelope also contained an admonition, e.g., "you are too stupid to pass this exam." Other envelopes contained information that was irrelevant to the questions but encouraging, e.g., "you will certainly pass this exam." Of course the subjects did not know if the envelopes contained any information. As expected, the subject's scores on questions which were attached to the envelopes containing incorrect information and negative admonition were significantly lower than the scores on questions that were associated with information not relevant to the questions and a positive sentence of encouragement.

Some other interesting experiments in this category are reported by Kreitler & Kreitler (1972). In a series of three experiments the Kreitlers attempted to test whether non-intentional psi could bias subject's responses in standard psychological experiments. The subjects were not told that they were participating in a psi test. They were under the impression that they were taking standard psychological tests. The psychological tests they took were in the areas of (1) subliminal perception, (2) autokinetic motor perception and (3) the Thematic Apperception Test. The ESP part of the experiment consisted of an attempt by senders in another room to telepathically transmit the correct answers to the subjects who were responding to ambiguous stimuli presented to them in one of the three procedures, viz., subliminal perception. The authors concluded that the responses of the subjects were indeed significantly affected by the senders' "transmission." The results of these experiments were replicated by Lübke & Rohr (1975).

Stanford's review thus suggests that subjects could succeed in responding to ESP targets to a statistically significant degree even if they did not know that they were participating in an ESP experiment; further, they could respond to aspects of the test hidden from them. Evidence for such non-intentional psi raises important questions about the dirigibility of psi. What is it that enables the subject's psi to focus on the target? How is the subject guided to the target? Traditionally, it was the intention of the subject that was assumed to be responsible for guiding the subject to the target. The possibility of non-intentional psi suggests that intentions, at least conscious intentions, are not required to guide psi to the target. Stanford, in his psi-mediated instrumental response (PMIR) model, capitalizes on the possibility of non-intentional psi and proposes that "the organism non-intentionally uses psi to scan its environment." "*In the presence of a particular need,*" according to the PMIR model, "*the organism uses psi (ESP), as well as sensory means, to scan its environment for objects and events relevant to that end and for information crucially related to such objects and events"* (Stanford, 1974a, p. 43, emphasis in the original). It follows from this that the subject does not have to know at the sensory level the ESP task on hand. All that is required is the need to succeed in a given ESP test. The rest is accomplished at an unconscious level as the organism's psi resources constantly monitor the environment and occasionally succeed in responding via psi.

Stanford's PMIR model also provides for psi experimenter effects. The experimenter who conducts an experiment to test a hypothesis may be presumed to have a need to find evidence in support of his hypothesis. He may therefore use his psi to obtain the results he expects to obtain, for example by psychokinetically biasing the responses of his subject to conform to his expectations. Stanford regards PK as a response mode for PMIR. He illustrates this by referring to telepathy where the agent, the person attempting to transmit a message to the subject (percipient), could influence the internal states of the subject by means of PK, so that there is conformance between the subject's calls and agent's transmission. This kind of telepathy is what Stanford calls the "active-agent" telepathy distinguished from "active-percipient" telepathy in which it is the subject's psi that scans and gets the information from the agent. Granted the possibility of "active-agent" telepathy, then, it would be hardly surprising if the results in psi tests show the experimenter's influence on the outcome of a psi experiment. Thus the psi experimenter effect is a natural corollary of agent-active telepathy.

Relevant to the experimenter psi hypothesis also is the Decision Augmentation Theory (DAT) proposed by May, Utts & Spottiswoode (1995). John Palmer (2009) provides a review of the application of DAT to psi.

Reviews of the Experimenter Effect

Increasing experimental evidence for experimenter effects in psi research, the possibility of non-intentional psi, and the likelihood that the experimenter effect may be mediated by psi, and Stanford's influential PMIR model set the stage for a serious and systematic review of the relevant literature. This was done admirably by Kennedy & Taddonio (1976) and by Rhea White (1976a; 1976b; 1977). The reviews have made a clearcut case for a variety of experimenter effects in parapsychological experiments. More importantly, they made a case in favor of *psi-mediated experimenter effects*. It seemed that it is not only the personality of the experimenter, how he or she handles the subjects, and other normal psychological and situational variables that would have possible influence on the experimental outcome, but that it might also be possible that the experimenter or others associated with the experiment could influence the results, not by normal means but by their psi ability.

The review by Kennedy & Taddonio (1976) distinguishes between two primary categories of experimenter effects. In the first category are effects mediated by psychological variables; in the second category are effects result from psi processes. The latter is termed the "psi experimenter effect." While acknowledging that there is sufficient evidence in the literature to suggest the occurrence of both categories of experimenter effects, Kennedy & Taddonio focus on the psi experimenter effect. The psi experimenter effect is defined as "non-intentional psi which affects experimental outcomes in ways that are directly related to the experimenter's needs, wishes, expectancies, or moods." The definition appears to be needlessly restrictive because even in cases where the experimenter's psi influence is intentional, the effect would still be a psi experimenter effect unless we restrict the use of "intentional" only to experimentally manipulated variables. Also, relating the effects to experimenter's needs, wishes, etc. is theoretically loaded inasmuch as it assumes that one's psi function is related to one's needs, wishes, expectancies or moods. It is entirely feasible to assume that a person's psi could exert an influence independent of that person's needs and wishes.

According to Kennedy & Taddonio, the review of literature suggests that studies in which the subjects seem to react differentially to experimenters as well as the successful studies involving unintentional psi tasks indicate psi experimenter effects. They also conclude that their review suggests that PK on the part of the experimenter can influence the outcomes in PK as well as precognition experiments. The reasons for assuming experimenter PK are threefold. First, the experimenters are typically more motivated than their subjects to obtain significant results. Second, PK can function in the absence of conscious intent. Third, Kennedy & Taddonio point out that most successful PK experimenters are themselves successful PK subjects.

Rhea White's survey of the experimental literature further suggests that the outcomes in some parapsychological experiments are significantly influenced by persons taking part in the experiments other than the experimenters. These include the observers invited to witness the experiment and the persons who randomize the targets, score the data sheets or serve as agents. The influence, she contends, is not merely of a psychological nature. It may involve direct and psi-mediated intervention (White, 1976a).

In a second review article, White (1976b) deals directly with the influence of the experimenter on the outcomes of psi experiments. She reviews non-intentional psi experiments in which the subjects were not aware of some of the important aspects of the experiments or might not even be aware that they are taking part in a psi experiment and are yet successful in them. She also reviewed studies in which the experimenter deliberately attempted to influence the results by his own psi. Finding evidence for psi in both the categories of studies, White concludes that "it may not be possible to differentiate between the experimenter and his experiment" (p. 333).

In another review of the literature on the influence of the experimenter on the results of psi experiments, White (1977) brings together a large number of studies bearing on the role of the experimenter, his attitudes toward the experiment, his methods of handling the subjects, and his motivation in eliciting psi. She concludes that the experimenter is

> the most important variable of all. Some experimenters have reported not being able to obtain significant results on ESP or PK tests while others often seem able to get significant results. Others are successful only with certain subjects or under certain testing conditions. It appears that whether or not a subject provides evidence of psi depends on how he is handled by the experimenter. A favorable subject-experimenter relationship favors psi test results. In addition, the motivation of the experimenter in carrying out his experiment appears to be an important factor in whether he will succeed or fail, although this supposition has not been tested [p. 297–298].

The Current Phase of Puzzlement

The above reviews brought into the open what several psi investigators have long suspected. There is unmistakable influence of the experimenter on psi test results. This is no surprise. The founding fathers of experimental parapsychology were mindful of this. However, they were reluctant to concede that the experimenter effect is any more than some kind of sensory influence. It would have been anathema to think otherwise, that it could be psi-mediated. The reasons for this are not far to seek. First, non-intentional psi and psi experimenter effects are inconsistent with the widely accepted experimental paradigm in parapsychological research. In order to carry out research in the area of the paranormal, it was necessary at the outset to draw the empirical contours of the field, operationally define the concepts and develop appropriate methods of research. J.B. Rhine's signal contribution to parapsychology is precisely this.

The experimental paradigm promoted by Rhine, which had such a powerful hold on psi investigators for a very long period of time, makes two crucial assumptions about psi. (1) Psi is an ability on the part of the subject; and it is amenable for empirical investigation pursuing the scientific method. Inasmuch as the *subject* is the *source* of psi, the study of the personality, attitudes, beliefs, and moods etc., of the subject, in their relation to his psi function, are legitimate areas of investigation. (2) Psi is triggered and guided by the intentions of the subject. The latter constitutes a significant difference between the spontaneous occurrence of psychic events and psi investigated in the lab. In an ESP experiment, for example, the subject is given a task such as guessing the symbol on a card in a deck. Sometime, the target decks are outside the room in which the subject is situated. How does the ESP guide the subject to the particular target card and the symbol on it as distinguished from other cards in the deck and other decks elsewhere? It is the problem of what Rhine called the dirigibility of psi. It is assumed that it is the intention of the subject that not only triggers psi but also guides it to the target. Thus, the two assumptions regarding the source and guidance of psi made by psi researchers for a long period of time come into direct conflict with non-intentional psi and the notion of psi experimenter effects.

Second, acceptance of the reality of psi experimenter effects opens up the Pandora's Box and raises serious and troublesome questions that are difficult to answer. Rhine argued persuasively against research on telepathy. His reasoning was simple and straightforward. It is difficult to unambiguously conclude that the results of a telepathic experiment are due to telepathy and not clairvoyance on the part of the subject. Now, if psi experimenter effects are indeed possible, the interpretation of test results as to the source of the psi becomes problematic. Who is the real source, the subject or the experimenter? How can we control the role of the experimenter to ensure that it is the subject who is the source? If we cannot assume that the subject is in fact the source of psi in a given experiment, what then is the point in studying subject beliefs, attitudes, personality and states of mind in their relation to psi scores? Rhine shelved research on postmortem survival on the ground that he was not aware of any methods that could give unambiguous evidence that the message received is from the deceased person and not from someone living. The possibility of psi on the part of a living person is a factor that should be controlled in order to seriously entertain a survival hypothesis. Since Rhine did not see how this can be done, he decided to wait until suitable methods are developed for this purpose. By the same logic one could argue that psi research should be shelved until we know how to control for the experimenter effect.

For these reasons, even after researchers were aware of the evidence for the reality of psi-mediated experimenter effects, there was understandable reluctance to discuss them. For example, Rhea White, writing for Wolman's *Handbook of Parapsychology* (White, 1977), in her chapter on the influence of the experimenter on psi tests, omits the mention of the psi experimenter effect from her review and discussion. The only indexed reference to psi-mediated experimenter effects in the *Handbook* of 967 pages is in the article by Rex Stanford on experimental psychokinesis, which refers to the study by Fisk & West (1958).

The matter of the psi experimenter effect remains a deeply troubling predicament, which few researchers were and are willing to confront. It was more than fifty years ago that the courageous investigator Jule Eisenbud (1963) did not hesitate to raise the question of experimenter psi in a straightforward way. He wrote: "Experiments are conducted on the curious assumption that the subjects in them will not use their ability that they are being tested for...." "By the same token," he continued, "it seems implicitly to be taken for granted that experimenters ... will not ... use any psi faculties *they* may have to muddy the field" (p. 258). These pertinent observations hardly evoked any response from any major research establishments in parapsychology at the time. If the subject can become aware of an ESP symbol in a non-sensorial way, why may not he also have psi awareness of the experimenter's moods, expectations and preferences? If the subjects can influence events by their psi abilities, why may not the experimenters influence the outcome of the experiments as well? It is not until the 1990s that these questions were seriously entertained.

Once we accept these possibilities, we are led to reexamine the foundational assumptions of experimental parapsychology. It would seem that Stanford, while arguing against what he called psychobiological model, was essentially calling for a new experimental paradigm in parapsychology.

There has been increasing recognition that psi researchers should confront the experimenter effect in parapsychology for what it is. John Palmer (1996; 1997) among others asserted that the experimenter effect is "the most important challenge" and that psi researchers themselves, who pay little attention to it in the design of their experiments, have not shown sufficient appreciation of experimenter psi. Also, there have been deliberate attempts to study the role of the experimenter in a more systematic way than in the past. The experiments conducted jointly by Wiseman and Schlitz (1997; 1999) are of some importance in this context.

In this research two experimenters, one who is known to be successful in eliciting psi effects in the past and the other who has a record of failures, participated. The study is built around the commonly experienced phenomenon of being stared at. A feeling of being stared at when no one is directly looking at you, is not an uncommon experience. In some surveys the percentage of those reporting such experiences is as high as 80 percent (Sheldrake, 1994) and 94 percent (Braud, Shafer & Andrews, 1990). Attempts to test experimentally the genuineness of this as a psi effect date back to 1913 when J.E. Coover at Stanford University unsuccessfully tested 10 subjects. Subsequently, J.J. Poortaman (1959) and D.M. Peterson (1978) reported results which showed that the subjects reported more often that they were being stared at when someone was covertly staring at them (i.e., unnoticed by the subjects) than during control periods when no one was staring at them.

William Braud, Shafer & Andrews (1990) designed a more sophisticated study in which they attempted to utilize autonomic nervous system activity as an indication of the subject's detection of covert staring, in place of conscious guessing by the subject. The reason behind this move is the belief that the detection may take place at the level of the unconscious and that it may manifest more readily in the form of spontaneous behavioral and body changes than in overt recognition. In fact, people often report tingling of the skin when they are stared at. Accordingly, the experimenters monitored the electrodermal activity of the subjects during periods of covert staring and non-staring, which were randomly interspersed. The results revealed that the electrodermal properties of the subjects correlated to a statistically significant degree with the intense attention of the remotely situated staring person.

In an attempt to replicate the above experiment of Braud *et al.* (1990), Schlitz & LaBerge (1997) tested 39 subjects in a total of 48 sessions. The subjects were randomly assigned to experimental and control periods and during these periods their phasic skin conductance responses were sampled once a second for the 30 second period of recording. During the experimental sessions, unknown to the subject, an observer situated in a different room from the subject stared intently at the television image of the subject. During the control periods, the observer spent the time reading a book and tried "to shift his or her attention from the subject." The results confirmed the hypothesis of greater skin conductance activity during periods of covert observation than during control periods. Thus there is already sufficient evidence of psi "staring at" effect before Schlitz and Wiseman embarked on their joint project.

Marilyn Schlitz has a long track record of being a successful psi experimenter. She has been successful in the remote staring experiments as well. Richard Wiseman is a skeptic about the claims of parapsychology and his attempts to replicate the remote staring experiments were unsuccessful in the past (Wiseman & Smith, 1994; Wiseman *et al.*, 1995). Now the two, the skeptic and the proponent of psi, joined together to replicate the remote staring phenomena. Each carried out a separate experiment; but they conducted them in the same location and used the same equipment. The subjects were drawn from the same pool.

The observed results are, however, different. Schlitz's series shows statistically significant evidence of a psi effect, whereas Wiseman's data are at chance (Wiseman & Schlitz, 1997, 1999).

It is suggested that the observed differences in the ESP scores obtained by Schlitz and Wiseman may be merely a psychological interaction effect between the subjects and the experimenter rather than a genuine experimenter psi effect. The experimenters did interact with the subjects during the briefing stage of the experiment. It is likely that the influence of Schlitz is more positive on the motivation and expectations of the subject compared to Wiseman's interaction with the subjects. Admittedly Schlitz put greater effort in developing a rapport with the subjects than did Wiseman (Watt *et al.*, 2002). Another confounding variable was that the experimenters also served as agents (Morris, 2002). However, two other studies attempting to manipulate the interaction between subjects and participants, creating positive and negative expectations (Schneider *et al.*, 2000; Watt & Baker, 2002) yielded insignificant results. Also an attempt by Watt and Wiseman (2002) at conceptual replication of the Wiseman-Schlitz results failed.

Caroline Watt and associates carried out a series of experiments to study the experimenter effect by manipulating the belief and personality variables of the experimenters and their interactions with the subjects. As referred to above, three of these studies were unsuccessful in eliciting any psi in the experiments; and no significant relationships were found between ESP scores and other variables investigated. However, the fourth study (Watt & Ramakers, 2003) did find evidence for ESP as well as the experimenter effect.

The typical experiment in this series consists of a "helpee" who focuses attention on a candle and presses a button whenever she or he gets a feeling of being distracted. During the same period, a remotely situated "helper" attempts to focus on the candle and at the same time "maintain the mental intention to help his or her friend focus" in sessions designated as help sessions. In control sessions the helper was asked "to break from focusing and to let his or her mind wander" (p. 106).

Nine persons who believed in psi and five who disbelieved were trained to conduct the experimental sessions, each carrying out 36 trials. The ESP hypotheses predicted that during "help" sessions there would be fewer button presses indicating distraction than in control sessions. As predicted, there were fewer button presses during the "help" period than in the "control" period. Again, as predicted, there were fewer distractions during the help periods when believers were the experimenters than in the control periods. With the believer experimenter there were on average 12.25 presses in "help" sessions compared to 14.54 in control sessions. The difference is statistically significant (p = .005).

Data relating to participants' beliefs in psi, participants' expected and perceived success in the test, and the experimenters' personality were collected by questionnaires. The results showed no significant differences between participants or experimenters on any of the questionnaire measures. Watt & Ramakers (2003) "suggest that the experimenter effect in psi research could only mean experimenter psi because the psychological measures seem to show no difference between conditions" (p. 111).

What Does All This Mean?

What can we conclude from the preceding review and discussion of the studies of the experimenter influence on the results of psi research? More specifically, first, what does the experimenter effect precisely mean in parapsychology? Second, how is it related to experimenter effects found in other behavioral sciences? Third, what are the known mediating factors involved in the observed experimenter influences on parapsychological results? Fourth, what are the ramifications of the reality of experimenter effects for psi research in general?

Taxonomy of Experimenter Effects

There is some confusion and controversy about the meaning of experimenter effects in parapsychology. These are fostered to a large extent by the fact that there are more than one type of experimenter effects and are further compounded by researcher's preconceptions and theoretical commitments.

The experimenter effect in its broadest sense refers to the influence (intended or not) of the experimenter on the experimental outcome (the results of the experiment). The resultant effects fall into two broad categories (see the accompanying chart). In one category are biased results attributable to experimenter's incompetence leading to errors in recording, reporting and interpreting the results. These may be designated as "error effects." This category also includes "cheating effects" arising from deliberate experimental misconduct and cheating on the part of the experimenter. These are obviously spurious effects. The second category refers to genuine experimenter effects. These may be classified further into two categories. In one category are genuine psychosocial effects mediated sensorially by the experimenter. Included in the other category are genuine effects mediated by psi on the part of the experimenter.

TAXONOMY OF EXPERIMENTER EFFECTS IN PSI RESEARCH

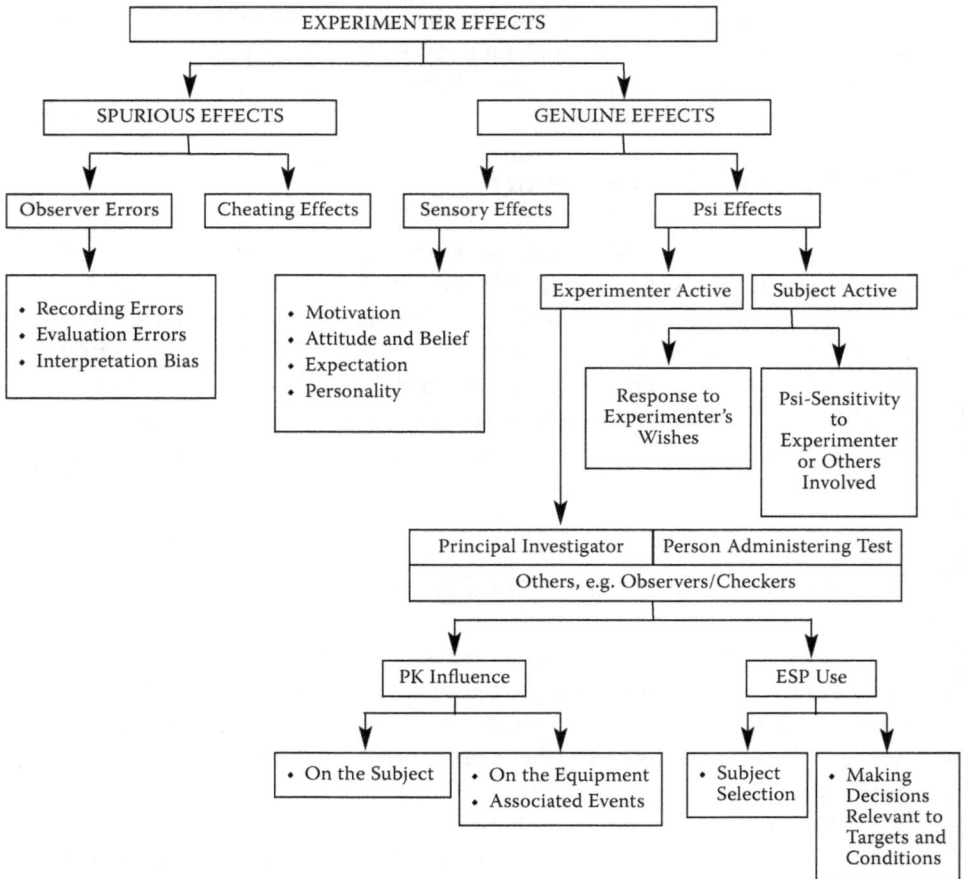

Spurious Experimenter Effects: In parapsychological literature the term "experimenter effect" refers to putative genuine effects and not to the spurious ones. The latter, however, are in the focus of critical evaluation of experimenter effects by skeptical writers on psi. Psychologist J.E. Alcock is a good example. Alcock (1981; 2003) repeatedly ridiculed the claimed evidence for experimenter effects in parapsychology as no more than a failure to replicate. "The psi-experimenter effect," according to him, "provides the ultimate Catch-22; if you find the psi effect you are looking for, well and good. If you do not find it, this might be because of the experimenter effect, and so this could be a manifestation of psi!" Alcock (2003) goes on to say that the experimenter effects, among other psi effects, are not "anything more than arbitrary, post-hoc labels to unexpected negative outcomes. The employment of arbitrary *post hoc* constructs to explain away failures and inconsistencies in the data is a serious problem when one considers the scientific status of parapsychology" (p. 39).

Alcock's use of the term experimenter effect is quite ambiguous. It may be understood in the restrictive sense of psi-mediated experimenter effect as, for example when he refers to "the psi-experimenter effect" (Alcock, 2003, p. 39). He also uses it in a broad and too vague a sense. He writes, for example, the experimenter effect "is said to occur when one experimenter is unable to replicate another's findings, or when two co-experimenters using the same procedures obtain different results" (Alcock, 1981, p. 124). The reason for the ambiguity, it would seem, is that Alcock does not accept either the genuineness of the experimenter effect or the reality of psi. This rejection of the experimenter effect, it would seem, is not based on a judicious review of studies bearing on the experimenter effect, but is prompted by his a priori beliefs about psi. Therefore, Alcock finds little justification for defining the experimenter effect or for examining the evidence for it. In another sense, Alcock eliminates the experimenter effect at the definitional stage itself when he characterizes it as an arbitrary and ad hoc excuse to replicate.

Contrary to Alcock's views, our review of parapsychological literature makes a strong case for the existence of the anomaly called psi (Rao & Palmer, 1987). The reviews and discussions in this chapter reveal that the experimenter effect is neither arbitrary nor a post hoc construct, but a genuine phenomenon in need of explanation. There may be differences of opinion in explaining the observed effect, but there could hardly be any doubt about the effect itself. Let us recall, for example, the careful studies by Wiseman & Schlitz (1997; 1999) that we referred to earlier. Both Schlitz and Wiseman, as mentioned, had well-known track records before they conducted these experiments. Schlitz was previously successful, having published numerous experimental reports with positive findings. Wiseman, on the other hand, was unsuccessful in a number of previous attempts to elicit psi in his experiments. Now, the two, the previously successful and the unsuccessful experimenters, team up to carry out a study with an identical experimental setup to test the role of the experimenter in psi testing. The results unambiguously confirm the hypothesis that: the previously successful experimenter will find in her data evidence for psi while the previously unsuccessful experimenter will not. Again, this finding of 1997 is reconfirmed in their second study of 1999. Thus these studies by Wiseman and Schlitz render untenable the contention of critics like Alcock that the experimenter effect is an arbitrary and ad hoc excuse for failure to replicate.

Obviously we have no way of empirically ruling out spurious effects in all cases. Spurious experimenter effects do occasionally surface in psi research as they do in other areas of behavioral research. An experimenter may be too trusting of his assistants and subjects or too careless in collecting and analyzing his data. He may allow himself to be fooled by preconceptions. In extreme cases, he may indulge in outright deception. Indeed there are documented cases of fraud in psi research (Rhine, 1974; Markwick, 1978), even though there is no reason to think that they are any more frequent than in other disciplines (Broad & Wade, 1982). Cheating and deception may occur in the form of falsifying data and tampering with the records (as in the case of S.G. Soal) or dishonestly manipulating equipment (as in the case of W.J. Levy). Of course it is entirely possible to invent and report an experiment without even conducting it. But to my knowledge there are no such instances in parapsychology. In any case, I am inclined to think that the extensive evidence for experimenter effects across several experimenters renders the fraud hypothesis no more convincing an explanation of experimenter effects than it is for explaining away evidence for ESP in general.

Again, experimenter error effects may not be ruled out in all cases. Some are detected and corrected, but there may be others that go unnoticed. The errors may occur at the time of recording data, or at the level of evaluation and interpretation of the data. Watt & Brady (2002) report an interesting incident that resulted in the detection of an artifact in one of their studies carried out to test some of the leads provided by the evidence for experimenter differences in the Wiseman & Schlitz (1997; 1999) experiments. The experimental setup and the testing procedure are similar to those in the study by Watt & Ramakers (2003) described earlier.

In the first of the two studies by Watt & Brady, the results showed a large effect in the expected direction, which is that there would be fewer distractions recorded by button presses during the "help" epochs compared to the control periods. The large and somewhat unexpected size of the effect led the investigators to modify the computer program in the second study to record the exact time of the button presses to ensure that the button presses are recorded during the influence periods only and not before. If the subject pressed the button before actual commencement of the session in the first study, the computer automatically assigned the press to the control condition. Therefore, an artifactual result in favor of the "help" condition would be obtained if subjects did in fact press the button before the actual commencement of the influence period. Since this was not controlled in the first experiment, the ESP test is methodologically flawed. This flaw, Watt and Brady say, was discovered because they felt that the results

> were unusually strong, and were therefore *unexpected.* If the remote helping effect size had been of similar magnitude to the previous two remote helping studies, we might have reacted quite differently. In that case, we might have regarded our results as successfully replicating the effect size of the previous two studies, and we might not have made any further attempts to check whether the results were valid [p. 70].

Watt and Brady deserve to be complimented for frankly admitting their procedural loophole and correcting it before publishing their study. The discovery of the artifact in an experiment carried out in one of the leading laboratories of psi research does suggest that errors do take place and that some of them get detected. However, to argue that all evidence for psi or the experimenter effect has its source in such errors is one that goes beyond evidence, clearly a nonfalsifiable hypothesis.

Genuine Experimenter Effects: As mentioned, the genuine experimenter effects may be further divided into two groups: (1) those mediated by known psychosocial variables and sensory processes and (2) those mediated by psi and unknown processes. These may be designated as experimenter sensory effects (ESEs) and experimenter psi effects (EPEs) respectively. ESEs and EPEs are genuine psi effects not attributable to sensory leakage, experimenter errors or cheating. Even though the ESEs are brought about or mediated by normal psychological factors or processes manipulated by or relevant to the experimenter, they involve a psi component, intentional or non-intentional, presumably on the part of the subject. In other words, the obtained results suggest a genuine psi effect and are not artifacts arising from known sensory or motor processes on the part of the subject, experimenter or anyone else. The source of psi in this case is the subject and the role of the experimenter is to trigger, facilitate or inhibit psi.

There is evidence that the experimenter sensory effects may be brought about by manipulating a subject's motivation, attitudes, beliefs and expectations. The personality of the experimenter, whether outgoing, involved and empathetic or reserved, unattached and disconnected, may enhance or inhibit subject's psi performance in a given task. In other words, how the experimenter interacts with subjects may have a decisive influence on the subject's psi performance. Experimenters with the right kind of personality and temperament, having positive beliefs and the right attitudes and expectations and by interacting with the subjects in a socially supportive and personally agreeable and nonthreatening manner are the ones who appear to obtain successful results in psi tests. These factors are not only anecdotally known and often observed on the part of previously successful experimenters, but they are also supported by experiments specially designed to study them. For example, the study by Honorton, Ramsey & Cabbibo (1975) showed that the subjects in ESP tests tended to score significantly higher when the experimenter interacted with them in a friendly and supportive manner than in a formal, abrupt and unfriendly way. Supportive evidence for experimenter expectancy effects in psi research are reported by Parker (1975) and Taddonio (1976). Also, there is reason to believe that Schlitz's success in her experiments along with Wiseman is due to her effort to build rapport with her subjects (Watt *et al.*, 2002).

The experimenter psi effects, unlike ESEs, are those believed to be mediated by psi on the part of the experimenter. The experimenter in ESEs is the person who tests and interacts with the subject. However, in EPEs, the term experimenter extends to anyone associated with or interested in the outcome of the experimental results, such as observers who witness a testing session or those who check the data, select a target or act as an agent to transmit a message in a psychic manner.

The EPEs may be further divided into "experimenter active" and "subject active" categories. *Experimenter active* psi effects are those in which the experimenter is believed to be involved and actively associated psychically in bringing about the experimental outcome. *Subject active* psi effects are those in which the subject is the true source of the effect and the experimenter is merely some kind of a "token object" to which subject's psi is sensitive or insensitive.

Such effects are different from ESEs in that the sensitivity factors influencing the subject in the latter case are of a sensory nature whereas in the case of the former, the sensitivity is unexplainable in normal psychological or social terms. In this context, we may recall that Ryzl & Pratt (1963a; 1963b) reported that certain target cards seemed to be good channels for psi to operate. Their subject PS was consistently more successful with certain cards than others. If subjects find certain target cards better suited to channel their psi, it is also possible that they may find some experimenters more conducive to manifesting psi than others.

I propose the term "subject active psi effects" to account for the results of experiments such as those conducted by West & Fisk (1953). The data in which Fisk was the experimenter show evidence for psi, whereas West's data are flat at chance. The subjects in this experiment were completely unaware of the role of West and consequently their sensitivity to him can only be paranormal. A similar explanation is plausible in the case of checker effects reported among others by Weiner and Zingrone (1986). This possibility once acknowledged would account for what Stanford (1974b) calls "active-agent" telepathy and makes it unnecessary to postulate two kinds of telepathy.

The experimenter active psi effects are those that were the focus of the reviews by Kennedy & Taddonio (1976) and White (1976b). The possibility that the experimenter could influence the subject by psi has been attested to by a number of experiments.

Schmeidler's experiments (1958, 1960, 1961) provide good evidence that "agents" could influence the outcomes of subjects' performance in clairvoyance tests by wishing success or failure. Also, it is possible that the experimenters themselves are the source of psi and act as the subject even when they are ostensibly testing subjects. The report of an experiment by Honorton & Barksdale (1972) concedes that the source of PK effect in this study may be attributed to Honorton himself rather than the participant subjects because the PK effect found when Honorton tested his subjects was also present when Honorton alone served as a subject as well as experimenter and not when another experimenter tested the subjects in the same study. This had led Honorton & Barksdale to conclude, as we have seen, that there is reason to question the "traditional boundaries between subjects and experimenters" (Honorton & Barksdale, 1972, p. 213).

There is evidence in the literature that the experimenter psi effects may be mediated or facilitated by experimenter ESP or PK. In the above mentioned study the experimenter's influence was likely mediated directly by the experimenter's PK influence on the REG. There are other experiments in which the communication between the subject and the experimenter is possibly carried out by ESP. For example, in an experiment reported by Stanford *et al.* (1975), the subjects participated in a very boring task after participating in a PK test. Unknown to the subject, a REG was switched on during this period. If the REG recorded seven consecutive hits in a total of ten trails, the subject was released from the boring task and was given a pleasant task. The subjects were not consciously trying to influence the REG because they were not informed about this part of the experiment. The results showed that the subjects were released significantly more times from the boring task than expected by chance, suggesting that the subjects were non-intentionally responding to the PK task set by the experimenter.

One plausible explanation for this is that the experimenter telepathically communicated to the subjects the intent of the experiment, even though they were sensorially blind to it. Of course, the theoretical possibility that the experimenter himself was directly influencing the REG by his PK cannot be ruled out. However, if we assume that psi is triggered by the need of the subject as an instrumental response to meet that need, it makes more sense to suggest that the PK influence on the REG is by the subject and not the experimenter and that the latter's role is best limited to initiating a telepathic communication. At the same time, we may not ignore the fact that the experimenter himself had the motivation to bring about the wished-for effects to confirm his theory. Such motivation on the part of the experimenter may even have a stronger influence than the mundane needs of the subjects.

The more direct avenues of an experimenter's ESP influencing the outcome of psi results may be in the selection of subjects. Some experimenters may use their psi to pick the kind of subjects that are likely to fulfill their predictions. Similarly, the experimenter's decisions about the time of randomization of targets and other experimental details may be prompted by his psi so that he will find the evidence he is looking for. The intuitive data sorting hypothesis advanced by Ed May supports such a possibility (May, Utts & Spottiswoode, 1995).

What are described above are the variety of experimenter effects for which there is some evidence in parapsychology. The taxonomy depicted here reveals how complex and intricate the mosaic of experimenter influence on psi results is. Psi studies suggesting the influence of experimenter on the results are too numerous to list. The range all the way from the checker effect beginning with West and Fisk (1953) and through Houtkooper & Haraldsson (1983), and Weiner & Zingrone (1986, 1989). They provide strong evidence for the occurrence of genuine experimenter psi effects. They also suggest that the effects may take diverse forms and are mediated in different ways. Thus it is difficult to speak of *the* experimenter effect. There appear to be multiple forms of experimenter effects. The evidence so far is hardly of any help in providing meaningful insights into the modus operandi of these effects. There is thus a crying need for a radical reexamination of the foundational assumptions of psi research. At this point, we have come to recognize some major issues that need to be resolved for making further progress in understanding experimenter effects.

The categorization of the experimenter effects as well as the attempted explanation of them revolve around the source of psi and the triggering and guidance instrumentalities, the dirigibility aspect of psi. The source of psi issue is pegged to the conceptual distinction between the subject and the experimenter. Triggering and guidance factors are seen in the intentions, needs, moods, motivations and so on of both the subject and the experimenter. There are serious problems with this kind of analysis. Honorton has insightfully observed that it is difficult to draw any meaningful boundaries between subject and experimenter. Add to this the problem of defining the experimenter in the context of the experimenter effects. It could be the principal investigator who designed and executed the experiment. It could be an associate involved at some stage of the experiment such as (1) administering the test, (2) randomizing the targets, (3) scoring/checking the data, (4) participating in the experiment as a mere observer, or (5) acting as an agent. (See White, 1976a). Therefore, the matter of making this distinction between subject and experimenter needs careful examination.

There is the possibility that all those involved in a psi experiment may be parts of a larger whole and are connected at some level in a profound manner, a level, possibly, at which psi manifests. F.W.H. Myers hinted at such a possibility; and William James was much more explicit (see Chapter 1). Gardner Murphy followed up on James and argued that the psi test situation is a holistic "interindividual reality." "From this point of view," wrote Murphy (1945), "a subject and an experimenter in a telepathy experiment represent phases of an organic whole both at the ordinary normal level of interaction and also, more profoundly, at the deeper level at which paranormal processes occur" (p. 198). On another occasion Murphy (1948) suggested that a

> clue to the paranormal process lies beyond the *realm of needs and barriers*, indeed that it does not lie inside of human personality at all, whether in this

generic or in its individualized aspects. I believe, on the contrary, that it is strictly interpersonal; that it lies in the relations between persons and not *in* the persons as such ... I suggest that it is not within the individual psychic structure, but within certain specific relations between the psychic structure of one individual and the psychic structure of another that our clue lies; or if you like, that the phenomena are, so to speak, transpersonal, just as they are, indeed, trans-spatial and trans-temporal [pp. 11–12, the flush left emphasis added].

The evidence for experimenter effects and their variety lend support to Murphy's suggestion that we reexamine our basic assumptions about the source of psi in designing psi tests.

Experimenter Effects in Human Sciences

Experimenter effects are not uncommon in the behavioral sciences. In psychology, for example, the Rosenthal effect is well known. Robert Rosenthal (1976) of Harvard University carried out extensive explorations into what are called interpersonal expectancy effects (IEES). The results of a large number of experiments confirm the hypothesis that "person A's expectation for person B's behavior can affect B's behavior in such a way as to increase the probability that B will behave as expected" (Rosenthal & Rubin 1978). In a target article appearing in *The Behavioral and Brain Sciences,* Rosenthal & Rubin (1978) summarize the results of 345 experiments investigating interpersonal expectancy effects (IEEs). The studies reviewed fall into eight broad areas of research such as reaction time studies, person perception and psychophysical judgments. The accumulated evidence for IEEs appears to be quite strong notwithstanding some of the persuasive criticisms on methodological grounds by psychologists like T.X. Barber (1973, 1978).

Rosenthal & Rubin do not include studies investigating similar effects in psi research. Clearly one category of experimenter effects among ESEs are very similar to IEEs. The study by Honorton *et al.* (1975) is a good example. Also, the experiments by Parker (1975) and Taddonio (1976) attempted to manipulate directly the expectations of the experimenters on ESP scores and found evidence for IEEs in parapsychology. Therefore, it was suggested (Rao, 1978) that psi research should be added to the other eight areas mentioned by Rosenthal & Rubin.

Further, the reality of experimenter psi effects raises the possibility that in some cases the IEEs may be mediated by psi. That the IEEs may have a psi source is also suggested by the following similarities between the experimenter expectancy effects in psychology and experimenter effects in parapsychology (Rao, 1978): (1) Apart from their somewhat elusive and evanescent nature, these effects seem to occur more frequently with certain experimenters than with others. (2) With some experimenters the effect may even be the opposite of what was expected. (3) The experimenters who produce negative effects seem to share some common characteristics, as distinct from those who produce positive effects.

There are, however, some significant differences between IEEs and ISEs. There is some evidence that interpersonal expectancy effects can be learned or improved with practice. There is no such evidence in the case experimenter effects in parapsychology. As Stanley Krippner (1978) succinctly remarked: "There is probably considerable experimenter effect in psi—there may be a bit of psi in the experimenter effect" (p. 399). Other writers on experimenter effects in psi research also referred to the work of Rosenthal and to others on IEEs in an attempt to find an explanation to experimenter effects involving psi (Smith, 2003).

Micro-Macro Mental Phenomena

That psi could influence test results in regular psychological experiments in areas such as subliminal perception, auto-kinetic motion and the Thematic Apperception Test (Kreitler & Kreitler, 1972; Lübke & Rohr, 1975) and that even students' answers to questions in academic examinations may be influenced by psi (Johnson, 1973) raise some serious issues of concern for controlling psi in such testing situations. In other words, psi may be seen as contaminating the results of a variety of common tests. White (1976b) in her review of experimenter influence on psi test results asserts that "unless psi itself can be ruled out, it is impossible to eliminate the influence of experimenter expectancies on experimental results" (p. 365). In a more recent review Mathew Smith (2003) writes:

> If psi experimenter effects are real, they have implications far beyond parapsychology. For example, more conventional experimental psychological research becomes difficult to interpret, as it would not be clear whether participants are the primary source of experimental findings (as is typically assumed) or whether the findings are simply an expression of the experimenter's own desires and expectations [p. 82].

Also, as Kennedy & Taddonio (1976) pointed out, the resolution of the above perplexing prospect of psi contaminating all kinds of test results depends to a large extent on our understanding the limits of the operation of psi. As mentioned earlier, J.B. Rhine attempted to make psi research a scientific endeavor by precisely setting up such limits and drawing the boundary conditions for psi. The assumptive base of experimental parapsychology, therefore, rested on restricting psi to the subjects' abilities, which are guided by their intentions. Non-intentional psi as well as psi mediated experimenter effects raise formidable questions about these foundational assumptions of psi research. Added to this is the issue of complexity. Does the outcomes of a psi task depend on the complexity of the task involved. For example, do subjects perform better when they are consciously aware of the target to influence in a PK trial, than when they are sensorially blind to the target? That latter task is much more complex than the former because the subject in this case has to use his ESP first to know about the target and then use his PK to influence it. Recognizing this, Kennedy & Taddonio (1976) say that "the complexity issue has important implications for many areas of parapsychology, as well as the problem of experimenter effects" (p. 28). They, however, were somewhat optimistic when they wrote: "If psi is *not* independent of complexity, however—and it should be noted that the evidence the authors are aware of is far from conclusive—one should be able to establish limits on its operation" (*ibid.*). The optimism appears to be short-lived because soon after the Kennedy-Taddonio review Stanford (1977) published a review of relevant literature and concluded that the efficiency of PK function is not reduced by an increase in the complexity of the target system.

With all these complications and the apparent ubiquity of psi, one begins to wonder why is it that by and large natural laws hold, that psychological test results are generally dependable without psi intrusion and that lottery outcomes are dependably random rather than PK driven. I am inclined to think that mental phenomena operate at two levels, as physical phenomena do—micro and macro levels. At the macro level, we may function as if there are no psi effects, just as Newtonian laws work pretty well without cognizance of quantum mechanics. At the micro level however, mental phenomena manifest characteristics that may not be intelligible in terms of macro level laws, which common psychological phenomena obey. At the same time, the study of micro level mental phenomena may not be fruitfully pursued with the assumptions that hold good at the macro level. There may be a need to postulate a new set of assumptions without which the complexities of psi may never be fully understood.

Micro-mental events may have macro effects. An understanding of the laws of micro-mental phenomena may give a more holistic understanding of the human mind. In the Indian tradition, there is a distinct recognition of the role of subtle psychophysiological processes. A distinction between subtle and gross aspects of human functioning is made and the role of subtle body (*sukṣma śarira*) in the manifestation of extraordinary mental events is recognized. It would seem therefore that classical Indian psychological thought may provide some of the new assumptions needed to make sense of psi and with it an understanding of the experimenter effects in parapsychology.

Summary

The evidence for genuine experimenter effects in psi research is as strong and as good as the evidence for the existence of psi. It could only be dismissed as a widespread conspiracy or pervasive incompetence among research scientists investigating psi. The areas and numbers involved are too broad and too many to take these allegations as serious alternatives to psi and the experimenter effects.

The question of what these effects mean is, however, much more difficult to answer. The issues involved are too complex and the crucial evidence in favor of one interpretation over another is fuzzy. The traditional assumptions about the *source* of psi and its *dirigibility* are being stretched to their limits; and strong pressure is building up to revise, revamp or even replace them with a new set of paradigmatically different assumptions.

It is difficult to conceive anyone other than the subject as the true source of psi. With the subject at the center, is there any way one can make sense of experimenter effects in parapsychology? The experimenter sensory effects (ESEs) are an easy fit; but the experimenter psi effects (EPEs) pose a real challenge. Among the two main categories of experimenter psi effects, if the experimenter does indeed seem to influence *directly* the psi outcome by his PK as in the case of the Honorton & Barksdale (1972) study, then the interpretation is not difficult within the existing "subject-source" paradigm. One may simply assume that the true subject is the experimenter, whose PK influences the output of the REG. The West-Fisk experiment in which success is recorded only in the data kept by Fisk is about the most challenging, but could be explained within the "subject-source" paradigm if one assumes that subjects are psi sensitive to experimenters in that they function psychically better with some experimenters than others. This may not be surprising because subjects are known to be psychically sensitive to certain targets and some target persons. Recall the case of "good" and "bad" targets in the work of Ryzl and Pratt with P.S. as the subject.

It may be argued in the case of West-Fisk study that the subjects are unaware of the involvement of the two experimenters and therefore the question of relative sensitivity between the two does not arise. But, then, there are too many studies that suggest that the subjects psychically discriminate between sets of targets even when they are not consciously aware that two different sets of targets are used. The operation of psi at the unconscious level is something on which there is a general agreement among parapsychologists. If psi functions at the level of the unconscious, then non-intentional psi would be a misnomer because the intentions of the subject relative to a given psi outcome may operate at the unconscious level.

So, the extended "subject-source" hypothesis would assume that the subject's psi may be activated at the level of the unconscious as well. Therefore intentions imply not only conscious but also unconscious motivations, desires, wishes, hostilities, and so on. Once psi is triggered by a situation or event such as a subject's involvement in an ESP test, his psi is influenced by a number of facts that include target, situational and test variables and experimenter differences. Therefore, further progress in finding a more viable explanation of the experimenter effects is predicated on a better understanding of the nonconscious functioning of psi.

The other alternative is to reexamine and replace the traditional assumptions of the sources of psi. Gardner Murphy (1949) among others has suggested that psi may be transpersonal as it is transtemporal and transspatial. The distinctions between subject and experimenter and others involved in an experiment may be artificial and arbitrary and that they might be linked at a deeper level of the unconscious. A.D. Price (1973) speculated about "a universal, transpersonal *structure* from which psi derives both its existence and its meaning. Thus it is the meta-process or the structure of a situation which should attract our theoretical and research attention rather than the processes in themselves" (p. 319). Indeed classical psychological ideas in the Indian tradition have much to offer to deal with the enigma of psi and the riddle of the experimenter effects.

Some Indian systems of thought assume that the distinction between subject and object disappears at some levels of awareness. Attaining such states of consciousness is believed to be associated with manifestation of psychic phenomena. Patañjali in his *Yoga-Sutra* describes that state as *saṃyama*, achieved by concentrated focus in a deeply absorbing *samadhi*.

8

Explanatory Quagmire

One wonders whether parapsychology is in a no-win situation despite its massive database. If the experimental results may be convincing to those who collected the data, but continue to be controversial in the minds of many scientists. It would seem that there is little hope that any more compelling evidence than what is already on the record would be available any time soon. Therefore, the haunting question that confronts those of us writing on this topic is: What do we make of the mountains of data that filled 80 volumes of the *Journal of Parapsychology* and 100-plus volumes of the *Journal of the Society for Psychical Research* and an equal number from its American counterpart? How may we explain (a) the data and (b) the continuing controversies surrounding them? In the previous chapters we referred to the available data bearing on possible relationships of psi with other variables; and some attempts at their theoretical understanding. In this chapter we will face head-on the explanatory quagmire, and see if there is any light at the end of the tunnel.

The attempts to explain psi phenomena range all the way from rejecting evidence as insufficient to reject the null hypothesis to postulating new and mysterious entities or processes to account for the phenomena, considering them real and the studies of them a genuine exercise. The attempts include on the one hand naturalistic explanations that seek either to explain away the data or account for them within the bounds of current science or with minor extensions of it. On the other hand, there are those that find it necessary to go way beyond the currently accepted principles that limit science and to embrace new epistemologies. We have discussed earlier the main arguments against the claims advanced by the critics of parapsychology.

Explaining psi away as some kind of an artifact has been the favorite pastime of many critics, who implicitly accept David Hume's celebrated statement on miracles. The Scottish philosopher stated unambiguously that no evidence is sufficient to establish a miracle. Applied to psi, the skeptical argument runs as follows: Miracles are a priori unreal. Parapsychological phenomena are miracles in that they purport in some way to defy all natural explanations. Therefore, they cannot exist. Any claim of their existence is a spurious artifact of a natural phenomenon. This is the basic argument behind the general skepticism about psychic phenomena. The more sophisticated among the critics of parapsychology, however, find it expedient on occasion to disclaim their Humean legacy.

For example, Paul Kurtz, the founder chairman of the Committee for the Scientific Investigation of Claims of the Paranormal in the U.S., which spared no effort to debunk parapsychology, points out that we cannot "legislate, antecedent to inquiry, what is true or false. One must always be open to unsuspected possibilities, novel theories, new kinds of discovery." "The history of science," he writes, "vividly demonstrates the fact that revolutions in thought can overturn even well-established beliefs, and that ideas once rejected may eventually be verified" (1977, p. 42).

Another critic of ESP research has pointed out that "modern parapsychological research is important. If any of its claims are substantiated, it will radically change the way we look at the world" (Diaconis, 1978, p. 135). Obviously, this opinion is not shared by all the critics. For example, Ray Hyman says that "if ESP were proven to be a reality it would not provide a serious threat to science or other accepted views" (1977, p. 18), and its import will tend to be "methodological, rather than theoretical or substantive" (1978, p. 645).

There is thus a degree of dissonance in the critics' minds. The belief in the openness of science is inconsistent with a priori rejection of phenomena for which an empirical claim is made. The simple way of dealing with such dissonance is to consider irrespective of facts that either the evidence is inadequate or that the phenomenon is too trivial to merit consideration.

Phillip Abelson's assertion that "extraordinary claims require extraordinary evidence" implies that the strength of evidence required to establish a new phenomenon is proportional to its incongruence with our prior notions concerning its existence. At the extreme, then, if one considers the existence of a phenomenon impossible, it is within one's right to demand evidence that would be impossible to obtain. This is what some critics of parapsychology have attempted to do. When the requirements set by a critic for acceptable evidence are met by further research, another critic comes up with new ad hoc explanations rejecting the positive results and averring that there is no good reason of accepting the existence of psi. This can go on endlessly because the unstated assumption is the one made by David Hume concerning miracles. The history of science, however, is replete with examples that render Hume's assumption untenable. Some of parapsychology's critics, who readily acknowledge the untenability of a priori denial of psi, do no better than mask their implicit Humean prejudice. While asserting the openness of science to anomalous phenomena, they make evidential demands that are impossible to meet. Cardeña (2011) soundly rejects the notion that psi is a priori unreal and that such a notion is indicative of epistemological totalitarianism.

Why Do We Think Psi Exists?

Psi experiences have been reported throughout recorded history. Evidence for the existence of psi has been obtained under controlled conditions by dozens of scientists widely scattered across the globe. Psi effects, such as declines and psi-missing (Rao, 1977a), not anticipated by the original investigator, have been later discovered in the data. People who were too afraid or too reticent to publish their data because of their controversial nature are known to have obtained significant psi results. It is difficult to see how someone like Kurtz could have any alternative to accepting the reality of psi if he looks at the available data objectively. C.E.M. Hansel (1966), who is often referred to for a final word on parapsychology by those who do not believe in psi, concluded in his magnum opus *ESP: A Scientific Evaluation* thus: "A great deal of time, effort and money has been expended but an acceptable demonstration of the existence of extrasensory perception has not been given. Critics have themselves been criticized for making the conditions of a satisfactory demonstration impossible to obtain. An acceptable model for future research with which the argument could rapidly be settled one way or the other has now been made available by the investigators at the United States Air Force Research Laboratories. If 12 months research on VERITAC can establish the existence of ESP, the past research will not have been in vain. If ESP is not established, much further effort could be spared and the energies of many young scientists could be directed to more worthwhile research" (p. 241).

If these are the final words of the critic, no one who is familiar with the recent parapsychological research could reasonably doubt the existence of psi. Helmut Schmidt (1969a, 1969b) and the work that followed his first experiment involving random event generators and the automatic recording devices, as we have noted, are no way inferior to the VERITAC.

They meet all the demands made by Hansel for an acceptable psi experiment. The overwhelming evidence that Schmidt and others such as Robert Jahn and his associates (Jahn, 1982; Jahn & Dunne, 1987) have accumulated since should suffice to convince any open-minded skeptic.

Whatever may be the shortcomings of parapsychological research, one fact emerges clearly and forcefully out of its huge database. The null hypothesis that ESP subjects under conditions of reduced sensory noise (e.g., ganzfeld stimulation) obtain scores that do not defer significantly from those expected by chance stands summarily rejected. Contrary to the skeptical stance, parapsychology has data in need of explanation. The only argument left is that the successful psi results are simply fraudulent. The explanation based on presumed, undetected fraud is believed to be more parsimonious than assuming the reality of psi inconsistent with and contrary to natural laws. However, the assumption that the possibility of psi is contrary to natural laws is vigorously contested in several reports. Some suggest that psi can be accounted within the quantum mechanical paradigm, and a few others feel that a paradigm shift may be warranted for accounting for psi as natural phenomenon (Carr, 2015).

What Needs Explanation?

Now accepting that the null hypothesis is rejected by available psi data, then we may ask what is it in the data that needs explanation? What are the basic aspects of psi that should be incorporated into any theory that attempts to explain psi? On the face of it, the first priority, it would appear, is to account for the different forms of psi such as ESP and PK. Indeed this issue was salient at one point; but now it does not seem that a psi theory must explain both ESP and PK as two separate forms of psi.

Take, for instance, the question of telepathy versus clairvoyance. The conceptual distinction between these two terms was made quite early in the history of systematic parapsychology. For many years there was a controversy over the state of evidence for one against the other. One could even identify national stereotypes on this question. The British by and large favored the telepathy hypothesis while the American researchers preferred clairvoyance.

After years of intense attempts to demonstrate "pure" telepathy and "pure" clairvoyance and the heated exchanges aimed at explaining telepathy by clairvoyance and precognition, and clairvoyance in terms of telepathy, we are now led to a position where the traditional distinction between the two as two distinct modes of psi seems to be rather pointless. Telepathy and clairvoyance simply appear as a single ability operating on diverse target materials. The range of targets seem to be immense indeed, as the subjects are known to succeed in guessing the images in someone's mind, as well as the electromagnetic activity inside a computer. Again, evidence seems to suggest that the distinction between ESP and PK may be misleading in some crucial ways. Already theoretical attempts to reduce one to the other have been made with a certain amount of plausibility (May, Utts & Spottiswoode, 1995; Schmidt, 1975; Stanford, 1977b, 1978; Walker, 1975; Roll, 1961).

Not all parapsychologists may agree on what is the single most significant aspect of psi that has been discovered so far. The most salient findings, however, seem in some sense to have a negative tone. We know more about the conditions that do not constrain psi functioning than those that enhance its manifestation. This is somewhat paradoxical because the occurrence of psi itself is sporadic and elusive. I have come to think that these findings are quite important in that they may lead us to an appreciation of the true place of psi in nature. The physical aspects of the target, such as size, shape, color and form do not seem to have any intrinsic effect on psi. Neither do space and time, and the causative complexity of the psi task. Any hypothetical relationship of distance to ESP must assume that there is some energy transmission between the subject guessing and the targets guessed. Such transmission should be inhibited by the distance factor, and there is no evidence for such an effect of distance on psi scoring. Further, if precognition is a fact, and we have strong evidence to believe that it is, what is the nature of this transmission that occurs between the subject and the not-yet-existing target? Thus, the evidence for precognition and the success of ESP experiments over long distances lead me to believe that space and time as we conceive them are not constraining variables as far as psi is concerned. Another significant negative non-limiting aspect is the relative ineffectiveness of task complexity in constraining psi. Stanford (1977b) who reviewed the relevant literature concluded that "the efficacy of PK function is not reduced by increases in the complexity of the target system" (p. 375). I have not seen anything since that may be taken to challenge Stanford's conclusion.

If psi is unconstrained by space, time or complexity of task, and if the psi situation is such that distinctions between thought and matter, cognition and action, subject and object become less than meaningful, it would seem that psi may function beyond the familiar categories of understanding and may point to a state of being which cannot be properly classed as either mind or matter. Psi phenomena do seem to raise the question whether there exists a realm of reality beyond the phenomenal world of appearance, a product of our information-processing capabilities and mechanisms. One may rightly wonder whether we are dealing here with the Kantian *Ding an sich* (the noumenon, the "thing in itself"). Also, it would seem that it is just for this reason that J.B. Rhine (1953) and others have emphasized the notion of the non-physicality of psi.

Another characteristic of psi phenomena is the apparent lack of any discernible connection between a psi event and its assumed cause. This led C.G. Jung to postulate that psi belongs to a class of synchronistic acausal events (Jung & Pauli, 1955). In order to make any sense of synchronicity as an explanatory hypothesis we have to assume a kind of omniscience on one's part and regard archetypes as nonlocal in the sense that they can function independently of space-time constraints (Rao, 1977b). Yet the problem of communication between the individual and the archetypes remains unresolved. We need to explain the dirigibility aspect of psi, i.e., the synchronization of archetypal activity with the wishes of the subject or the experimenter in a successful psi test.

Walter Lucadou (1987, 2015) provides "The Pragmatic Information Model" (PMI), a development of Jung's synchronicity. Unlike other observational theories of psi, the PMI does not begin at the level of quantum theory, but at the general level of systems theory.

Unlike spontaneous psi events, laboratory effects involve a connection between someone's intention and the subsequent observation of an effect. Without such an intention or expectation, observed effects would be no more than improbable coincidences. It is this intentionality, often stated in terms of expectations and experimental hypotheses, that gives *meaning* to coincidences. But the intention itself, it seems to me, is not the cause of the observed effect in the sense of a formal or efficient cause. Only in a teleological sense can the intention be considered the cause of psi effect. This point is apparent in the theoretical attempts to regard psi as goal-oriented.

Then, what about non-intentional psi effects? Non-intentional psi events may occur in real life. However, in the sense of an effect obtained in a planned laboratory experiment, non-intentional psi is a misnomer. The usefulness of this concept is at best limited to focusing attention on the possibility that the source of a psi effect may not be the subject, as is traditionally assumed, but the experimenter or some other one involved in the experiment. Insofar as the experimenter intends or expects a particular outcome in an experiment he or she carries out, whatever psi may be evidenced by that experiment cannot be regarded as non-intentional.

One thing that seems to stand out prominently in the ESP database among numerous other claims is the observation that subjects tend to score significantly under conditions of reduced sensory noise as, for example, when they are under ganzfeld stimulation, or after they meditate, and are relaxed. This is important; it needs to be taken into account while attempting to account for psi.

Nature of Explanation

Generally, explanation of a phenomenon involves the statement of a *theory*. Theories are derived from explicit or implicit *models*. *Paradigms* provide the principles of orientation for building models. Theories have greater generality than hypotheses. However, the terms *paradigm, model* and *theory* do not seem to have a sufficiently precise and agreed-upon meaning to permit a consistent usage. Even among philosophers of science there does not seem to be a consensus about the criteria for paradigms, models and theories (Chari, 1977).

According to Thomas Kuhn (1970), paradigms are the "universally recognized scientific achievements that for a time provide model problems and solutions to a community of practitioners" (p. viii). A paradigm in this sense transcends the narrow confines of a discipline and encompasses the whole range of "normal science." A model is less generalized than a paradigm and is usually oriented towards a discipline or a problem area. A model is an abstract, mathematical formalism or a descriptive and typological scheme. Like the paradigm, a model is neither true nor false. Insofar as models determine the kinds of research one does and the types of theories one develops, their value is a function of the importance of the research they engender and the value and validity of the theories they lead to. Models in their formulation are independent of empirical events. Theories provide the connection between the terms of a model and their operational and empirical equivalents. Theories generally serve two functions. They enable us to make (a) *generalized* statements about observed relationship between variables and (b) *predictions* about unexamined relationship. A theory is true to the degree to which it enjoys empirical support. It is fruitful to the extent of its predictive generality. It is scientific if it is testable.

Opinions differ on the value of models and theories in a given scientific enterprise. Those critical of their value argue that they are closed gateways that restrict the investigator to narrow confines. Commitment to a theory sometimes leads to overlooking data that conflict with the theory. This argument is more against the misuse of a theory than against its intrinsic value. Generally, theory and research should go together. The priority—which comes first—is not important in itself. Research findings sometimes lead to new theories; theories in their turn start fresh research.

Among parapsychologists, there is a degree of ambivalence about the value of theories. The point that parapsychology has "a factual basis on which there is yet to be built a great theory" (Scriven, 1976, p. 73) has been made quite often. "The theoretical side of psychical research," wrote H.H. Price (1949), "has lagged far behind the evidential side. And that, I believe, is one of the main reasons why the evidence itself is still ignored by so many ... highly educated people. It is because these queer facts apparently" make no sense "...that they tend to make no permanent impression on the mind... If we could devise some theoretical explanation ... in terms of which the facts did make sense ... it would be a great gain. Such an explanation is needed for its own sake; and it is also needed to get the evidence attended to and considered."

This view, though shared by many, was questioned by C.W.K. Mundle (1976), among some others. He doubts "whether we shall persuade many scientists to pay heed to the facts by explaining them in terms of theories which are themselves so hard to believe. What scientists want," Mundle declares, "are not metaphysical theories but verifiable hypotheses" (p. 96).

All this does not mean that there is any lack of speculative thinking in parapsychology. If anything, it has been rampant, even wild, on occasions. What are lacking are (a) a consensus of acceptance and (b) systematic attempts to ask questions, raise problems, and expect answers that would strengthen a stated theoretical position. The absence of such attempts because of the inherent difficulties involved in making generalized statements about phenomena that seem to be capricious and largely uncontrollable may have been at the root of this ambivalence to theory building in parapsychology.

As is often said, parapsychology has no paradigm; but its data do conflict prima facie with the paradigm of what Kuhn calls "normal science." It would appear that parapsychological events ought not to occur if the world is what the physicists think it is. Thus, the critics of parapsychology have a paradigm which gives them a number of ad hoc theories to explain the "alleged" psi phenomena. These include sensory cueing and inadequate experimental controls, statistical artifacts and outright fraud. It is, however, increasingly realized that parapsychological phenomena pose no serious threat to contemporary physics, especially quantum theory and the behavior of subatomic particles. Richard Shoup (2015), for example, presents a plausible case that with some "modest changes" to the assumptions and formalism of quantum mechanics, we can find much better understanding of psi and its observed effects.

Parapsychological theories can be placed into distinct categories of varying value. They seem to fit into three descriptive models. The primary thrust of parapsychological theorizing so far has been directed toward explaining how psi may function in a manner relatively unaffected by time-space limitations. Many theorists have felt it necessary to postulate new entities that can transcend time and space or new media that enable an individual to interact with his environment independently of time and space. These theories fall into what may be called the mental or vitalist model. They are essentially paranormal in nature, even though they may contain some crucial psychological component.

A few others have expressed the hope that an extension of the principles of the physical sciences will suffice to account for psi occurrences. This is the physical model. The physical and mental models, whether normal or paranormal, assume an interaction between the subject and the object of psi cognitions. Both are, in a sense, causative models.

The third, the acausal model, does away altogether with such an interaction to explain psi.

Subsumed under these models are varieties of theoretical attempts to explain psi or some aspects of it. A few of them were developed by those who were actively involved in the investigation of the phenomena. Several were suggested, however, by those whose primary involvement was in other disciplines, such as philosophy and physics, but who were attracted to parapsychological phenomena because of their theoretical significance and implications. In this sense, a good many theories in this field have an extraneous significance, which may explain why so few of them have generated any research to test them. The trend seems to be changing a bit as more parapsychologists are tending to raise theoretical questions. Volume 2 of *Extrasensory Perception* edited by May and Marwaha (2015) contains ten different theories and models toward explaining psi.

Physical Models

Quite early in the history of psi research it seemed that the basic characteristics of psychic phenomena are nonphysical in nature. Consequently, they saw little hope of finding viable physical explanations. For example, influential thinkers like H.H. Price (1967) wrote that psi simply does not fit into a physicalistic worldview and that no extension of "physical" principles would be able to provide a satisfactory explanation of psi. J.B. Rhine, who began in psychical research as a biological mechanist, says that he was eventually led by the cumulative results of psi testing to conclude that no physical correlates of psi have so far been found and confirmed. While Rhine recognized that the absence of any reliable physical quality of psi did not warrant the conclusion that psi is absolutely extraphysical, he was impressed by the evidence that psi is nonphysical, until such time as new research alters this picture. While this view is shared by several psi theorists, an increasing number in recent years seem to think that the nonphysical notion of psi is more a reaction to classical than to contemporary physics. In the "weird wonderland" of subatomic and supergalactic physics, as Arthur Koestler (1972) puts it, phenomena which appear to be more "occultish" than psi are known to exist. It is therefore argued that no intrinsic incompatibility between physical laws and psi need be assumed and that the manifest anomalies may be resolved by suitably extending or amending physical principles. More recent advocates of this view include Ed May (May, Utts & Spottiswoode, 1995b).

Also, it makes sense that we first look into known energetic interactions for an understanding of psi before postulating more esoteric entities or extra-physical energies. So, we find quite early in the history of parapsychology earnest attempts to find physical explanations of psi within the boundaries of electromagnetism, and by extending quantum physical theories. The former are referred to as signal theories by Douglas Stokes (1987; 1997) because they assume implicitly or explicitly that the target and the subject are separate entities and that signals from the target somehow reach the subject in case of psi communication or that the subject exerts influence on the target in the case of PK.

Electromagnetic Theories: On the analogy of the radio, it is suggested that in telepathy some kind of electromagnetic wave transmission may take place between the subject and the agent. According to the Russian scientist B. Kajinsky, the neuron system is vibratory in nature. There are closed electrical circuits in the nervous system. Every thought in this view is accompanied by electromagnetic waves generated in the nervous system; and the waves thus generated in one brain are afferently received by another brain resulting in a telepathic kind of experience.

There are several problems with an electromagnetic theory like the above. Electromagnetic transmission between brains, if it is possible, must be subject to the inverse square law. It is not known, however, that the effectiveness of telepathic communication decreases with distance. Another Russian physiologist, L.L. Vasiliev (1963/1976) reported that he was able to induce hypnotic trance over long distance (1700 km) by telepathic suggestion, and that he found no diminishing of the effect when double metal screens were used to shield electromagnetic wave transmission. Again, ESP is known to manifest in the form of clairvoyance, where the information is not generated in the brain but comes from objects that do not have brain-like structures to transmit electromagnetic waves.

Other versions of electromagnetic theory appear in I.M. Kogan (1966) and Robert Becker (1992). Kogan postulated the existence of "the electromagnetic field of extra-long waves excited by bio-currents' (p. 81). In a similar vein, Becker proposed that extremely low frequency (ELF) waves are involved in psi communications. The ELF waves are assumed to be of such great length that they are not impeded by physical obstructions. In Becker's view, psi signals are not processed by the neurons in the brain, but by a more primitive system involving possibly the glial cells. It is hypothesized that such a primitive communication system consisting of electromagnetic field effects may function more effectively during periods of less turbulent geomagnetic activity. Significant correlations are in fact observed between the occurrence of spontaneous ESP experiences and quiet geomagnetic activity (Persinger, 1985, 1989) and between successful psi tests in the laboratory and low levels of geomagnetic activity at the time the tests were conducted (Persinger, 1985; Persinger & Schaut, 1988; Berger & Persinger 1991; Persinger & Krippner, 1989). According to Persinger (1979), the person (agent) attempting to send a telepathic message to another person (subject) would impose a low frequency electromagnetic wave on a geophysical system. In a successful telepathic transmission, this wave would be carried to the subject. Alternatively, Persinger suggests that the brains of the agent and the subject would resonate a geophysical wave resulting in a similar brain state in the agent and the subject. However, Wilkinson & Gauld (1993) criticized the results of studies supporting such a contention on the ground that the geomagnetic activity measurements tend to be quite skewed and cannot be taken as evidence in support of the ELF hypothesis.

There are several other less known signal theories of psi, which postulate that some localized particle or wave carries psi signal across, overcoming the normal time-space constraints. These include postulation of tachyons, psitrons and advanced waves. For a brief discussion of them see Stokes (1977). More recently, Daniel Sheehan (2015) discussed the case for retrocausation in the light of evidence for precognition.

Quantum Theories: Unlike classical physics, quantum mechanics does not postulate that the universe consists of localized, mutually isolated and discrete particles of matter. Rather, quantum mechanics suggests that protons, for example, constitute a unified system even if they are separated by light years of space. This gives rise to the notion of non-locality. Suggested non-locality of micro-matter on which the usual space-time constraints do not seem to have an influence, has direct relevance to parapsychological phenomena, which are also unaffected by space-time factors. This apparent similarity between micro-physical phenomena and psi has led some physics-trained parapsychologists to come up with quantum theories of psi. These are referred to as the observational theories.

It may be recalled that classical mechanics assumes that the future state of a physical system can be determined if we have a complete description of the preceding state of the system. In quantum mechanics, however, a given system develops into one of several possible subsequent states and, according to the widely accepted Copenhagen interpretation, the ultimate description, or state vector of the system incorporates all the potential states. However, when a measurement or "observation" of the system is made, the state vector loses this undefined probabilistic quality and gets "reduced" to one real outcome. Unfortunately, the mathematical formalism of quantum mechanics does not specify what exactly constitutes an "observation," and the resulting difficulties lead to the well known "measurement problem" in quantum mechanics.

One attempt to overcome this problem is to introduce the concept of "hidden variables," the hypothetical factors that reconcile the demands of the deterministic and stochastic conceptions of the development of the state vector. Harris Walker takes off from here and locates the hidden variables in consciousness and equates them with the "will." In Walker's view, the will is responsible for the collapse of the state vector for a physical system. PK is an instance of such collapse brought about by human volition. Since the hidden variables are "nonlocal," they are unconstrained by space-time factors, and are capable of coupling two observers or an observer and an object separated by distance or time. In telepathy, for instance, "the will of the subject and the experimenter act together to select a particular state into which the system collapsed" (Walker 1975, p. 10). In psi, whether ESP or PK, there is no transfer of energy; only information is transferred. The magnitude of a psi effect, in Walker's view, depends on the amount of information transferred through the will channel and the amount needed to collapse the state vector of a given system. Walker suggests that quantitative predictions of psi effects can be made based on a detailed analysis of the psi task and an estimate of the observer's abilities and will.

Helmut Schmidt and others, notably Mattuck, have proposed varying versions of observational theory. According to Schmidt (1975, 1984), in situations involving two quantum processes with known probability values of their occurrence, a gifted subject could psychically alter their probabilities in the desired direction. Schmidt offers a mathematical formalism to estimate the expected psi of such effects. He argues that such effects are independent of spatio-temporal considerations and provide evidence for the occurrence of retroactive PK, which his theory predicts. But a number of important questions arise. How does the subject bring about this shift in probabilities? An observational theorist would hold that it is brought about by the subject's observations, as, for example, when the subject receives the feedback of the outcome. What happens when more than one person observes? Do successive observations by the same subject or subsequent observations of other subjects also influence the outcome? Schmidt allows for the possibility of multiple observations influencing the outcomes. He, however, suggests that successive observations can influence the probability outcomes as long as the prior observations are not complete. According to Schmidt's theory, there is an optimum limit to psychic influence. When that limit is reached, the observation is complete and subsequent observations will have no effect on the outcomes.

Building on the ideas of Walker and Schmidt, Mattuck (1977, 1982) suggests that the psychokinetic influence is exerted by the action of the mind to restructure thermal noise. According to Mattuck, his theory "does not operate by selection of individual molecules, but rather by the selection of *macroscopic* pure states" (1977, p. 192). Like Schmidt, Mattuck also develops a mathematical formalism and asserts that his theory makes testable predictions. However, as it is pointed out, no tests have been reported validating the basic predictions of Schmidt or Mattuck (Stokes, 1987).

The observational theories of psi are stated to be experimentally testable, as they are formulated in mathematical terms. Indeed, Walker's theory and modifications of it by others did stimulate a significant amount of research, especially in the area of PK. However, the validity of any of the versions of the observational theory is yet to be established (Irwin, 1999). Even in the liberal version of quantum mechanics, it is highly controversial whether the collapse of the state vector involves consciousness in the sense the observational theories require for explaining psi. Further, the question of what constitutes an "observation" that is necessary to bring about the collapse of the state vector is not answered with any degree of clarity by theorists in this area. Even granting some validity to the observational theories of psi, it is difficult to see them as mere extensions of current physical theory. Walker's theory, for example, sounds clearly dualistic. The "will" and the "hidden variables" seem to have the same ontological primacy as energy, which accounts for events in the physical world. That the "will" influences only the micro-level quantum systems is beside the point. What is important is that even the physical theories do seem to assume principles and processes that are not a mere extension of what is ordinarily understood as physical, but things that are commonly regarded as mental in the Cartesian model. In an important sense, Walker's theory is a significant reversal of the physical model. One could even characterize it as vitalist, because the central principle that accounts for psi is located in the "will" of the subject. This shift away from the stimulus-centered approach gives Walker's theory a vitalist look. Note that Walker is not looking at the process by which the energy emanating from objects reaches the subject, but rather at the subject and his "will" variables. The development of a dualistic physics (which is what this theory attempts to develop) would indeed constitute a paradigmatic shift, and its acceptance would have revolutionary consequences for physics.

More recent renderings of quantum theories of psi include Lucadou (1995) and Walach & Stillfried (2011). A hybrid theory with a physical base may be found in the "Decision Augmentation Theory (DAT) proposed by Edwin May and colleagues (May, Utts & Spottiswoode, 2014). The theory assumes that humans integrate information obtained by ESP into their usual decision making process. This assumption is basically what the PMIR model of Stanford suggests. May and associates, however, go further and suggest some hypotheses that may be derived and experimentally tested. They further add that these hypotheses differ from those derived from "force-like" models. However, May et al. (1995) tend to reduce all forms of psi to precognition; and this tends not only to contradict the traditional assumptions about psychokinesis, but also to conflict with observed macro-physical psi effects.

Psychological Models

Some attempts have been made by parapsychologists to explain psi within the framework of an information-processing model (Schmeidler, 1991; Irwin, 1979, 1999; Lucadou, 1995, 2015). In fact, the concept "extrasensory perception" presupposes a perceptual model, that psi operates in a sensory-like fashion, even if it is not mediated by any known senses. This model has shown little promise and attracted only negligible support within the parapsychological community. In a sense, it is paradoxical to consider psi as a species of perception and at the same time regard it as non-sensory. In fact, the lack of any sensory orientation, and the absence of any systematic effects of color, shape, size and location of the target on ESP performance, clearly suggest that no sensory processing of the kind that goes on in perception is involved in psi. For this reason, I have argued elsewhere (Rao, 1966) that psi in its cognitive aspect is more like imagination than perception.

H.J. Irwin (1979, 1999) suggested that psi fits better with the information-processing model in its ideational mode than in its sensory mode. Irwin recommends a memory model of psi such as the one proposed by W.G. Roll (1966, 1987). Roll suggested that ESP is more like remembering than perceiving. The mediation of psi into awareness may involve essentially similar cognitive processing as in memory and be subject to similar laws, e.g., laws of association and frequency. In support of this theory, it is claimed that exceptionally successful subjects appear to have excellent memories. At least one experimental study (Feather, 1967) reported a positive correlation between subjects' memory scores and ESP scores. All this is well taken, and there may be some genuine similarities in the way memories and ESP information are mediated into awareness. The memory model, however, does not really explain ESP without invoking something more fundamental, something that is entirely beyond what memory can do. As Irwin himself recognizes, the memory model at best attempts to account for the mediation phase of psi, but not how the subject has access to extrasensory information in the first place. The latter does seem to require a paranormal process.

PMIR and the Conformance Model: Emphasizing that we should depart from the notion that ESP is a kind of information processing ability, Rex Stanford (1977c) proposes that psi is a disposition subserving function. He attempts to make explicit the assumptions implied in the traditional model, which he calls the *"psychobiological* paradigm." Crediting this paradigm with a strong and constraining influence on the course of parapsychological research in the past, he identifies the following preconceptions it is believed to imply: (1) that ESP is an information-receiving capacity and that "in some sense either a specialized receptor or the brain and nervous system must have the capacity to receive and process such information" (p. 2), and (2) that "extrasensory information is used, albeit unconsciously, to guide and thus to control the outcome" (p. 2). Stanford refers to J.B. Rhine's view that assumes ESP and PK to be the nonphysical analogues of sensory perception and motor action, as an example of the psychobiological paradigm that, he says, has been rarely questioned by parapsychological researchers.

Stanford (1974a, b; 1977a, c) has proposed instead his own model for understanding psi, which he believes circumvents the limitations of the psychobiological model. This PMIR model was alluded to while discussing the experimenter efforts in parapsychology in a previous chapter. Stanford postulates that the organism uses psi to scan its environment, as it does with its available sensory resources. This scanning, according to him, is need-based. *"In the presence of a particular need,"* writes Stanford (1974a), *"the organism uses psi (ESP),as well as sensory means, to scan its environment for objects and events relevant to that need and for information crucially related to such objects and events* (p. 43)" (emphasis in the original). When extrasensory information is obtained to subserve a need, the organism tends to behave in ways to satisfy the need, resulting in what Stanford calls the psi-mediated instrumental response or PMIR. In other words, when an organism receives psi information, it tends "to act in ways which are instrumental in satisfying its needs in relation to the need-relevant object or event" (1974a, p. 44). Stanford goes on to state several other propositions that develop this basic idea of PMIR, to explain some of the experimental results in terms of PMIR concepts, and also to suggest further areas of research.

Stanford (1974b) extends his model to explain psychokinesis. PK is regarded as "a response mode for PMIR." PMIR may be any kind of goal-relevant response made possible through extrasensory means by PK. Stanford distinguishes two kinds of telepathy: the "percipient-active" and the "agent-active" forms. Telepathy, where the percipient actively scans the internal states of the agent, is the first kind. The second form of telepathy is one in which the agent actively influences the internal states of the percipient by means of PK. In other words, the agent-active telepathy is really a form of PK. An important aspect of Stanford's theory is that PMIR is conceived as disposition-subserving rather than intrinsically perceptual or cognitive in character and that psi tends to influence behavior in appropriate ways, not necessarily striving for perceptual-cognitive expression.

The central idea in this model is that all psi responses are mediated, that they are instrumental and that they subserve the "entire range of needs." The emphasis on the non-intentional character of psi scanning reiterates the assumptions that psi is somewhat similar to the autonomic nervous system activity, in that it functions without our conscious intent and that the extrasensory information received at the level of the unconscious requires a mediating instrument for it to manifest in consciousness. It is not clear, however, whether Stanford rules out completely the possibility of having direct awareness of extrasensory information, and if he holds that ESP can only be inferred from the responses it is believed to mediate.

Stanford brings together a number of psi findings with commendable ingenuity and candor. His stress on the non-intentional character of psi makes sense. Yet the basic model is hardly an advance over the psychobiological model he criticizes. While Stanford may be correct in his thinking about the goal directedness of PMIR, one will find it hard to believe that the strength and importance of the need is as relevant to psi as Stanford's model implies. Many subjects who are successful on trivial psi tasks have reported no psi experiences on matters that must have been tremendously important to them in life. In defense of Stanford's theory, it may be pointed out that the theory makes several assumptions concerning the conditions that block psi functioning, which presumably explain why we do not always experience psi in response to our need demands.

Subsequent to the publication of the PMIR theory, Stanford has developed his theory to include assumptions explaining the underlying character of psi phenomena. These new ideas make it clear that the "scanning" mentioned in the PMIR model is not literal. Psi often occurs so that it looks *as if* scanning has occurred, but that scanning is not what actually activates psi response (Stanford, 1977a, 1977c).

Extending and revising his PMIR model, Stanford has proposed the theory of "conformance behavior," which attempts to explain ESP in the following way. The nervous system or the brain is a complex and sophisticated random event generator (REG). The ESP subject (or the experimenter), insofar as he or she has a need, wish or desire to succeed in the test, is a disposed system. A disposed system is contingently linked to an REG under circumstances that are favorable in such a manner that the outputs of the latter fulfill the dispositions of the former. When such conformance behavior manifests, we have ESP. In other words, if the subject has a wish or need to succeed in an ESP test, under favorable circumstances his or her brain or nervous system will be biased to make correct calls. This is possible because a "contingent linkage" exists between a successful subject's disposition and brain, or between a successful experimenter and his or her subjects in the case of experimenter effect, or between the agent and the percipient in some forms of telepathy.

Stanford claims that his "conformance behavior" model is an alternative to the psychological model he criticizes. However, the concept of contingent linkage makes some of the same assumptions made by the variety of hypotheses based on the so-called psychobiological model. How the linkage between the subject and the target is established remains equivocal, considering the non-intentional aspects of psi. Again, what is the channel and the mechanism involved in bringing about the conformance? If the conformance is a product of a chain of causation, that is left unstated. If psi effects result non-causally, then Stanford needs to deal with the nature of such non-causality in bringing about psi effects paranormally.

James Carpenter (2012) in his book *First Sight: ESP and Parapsychology in Everyday Life* develops a theory for explaining parapsychological phenomena. The theory makes two basic assumptions. First, psi is primary and common in everyday experience and not something exceptional. Second, it functions at the unconscious level as well as at the level of consciousness. In a significant sense, Carpenter asserts that the unconscious psi plays an important role in conscious experiences.

Lucadou (2015) contends that his model of pragmatic information (MPI) accounts for physical as well as psychological aspects of psi. The model assumes that there is a structure underlying psi and that this structure is able to exchange information with some others.

Paranormal Explanations

If psi phenomena are anomalous, as they appear to be, and do not fit into physical and psychological models, one is tempted naturally to conclude that consciousness is not completely contained in our cortical structures or the rest of the nervous system. Indeed, several psychical researchers from F.W.H. Myers (1903/1915) and William James to R.H. Thouless (Thouless & Weisner, 1948) and Larry LeShan (1976) felt it necessary to postulate a hitherto unknown "entity" or a hitherto unrecognized principle or medium operating when one has a psi experience. The primary thrust of the theories in this area has been directed toward explaining how psi functions relatively unaffected by space-time constraints. Since there are too many theories to review here, we consider here only the prominent ones (see Rao, 1977b; Stokes, 1987 for a more detailed discussion of parapsychological theories). *Parapsychology: A Handbook for the 21st Century*, edited by Cardeña, Palmer & Marcusson-Clavertz (2015), contains no discussion of paranormal theories of psi.

Subliminal Self: In his monumental work *Human Personality and Its Survival of Bodily Death,* F.W.H. Myers (1903/1915) attempted to lay the foundation for a comprehensive science of consciousness. Myers believed that consciousness is more than that of which we are ordinarily aware. Our ordinary consciousness, which Myers called *supraliminal consciousness,* "does not comprise the whole of consciousness or of the faculty within us. There exists a more comprehensive consciousness, a profounder faculty" (p. 12), which he refers to as *subliminal* or *ultramarginal consciousness.* Consciousness is like radiation beyond the visible spectrum. According to Myers, the conscious human faculty can be represented "as a linear spectrum whose red rays begin where voluntary muscular control and organic sensation begin, and whose violet rays fade away at the point at which man's highest strain of thought or imagination merges in reverie and ecstasy" (p. 18). Thus, at either end of the psychological spectrum, Myers sensed a wide variety of conscious states that go beyond sensation and intellect.

The ultramarginal consciousness, which remains for the most part only as potential, is what Myers calls the *subliminal self.* "I mean by the subliminal self," he wrote, "that part of the self which is commonly subliminal. And I conceive also that no self of which we can have cognizance is in reality more than a fragment of a larger Self,—revealed in a fashion at once shifting and limited through an organism not so framed as to afford its full manifestation" (p. 15).

In his conception of the subliminal self, Myers postulates an "inward extension of our being," as James put it, "cut off from common consciousness by a stream or diaphragm not absolutely impervious but liable to leakage and to occasional rupture" (Murphy & Ballou, 1960, p. 230). However, Myers was vague as to how the subliminal self makes contact with the "cosmic" environment to bring about paranormal events. Various alternatives suggest themselves. (1) The subliminal selves are but waves in a sea of consciousness. (2) The subliminal selves themselves are discrete and discontinuous, but can interact because they are submerged or situated in a common medium of consciousness. (3) The subliminal self is a discrete center of consciousness inherently capable of interacting with others without being limited by space or time. For his time, the ideas of Myers were provocative and seminal. They inspired a number of subsequent thinkers from William James to G.N.M. Tyrrell (1947a, 1947b) and Jan Ehrenwald (1947, 1978) and David Kahn (1976).

S. David Kahn (1976) plausibly argues that Myers' hypothesis can be further extended if we assume, as James did, that we are linked together in a far more fundamental way than we have hitherto imagined. The subliminal influence on our being may not be conceived of merely as the "subliminal uprush" on rare occasions. Rather, according to Kahn, it is more pervasive than that, and is, in fact, "an intrinsic component to the human condition" (p. 225). "Here the emphasis," writes Kahn, "is on a constantly impinging heteropsychic set of stimuli which occasionally may break through, but which ordinarily press on the stream of thought in such a way as to steadily distort, modify, emphasize, and deflect the ongoing process of consciousness. Here the occasional breakthrough is less important than the constant interaction between the psi level and the stream of consciousness itself, which now becomes the focus of our attention" (p. 224).

The Compound Theory: The British philosopher with an interest in psychical research, C.D. Broad (1925/1951), proposed what he called the "compound theory" of the mind. According to this theory, the mind is not a single substance. It is a compound of two substances, and neither of them by itself has the characteristics of the mind. The two substances are the *psychic factor* or *psi component,* as he later called it, and the *bodily factor*.

Such actions as perception, reasoning, and remembering are not the functions of either of the factors by itself. Just as a chemical compound possesses characteristics that do not belong individually to either of the constituents, the functions of the mind are not to be found solely in one or another of its constituent elements.

Broad goes on to suggest that the psychic factor could persist even after the cessation of the body at death. When a psychic factor is united with a body, it functions as a mind, and certain traces are formed. When the person dies, this factor separates. Consequently, a discarnate psychic factor does not have a mind or conscious awareness. Let us suppose that a psychic factor, after its separation from the body with which it has so long been associated, comes into contact with the body of another living organism, as would be in the case with an entranced medium. The newly formed "mind," in virtue of the impressions this psychic factor had in the form of traces, may recall the experiences of the deceased person with whose body the psychic factor had been associated.

It is possible to extend this hypothesis and argue that the psychic factor has also the ability to psi-cognize and psi-kinetize without being conscious of their effects. However, we then have to assume that the psychic factor goes out to reach for the object or thought in psi cognitive operations or that it is in constant touch with all things and thoughts at all times. If we assume the former, we have to argue that when a thought, memory or experiential event is extra-sensorially transferred from one person to another, as in telepathy, the psychic factor in the mind of the former must have come into contact with the body of the latter, replacing its mind temporarily. But this could be possible, so far as we know, only if one of the persons involved in the situation were deceased or had temporarily lost their mind or were at least in the state of deep sleep. That this is not the case in successful ESP experiments, and even in some spontaneous cases, argues against the plausibility of this alternative. If we admit the second possibility, that of universal and omniscient ESP, there would be no need for any traces in the psychic factor in order to recall the experiences, since it is actually in touch with all that is. An escape from the predicament is to assume that the psychic factor is in some sense "nonlocal" and can enter into a relationship with other bodies without actually leaving the mind of which it is a constituent.

The Shin Hypothesis: Psychologist R.H. Thouless and his associate B.P. Weisner advocate a radical dualistic postulation of the mind-brain relationship. Thouless & Weisner (1948) suggest that an entity, which they call "shin," is involved in all our cognitive processes, normal as well as paranormal. They argue that in all normal processes of volition and perception, shin functions through the medium of the brain and the nervous system. Anomalous cognitive experiences occur when shin bypasses the brain and the nervous system and directly interacts with the environment. In this view, shin becomes aware of the brain states by a clairvoyant type of monitoring of neural activity in a manner that is similar to a theory proposed by neurophysiologist John Eccles (1976, 1977). Similarly, the psychokinetic type of influence on neural events by shin results in volitional activity. In normal perception, stimuli from the object act on the sensory part of the nervous system. The processes in the nervous system and the brain inform shin. In clairvoyance, however, direct connections are established between shin and the objects, without the mediation of the brain and the nervous system. Thus, psi cognitions are no more supernormal than ordinary perceptions, but they are, as Thouless and Weisner put it, "exosomatic forms of processes which are normally endosomatic" (1948, p. 199).

"*In normal thinking and perceiving*," Thouless & Weisner write, "*I am in the same sort of relation to what is going on in the sensory part of my brain and nervous system as that of the successful clairvoyant to some external event, and ... this relation is established by the same means*" (p. 196, emphasis in the original). In an act of perception, they point out, we are not aware of the immediate cause of our perceptions, the cause being the changes in the brain and nervous system. So also, a successful clairvoyant is not aware of the object of his or her cognition. Thus, normal perception differs from clairvoyance only in that the brain and the nervous system mediate the former, whereas in clairvoyant perception a direct contact between the subject and the object is established.

It would appear that shin is more like the mind in the state of what may be referred to as pure consciousness. The question remains, however, whether shin is a discrete center of consciousness like Broad's psychic factor or a common medium that envelops the multitude of beings with cognitive abilities. Shin, as a discrete entity, is consistent with the notion of the plurality of selves. But plurality of nonlocal selves, whose normal cognitive processes manifest only in association with particulate brain structures, will be hardly noticeable as functional plurality. At the nonlocal or transcendental level, the question of the one and the many may be meaningless if discreteness and multiplicity are the result of the union of pure consciousness with the brain.

What is important, however, is the recognition that there is another source of awareness that is different from and runs parallel to sensorially processed cognition. It involves a process that appears to give direct and unmediated access to reality. Such a process involving a transcendental transaction, as it were, may be designated as the paranormal process. The paranormal process is possibly the one that leads to a state of "knowing by being." This is a state that mystics are believed to be capable of experiencing. In the case of psychical phenomena, such as ESP, we have reason to believe that the normal and paranormal processes work in a complementary manner. G.N.M. Tyrrell and L.E. Rhine, among others, recognized that psi is a two-stage process. Tyrrell (1947a), for example, suggested that ESP phenomena first occur at the subliminal level and then are obliged "to pass through the bottleneck at the threshold if they are to reach the normal consciousness" (p. 331). They pass over the threshold by making use of what he called the "mediating vehicles." The second stage is a form of cognitive processing that enables the subliminally received material to manifest in awareness. An ESP experience thus seems to involve both normal and paranormal processes. Inasmuch as parapsychological phenomena involve both these processes, they may be useful in providing the bridge connecting cognitive psychology at one end and transpersonal psychology at the other.

Theories of Collective Mind

As Myers and James suspected, the individual minds may be surface appearances of a more profound and pervasive entity underlying them.

They may be connected at a deeper level by a common medium. In virtue of such association, paranormal communication between people might be possible. This possibility appealed to several theorists.

"Out of my experience," wrote James, "one fixed conclusion dogmatically emerges, and that is this, that we with our lives are like islands in the sea, or like trees in the forest. The maple and the pine may whisper to each other with their leaves, and Conaniqut and Newport hear each other's foghorns. But the trees also co-mingle their roots in the darkness underground, and the islands also hang together through the ocean's bottom. Just so there is a continuum of cosmic consciousness, against which our individuality builds but accidental fences, and into which our several minds plunge as into a mother-sea or reservoir. Our normal consciousness is circumscribed for adaptation to our external earthly environment, but the fence is weak in spots, and fitful influences from beyond leak in, showing the otherwise unverifiable common connection. Not only psychic research, but metaphysical philosophy, and speculative biology are led in their own ways to look with favor on some such 'panpsychic' view of the universe as this" (Murphy & Ballou 1960, p. 324).

The Common Unconscious: Another British philosopher H.H. Price, who took anomalous phenomena such as ESP seriously, felt that the evidence suggestive of mind-to-mind communication (telepathy) makes it foolish to argue for the plurality of minds. Between one mind and another there are no clear-cut boundaries. The division of minds is not "absolute and unconditional, either." The illusion of the individual mind arises out of the superficial nature of self-consciousness (Price, 1940, 1948).

Price thinks that the unconscious portion of one mind may interact with that of another because they share the "collective unconscious" and that the collective unconscious, which connects all the apparently individual minds, is responsible for telepathic cognition. The collective unconscious, according to Price, is not an "entity" or a "thing" but a "field of interaction." Minds are not causally isolated entities. Unconscious events in one mind may produce unconscious events in another mind.

Why then are we not aware of others' thoughts all the time? Following Bergson (1921), Price argues that the human mind has developed a repressive mechanism that suppresses the continual flow of telepathic impact from one mind to another. There is a biological need for such a mechanism. Otherwise, everyone would constantly receive the thoughts and emotions experienced by all minds; life would very likely become chaos, and action impossible. Psychoanalysts have indicated that repressive mechanisms are partly in abeyance during states of relaxation and dreaming. If telepathic influences are suppressed by similar repressive mechanisms, the former should come through more often when the latter are in relative abeyance. Price points out that, in fact, many spontaneous cases of a telepathic nature do occur during dreams. The existence of a repressive mechanism, he says, is also suggested by the fact that most mediums known for their psychic abilities enter a state of dissociation that seems to release them from the repressive controls. As we have noted, sensory noise appears to act as a psi detractor and procedures of relaxation and sensory deprivation are psi conducive.

Price suggests that the unconscious part of our minds may be capable of perceiving everything, however remote in space, for the simple reason that the unconscious may be in contact with all things. However, we do not see all things at once because the nervous system and the sense organs may be preventing us from doing so and this process is, of course, biologically useful to us. Occasionally, however, when the physiological mechanism allows it, these unconscious contacts may actualize themselves in the form of anomalous experiences.

A variant of the idea of H.H. Price is developed by Carington which is more positivistic than Price's notion of the collective unconscious. The fundamental postulate of Carington's (1949) "radical positivism" is that what is meaningful must be verified by sensation or introspection. He says that an analysis of our perceptions reveals to us that the real or the meaningful in them is only sense data or "cognita." Carington then proceeds to put forward a conception of the mind in terms of cognita and cognitum sequences. He argues that to regard the mind as something other than sense cognita is entirely metaphysical and has no meaning.

"The mind," he suggests, could be viewed as "an immense assemblage of discrete particles..." (1949, p. 155). Individual minds are the "condensations" formed of cognita. They are not completely "discrete" and "isolate" but are so formed as to possess a common something that may be called the common unconscious or subconscious.

Carington (1949) thinks that this new conception of mind affords a simple and meaningful explanation of the perplexing phenomenon of telepathy. When two or more individuals are faced with similar circumstances they are likely to have similar thoughts or mental images. For example, two persons looking at the sea or thinking about it are likely to imagine boats, waves or beaches. In a telepathy experiment, the agent concentrates on a target (for example, a picture). The idea of this target is probably associated with various thoughts and ideas about the telepathy experiment. The percipient is therefore likely to have similar thoughts and ideas. Now, granted that the minds of the agent and percipient are related in the common unconscious or subconscious, it is likely, says Carington, that the idea of the target will be brought to the percipient's mind because of its association with the idea of the experiment in the agent's mind. Carington argues that the principle of association of ideas renders this view plausible.

Carington introduces the concept of "K-ideas" to render the association theory of telepathy more intelligible. The K-idea is a connecting link, or an associative bond, between the agent and the percipient. The greater the number of K-ideas, the greater would be the probability of success in telepathy experiments. Carington explains the function of K-ideas by the following analogy. If an individual who is sailing in a boat wishes to send a heavy object to a person, who is in another boat, he would naturally tie a rope to the object and throw the free end to the other boat. Now, the two boats are like the minds of the agent and the percipient; the rope is the connector or the K-idea, and the tying of the rope is the formation of an associative bond. Carington hoped that his version of the collective unconscious has testable implications and empirical ramifications for psi research. Unfortunately, this hope was not fulfilled to any great extent. The collective unconscious remains just a concept with interesting theoretical promises but little empirical support.

Roger Nelson and others in their "global consciousness" project have embarked on extensive field research based on the notion of collective or group mind. Dean Radin (1997b) in his book *Consciousness Universe* describes the theoretical base of the project. The central assumption is that "there is a fundamental interconnectedness among all things" (p. 157–158). According to Radin, consciousness has the following properties:

1. Consciousness is not individually localized.
2. It has quantum field-like properties and is able to influence the probability of the occurrence of events.
3. The influence of consciousness is one of injecting order into the system.
4. Such influence is proportional to the strength of consciousness present.
5. The strength of consciousness is not static, but fluctuates.
6. The fluctuations of consciousness are regulated by attentional focus of the people involved.
7. In the event a group of people focuses its attention on a common object or event, there emerges group consciousness.
8. The degree of group coherence is related to the number of

persons in the group and the strength of the members'
attentional focus (coherence) as well as on other unspecified
environmental, psychological and physiological factors.
9. In sum, physical systems of all kinds respond to a conscious
field by becoming more ordered. The stronger or more coherent
a conscious field, the more the order will be evident [Radin,
1997, p. 160].

Assuming that a random event generator is a chaotic system without
order, the theory postulates that a coherent group generates a conscious
field that will bring order into the REG system, such as producing more
hits than misses. Radin claims that a number of his experiments support
the above prediction.

Radin's postulation of "field consciousness" is cleverly stated. His notion
that the influence of consciousness on physical systems is to "inject order"
into them fits well with much of micro-PK data. However, there are dis-
concerting ambiguities and unaddressed issues that need attention. These
include: What is consciousness? How is it related to the field it generates?
How does field consciousness "inject order" into physical systems? Can
consciousness inject disorder in systems that have order? Is the influence
exerted by the field causative in nature? Is there a distinction between
mind and consciousness? Is the field of consciousness physical like electromagnetic fields? Does it influence conscious systems as it does physical
systems? Thus, the field consciousness theory, as noted above, raises more
questions than it answers.

Acausal Theories

The normal as well as the paranormal theories of psi discussed so far
find it necessary to postulate an agency that is endowed with the ability
to make a direct contact with the target, transcending the inhibitory effects
of space and time, or a medium that provides the necessary link of contact
between the subject and the target. In either case some kind of causal
interaction is assumed or implied. There are, however, a few who question
the basic assumptions underlying these theories and argue for acausal
models. For example, Dommeyer (1977) suggests that the anomalies of
psi that arouse the antagonism of scientists could be resolved by an acausal
theory of ESP and PK. He proposes "acausal uniformity" to supplement
the well-known causal uniformity.

Dommeyer distinguishes among three types of acausality. The first type is implied in the kind of uniformity that exists between two clocks showing the same time, even though one is not the cause of the other. The second type of acausal relationship is one where two causally independent events have a common causal antecedent(s), as in two apple trees blooming about the same time. The third type of acausality involves "intermittent acausal uniformity." "In this sort," says Dommeyer, "the uniform occurrence of the kind of events that A and B are is not constant. It can be sufficiently present, however, to be statistically significant" (p. 90). Dommeyer argues that the fact that no intelligible causal relationship is found between a psychic event such as a premonition and the verifying referent indicates that there may be no causal relation between them. This would call for a change in our interpretational framework from a causal model to an acausal one.

Another critic of vitalistic theories in parapsychology is Antony Flew (1951, 1953, 1954), who has characterized the "mind talk" of Rhine and others as "philosophical sensationalism" born out of inappropriate explanatory models and a misunderstanding of the "logic of terms."

The concept of extrasensory perception, Flew argues, suggests an explanatory model of perception, but ESP is very different from perception in essential respects. He goes on to say that such paradoxes as serial concepts of time are patently due to taking seriously the perceptive models of ESP. If we cannot explain ESP on the model of perception, how else can we explain it? Flew thinks that it is more fruitful to consider ESP a "species of guess work." But one fails to see, even granting an explainable connection between the subject's guesses and some other psychological factors associated with it, what purpose this new model would serve for ESP. As Mundle (1952) succinctly points out, Flew's "guesswork" model could neither *describe* nor *explain* the facts of ESP any more appropriately than the perception model of the parapsychologists.

Synchronicity and Meaningful Coincidence: The best-known acausal explanation of psi is Jung's synchronicity hypothesis. Jung, once a prominent disciple of Freud, broke with his teacher and postulated the existence of a "collective unconscious" at a deeper level of the psyche. The collective unconscious with its archetypes is more than Freudian unconscious with its repressed wishes and childhood fantasies. It is a consummate source of our collectivity and interconnectedness.

According to Jung (Jung & Pauli, 1955), any causal explanation of paranormal phenomena such as ESP is "unthinkable," because a causal interaction is always an "energetic" phenomenon bound by space-time limitations. The nonlocal nature of parapsychological phenomena—i.e., their presumed independence of space and time—suggests that they belong to another order of the universe. In contradistinction to the familiar causal order, Jung postulates a noncausal order that is composed of synchronistic phenomena. By synchronicity Jung means a noncausal relationship that links two events together in a meaningful way. It is a sort of meaningful coincidence, a coincidence that makes sense. Synchronicity, says Jung, applies to those cases of simultaneous occurrence of a certain psychological condition with one or more objective phenomena in which the meaning of the first is similar to the others that follow.

Synchronistic coincidences include the significant results in psi experiments and spontaneous psi occurrences but also the omens, successful astrological predictions, *I Ching* readings, and all kinds of physical effects that have no normal causal explanation. The following is one of the several personal experiences of synchronicity Jung (1963) reports, one that occurred in 1909 when Jung and Freud were discussing paranormal phenomena:

> While Freud was going on this way, I had a curious sensation. It was as if my diaphragm were made of iron and becoming red-hot—a glowing vault. And at that moment there was such a loud report in the bookcase, which stood right next to us, that we both started up in alarm, fearing the thing was going to topple over on us. I said to Freud: "There, that is an example of a so-called catalytic exteriorization phenomenon." "Oh come," he exclaimed. "That is sheer bosh." "It is not," I replied. "You are mistaken, Herr Professor. And to prove my point I now predict that in a moment there will be another such loud report!" Sure enough, no sooner had I said the words than the same detonation went off in the bookcase [Jung, 1963, p. 155].

Even though synchronous events literally mean those events that are simultaneous occurrences, Jung uses the concept of synchronicity to include even precognitive events. In the experience cited above, for example, the second explosion occurred after Jung's prediction of it. Spontaneous precognitive events do sometimes occur considerably later in time than their predictions. Jung did not seem to be concerned about the extent of duration between the event and its foreknowledge as a precondition for synchronistic precognition.

Flew (1953–1954) criticized this concept on the ground that "meaningful coincidence" is a tautology. He argued that coincidences are coincidences because they are meaningful. But by *meaningful* Jung seems to imply more than what Flew grants him, even though some examples of synchronicity given by Jung himself, devoid of their symbolism, appear to be no more than mere coincidences. In Jung's experience narrated above, the meaningfulness of the coincidence is derived by three factors: (1) The explosions occurred when the two men were discussing paranormal phenomena; (2) Jung predicted the occurrence of the second explosion with no ordinary means of knowing that such an explosion would occur again; and (3) no causal relationship is discernible between the discussion of paranormal phenomena by Jung and Freud and the first explosion or between Jung's awareness of the impending explosion and the subsequent detonation in the bookcase.

While Jung is unequivocal in his denial of any causal relationship between the synchronistic events, he does not deny that each of the synchronistically related events may have its own causal ancestors. For example, it is possible that the explosions may have had natural explanations; but what is of interest is that they happened when they did.

Even granting Jung's assumption that it is futile to look for causal connections between synchronistic events, we are still left with the problem of distinguishing true synchronistic events from chance coincidences; i.e., the coincidences that are "meaningful" from those that are not. The concept would make sense if we could explain how the synchronistic events, as opposed to non-synchronistic events, come to pass. This is the most crucial aspect of synchronistic theory and unfortunately the most difficult one from the point of view of knowing what precisely Jung's views were. It is no easy task to reconcile Jung's own writings on this subject or the interpretations given by his followers. One reason for this state of affairs is that, for Jung, synchronicity is a metaphysical principle and is intended to explain more than what we now regard as parapsychological phenomena.

A parapsychological situation, whether it is causal or synchronistic, has two elements that need to be related: a series of mental events within the subject and one or more events outside of the subject. The subjective psychic events have their own causation. According to Jung, in a synchronistic situation the psychic events are mediated by the archetypes, which are dispositions of the collective unconscious. The archetypes are not themselves in consciousness but are represented in it by archetypal images and symbols. As mediators or vehicles, the archetypes themselves are insufficient to account for the content of the synchronistic psychic event. The true source is located at the deeper levels of our psyche—the psychoid level. At this level, the psyche, a microcosm, "reflects" the universe, the macrocosm. While discussing Swedenborg's vision of the Stockholm fire, Jung (1969) says, "The fire in Stockholm was, in a sense, burning in him too" (p. 481). As Progoff has pointed out, Jung seems to be providing the psychological phenomenology of Leibniz's concept of the monad "mirroring" the universe. To quote Progoff (1973): "Once the functioning of a significant part of the psyche has dropped to the psychoid depth, the individual, as microcosm, is in a condition at which a part of his psyche is able to "catch" the "reflections" of the surrounding macrocosm to describe them and make them articulate" (p. 115).

The basic assumption, then, is that there is latent in the unconscious a capacity for foreknowledge that can operate without such intermediaries as the senses. In extrasensory perception, we draw on this latent capacity by the process of *abasement*, a "lowering of the mental level." Since the psyche functions by means of a "dynamic balancing process," a lowering of consciousness on one side leads to a corresponding intensification of consciousness on the other. Such a "lowering," then, makes the psyche open to the full impact of the archetypal factors at the psychoid level. It activates the latent capacity for extended awareness without the usual intermediaries. This becomes possible because the psyche at its deepest level is a microcosm that "reflects" the macrocosm, the universe.

Thus, in his attempts to avoid any explanation of the paranormal based on "magical causality," Jung is led to assume that our unconscious in a significant sense is capable of omniscience, which on occasions becomes available to conscious experience through archetypal images and symbols. The emergence of these images into consciousness at the experiential level may be simultaneous with, prior to, or after the occurrence of the related external event. So we have contemporaneous, precognitive, or retrocognitive psi experiences. The "meaningfulness" of the coincidence is then a function of the "mirroring" effect—i.e., the reflection of the macroscopic event in the microcosm of our unconscious. In nonsynchronistic coincidences there are presumably no such reflections.

Now, let us consider the event, the detonation in Freud's bookcase, as an example of a paranormal event and attempt to interpret it in synchronistic acausal terms. The knowledge of the detonations is potentially available to the unconscious of Jung as well as of Freud. But this knowledge was mediated into Jung's awareness alone after the first detonation and shortly before the second. Therefore, the coincidences became meaningful to Jung and not to Freud, who apparently did not experience a similar "reflection" of his unconscious. The alternative explanations to this are (1) that the impending detonation somehow caused awareness in Jung, or (2) that Jung himself in some paranormal way caused the explosion in the bookcase. The first of these two is ruled out because it is impossible for a nonexistent external event to cause awareness. The second involves some sort of a PK effect, which would imply again a cause-effect relationship. If a natural sequence of events is shown to have caused the detonation in the bookcase, then, of course PK is ruled out. However, whether PK occurred in this instance or not, in the light of substantial evidence for PK, Jung's hypothesis that in synchronistic situations external events are experienced as reflections in the unconscious through the mediation of the archetypes needs extension.

As Aniela Jaffe (quoted by Bender, 1977) points out, synchronicity is scarcely an explanation of PK:

> Jung's hint at the psychical relativity of time and space, "then the moving body must possess, or be subject to, corresponding relativity," does not lead us much further. He did not mention the question of psychokinesis with much more than this short remark. But in his work as well as in his letters he does hint at a possibility that the psyche can influence nonpsychical things in some way and that, therefore, there may exist some so-to-speak causal relation [Bender, 1977, p. 75].

In order to explain PK, Jung would have to assume that the archetypes, which are assumed to be capable of mediating the unconscious "knowledge" into consciousness, might also be able to exert their influence on and create events extending beyond the experiencing subject. This idea is implied in the concept of archetype as "psychoid." Being at the limits of our observational ability, it eludes our categorization into physical or psychical. When an archetype is activated, it may influence the external events as well as the images in the mind of the person involved in the synchronistic situation.

The omniscience of the unconscious and its capacity to effect changes in the environment are no new assumptions in parapsychology. What seems to be important in Jung's theory is the suggestion that the archetypes are involved as mediating agents and that the process of *abasement* is important for archetypal activation that would result in paranormal experiences. These ideas are capable of empirical testing and provide the basis for interaction between Jungians and parapsychologists.

L.L. Gatlin (1977) makes use of Jung's synchronicity concept for a generic interpretation of psi. She argues that the failure to identify a physical carrier of psi information suggests that there is no such carrier and that no transmission of information takes place in ESP. Instead, information is created via the mechanism of synchronicity. Gatlin questions the commonly made assumption that there is some kind of an interaction between the target and the subject. The possibility of success in a precognitive situation rules this out because meaningful information cannot be transmitted backward in time.

Psi situations may be regarded as hierarchically structured situations of ascending levels of complexity where a unit can be seen either as a part of a larger whole or as the whole of some parts. A hit is ordinarily considered to be the elementary unit of psi, and the parapsychologists had hoped to find an explanation in an interaction that would bring about the target-response match. Gatlin argues that this is a wrong way of looking at the psi situation. The subject's response is not caused by the target; at the same time the response is not causeless. Again, Gatlin suggests, the target sequence is not so random as we often tend to believe. The concept of a "random finite sequence is an unattainable ideal" (p. 8). Thus, once we realize what the hierarchies involved are, we could see that the individual hits are acausal inasmuch as the target response matchings may now be seen as the matching of bias in target and response sources. Gatlin points out:

> It does seem intuitively reasonable that two biased sources chosen at random from nature would not match to the extent we sometimes observe, but have been tuned to synchronize by some kind of interaction. However, and this is the heart of the matter, this tuning process does not have to occur (a) during the course of the experiment per se (ESP, PK, etc.). It does not even have to occur (b) in the pre-experiment subject-experimenter-environment interaction. It could possibly have occurred (c) even further back in time by slow evolutionary processes which have sorted biological sources into a finite number of discrete informational categories such that the probability is high that two of them will match by coincidence without significant interaction in the present [Gatlin, 1977, p. 14].

Gatlin recognizes that the matching of target and response bias may itself be acausal and that such a matching, in its turn, may be traced to "higher level synchronistic mechanisms which operate on a cosmic scale" (p. 15).

While Gatlin's conjecture may seem prima facie plausible to explain spontaneous ESP, particularly of the telepathic kind, where one could assume synchronization between the built-in biases of the two biological sources (the percipient and the agent), it is difficult to conceive that in an experimental psi situation the subjective and genetic bias of the subject somehow mysteriously synchronize with the assumed bias of the target sequence. Gatlin has not been convincing in explaining how and at what level of the hierarchical organization the acausal relation between the subject source and the target sources becomes causally related. One implication of Gatlin's theory, however, has some merit. It makes sense to assume that in some cases the subject may not respond in a target-by-target fashion. In fact, psi may simply instigate a bias in the subject's response pattern, a bias that would synchronize with the inherent bias of the target sequence so that more of his responses would match with the targets than otherwise. Some research on this question is clearly called for. May, Utts & Spottiswoode (1995) have already made a beginning in this regard with their decision augmentation theory.

Koestler (1972) found it painful to see Jung entangle himself in the verbiage of causality when he seems to assign a causative role to archetypes in producing psi effects. Koestler argued that synchronicity is an ultimate and irreducible principle and is complementary to mechanical causation. He saw in parapsychological phenomena the highest manifestation of nature's integrative tendency to create order out of disorder. He argued that recent developments in physics and biology as well as parapsychology seem to point this out. "Everything," writes Koestler, "hangs together; no atom is an island; microcosm reflects macrocosm, and is reflected by it" (Hardy, Harvie & Koestler, 1973, p. 261). Elsewhere he writes about some sort of "psychomagnetic field" that is credited with producing synchronistic or confluential events that are not subject to the laws of classical physics. Its modus operandi at this time is unknown, but it may be "related to that striving towards higher forms of order and unity-in-variety which we observe in the evolution of the universe..." (Koestler, 1972, p. 128). For a more detailed discussion of the psychological aspects of synchronity and psychic experiences see Atmanspacher & Fach, 2013).

Summary

Writing about theories and models of psi, C.T.K. Chari (1977) observed that the "field is strewn with dead and dying hypotheses and desperate expedients" (p. 806). Many of the theories we have surveyed are tentative and exploratory, often no more than descriptions. While none is entirely satisfactory in explaining psi, each of them seems to contain some fruitful ideas. The growing emphasis on testable hypotheses and falsifiable models augurs well for the advancement of psi research. The factor that distinguishes parapsychology from the occult is the former's commitment to scientific method. A theory that permits no deductive development and makes no verifiable predictions can seldom contribute to the growth of a science. The critical need is for theory and research to go hand in hand. Psi researchers are trying hard to do just this. So far their attempts have not been very successful either because of the inappropriate models they are working with or because of inadequate methods to test the implications of their models.

In the above discussions of theories of psi one thing seems to stand out prominently. That is, at some level, we function as if we were omniscient or omnipresent. Even the physical theories such as the observational theories, inasmuch as they postulate non-locality, are conceding the possibility of pervasive interconnectedness in the universe. Such an interconnectedness is a necessary precondition for any kind of omniscience for apparently isolated individuals. The psychological models, including Stanford's conformance behavior model, do seem to imply and warrant a paranormal process as stage one in the two-stage psi process. The paranormal process in turn requires a universal matrix such as the collective unconscious or omniscience at the level of individual consciousness. The acausal theory of Jung, as discussed, must also concede that the individual psyche is a microcosm that reflects the macrocosm, the universe. The major problems the theories face include the question of dirigibility and the selection mechanism in the case of collective consciousness and the matter of non-locality in the case of individual consciousness. Thus, the crucial issue, it would seem, is the relationship between consciousness at the level of the individual and consciousness that encompasses the universe. It is on this problem that the attempts to explain psi appear to falter.

Investigation of the "physical" hypotheses, directed toward finding a new medium of psi communication, will at best reveal the limiting conditions of psi. Today, no one really knows what the outer boundaries of psi are. To assume a priori that ESP can reach any object, however remote it may be in space or time, that it can make possible such feats as speaking in unknown languages and exhibiting unlearned skills, or that PK can influence any target without regard to its size and kind, indicates a naïve optimism. It is just as important to learn what psi cannot accomplish as it is to discover what it can. Testing for psi within the physical paradigm is best suited for such determination.

The psychological hypotheses are likely to be the ones that will give us insights into the psychological processes involved in psi cognitions. It is not unlikely that psi is a manifestation of not one process but two. If indeed psi involves a two stage process, one that accounts for the information content of psi and the other for explaining the actual manifestation of that content either as awareness or response, then the psychological theories may provide helpful insights into the second stage of the psi process.

The paranormal theories are likely to be the ones that are best suited to explain the stage one psi process. For example, the theories that postulate the common or collective unconscious offer explanatory models that provide for the observed lack of space-time constraints that govern psi manifestation. They are confronted, however, with the problem of explaining the selection process involved in receiving psi messages. Projection hypotheses, such as those contained in the shin theory, attempt to overcome this problem. The testing of the projection hypotheses, which place the principle of psi operation and its energetic source in the individual rather than in the target object, will likely provide important information about subject variables.

Most of the paranormal hypotheses, like the physical ones, are derived from what may be called the *interaction model*—a model that assumes the independence of the subject and the target in a psi situation and regards the subject-target interaction as essential for psi manifestation. Acausal theories plead for abandoning the interaction model in favor of what may be called the *intuition model.*

Acausal hypotheses have the merit of questioning some of the classical assumptions concerning subject-target relationships. They, more than any others, show the basic inappropriateness of the stimulus response model of psi. In a significant sense there is a prima facie absurdity in any attempt to connect the subject and the target in a psi situation. Take for example the question of precognition. The target by definition is nonexistent at the moment of the subject's cognition of it. The vain attempts to connect the subject with a nonexisting event lead us to such paradoxical notions of other dimensions of time and different orders of reality (Flew, 1976). Acausal models assume a subject-target identification. Thus there is no distance to travel or no time to scan between the subject and the target. Every subject is a microcosm, potentially capable of reflecting the whole cosmos. This potential is not realized because we are habitually and constitutionally given to respond to and interact with our environment rather than to probe within to discover hidden knowledge. Our sensory and motor systems are eminently suited for this and we have learned to depend on them through our developmental process. Psi events do seem to indicate, however, that this is not an irreversible process and that on occasion knowledge can be had by tapping one's inner resources.

Whether we opt for an interaction model or for the intuition model, we are in a theoretical quagmire because of the inherent limitations of these models. The interaction models are caught in the perceived absurdities of action at a distance and knowing about nonexistent objects and events. The intuition model suffers from the neglect of the dirigibility aspect of psi and the role of human intentions in psi manifestations. The root problem, however, may rest with our obsession for a unified theory of awareness. It is possible that there are different sorts of awareness, each with its own unique characteristics. Consciousness may look like a "stream" from one perspective and as the "mother sea" from another perspective. There may be then a need for different conceptual maps and methodological tools for describing and investigating the various forms in which consciousness manifests. Therefore, from the above review, it would seem that proper and unambiguous understanding of what consciousness is and how it manifests may be a precondition for understanding and explaining psi.

The discussion of cognitive anomalies in this work has been restricted so far primarily to the attempts in the West to scientifically study them, which are of relatively recent origin. There is a long and continuing tradition in India that accords a distinctive place for psychic phenomena in its epistemologies. The ideas relevant to psi and its application are embedded in the epistemologies of the different schools of Indian thought.

Western theories are meant mostly to explain statistical psi. Indian theory deals essentially with macro-events. The possibility exists that these two models may be utterly different and that the anomalous statistical deviations observed in the scientific investigations in the West may refer to something radically different from the *siddhis* practiced in the Indian psychological tradition. At any rate, this author now thinks that the statistical research of the kind reviewed herein may do no more than suggest the existence of an anomaly. Its process and what it means may not be fully known. Replication and application may remain elusive goals. However, from the traditional Indian perspective the situation is very different. Replicability and application are built into the very conception of *siddhis*. It took over half a century of direct involvement in the statistical type of psi research for me to realize this. It will be discussed in some detail in the following chapter. What has been reviewed and the discussions bearing on them are my reflections before new insights incorporating the Indian tradition of *siddhis* had dawned.

9

The Unsettled State: Postscript to Sixty Years in Parapsychology

What this author has described and discussed so far is almost entirely the inquiry into psychic abilities in the Western tradition. Parapsychological phenomena, however, are observed worldwide. The attempts to systematically study psychic events in India are at least as old as yoga. Parapsychology itself, however, as we have seen, is of relatively recent origin, which can be justifiably traced to the founding of the Society for Psychical Research (SPR) in 1882 in England. The roots of SPR and the motivation for starting it may not be traced to yoga, which undoubtedly is the earliest—and in a significant sense the continuing—science of psychic phenomena (*siddhis*).

The starting point of the SPR researchers was the reported experiences of people and their important bearing, if true, on religious beliefs and spiritual practices. While there is thus little connection between the Indian science of *siddhis* and Western psychical research, which came to be known as parapsychology, the reports of the SPR and the publication of the results of scientific research into paranormal phenomena has had profound impact on Indian philosophers and scholars like S. Radhakrishnan who were exposed to research reports coming out of the SPR and related work in Europe and the United States. Because of the traditional beliefs in the possibility of the *siddhis* and their acquisition through certain mind-body controlling practices, the results of psychical research are readily taken in India as modern scientific proof for *siddhis*, whereas in the West they remained essentially as anomalies.

I am one of those caught in the cross-currents of Western psychical research and classical Indian thought. Having received for nearly sixty years significant inflows from both sides, experienced the trials and turbulence, and faced the challenges and successes that came in the way, I am tempted to offer an autobiographical account of my sixty-plus years in parapsychology as a postscript to the book. Such an account may have some historical relevance and some lessons may be learned for the future of the field.

My first research publication in this area appeared 62 years ago as I wrote (Rao, 1955). Interestingly it starts with an East-West dialogue, discussing *Vedanta* and parapsychology. Since then, I had the privilege of (a) studying and working with J.B. Rhine, the acknowledged father of experimental parapsychology, at Duke University, (b) being elected on three different occasions as the president of the Parapsychological Association (PA), the international professional society of scientists engaged in parapsychological research around the world with its base in the U.S., (c) establishing and heading the one and only statutory department for studying parapsychology in India at Andhra University, (d) heading the premier parapsychology research establishment founded by Rhine for nearly twenty years, and (e) editing the *Journal of Parapsychology* for eighteen years. How did I come to play these different roles? What have I learned? What is the progress made by parapsychologists over this period? Where is the field now heading?

The first ten years or so of my parapsychological study and research was a period of preparation. The next 25 years represent active professional participation in advancing parapsychological research. The last twenty-five years have been a period of reflection and puzzlement. The following biographical reminiscence and review of these three periods may be of some historical and professional interest.

The Beginning

My entry into parapsychology is neither by accident nor premeditated. As a graduate student in philosophy and psychology at Andhra University, I was studying Indian philosophy with Prof. Saileswara Sen, the outstanding scholar with special interest in *Navya-Nyaya*. I recall Karl Potter, a student at Harvard University then, came to study with Prof. Sen. In his classes we were discussing *Vedanta* and *Brahman*. We were told that *Brahman* is the absolute underlying reality, pure consciousness, realizable only in transcognitive states. The very next hour, following Indian philosophy classes, I was attending psychology classes. It was the heyday of behaviorism. We were studying behavior in a deterministic paradigm and within the stimulus-response framework. Conditioning is the over-arching law governing behavior, we were taught. There is no place for mind or consciousness. So this sudden shift from one hour to the next, day after day, from *Brahman* to behaviorism was not easy to handle, because my interest was more than passing the exams and getting a good grade. The gap between Brahman consciousness and stimulus driven behavior appeared too wide to bridge.

The incompatibility of the two worldviews concerning human nature, one expounded in my Indian philosophy classes and the other implied in the Western psychology I was learning, and the consequent experience of cognitive dissonance led me to confront Prof. Sen. One morning as he was eloquently elaborating the *Advaita* concept of *Brahman* and the *Saṃkhya–Yoga* concept of *Puruṣa* as pure consciousness I tried to argue that in light of the developments in psychology, which is a scientific study of human nature, it is time that we abandoned the worn out speculations of a bygone age and move on to embrace a worldview consistent with the scientific understanding of the universe and our place in it. I was afraid that I might have offended the professor whom I admired in many ways. He was visibly startled and taken aback a little because we seldom raised such questions in the class. He quickly regained his composure, as I recall, simply smiled and did not attempt to rebut. He said, "Yes, I understand what you are saying. I want you to read two books written not by Indian authors but by a British scholar and an American scientist, and then come back. Then we will discuss the questions you raised." I was humbled, but glad that there might be a way to reduce my dissonance. The two books he mentioned were *Human Personality and Its Survival of Bodily Death* by F.W.H. Myers (1903/1915) and *Extrasensory Perception,* a monograph by J.B. Rhine (1934).

That was my first introduction to parapsychology. When I met Prof. Sen a few weeks later, he explained to me how parapsychology could be a bridge to connect *"Brahman"* and "behavior," the apparently opposing perspectives, and reconcile some salient features of Indian tradition concerning human nature with scientific understanding of the mind. I was relieved and excited. I was relieved because my questioning took a positive turn; and was truly excited at the prospect of exploring this uncharted territory in East-West dialogue. I began reading parapsychology books and the *Journal* and the *Proceedings* of the *Society for Psychical Research* and opted to write my M.A. (Hons.) dissertation on the subject of parapsychology. Prof. Sen died soon after I settled on this topic. Dr. Satchidananda Murthy supervised my dissertation. It was published in 1957 under the title *Psi Cognition* (Rao, 1957) with a foreword by J.B. Rhine. My deepest disappointment was that Prof. Sen did not live to see the completion of my dissertation and the publication of the book, which would have pleased him immensely.

Andhra University Library had a good collection of books on parapsychology and a complete set of the *Journal* and *Proceedings* of the Society for Psychical Research dating back to 1882. Dr. S. Radhakrishnan, an outstanding exponent of Indian philosophy, served earlier as vice-chancellor of Andhra University. During his tenure he helped to build this excellent collection. Later when Dr. Radhakrishnan was the president of India, I had the privilege of presenting to him a copy of my book *Psi Cognition.* He encouraged me to continue to work in this field, which he saw, as Prof. Sen did, as a viable bridge between contemporary Western science and classical Indian thought.

My readings in parapsychology, as I prepared for writing my dissertation, convinced me of the reality of ESP. I could not for example conceive of any possible alternatives to ESP to explain the results of the Pearce-Pratt experiment. I was enthusiastic about getting professionally involved and was eager to study with Rhine and observe and learn firsthand the exciting new science. In 1956 I applied for a Smith-Mundt Fulbright Scholarship and was chosen. I sent in my application for admission to the Ph.D. in psychology program at Duke University with an explicit statement of interest in working in parapsychology with Rhine. I was selected and was all set to sail to the U.S. in June of 1957. Hardly a month before my expected departure, there came a telegram from the Fulbright administrator in India, Dr. Olive I. Reddick, advising me to stop making further preparations to go to the U.S. The fellowship was withdrawn, as they could not find a placement for me at Duke, the only university I chose to attend. Then, I learned from Rhine that though he was a professor at Duke, his establishment was separate from the psychology department, he no longer taught in that department, and there was no teaching program available at Duke to do a doctorate in parapsychology. This was my first encounter with the uneasy relationship between parapsychology and the mainstream academic psychology in the U.S.

I was disappointed but did not despair. The next year I applied again but this time to study philosophy at the University of Chicago. By then, I had come to know Prof. Richard McKeon, an Aristotelian scholar and a distinguished professor of philosophy at Chicago. Prof. McKeon visited our department in India during 1957 when I was a provisional (temporary) head. We took a liking to each other and he encouraged me to apply again for a Fulbright fellowship and to give his name as a reference. By then I also applied for a British Council Fellowship to study parapsychological concepts at Oxford with Gilbert Ryle. I was fortunate to have been selected for both. I chose to go to the United States rather than to Oxford because my mind was set on Rhine, Duke and parapsychology. As soon as I arrived in the U.S. during the summer of 1958, even before going to Chicago, I went to Durham and spent two weeks with Rhine and his colleagues at Duke's Parapsychology Laboratory. That was love at first sight. I admired Rhine even before; but I now became very fond of him as a person and scientist. Rhine was not disappointed with me either. He gave me an open invitation to come back and join him any time I wanted. As soon as I completed my work at the University of Chicago, I went back to Duke for a few months' stint, before I left for India at the end of 1960.

My stay at the University of Chicago was uneventful as far as parapsychology was concerned, even though I kept in touch with the developments in the field and the people working in it. However, it was possibly the most important period in laying a solid foundation for theoretical and philosophical scholarship. The training I received at Andhra University was no match to the logical rigor and the intellectual and scholarly demands at the University of Chicago. If my philosophical mind was cast at Andhra University, it was shaped and sharpened at the University of Chicago.

While at Duke with Rhine, I had firsthand exposure to the field and to the research that was ongoing. I met many of the people involved in actively contributing to research at the time—such as J.G. Pratt, L.E. Rhine, Karlis Osis, Gertrude Schmeidler, Robert McConnell, Margaret Anderson, Rhea White, William Roll and others. I was duly impressed by their credentials, commitment, competence and professionalism.

On return to India, I attempted to carry out some research in parapsychology on my own; but found myself alone and inadequately equipped. I felt I needed more training in research methodology and better grounding and sophistication in statistical applications. So I went back again to Duke, taking advantage of Rhine's open invitation to complete the final phase of preparation to become a full-fledged parapsychologist. On leave from Andhra University, I spent three years, 1962 to 1965, working in Rhine's Parapsychology Laboratory at Duke University as a postdoctoral fellow.

This period saw me grow as a scientist. A tender-minded scholar with interests in philosophy and theoretical psychology was transformed into a tough-minded empirical researcher. I carried out several successful experiments and wrote the book *Experimental Parapsychology* (Rao, 1966), a review and interpretation of research during the preceding quarter century. I was also elected as president of the Parapsychological Association, the U.S.-based international organization of professional parapsychologists.

Many other interesting and eventful things happened during my three years with Rhine at Duke. At a personal level, unaware and unappreciated at the time, my theoretical interests, which started me in parapsychology, receded into the background. I began whole-heartedly embracing methodological behaviorism. Notwithstanding the frequent talk about the nonphysicality and nonmaterial nature of psi that Rhine indulged in via his popular writings, his research methods were completely positivistic and behaviorist. Rhine was intent on uncompromisingly pursuing the goal of "naturalizing the supernatural" that his mentor William McDougall had set for the field of parapsychology. It would seem that I went further than Rhine in taking a positivist stance. The *Brahman* was forgotten. I was left with just behavior. While at Duke, I confess that I developed a "holier than thou" attitude and was ready to go beyond the methodological behaviorism that Rhine practiced. I characterized him as a vitalist with all his obsession with the concept of the mind. I criticized his notion of nonphysicality of *psi* as inconsistent and in a sense clearly nonsensical. This of course did not endear me to Rhine. His displeasure showed up in the Foreword he wrote at my request to be published in my book *Experimental Parapsychology*. I politely declined to use it; and neither of us was unhappy with that alternative.

Indian Interest

At another level also, the events during those years were of great consequence. Dr. D.S. Kothari, chairman of the University Grants Commission (UGC), happened to read a review of my earlier book *Psi Cognition* in the *Main Currents of Modern Thought*. He wrote me congratulating and complimenting me on my work. Dr. Kothari was a distinguished theoretical physicist who had worked at Delhi University. At the time, he was heading the University Grants Commission, an autonomous body of the government of India, which provides major developmental funding to Indian universities. Thrilled by this unexpected positive feedback from Dr. Kothari, I thanked him for his generous compliments and encouraging words and informed him of what I was doing at Duke University in Rhine's Laboratory.

Quickly I got another letter asking if I could come back to India and help to start a parapsychology research center at one of the Indian universities with the financial support of the UGC. When I told Rhine about this, he enthusiastically endorsed the proposal and expressed his willingness to support it. So, I traveled to India and J.G. Pratt, who also happened to be in India at that time, joined me. We two visited a number of universities in India and gave a report to the UGC on starting a parapsychology center. Based on our report, the UGC sanctioned funds to start the Department of Psychology and Parapsychology at Andhra University.

During my visit to New Delhi, Prof. Kothari arranged for me to meet among others, Sri Gulzarilal Nanda, the Minister for Home, the second in command in the government of India, Dr. Srimali, the minister in charge of education, Prof. Mahalnobes, a statistician of great distinction, and Dr. B.K. Anand, a physiologist at the All India Institute of Medical Sciences whose work on Indian yogins was beginning to be known. All of them were very supportive of the new venture and gave me lots of suggestions as how I should go about organizing this center. Similarly, when I and Gaither Pratt visited several universities across the country, all of them without exception came forward to host the center if the UGC decided to give them the required funds.

Back at Duke, Rhine and I embarked on the process of training prospective researchers from India who might work at the Indian center. Ms. Kanthamani, Ms. Sailaja and Mr. Bhadra were given fellowships to enable them to study at the Parapsychology Laboratory at Duke. A senior professor of psychology from Sri Venkateswara University, Prof. S. Parthasarathi joined. We the Indians were the largest group at Rhine's lab during that period.

I returned to India in July 1965. Kanthamani and Sailaja joined me; and they were enrolled as Ph.D. students. There were some delays and uncertainties in setting up the center, largely because of local conditions in Visakhapatnam and Andhra University, but eventually the Department of Psychology and Parapsychology came into being with full financial support from the University Grants Commission. It should be mentioned that this Department came into being solely to develop parapsychology at the level of teaching and research. I added psychology to it because of my interest in pursuing parapsychology as a branch of psychology.

As I moved back to India, Rhine, who had retired from Duke, was making his moves to organize the Institute for Parapsychology under the auspices of the Foundation for Research on the Nature of Man, across the east campus of Duke. Pratt left Rhine to join Ian Stevenson at the University of Virginia. Chuck Honorton, Rex Stanford, and Sally Feather and Robert Brier joined Rhine's new establishment.

The Department of Psychology and Parapsychology (DPP) at Andhra University began admitting students for master's and doctoral programs. Soon the DPP carved for itself an important niche at Andhra University. It acquired its own building and a well equipped lab and an excellent collection of books. There was a large output of research publications. Six students were awarded Ph.D. degrees for their work in parapsychology. The first two of them received gold medals for having the most outstanding dissertations among all those submitted in the disciplines of social sciences and humanities at Andhra University for two consecutive years. The Department became a showpiece for the University. The chief-minister of Andhra Pradesh at that time, Sri Vengala Rao, came to witness the ongoing research on a yogin. I was proud of what we were able to achieve within a short span of time.

The Institute for Parapsychology at the FRNM was started with some very dedicated and competent young researchers well groomed and trained by Rhine. However, there were soon some problems. Many of the young people, including Honorton and Stanford, left the FRNM, in what appeared to be a revolt against and a defiance of Rhine. Undaunted by this unexpected and clearly severe setback, Rhine continued to attract needed personnel to work at the institute, such as Helmut Schmidt. Among the new recruits was Jay Levy, a medical graduate who soon impressed Rhine as a very capable and committed researcher. Levy began to work with animals, published several papers and was groomed to succeed Rhine to lead the Institute.

Things looked brighter and more promising than ever for the field of parapsychology. The Parapsychological Association (PA) grew into a viable professional body, holding its annual conventions in different parts of the world. The PA was admitted as an affiliate member of the American Association for the Advancement of Science with support from people like anthropologist Margaret Mead. The Parapsychological Foundation established by Eileen Garrett, and the American Society for Psychical Research with Karl Osis as the director of research were active. The group headed by Montague Ullman at Maimonides Medical Center in Brooklyn, New York, was making important strides exploring ESP in dreams. In other places Gertrude Schmeidler, Charles Tart, William Roll and William Braud were making important research contributions. John Beloff at the University of Edinburgh started his own program. Ian Stevenson and his team at the University of Virginia were vigorously pursuing their reincarnation research.

As I began organizing the new department at Andhra University, I started refocusing on the larger context that brought me into parapsychology, going beyond the narrow confines of experimental parapsychology. It seemed that I was rediscovering my roots again. The very fact that I chose to set up the Department of Psychology and Parapsychology and not just a department or center for parapsychology, is indicative of the implicit desire that parapsychology grow along with mainstream psychology. I was beginning to refocus on consciousness studies and Indian psychology with the goal of integrating parapsychology with broader nonreductionist psychology. Three of my students received Ph.D. degrees for their research in the area of nocturnal dreaming. Things were going well for me personally and professionally at Andhra University and in India. I was elected as a member of the Syndicate, the Executive Council of Andhra University and was just a step away from being the vice-chancellor, the academic and the executive head of the University.

Jay Levy

Professionally, things never looked so good for parapsychology around the world. We were all upbeat. Then suddenly tragedy struck at the place it was least suspected. Jay Levy, the designated successor to Rhine, was at the center of the storm that shook the very foundations of the Institute that Rhine was attempting to build as the world center for parapsychology. People assisting Levy in his experiments to study ESP in animals became suspicious that Levy might be manipulating the results of his experiments. They laid out and executed a cleverly conceived trap, and were convinced that their suspicions were well founded. Confronted with the data and the circumstances, Rhine agreed with the junior colleagues of Levy and fired Levy. And it was national news, carried among others by *Time* magazine.

At age 75, this was a severe blow to Rhine. His foes inside and outside the field did not take it kindly. Honorton, a former student protégé of Rhine, was the president of the Parapsychological Association and chairman of the Program Committee of the ensuing PA annual convention in Santa Barbara, California. Honorton rejected the papers submitted by researchers working at Rhine's Institute for Parapsychology for presentation at the convention. It was a brazen and unwise attempt to isolate Rhine.

Around this time, I happened to be in the U.S., primarily to attend in Los Angeles an international parapsychology conference convened by the Parapsychology Foundation (PF). Before going to Los Angeles I spent a few weeks at Rhine's Institute. I was informed about the Levy affair in all its detail and the fallout from it by Rhine and others working at the Institute including those who exposed Levy. I also visited Honorton in New York and had a chance to know his stance vis-à-vis the papers submitted by people at Rhine's Institute. I counseled Honorton against the rejection and gently warned him of the consequences for the field, apart from the unfairness involved. He did not relent.

After the PF sponsored conference in Los Angeles, I attended the PA Annual Convention in Santa Barbara. As the president of the PA, Honorton opened the conference with a statement that he had rejected the submissions from the FRNM. He gave his reasons for it. I was incensed and angry as were many others. I got up and raised my hand. Honorton graciously recognized me and I was given a chance to speak my mind. With equal bluntness and undisguised outrage, I accused Honorton of playing politics, undermining the PA, and harming the field. I was pleasantly surprised at the spontaneous loud applause and cheering at the conclusion of my comments that clearly showed that most of the people in attendance were with me and felt that Honorton had erred.

The damage was already done, however. Levy's exposé set the house on fire. Rhine responded forthrightly and in a statesmanlike manner that helped in important ways to save his own image and to a lesser extent that of his Institute. However, my own assessment is that the field as a whole suffered. The leadership of the field at the time did not show the same maturity and wisdom as Rhine did.

Soon after the Parapsychological Association annual convention, I returned to India and back to work at Andhra University. Of course, our work was not affected in any way by the Levy scandal. For one thing, we were geographically remote and for another, our group was not dependent on external funding. We were fully supported by the University and the University Grants Commission. As an active member of the Executive Council (then called the University Syndicate) of Andhra University—its main governing body—I was able to ensure the continued support of Andhra University to the Department of Psychology and Parapsychology.

In our continued exchanges, Rhine told me that he was looking for a suitable person to head his Institute and sounded me out for possible interest. He fully realized my commitment to what we were doing in India, but always felt that somehow the center of action was FRNM and no other place in the world. Rhine attempted to impress on me why it was so important to "save" FRNM and secure for it the coveted place of pride for parapsychology. I was flattered when he said during my visit to his office in Durham, North Carolina, that I was the person who could help him complete the job he started. Rhine was known to be very forceful and persuasive. He certainly was on this occasion. I relented and agreed to spend three years at the FRNM's Institute for Parapsychology as its director, on leave from Andhra University. Once again Andhra University was generous to sanction leave for three years.

No one in the Department of Psychology and Parapsychology was ready at the time to take the mantle of heading it. So, it was a tough decision to take. The parapsychology program at Andhra had a good start. It was ready to take off. Unlike many other centers, we had complete financial security to continue the program indefinitely. I began playing an increasingly prominent role in the affairs of the university. Already the most important of my colleagues in the group, Dr. Kanthamani, left Andhra University and joined Rhine's Institute. The reasons for my decision to temporarily join Rhine's establishment included (a) strong persuasion from Rhine that my being at his Institute at that critical juncture was more important for the field of parapsychology than my staying at Andhra University; (b) I felt that I should entrust more responsibility and give more visibility to my colleagues and also (c) I was confident that I could ensure that the program at the University would not suffer because I was going to be away only for a few years and that Prof. S. Parthasarathy, whom I persuaded to deputize for me, had agreed to move to Visakhapatnam and help. To facilitate his move, we found a place for his daughter Dr. Mythili in the Department at Andhra University as a lecturer. Dr. Sailaja was given the temporary responsibility to head the program.

In hindsight, it would appear, I was wrong. Whether or not I succeeded in "saving" the FRNM as J.B. Rhine wished, I clearly failed in my responsibilities for the Department of Psychology and Parapsychology and especially to the parapsychology program there that was entrusted to me by D.S. Kothari and the University Grants Commission. There were several reasons for this unexpected outcome. First and foremost is my decision to stay back in the U.S. beyond the initial three-year period. This was again at the urging of Rhine that I should not leave in the middle but should stay until a successor was groomed, which we hoped would take place within two or three years. Andhra University had agreed to extend my leave of absence further, until 1982. Then Rhine died; the complete burden of managing the FRNM, beyond directing research at the Institute for Parapsychology, I had to shoulder. I felt that I had no choice but to stay in the United States and stay for good. So with utmost reluctance and sadness I had to give up my position at Andhra University.

Thus I was guilty of leaving the ship in mid-voyage as far as the program of parapsychology at Andhra was concerned. Without the captain the ship drifted and in significant ways it changed course. Parapsychology was sidelined. Except for the four students who enrolled for their Ph.D. degrees in parapsychology when I was there, no fresh research in parapsychology was undertaken. Enthusiasm for parapsychology that was so much in the air during my tenure as the head of the Department had gradually declined to almost the point of disappearance.

Back in the U.S., I continued strictly the Rhinean experimental legacy, shelving my personal preference for integrating psi research into related areas of human science because it did not appear prudent or feasible in the American setting. We continued to accumulate more and more data testing what now seem to me trivial hypotheses. Our work, as most of the work in parapsychology, was fundamentally data-driven, rather than theoretically oriented. It was methodologically sound and rigorous, but theoretically lacking strength and significance. By and large, the posture of those in the field was defensive maundering to the groundless surmises and gratuitous suggestions of the critics, when they should be aggressively pursuing the challenges the phenomena posed. We were too timid to draw the logical conclusions of the reality of psi. The goal, it seemed, was to seek admission into the portals of science rather than try to make a difference. The cry by the "guardians of science" to drive the "pseudos" out— rather than an attempt to absorb the leads provided by the reality of psi to unlock the mocking mysteries of the human mind—is, I believe, the direct consequence of parapsychology's posture to gain scientific respectability rather than show its practical utility and theoretical relevance.

In parapsychology there has been a continuing obsessive concern with methodology rather than with the meaning of their search. Parapsychologists were overly defensive. They continue to fear the sacred and the spiritual. Their insulation within the protective walls of their own limited professional group reminds of the creatures caught in the cocoons of their own creation. I was no exception, remarkably content with the snail's progress we had made, blaming others for the state of the field rather than owning responsibility for it. We parapsychologists just could not accept the fact that the field is on a dead end road.

Return to India

We were thus sitting behind the silk screen hoping for a breakthrough that would take us out into the mainstream. It was near the end of 1984,

Thanksgiving time. There was an unexpected call from the newly elected chief-minister of Andhra Pradesh, N.T. Rama Rao. He asked me to return to India and assume charge as the head of Andhra University, my alma mater. What would I do? The chief-minister, "NTR," as he was popularly known, was as persuasive as J.B. Rhine. The situation was very similar when I made the decision to accept Rhine's invitation. Again, by taking a three-year leave of absence, this time from the FRNM, I returned to Andhra University.

The move was not to the narrow strip trailing for psi, but to the broader vistas of administering higher education. It was a march into the world of public life and university administration. Even though I had not met NTR before, we instantly took a liking to each other and I soon became his principal advisor on education, a role that was to continue until his death in 1996. My hands were full with the administration of a university in turmoil and with drawing blueprints for overhauling higher education in the entire state. Not surprisingly there was little time for parapsychology during this three-year period.

I had of course continued to be in regular touch with the affairs of the FRNM and the work at the Institute for Parapsychology in Durham. I attended the annual meetings of the Board of Trustees of the FRNM. The day-to-day management, however, was left to Richard Broughton, H. Kanthamani and John Palmer. Back in India, I realized quickly how parapsychology lost its shine and glamour at the University. There was little interest or enthusiasm in the Department of Psychology and Parapsychology I founded. I arranged for an international conference sponsored by the Parapsychological Association at Andhra University and appointed a couple of additional faculty with parapsychology specialization. These efforts did not ignite the necessary interest to set parapsychological research in motion again. As the head of the University, I did not wish to interfere in the workings of the Department, academically or administratively at the personal or professional level. At the same time, my interest in and commitment to exploring extraordinary human abilities was too intense to accept the unexciting prospects for parapsychology at Andhra University.

Making use of my influence with NTR and the state government, I proposed to establish a separate institute within the university with a focus on parapsychology along with its related disciplines yoga and consciousness studies. I soon secured necessary funding from the Andhra Pradesh government and the University Grants Commission to set up the Institute for Yoga and Consciousness. While the central theme and the main thrust of the Institute is psi research, as is explicitly stated in its descriptive brochure, I advisedly left out parapsychology in naming the institute. The reason for this is twofold. First, the word "parapsychology" is already tied with psychology and I wanted it to stay that way, because the Department of Psychology and Parapsychology came into being with the sole purpose of pursuing parapsychology at teaching and research levels. I hoped that sooner or later parapsychology would take center stage at the Department, as was the case when it began and continued for about a decade after that. Second is my interest in integrating parapsychology with related disciplines and breaking the crippling insulation of the field and helping parapsychologists to come out of the cocoons of their own making. I thought that parapsychology belonged as an integral and indispensable core of consciousness studies. Yoga indicated the possibility of developing psychic technologies for the development of the mind. The president of India, Mr. Zail Singh, flew in from New Delhi to inaugurate the Institute for Yoga and Consciousness. The governor of Andhra Pradesh, Dr. Shankar Dayal Sharma, came from Hyderabad to preside over the inaugural function. I picked Prof. P.V. Krishna Rao who received his Ph.D. in parapsychology and spent a year at the Institute for Parapsychology in Durham, North Carolina, as the director. I put myself up as the honorary director with the expectation to keep in touch and help guide the Institute.

As I neared the end of my three-year tenure as the vice-chancellor of Andhra University, NTR wanted me to move to Hyderabad and help him to reorganize higher education at the state level. On the recommendation of the committee chaired by me, the state government set up an autonomous body, now called the Andhra Pradesh State Council of Higher Education. I was its chairman and later took charge as the advisor to the Andhra Pradesh government on Higher Education in the rank of Chief-Secretary. All this necessitated the extension of my stay in India by six more months beyond the three-year period. Then I had to return to the United States. Not happy about my leaving, NTR extracted a promise from me at a farewell meeting on February 22, 1988, in the Jubilee Hall attended by the governor and the elite of Hyderabad. It was arranged collectively by all the vice-chancellors of universities in Andhra Pradesh. I told the gathering that I would return later and that I would in the meanwhile continue as honorary advisor on higher education and visit NTR at least once a year.

Back and Forth

I was back in North Carolina in March of 1988. The contrast between my roles and activities in India and the U.S. is as stark as one could imagine in terms of the annual budget, the number of employees I had the responsibility for, the public and media exposure, and so on. Even so, I felt quite at home whether I lived in the comforts and conveniences of America or the hardships of rural India, whether the universe of my activities was as large as Andhra Pradesh or as small as the FRNM. Back in the U.S., I was no longer content with pursuing the narrow line of inquiry as in the past. I began looking into possibilities of bringing parapsychology and other related disciplines together on a common platform. The resurgence of interest in consciousness studies among the Western academia appeared to me as the most promising for fruitful interaction. I arranged on behalf of the FRNM a major conference on consciousness in Durham. The papers presented at the conference were published under the title *Cultivating Consciousness* (Rao, 1993). Also, in my presidential address at the annual convention of the Parapsychological Association I dealt extensively with the general need to build bridges between parapsychology and related disciplines and draw attention to the inherent synergy between psi research and consciousness studies (Rao, 1991).

By this time consciousness had come to be my major interest. I spent a significant amount of time reading and thinking about the relevant issues binding consciousness and psi. It seemed obvious to me that the reality of psi has important ontological and epistemological implications bearing on consciousness. At the ontological level, consciousness no longer appeared to be reducible to physical states. Whether or not psi research findings warrant dualist metaphysics, they seem to lend strong support to the notion that consciousness is a primary principle governing reality and that epistemological dualism is a necessary corollary of the existence of psi. The ESP results with their ostensible independence of time, space and sensory-motor variables appear to point to a qualitatively different source of knowledge from sensory knowing or what James called the "non-rational" forms of awareness.

Again, the relevance of classical Indian thought to the study of consciousness as well as psi, which was in the background all along, came to the fore and led me to refocus on Indian psychology. Therefore, I welcomed the opportunity to contribute a chapter to Janak Pandey's three-volume *Psychology in India: State of the Art*. I reviewed in that chapter the continuing relevance of classical Indian ideas to contemporary concerns in psychology (Rao, 2001). The next step was a full-fledged book on *Consciousness Studies: Cross-Cultural Perspectives* (Rao, 2002).

Having thus moved somewhat away from mundane experimental psi research to broader theoretical concerns pertaining to human nature in general and Indian psychology in particular, I began thinking about retirement and returning to India. I was no longer worried about leadership at FRNM's Institute for Parapsychology. We were able to assemble what seemed to me to be a well-trained team of researchers who with years of research experience behind them are ready to take over. The team at the time included H. Kanthamani, R. Broughton and J. Palmer. Kantha had an outstanding track record as an experimental parapsychologist. Richard showed a flair for public relations and management. He was also given the role of research director. John seemed ready to take over the editorial responsibilities for the *Journal of Parapsychology* and lead the educational programs at the Institute.

Back in India, NTR won a landslide victory in the 1994 general election and wanted me to join him as his principal advisor and head of the Andhra Pradesh State Planning Board with the rank of cabinet minister. So, even before my retirement from the FRNM became official, I landed in India in December of 1994 to occupy a position few nonpolitically involved academics in India could dream of.

Even though I was disinclined toward electoral politics, I had a penchant for public service. J.B. Rhine noticed it many years before and predicted that I was destined for an administrative career in government. I recall Prof. Sen making a similar prediction. I was glad to have this opportunity to give back something to the society and serve the poor and the underprivileged, the primary goal I shared with NTR. I supported wholeheartedly the implementation of the twin pre-election promises of NTR, a total prohibition of the consumption and sale of alcohol in the state, and a supply of basic food requirements to poor people at a highly subsidized, affordable prices. Though these policies seemed economically imprudent, we felt that they were morally imperative to save the rural poor from abysmal poverty and avoiding starvation on the one hand and rampant alcoholism on the other. So up to my neck in public life, my plans for the book on consciousness had to be shelved. So was my grandiose vision of a combined, somewhat revolutionary platform for a radical human science.

Before the end of 1995, there was another twist—a sad end to NTR's political saga. NTR left the government and died in January 1996. I resigned from the government and returned to my home base in Visakhapatnam, once again with enough time on hand to pursue my academic interests. Thus began the current phase, which takes me back to the basics. Now, my interests include consciousness studies and yoga in order to find the place of psi in the universe. My most recent effort is the book *Foundations of Yoga Psychology* (2017).

At the end of this fifty-plus years' journey in parapsychology, what have I learned? Where is the field heading? What is its future? Are we on the right course? Is parapsychology a viable scientific discipline? Are the people involved in parapsychology ready to face up to the challenges and take on the responsibilities of pioneers pursuing a paradigmatic science? In retrospect, was it a wise thing to have spent that much time in parapsychology? If I were to begin all over again, would I do any differently?

I have no regret that I spent a better part of my life doing parapsychology. It has been a great learning experience. I have learned that it is easy to choose to be a parapsychologist, but difficult to survive as one. I have seen several highly competent and outstanding contributors to the field constantly struggling to keep their research programs going for want of adequate academic and financial support. Because of the limited opportunities available, I have seen some bickering, backbiting and pettiness. I have also seen uncommon courage, caution, courtesy and comradeship. I have in the field come across extraordinary ingenuity in research; and there has also been some callous chicanery. The field is an unusual blend of good, bad and indifferent. To survive a lifetime struggle amidst insecurity, lack of recognition, extremely limited funding, uncertain future and lackluster progress is indeed a big challenge. Therefore, it is not surprising that there are a very few fulltime professionals who have committed their lives to pursuing parapsychology. Fewer still are those who can look back and say that they had a satisfying career. Perhaps it was an exception in my case.

My situation has been somewhat different. I did not face professional hostility or ostracism because of my involvement in parapsychology. I was not denied employment or tenure as some parapsychologists were. In fact many opportunities came my way without my actively seeking them. Also, I was more fortunate than most others in receiving funding when I needed it. I had few problems in publishing in the mainstream journals. While my commitment to and involvement in parapsychology is very strong and for many years was full time, it did not consume all of me. I was left with time for other things which on occasion proved more consequential in terms of their wider-ranging influence. I was involved in educational administration and reform. At 85 (in 2017), I am the Chancellor of GITAM University and chairman of the School of Gandhian Studies.

Where Is the Field of Parapsychology Heading?

During the past decade I have been more on the sidelines. The last PA annual convention I attended was the Heidelburg meeting in 1993, in

Germany. I discontinued my membership in 1995. Therefore, for a change, I have something of an outsider's look and presumably a more objective understanding of the field and where it is heading. I have kept up with the publications and continued my writing on the subject and contacts with a few friends in the field. A few years, I have been involved even in empirical research of psi at the institute for Human Science and Service here at home. Thus, though technically I may claim the privilege of being an outsider, I am very much familiar with what is going on; and my identity as a parapsychologist is well intact.

Looking at the massive empirical experimental data boosted by the multitude of meta-analyses, my confidence in the existence of cognitive anomalies has continued to grow throughout my career. Indeed, I believe, a better case has been made, based not so much on new breakthroughs made or fresh experimental results obtained, but by reanalysis of already existing data with more robust statistical tools. Do these new analyses and their more improved and impressive outcomes bring parapsychology any closer to the long-sought entry into mainstream science? I am afraid not. Statistical estimates of the improbability of psi's nonexistence based on the data of the kind we now have are unlikely to be convincing to someone who accords a very low subjective probability for its existence. The skeptic could continue to experience little cognitive dissonance no matter how small the claimed probability (p value) is in favor of rejecting the null hypothesis. Therefore, the key to psi's entry into the portals of science rests, I think, in raising the subjective probability estimates of psi, which can be influenced by a paradigm shift in people's worldview and the pragmatics of psi. The latter is realized when one perceives and appreciates the practical applications of psi in life.

If psi has a place in one's overall worldview, the existing data are sufficient to be convincing. Otherwise, it is unlikely that the presently available data or more of the same would render parapsychology a legitimate science, if by legitimacy we mean mainstream acceptance. However, applications of psi, whether in improving health or generating wealth, would significantly alter one's skeptical perceptions of psi and consequently reduce the resistance for accepting psi research as a scientific pursuit. Thus pursuing the pragmatics of psi is potentially a more plausible endeavor for promoting parapsychology. What researches in the lab did not accomplish, applying psi in life might. But then what are the realistic chances of applying psi in life?

In my view, it is not unlikely that we all use psi in our lives; but it goes undetected as it is built into our unconscious intuitive decision-making.

This is an area that received little attention in the past, but deserves to be explored systematically. Carpenter (2015) has brought attention to it; and his *First Sight Theory* is an attempt to address it. Research into the role of psi in real life is thus one avenue of applied psi research. There may be some inherent and even insurmountable hurdles in exploring applied psi. It is possible that a deliberate intention to involve psi in a given task may itself be a hurdle that impedes the manifestation of psi in an appreciably large scale, thus rendering voluntary control of psi an essentially unrealizable goal.

Keeping this possibility in perspective we may distinguish between two kinds of real life psi studies—*mapping psi* in life and *making use of psi* in life. The former is natural and unmanipulated. It is the recording of psi events in life. Spontaneous case collection is one kind of recording psi events in life. This has been done since the beginning of psychical research. Another kind of recording involves analyses of contemporaneous events to distill psi as a possible source. These kinds of studies have yet to be systematized. This is a methodological challenge that psi researchers should take seriously. Here again, post hoc detection of psi in life is less likely to lower skeptical thresholds than the predictive detection. Thus we are back again to the same issues discussed in relation to replication of experimental results.

Making use of psi in a skeptical cultural climate might be rendered difficult inasmuch as skepticism is known to be an impeding influence on the occurrence of psi. Thus we appear to be caught in a circle and are in a "no-win" situation. To reduce skepticism, we need psi to work. For psi to work we need a positive climate of belief in the possibility of psi. How can we break this deadlock?

Fortunately, there are societies in which science and belief in psychic phenomena coexist without conflict. I recall discussing psychic phenomenon with Nobel laureate in physics Sir C.V. Raman some years before his death. He saw no difficulty in accepting psi as a scientific truth because in his mind there was no culturally conditioned antecedent improbability of psi. His concluding statement to me was, "If there are these results, as you say, it [ESP] must be real." Raman did not look for alternative explanations as Western scientists generally tend to, because to him psi did not appear a priori improbable. I have a similar experience with the Indian physicist D.S. Kothari, who had no difficulty in accepting the possibility of psi. It would seem therefore that applied psi research has a better chance of success in Eastern nonskeptical cultures than in the Western societies where psi research as a scientific endeavor began but is struggling to survive.

It should be kept in mind that the majority of people even in the West are not skeptical of psi; but it is the science establishments that are. So the problem is not with the beliefs of people, but with the guardians and gatekeepers of science who either continue to ignore psi research results or dispute their veracity. It might look odd that in Western democratic societies, where the will of the people is supposed to prevail ultimately, the dictatorship of the establishments in science goes unchecked and unabated. It is indeed a paradox that public opinion and science policy decisions appear to be little related in societies that place a premium on the people's mandate, just as the freedom of the individual considered fundamental and foundational is often lost in corporate mazes in developed democratic societies.

The conundrums of cognitive anomalies continue to clog the minds of Western psi researchers. The mother of them all, it is generally thought, is inherent in the very paradox of naturalizing the supernatural. The major riddle is how to evaluate scientific evidence for psi, which, if true, would undermine science itself by raising doubts about its assumptive base. How can we have a science that supports antiscience assumptions and thus destabilizes science itself?

This, as we have noted, is a wrong assumption. An obsession to gain scientific acceptance has led psi researchers to become more and more data driven rather than theoretically attuned. What has attracted parapsychologists in the first place are the profound theoretical ramifications of the reality of psi. At the same time, what keeps them theoretically mute is the realization of the enormity of psi's theoretical importance and the fear to face the consequences. Parapsychologists persistently sought to gain scientific respectability but feared to face the potential for practical utility and implied challenges to science. In the Western scientific mindset psi will remain an anomaly. The resolution to this riddle is no less than a significant paradigm shift. The paucity of funding and the limited human resources available are simply inadequate for the required shift to come about in the short run.

If the power of the prevailing paradigm in science propels the resistance for psi research in the West, why is it, we may then ask, that psi research has made little headway in Eastern cultures that are presumably less skeptical? Eastern societies which accord no a priori improbability for psi have obviously not done any better than Western societies in promoting parapsychology, with very few exceptions. The reason is that they, as developing societies, are focused rightly in my opinion on improving economic and health conditions in the short term—quickly—by applying

Western science and technologies with proven potential to make a difference in the life of their people rather than exploring new and controversial areas with distant promises. Thus we find a benign neglect of the psychic realm in the East.

Caught between the belligerent resistance in the West and the benign neglect in the East, parapsychology has not made the progress I had hoped for it when I first began my journey sixty plus years ago. The flight that would take me to the promised land of the paranormal, I am afraid, is late, judging by my life span. Whether the next generation of psi researchers would be able to catch that flight depends on (a) the improvement of the weather conditions in the West that are at present turbulent for psi research, (b) developments in the methodological and design changes that would give a new kind of vehicle that can fly in inclement weather conditions, or (c) a change in the place of departure so that the flight can take off from more culturally friendly skies in the East.

To conclude, there is unassailable empirical evidence for the existence of psi. There is an equally strong resistance to accept it. From my perspective, no amount of the same research will help in breaking that resistance. Parapsychology in the West started its journey on a road without realizing that it is a dead-end. Having garnered enough evidence for the existence of paranormal phenomena, we are stranded with the discovery of an anomaly, without knowing what it means and where we are headed.

I would like to see future efforts to include (a) a strategic shift in the techniques and technologies based on the assumption that psi is neither an anomaly nor an aberration but a genuine, inherent principle embedded in reality and accessible to human experience, (b) an empathic appreciation of the relevance of the reality of psi to an interdisciplinary understanding of who we are and where our destiny lies, and (c) a judicious application of psi for personal transformation as well as enhancement of human potential. We need a mind set free from the fear of the paranormal and the courageous conviction to face squarely its theoretical ramifications. In this endeavor, one step is to find the interconnectedness of psi with related phenomena of consciousness that appear to defy physicalism. Another is to venture boldly into the applied aspects of psi research. If the utility value of psi is established, for example, in the area of healing or education, then it would generate a level of interest and momentum that could not be resisted by a priori theoretical improbability estimates.

For me, all this fits very well. The conundrums of cognitive anomalies, the complexities of consciousness and the mysteries of yoga hang together. This calls for a paradigmatic shift in our search for solutions and answers to the apparent paradoxes, the genuine puzzles, and the challenging implications. A lifetime of involvement in these three areas has not yet given me the answers I am seeking; but at the end of this I am convinced more than when I started the journey, that psychic phenomena are neither aberrations nor anomalies, but genuine pointers to something hidden that is no less profound and fundamental than those aspects of our being that characterize and consume much of what we do.

References

Akers, C. (1985). Can meta-analysis resolve the ESP controversy? In P. Kurtz (Ed.), *A skeptic's handbook of parapsychology* (pp. 611–627). Buffalo, NY: Prometheus Books.

Alcock, C.J., & Quartermain, D. (1959). Some problems in group testing of ESP. *Journal of Parapsychology*, 23, 251–56.

Alcock, J.E. (1981). *Parapsychology: Science or magic? A psychological perspective*. New York: Pergamon Press.

Alcock, J.E. (1985). Parapsychology as a "spiritual" science. In P. Kurtz (Ed.), *A skeptic's handbook of parapsychology*, 537–565. Buffalo, NY: Prometheus Books.

Alcock, J.E. (1987). Parapsychology: Science of the anomalous on search for the soul? *Behaviour and Brain Sciences*, 10, 553–565.

Alcock, J.E. (2003). Give the null hypothesis a chance. In J.E. Alcock, J.E. Burns & A. Freeman (Eds.), *Psi wars: Getting to grips with the paranormal* (pp. 2950). Exeter (UK): Imprint Academic.

Alexander, C.H., Persinger, M.A., Roll, W.G., & Webster, D.L. (1998). EEG and SPECT data of a selected subject during psi tasks: The discovery of a neurophysiological correlate. In *Proceedings of the presented papers: The Parapsychological Association 41st annual convention* (p. 3–13). Durham, NC: Parapsychological Association, Inc.

Allison, P.D. (1973). *Social aspects of scientific innovation: The case of parapsychology*. Madison: University of Wisconsin Press.

Altom, K., & Braud, W.G. (1976). Clairvoyant and telepathic impressions of musical targets. In J.D. Morris, W.G. Roll & R.L. Morris (Eds.), *Research in parapsychology*. Metuchen, NJ Scarecrow Press.

Ambach, W. (2008). Correlations between the EEGs of two spatially separated subjects: A replication study. *European Journal of Parapsychology*, 23, 131–146.

Anand, B.K., Chhina, G.S., & Singh, B. (1961a). Studies on Sri Ramanand yogi during his stay in an airtight box. *Indian Journal of Medical Research*, 49(1), 8289.

Anderson, M.L., & Gregory, E. (1959). A two-year program of tests for clairvoyance and precognition with a class of public school pupils. *Journal of Parapsychology*, 23, 149–77.

Anderson, M.L., & White, R.A. (1956). Teacher-pupil attitudes and clairvoyance test results. *Journal of Parapsychology*, 20, 141–157.

Anderson, M.L., & White, R.A. (1957). A further investigation of teacher-pupil attitudes and clairvoyance test results. *Journal of Parapsychology*, 21, 81–97.

Anderson, M.L., & White, R.A. (1958). ESP score level in relation to students' attitude toward teacher-agents acting simultaneously. *Journal of Parapsychology*, 22, 20–28.

Atmanspacher, H., & Fach, W. (2013). A structural-phenomenological typology of mind-matter correlations. *Journal of Analytical Psychology*, 58, 219–244.

Baptista, J., Derakhshani, M., & Tressoldi, E.P. (2015). Explicit anomalous cognition: A review of the best evidence in ganzfeld, forced-choice, remote viewing and dream studies. In E. Cardeña, J. Palmer, & D. Marcusson-Clavertz, *Parapsychology: A handbook for the 21st century*, 192–214. Jefferson, NC: McFarland.

Barber, T.X. (1969). *Hypnosis: A scientific approach.* New York: Van Nostrand Reinhold.

Barber, T.X. (1973). Experimental hypnosis. In B.B. Wolman (Ed.), *Handbook of general psychology* (pp. 942–963). Englewood Cliffs, NJ: Prentice Hall.

Barber, T.X. (1978). Hypnosis, suggestions and psychosomatic phenomena: A new look from the standpoint of recent experimental studies. *American Journal of Clinical Studies*, 21, 13–27.

Barrett, W. (1911). Poltergeists, old and new. *Proceedings of the Society for Psychical Research*, 25, No. 64.

Barry, J. (1968). General and comparative study of the psychokinetic effect on a fungus culture. *Journal of Parapsychology*, 32, 237–243.

Becker, R.O. (1992). Electromagnetism and psiphenomena. *Journal of the American Society for Psychical Research*, 86, 1–17.

Beloff, J. (1962). *The existence of mind.* London. MacGibbon & Kee.

Beloff, J. (1974). The subliminal and the extra-sensory. In A. Angoff & B. Shapin (Eds.) *Parapsychology and the sciences.* New York: Parapsychology Foundation.

Beloff, J. (1989). "Dualism: A parapsychological perspective." In J. Smythies & John Beloff (Eds.), *The case for dualism.* Charlottesville: University of Virginia Press.

Beloff, J. (1993). *A concise history of parapsychology.* New York: St. Martin's.

Belvedere, E., & Foulkes, D. (1971). Telepathy and dreams: A failure to replicate. *Perceptual and Motor Skills*, 33, 783–789.

Bem, D.J. (2011). Feeling the future: Experience for anomalous retroactive influences on cognition and affect. *Journal of Personality and Social Psychology*, 100(3), 407–425.

Bem, D.J., & Honorton, C. (1994). Does psi exist? Replicable evidence for an anomalous process of information transfer. *Psychological Bulletin*, 115(1), 4–18.

Bem, D.J., Palmer, J., & Broughton, R.S. (2001). Updating the ganzfeld database: A victim of its own success? *Journal of Parapsychology*, 65, 207–218.

Bender, H. (1977). Meaningful coincidences in the light of the Jung-Pauli theory of synchronicity and parapsychology. In: B. Shapin & L. Coly (Eds.), *The philosophy of parapsychology* (pp. 66–84). Parapsychology Foundation.

Bengston, W.F., & Krinsley, D. (2000). The effect of the "laying-on of hands" on transplanted breast cancer in mice. *Journal of Scientific Exploration*, 14, 353–36.

Benson, H., Dusek, J.A., Sherwood, J.B., Lam, P., Bethea, C.F., Carpenter, W., Levitsky, S., Hill, P., Clem, D.W., Jr., Jain, M.K., Drumel, D., Kopecky, S.L., Mueller, P.S., Marek, D., Rollins, S., & Hibberd, P.L. (2006). Study of the therapeutic effects of intercessory prayer (step) in cardiac bypass patients—A multi-center randomized trial of uncertainty and certainty of receiving intercessory prayer. *American Heart Journal*, 151(4), 934–942.

Berger, R.E., & Persinger, M.A. (1991). Geophysical variables and behavior: LXVII. Quieter annual geomagnetic activity and larger effect size for experimental psi (ESP) studies over six decades. *Perceptual and Motor Skills*, 73, 1219–1223.

Bergson, H. (1921). *Mind energy.* London, Macmillan.

Berkeley, G. (1975). *Berkeley: Philosophical works.* Edited by M.R. Ayers. London: Dent and Sons.

Bhadra, B.J. (1966). The relationship of test scores to belief in ESP. *Journal of Parapsychology*, 30, 1–7.

Bhadra, B.R, & Parthasarathy, S. (1965). ESP and attitudes. Paper presented at the *Eighth Annual Convention of the Parapsychological Association*, New York.

Bierman, D.J. (1996). Exploring correlations between local emotional and global emotional events and the behavior of a random number generator. *Journal of Scientific Exploration*, 10, 363–373.

Bierman, D.J. (2000). Anomalous baseline effects in mainstream emotion research using psychophysiological variables.

Paper presented at the *43 Annual Convention of the Parapsychological Association,* Freiburg Breslau; Germany, August 1720 (pp. 34–47).

Bierman, D.J., & Rabeyron, T. (2013). Can psi research sponsor itself? Simulations and results of an automated ARV-casino experiments. *Proceedings of the 56th Annual Convention of the Parapsychological Association* (p. 15).

Bierman, D.J., & Radin, D.I. (1997). Anomalous anticipatory response on randomized future conditions. *Perceptual and Motor Skills,* 84, 689–690.

Bierman, D.J., & Scholte, S.H. (2002). Anomalous anticipatory brain activation preceding exposure of emotional and neutral pictures, *Parapsychological Association Convention, Abstracts.*

Bisaha, J., & Dunne, B.J. (1979). Multiple subject and Long distance precognitive remote viewing of geographical locations. In C.T. Tart, M.E. Puthoff, & R. Targ (Eds.), *Mind at Large,* 107–124. New York: Praeger.

Blackmore, S.J. (1981) The effect of variations in target material on ESP and memory. *Research Letter,* 11, 126.

Bohm, D.J. (1980). *Wholeness and the implicate order.* London: Routledge & Kegan Paul.

Boring, E.G. (1966). Introduction. Paranormal phenomena: Evidence, specification, and chance. In C.E.M. Hansel, *ESP: A scientific evaluation* (pp. xiii–xxi). New York: Charles Scribner's Sons.

Bösch, H., Steinkamp, E., & Boller, E. (2006). In the eye of the beholder: Reply to Wilson and Shadish (2006) and Radin, Nelson, Dobyns, & Houtkooper (2006). *Psychological Bulletin,* 132, 533–537.

Bowles, N., & Hynds, F. (1978). *The new investigation of psychic phenomena that separates fact from speculation.* New York: Harper & Row.

Braud, L.W., & Boston, D.A. (1986). Target preference and clairvoyance in selected subjects following relaxation induction. In D.H. Weiner and D.I. Radin (Eds.), *Research in parapsychology,* 1985, p. 25–28. Metuchen, NJ: Scarecrow Press.

Braud, W.G. (1975). Psi-conducive states. *Journal of Communication,* 25, 142–152.

Braud, W.G. (1979) Conformance behavior involving living systems. In W.G. Roll (Ed.), *Research in parapsychology* (pp. 111–115). Metuchen, NJ: Scarecrow Press.

Braud, W. G. (1984). The two faces of psi: Psi revealed and psi obscured. In B. Shapin & L. Coly (Eds.), *The repeatability problem in parapsychology* (pp. 150–175). New York: Parapsychology Foundation.

Braud, W.G. (1985). ESP, PK, and sympathetic nervous system activity. *Parapsychology Review,* 16, 8–11.

Braud, W.G. (1990). Meditation and psychokinesis. *Parapsychology Review,* 21, 9–11.

Braud, W.G., & Braud, L.W. (1973). Preliminary explorations of psi-conducive states: Progressive muscular relaxation. *Journal of the American Society for Psychical Research,* 67, 6–46.

Braud, W.G., & Braud, L.W. (1974). Studies of psi facilitating states: Hypnosis, muscular relaxation, and an experimentally induced hypnagogic state. *Proceedings of the First International Congress of Parapsychology and Psychotronics.* 204–207.

Braud, W.G., Davis, G., & Wood, R. (1979). Experiments with Matthew Manning. *Journal of the Society for Psychical Research,* 50, 199–223.

Braud, W.G., & Schlitz, M.J. (1983). Psychokinetic influence on electrodermal activity. *Journal of Parapsychology,* 47, 95–119.

Braud, W.G., & Schlitz, M.J. (1991). Consciousness interactions with remote biological systems: Anomalous Intentionality Effects. *Subtle Energies* 2(1), 1–46.

Braud, W.G., Shafer, D., & Andrews, S. (1990). Electodermal correlates of remote attention: Autonomic reactions to an unseen gaze. *Proceedings of the Parapsychological Association 33 Annual Convention,* 14–28.

Braud, W.G, Shafer, D., & Andrews, S. (1993a). Reactions to an unseen gaze (remote attention): A review with new data on autonomic staring detection. *Journal of Parapsychology,* 57, 373–390.

Braud, W.G., Shafer, D., & Andrews, S.

(1993b). Further studies of autonomic detection of remote staring: replications, new control procedures, and personality correlates. *Journal of Parapsychology*, 57, 391–409.

Braud, W.G., Wood, & Braud, L.W. (1975). Free-response GESP performance during an experimental hypnagogic slate induced by visual and acoustic ganzfeld techniques. A replication and extension. *Journal of the American Society for Psychical Research*. 69, 105–13.

Braude, S.E. (1979b). *ESP and psychokinesis: A philosophical examination*. Philadelphia: Temple University Press.

Breslin, M.J., & Lewis, C.A. (2008). Theoretical models of the nature of prayer and health: A review. *Mental Health, Religion & Culture*, 11(1), 9–21. (Abstract). www.informaworld.com/smpp/content~content=a788556061~db=all

Bro, H.H. (1989). *A seer out of Searon*. New York: Penguin, New American Library.

Broad, C.D. (1925/1951). *Mind and its place in nature*. New York: Humanities Press.

Broad, C.D. (1946). Discussion of Prof. Rhine's paper and the foregoing comments upon it. *Proceedings of the Society for Psychical Research*, v. 48, 20–25.

Broad, C.D. (1953). *Religion, philosophy and psychical research*, 308. New York: Harcourt Brace.

Broad, C.D. (1962). *Lectures of psychical research*. London: Routledge & Kegan Paul.

Broad, W., & Wade, N. (1982). *Betrayers of the truth*. New York: Simon & Schuster.

Broughton, R. (1978). Repeatability and experimenter effect: Are subjects really necessary? *Parapsychology Review*, 10(1), 11–14.

Broughton, R., Millar, B., Beloff, J., & Wilson, K. (1977). PK investigation of the experimenter effect and its psi-based component. *Research in parapsychology*, 41–48.

Broughton, R.S. (2004). Exploring the reliability of the "presentiment" effect. *Proceedings of Presented Papers for the Parapsychological Association 2004 Annual Convention*, 15–26.

Brown, B. (1970). Recognition of aspects of consciousness through association with EEG alpha activity represented by a light signal. *Psychophysiology*, 6, 442–452.

Brown, H.I. (1979). *Perception, theory and commitment: The new philosophy of science*. Chicago: University of Chicago Press.

Brugmans, H.J.F.W. (1921). "Some experiments in telepathy performed in the Psychological Institute of the University of Groningen." *Compte-Rendu du Premier Congrès International des Recherches Psychiques*.

Burdick, D.S., & Kelly, E.F. (1977). Statistical methods in parapsychological research. In B.B. Wolman (Ed.), *Handbook of parapsychology*, 81–130. New York: Van Nostrand Reinhold.

Byrd, R.C. (1988). Positive therapeutic effects of intercessory prayer in a coronary care unit population. *Southern Medical Journal*, 81, 826–9.

Cadoret, R., & Pratt, J.G. (1950). The consistent missing effect in ESP. *Journal of Parapsychology*, 14, 244–56.

Calkins, J. (1980). Commentaries on the paper by Professor Karnes *et al.* Comments by James Calkins. *Zetetic Scholar*, No.6 (pp. 77–81).

Callaway, H. (1868). *The Religious system of the Amazulu I Unkulunkulu: or, The tradition of creation as existing among the Amazulu and other tribes of South Africa, in their own words, with a translation into English, and notes*. Natal: Blair.

Camp, B.H. (1937). (Statement in notes section). *Journal of Parapsychology*, 47–64.

Cardeña, E. (2011). On wolverines and epistemological totalitarianism. *Journal of Scientific Exploration*, 25, 539–551.

Cardeña, E., Marcusson-Clavertz, D., & Wasmuth, J. (2009). Hypnotizability and dissociation as predictors of performance in a precognition task: A pilot study. *Journal of Parapsychology*, 73, 137–158.

Cardeña, E., Palmer, J., & Marcusson-Clavertz, D. (Eds). (2015). *Parapsychology: A handbook for the 21st century*. Jefferson: McFarland.

Carington, W. (1949). *Mind, matter and meaning*. New Haven: Yale University Press.

Carington, W.W. (1946). On J.B. Rhine's "Telepathy and clairvoyance reconsidered," *Proceedings of the Society for Psychical Research*, v. 48, 8–10.

Carpenter, J.C. (1971). The differential effect and hidden target differences consisting of erotic and neutral stimuli. *Journal of the American Society for Psychical Research*, 65, 204–214.

Carpenter, J.C. (1975). Toward the effective utilization of enhanced weak signal ESP effects. Paper presented at the meeting of the *American Association for the Advancement of Science*, New York: January 1975.

Carpenter, J.C. (1977). Intrasubject and subject-agent effects in ESP experiments. In B.B. Wolman (Ed.), *Handbook of parapsychology* (pp. 202–272). New York: Van Nostrand Reinhold.

Carpenter, J.C. (2012). Spontaneous social behavior can implicitly express ESP information. Paper presented at the annual conference of the Parapsychological Association, Durham, NC.

Carr, B. (2015). Higher dimensions of space and time and their implications for psi. In E.C. May and S.B. Marwaha (Eds.), *Extrasensory perception: Support, skepticism, and science, volume II—Theoretical frameworks*. Santa Barbara: Praeger.

Casler, L. (1962). The improvement of clairvoyance scores by means of hypnotic suggestion. *Journal of Parapsychology*, 26, 77–87.

Casler, L. (1964). The effects of hypnosis on GESP. *Journal of Parapsychology*, 28, 126–34.

Casper, G.W. (1951). A further study of the relation of attitude to success in ESP scoring. *Journal of Parapsychology*, 15, 139–145.

Casper, G.W. (1952). Effect of receiver's attitude toward sender in ESP tests. *Journal of Parapsychology*, 16, 212–18.

Cayce, D. (1969). *Edgar Cayce on ESP*. New York: Paperback Library.

Chalmers, A.F. (1978). *What is this thing called science: An assessment of the nature and status of science and its methods*. Milton Keynes, Eng: Open University Press.

Chalmers, D.J. (1995). The puzzle of conscious experience. *Scientific American*, 273, 62–68.

Chari, C.T.K. (1977). Some generalized theories and models of psi: A critical evaluation. In B.B. Wolman (Ed.), *Handbook of parapsychology* (pp. 803–822). New York: Van Nostrand Reinhold.

Chauvin, R. (1961). ESP and size of target symbols. *Journal of Parapsychology*, 25, 185–89.

Chibnall, J.T., Jeral, J.M., & Cerullo, M.A. (2001). Experiments in distant intercessory prayer: God, science, and the lesson of Massah. *Archives of Internal Medicine*, 161, 2529–2536.

Child, I. (2001). Psychology and anomalous observation: The question of ESP in dreams. In K.R. Rao (Ed.), *Basic research in parapsychology* (2nd edition), 157–180. Jefferson, NC: McFarland.

Collins, H.M. (1978). Replication of experiments: A sociological comment. *The Behavioural and Brain Sciences*, 3, 391–2.

Coover, J.E. (1917). *Experiments in psychical research at Leland Stanford Junior University*, Leland Stanford Junior University Publications Psychical Research Monographs No. 1. Stanford, California: Stanford University Press.

Cox, W.E. (1954). A comparison of spheres and cubes in placement PK tests. *Journal of Parapsychology*, 18, 234–239.

Crookes, W. (1874). *Researches in the Phenomena of Spiritualism*. London: J. Burns [(1926). Manchester, England: Two Worlds Pub].

Crowther, J.G. (1955). *Six great scientists: Copernicus, Galileo, Newton, Darwin, Marie Curie, Einstein*. London: Hamilton.

Dale, L.A. (1946). The psychokinetic effect. *Journal of the American Society for Psychical Research*. 40(3), 123–51.

Davis, J.W. (1979). Psi in animals: A review of laboratory research. *Parapsychology Review*, 10, 1–9.

Dean, D., & Mihalsky, J. (1974). *Executive ESP*. Englewood Cliffs, NJ: Prentice-Hall.

Dean, E.D. (1962). The plethysmograph as an indication of ESP. *Journal of the Society for Psychical Research*, 41, 351–353.

Deguisne, A. (1959). Two repetitions of the Anderson White investigation of teacher-pupil attitudes and clairvoyance test results. Part I. High-School Tests, *Journal of Parapsychology*, 23: 196–207.

Del Prete, G., & Tressoldi, P.E. (2005). Anomalous cognition in hypnagogic state with OBE induction: An experimental study. *Journal of Parapsychology*, 69, 329–339.

Delanoy, D.L., & Morris, R.L. (1998–99). A DMILS training study utilizing two shielded environments. *European Journal of Parapsychology*, 14 (pp. 52–67).

Devereux, G. (Ed.) (1953). *Psychoanalysis and the occult*. New York: International University Press.

Diaconis, P. (1978). Statistical problems in ESP research. *Science*, 201, 131–136.

Dixon, N.F. (1979). Subliminal perception and parapsychology: Points of contact. *Parapsychology Review*, 10, 1–6.

Dobyns, Y., Dunne, B., Jahn, R., & Nelson, R. (1994). Reply to Hansen, Utts and Markwick's "Statistical and methodological problems of the PEAR remote viewing (sic) experiments." In E.W. Cook and D.L. Delanoy (Eds.), *Research in Parapsychology*, 1991, 108–111. Metuchen, NJ: Scarecrow Press.

Dobyns, Y.H. (1996). Selection versus influence revisited: New methods and conclusions. *Journal of Scientific Exploration*, 10(2): 258–68.

Dodds, E.R. (1971). Supernormal phenomena in classical antiquity. *Proceedings of the Society for Psychical Research*, 55, 189–237. University of Glasgow Press.

Dommeyer, F.C. (1977). An acausal theory of extrasensory perception and psychokinesis', i: In B. Shapin & L. Coly (Eds.), *The philosophy of parapsychology. Proceedings of an international conference held in Copenhagen, Denmark, August 2527, 1976.*(pp. 85–105). New York: Parapsychology Foundation, Inc.

Don, N.S., McDonough, B.E., & Warren, C.A. (1998). Event-related brain potential (ERP) indicators of unconscious psi: A replication using subjects unselected for psi. *Journal of Parapsychology*, 62, 127–145.

Duval, P., & Montredon, E. (1968a). ESP experiments with mice. *Journal of Parapsychology*, 32, 153–166.

Duval, P., & Montredon, E. (1968b). Further psi experiments with mice. *Journal of Parapsychology*, 32, 260 (Abstract).

Ebbinghaus, H. (1964/1885). *Memory*. New York: Dover. Eccles, J.C. (1953). *The neurophysiological basis of mind*. Oxford: Clarendon.

Eccles, J.C. (1976). Brain and free will. In C.G. Globus, G. Maxwell, & I. Savodnik (Eds.), *Consciousness and the brain: A scientific and philosophical inquiry* (pp. 101–121). New York: Plenum Press.

Eccles, J.C. (1977). The human person in its two-way relationship to the brain. In J.D. Morries, W.G. Roll & R.L. Morris (Eds.), *Research in parapsychology* 1976. Metuchen, NJ: Scarecrow Press.

Edge, H.L. (1980). The effect of laying-on-of-hands on an enzyme: An attempted replication. In W.G. Roll (Ed.), *Research in parapsychology*, 1979, 137–139. Metuchen, NJ: Scarecrow Press.

Egger, M., Smith, G.D., Schneider, M., & Minder, C. (1997). Bias in meta-analysis detected by a simple graphical test. *British Medical Journal*, 315, 629–634.

Ehrenwald, J. (1947). *Telepathy and medical psychology*. London: George Allen & Unwin.

Ehrenwald, J. (1976). *History of psychotherapy: From healing magic to encounter*. New York: Jason Aronson.

Ehrenwald, J. (1978). The ESP experience: *A psychiatric validation*. New York: Basic Books.

Eilbert, L., & Schmeidler, G.R. (1950). A study of certain psychological factors in relation to ESP performance. *Journal of Parapsychology*, 14, 53–74.

Eisenbud, J. (1963). Psi and the nature of things. *International Journal of Parapsychology*, 5, 245–273.

Eisenbud, J. (1965). Perception of subliminal visual stimuli in relation to ESP, *International Journal of Parapsychology*, 7, 161–181.

Eliade, M. (1969). *Yoga: Immortality and freedom*. Bollingon Series LVI. Princeton University Press.

Eliot, C. (1959). *Japanese Buddhism*. New York: Barnes & Noble.

Emerson, N. (1974). *Intuitive archaeology: A psychic approach. New Horizons*, 1(3), January.

Estabrooks, G.H. (1927). *A contribution to experimental telepathy*. Boston: Boston Society for Psychic Research.

Estabrooks, G.H. (1961). A contribution to experimental telepathy. *Journal of Parapsychology*, 25, 190–213.

Evans, C. (1973). Parapsychology: What the questionnaire revealed. *New Scientist*, 57, 209.

Eysenck, H.J. (1967). Personality and extrasensory perception. *Journal of the Society for Psychical Research*, 44, 55–71.

Fahler, J. (1957). ESP card tests with and without hypnosis. *Journal of Parapsychology*, 21, 179–185.

Fahler, J., & Cadoret, R.J. (1958). ESP card tests of college students with and without hypnosis. *Journal of Parapsychology*, 22, 125–136.

Feather, S.R. (1967). A quantitative comparison of memory and psi. *Journal of Parapsychology*, 31, 9398.

Feather, S.R., & Brier, R. (1968). The possible effect of the checker in precognition tests. *Journal of Parapsychology*, 32, 167–175.

Feyerabend, P.K. (1975). *Against method: Outline of an anarchistic theory of knowledge*. London: New Left Books.

Feyerabend, P.K. (1980). Comments on "Pathological science: Towards a proper diagnosis and remedy." *Zetetic Scholar*, 6, 52–54.

Figar, S. (1959). The application of plethysmography to the objective study of So-called extrasensory perception. *Journal of the Society for Psychical Research*, 40, 162–172.

Fisk, G.W., & West, D.J. (1958). Die-casting experiments with a single subject. *Journal of Society for Psychical Research*, 39, 277–287.

Flew, A.G.N. (1951). Minds and mystifications. *The Listener*, September 27, October 4, 1951.

Flew, A.G.N. (1953). *A new approach to psychical research*. London: Watts & Company.

Flew, A.G.N. (1953–54). Coincidence and synchronicity. *Journal of Society for Psychical Research*, 38: 198–201.

Flew, A.G.N. (1976). Parapsychology revisited: Laws, miracles, and repeatability. *The Humanist*, XXXVI(3), 28–30.

Forwald, H. (1955). A study of psychokinesis in its relation to physical conditions. *Journal of Parapsychology*, 19, 133–54.

Forwald, H. (1961). A PK experiment with die faces as targets. *Journal of Parapsychology*, 19, 133–54.

Freeman, J.A. (1962). An experiment in precognition. *Journal of Parapsychology*, 26, 123–130.

Freemen, J.A., & Nielsen, W. (1964). Precognition score deviation as related to anxiety levels. *Journal of Parapsychology*, 28, 239–249.

Gardner, M. (1989). *How not to test a psychic*. Buffalo, NY: Prometheus Books.

Gatlin, L.L. (1977). Meaningful information creation: An alternative interpretation of the psi phenomenon. *Journal of the American Society for Psychical Research*, 71, 1–18.

Gauld, A. (1968). *The founders of psychical research*. London: Routledge and Kegan Paul.

Gauld, A., & Cornell, A.D. (1979). *Poltergeists*. London: Routledge & Kegan Paul.

Gibson, E.P. (1937). A study of comparative performance in several ESP procedures, *Journal of Parapsychology*, 1, 264–75.

Goldbourt, U., Yaari, S., & Medalie, J.H. (1993). Factors predictive of long-term coronary heart disease mortality among 10,059 male Israeli civil servants and municipal employees. *Cardiology*, 82, 100–121.

Goldstone, G. (1959). Two repetitions of the Anderson White investigation of teacher-pupil attitudes and clairvoyance test results: Part II, grade-school tests. *Journal of Parapsychology*, 23: 208–213.

Goodman, J. (1977). *Psychic archeology: Time machine to the past*. New York: Berkley Pub. Corp.

Grad, B. (1967). The "laying on of hands": implications for psychotherapy, gentling, and the placebo effect. *Journal of the American Society for Psychical Research*, 61, 286–305.

Grad, B. (1977). Laboratory evidence of "laying-on-of-hands." In N.M. Regush (Ed.), *Frontiers of healing*, 203–213. New York: Avon Books.

Grad, B., Cadoret, R.J., & Paul, G.K. (1961). The influence of an unorthodox method of treatment on wound healing in mice. *International Journal of Parapsychology*, 3, 5–24.

Green, C.E. (1968). *Lucid dreams*. London: Hamish Hamilton.

Green, S., Benedetti, J., & Crowley, J. (2003). *Clinical trials in oncology* (2nd ed.). New York: Chapman & Hall/CRC.

Greenley, A.M., & McCready, W.C. (1975). Are we a nation of mystics? *New York Times Magazine*, January 26, p. 12.

Greenwood, J.A. (1939). Some mathematical problems for future consideration suggested by ESP research. *Journal of Parapsychology*, 3, 92–95.

Greenwood, J.A., & Greville, T.N.E. (1979a). On requirements for using statistical analysis in psi experiments. *Journal of Parapsychology*, 43, 315–321.

Greenwood, J.A., & Greville, T.N.E. (1979b). Reply to Dr. Burdick, *Journal of Parapsychology*, 43, 325.

Grela, J.J. (1945). Effect on ESP scoring of hypnotically induced attitudes. *Journal of Parapsychology*, 9, 194–202.

Greville, T.N.E. (1939). A summary of mathematical advances bearing on ESP research. *Journal of Parapsychology*, 1, 86–92.

Gurney, E., Myers, F.W.H., & Podmore, F. (1886). *Phantasms of the living* (2 vols.). London: Trübner.

Guthrie, M., & Birchall, J. (1883). "Record of experiments in thought-transference. *Proceedings of the Society for Psychical Research*, 1, 263–283.

Hall, T.H. (1962). *The spiritualists*, p. 188. London, Duckworth.

Hallett, S.J. (1952). A study of the effect of conditioning on multiple aspect ESP scoring. *Journal of Parapsychology*, 16, 204–211.

Hansel, C.E.M. (1966). *ESP: A scientific evaluation*. New York: Scribner's.

Hansel, C.E.M. (1980). *ESP and parapsychology: A critical re-evaluation*. Buffalo, NY: Prometheus.

Hansel, C.E.M. (1981). A critical analysis of H. Schmidt's psychokinesis experiments. *Skeptical Inquirer*, 5(3), 26–33.

Hansel, G.P., Utts, J., & Markwick, B. (1994). Statistical and methodological problems of the PEAR remote viewing experiments. In E.W. Cook and D.L. Delanoy (Eds.), *Research in parapsychology*, 1991, 103–107. Metuchen, NJ: Scarecrow Press.

Haraldsson, E. (1978). ESP and the Defense Mechanism Test (DMT): A further validation. *European Journal of Parapsychology*, 2, 104–114.

Haraldsson, E., & Gissurarson. L.R. (1987). Does geomagnetic activity effect extrasensory perception? *Personality and Individual Differences*, 8, 745–47.

Haraldsson, E., & Houtkooper, J. (1995). Meta-analysis of ten experiments on perceptual defensiverrness and ESP: ESP scoring patterns, experimenter and decline effects. *Journal of Parapsychology*, 59(3) 251–271.

Haraldsson, E., & Houtkooper, J.M. (1992). Effects of perceptual defensiveness, personality and belief on extrasensory perception tasks. *Personality and Individual Differences*, 13, 1085–96.

Haraldsson, E., Houtkooper, J.M., Schneider, R., & Bäckström, M. (2002). Perceptual defensiveness and ESP performance: Reconstructed DMT-ratings and psychological correlates in the first German DMT-ESP experiment. *Journal of Parapsychology*. 66(3), 249–270.

Haraldsson, E., & Thorsteinsson, T. (1973). Psychokinetic effects on yeast. An exploratory experiment. *Research in Parapsychology*, 1972, 20–21. Metuchen, NJ: Scarecrow Press.

Harding, S.E., & Thalbourne, M.A. (1981). Transcendental meditation, clairvoyant ability and psychological adjustment. In W.G. Roll and J. Beloff (Eds.), *Research in parapsychology*, 1980, p. 71–73. Metuchen, NJ: Scarecrow Press.

Hardy, A., Harvie, R., & Köestler, A. (1973).

The challenge of chance. London: Ilutchinson.

Hardy, G.H. (1959). *Ramanujan: Twelve lectures on subjects suggested by his life and work.* New York: Chelsea.

Harman, W., & Rheingold, H. (1984). *Higher creativity.* Los Angeles: Tarcher.

Harris, W.S., Gowda, M., & Kolb, J.W. (1999). A randomized, controlled trial of the effects of remote, intercessory prayer on outcomes in patients admitted to the coronary care unit. *Archives of Internal Medicine,* 24: 79–88.

Heinlein, C.P., & Heinlein, J.H. (1938). Critique of the premises and statistical methodology of parapsychology. *Journal of Parapsychology,* 2, 171–183.

Henkel, A., & R.K. Berger (Eds.) (1988). *Research in parapsychology* (pp. 121–156). Metuchen, NJ: Scarecrow Press.

Herr, D.L. (1938). A mathematical analysis of the experiments in parapsychology. *Journal of Experimental Psychology,* 22, 491–496.

Hettinger, J. (1946). On J.B. Rhine's "Telepathy and clairvoyance reconsidered," *Proceedings of the Society for Psychical Research,* v. 48, 10–15.

Hickman, J.L. (1979). Plant growth experiments with Matthew Manning. In J. Mishlove (Ed.), A month with Mathew Manning: Experiences and experiments in Northern California during May-June 1977.

Hitchman, G.A.M., Roe, C.A., & Sherwood, S.J. (2012). A reexamination of nonintentional precognition with openness to experience, creativity, psi beliefs, and luck beliefs as predictors of success. *Journal of Parapsychology,* 76, 109–145.

Honorton, C. (1964). Separation of high- and low-scoring ESP subjects through hypnotic preparation. *Journal of Parapsychology,* 28, 250–57.

Honorton, C. (1965). The relationship between ESP and manifest anxiety level. *Journal of Parapsychology,* 29, 291–292.

Honorton, C. (1966). A further separation of high-and low-scoring ESP subjects through hypnotic preparation. *Journal of Parapsychology,* 30, 172–183.

Honorton, C. (1969). Relation between EEG alpha activity and ESP card-guessing performance. *Journal of the American Society for Psychical Research,* 63, 365374.

Honorton, C. (1976). Has science developed the competence to confront claims of the paranormal? In J.D. Morris, W.G. Roll, & R.L. Morris (Eds.), *Research in parapsychology,* 1975 (199–223). Metuchen, NJ: Scarecrow Press.

Honorton, C. (1977). Psi and internal attention states. In B.B. Walmon (Ed.), *Handbook of parapsychology* (pp. 435–472). New York: Van Nostrand Reinhold.

Honorton, C. (1985). Meta-analysis of psi ganzfeld research: A response to Hyman. *Journal of Parapsychology.* 49, 51–91.

Honorton, C. (1993). Rhetoric over substance: The impoverished state of skepticism. *Journal of Parapsychology,* 57, 191–214.

Honorton, C., & Barksdale, W. (1972). PK performance with waking suggestions for muscle tension versus relaxation. *Journal of the American Society for Psychical Research,* 66, 208–214.

Honorton, C., Davidson, R., & Bindler, P. (1971). Feedback augmented EEG alpha, shifts in subjective state, and ESP card-guessing performance. *Journal of the American Society for Psychical Research,* 65, 308323.

Honorton, C., & Ferrari, D.C. (1989). "Future telling": A meta-analysis of forced choice precognition experiments, 1935–1987. *Journal of Parapsychology,* 53(28), 281–308.

Honorton, C., Ferrari, D.C., & Bem, D.J. (1998). Extroversion and ESP performance: A meta-analyses and a new confirmation. *Journal of Parapsychology,* 62, 255–276.

Honorton, C., & Harper, S. (1974). Psi-mediated imagery and ideation in an experimental procedure for regulating perceptual input. *Journal of the American Society for Psychical Research,* 68, 156–168.

Honorton, C., Krippner, S., & Ullman, M. (1971). Telepathic transmission of art prints under two conditions. In E. Malinoff (Ed.), *Proceedings of the 80th Annual Convention, American Psychological Association,* p. 319–320. Washington, D.C.: American Psychological Association.

Honorton, C., Ramsey, M., & Cabibo, C. (1975). Experimenter effects in extrasensory perception. *Journal of the American Society for Psychical Research*, 69, 135–150.

Houtkooper, J.M., Schienle, A., Stark, R., & Vaitil, D. (1998). Atmospheric electromagnetism: The possible disturbing influence of natural sferics on ESP. *41st Annual Parapsychological Association Convention Halifax, Nova Scotia.*

Hume, D. (1825). *Essays and treatises on several subjects.* Edinburgh: Printed for Bell and Bradfute; [etc., etc.].

Hume, D. (1939). *Treatise on human nature.* London: Dent.

Hume, D. (1978/1739). *A treatise on human nature* (Edited by L.A. Selby-Bigge, revised by P.H. Niddtich). Oxford: Oxford University Press.

Humphrey, B., & Rhine, J.B. (1944). The evolution of salience in Doctor Schneidler's ESP data. *Journal of Parapsychology*, 9, 124–132.

Humphrey, B.M., & Rhine, J.B. (1945). PK tests with two sizes of dice mechanically thrown. *Journal of Parapsychology*, 9, 124–132.

Humphrey, B.M. (1943). Patterns of success in an ESP experiment. *Journal of Parapsychology*, 7, 5–19.

Humphrey, B.M. (1951). Introversion-extroversion ratings in relation to scores in ESP tests. *Journal of Parapsychology*, 18, 252–62.

Humphrey, B.M. (1964a). Success in ESP as related to form of response drawings. I. Clairvoyance experiments. *Journal of Parapsychology*, 10, 181–196.

Humphrey, B.M. (1964b). Success in ESP as related to form of response drawings. II. GESP experiments. *Journal of Parapsychology*, 10, 78–106.

Humphrey, B.M., & Pratt, J.G. (1941). A comparison of five ESP test procedures. *Journal of Parapsychology*, 5, 267–93.

Hyman, R. (1977) Psychics and scientists: "Mind-reach" and remote viewing. *The Humanist.*

Hyman, R. (1978). Psi: A challenge to critics and believers (Review of Handbook

of parapsychology edited by B.B. Wolman). *Contemporary Psychology.*

Hyman, R. (1985). The ganzfeld psi experiment: A critical appraisal. *Journal of Parapsychology*, 49, 3–49.

Hyman, R. (1986). Outracing the evidence: The muddled mind race. In P.K. Frazier (Ed.), *Science confronts the paranormal.* Buffalo, NY: Prometheus Books.

Hyman, R. (1996). Evaluation of a program on anomalous mental phenomena. *Journal of Scientific Exploration*, 10, 31–58.

Hyman, R., & Honorton, C. (1986). Joint Communiqué: The psi ganzfeld controversy. *Journal of Parapsychology*, 50, 351–364.

Inglis, B. (1977). *Natural and supernatural: A history of the paranormal from earliest times to 1914.* London: Hodder and Stoughton [(1992). Rev. ed. London: Prism].

Irwin, H.J. (1979). *Psi and the mind: An information processing approach.* Metuchen, NJ: Scarecrow Press.

Irwin, H.J. (1994). *An introduction to parapsychology* (2nd ed.). Jefferson, NC: McFarland.

Irwin, H.J. (1999). *An introduction to parapsychology* (3d ed.) Jefferson, NC: McFarland.

Jahn, R.G. (1982). The persistent paradox of psychic phenomena: *An Engineering Perspective Proceedings of the IEEE.* 70, 136–70.

Jahn, R.G., & Dunne, B.J. (1987). *Margins of reality: The role of consciousness in the physical world.* New York: Harcourt Brace Jovanovich.

Jahn, R.G., & Dunne, B.J. (1999). *Two decades of pear: An anthology of selected publications.* Princeton, NJ: Princeton Engineering Anomalies Research Laboratory, Princeton University.

James, W. (1886). Report of the Committee on Mediumistic Phenomena. *Proceedings of the American Society for Psychical Research*, 1, 102–106.

James, W. (1890/1952). *Principles of psychology.* New York, NY: Holt.

James, W. (1892). What psychical research has accomplished. *Forum*, 13, 727–742.

James, W. (1896). Address of the president

before the Society for Psychical Research. *Science*, 3, 881–888.

James, W. (1911). Final impressions of a psychical researcher. In W. James, *Memories and studies* (pp. 173–206). Cambridge, MA: The Riverside Press.

Jephson, I. (1929). Evidence for clairvoyance in card-guessing: A report on some recent experiments. *Proceedings of Society for Psychical Research*, 38, 223–68.

Johnson, M. (1971). An attempt to manipulate the scoring direction of subjects by means of control of motivation of the subjects. *Research Letter of the Parapsychological Division of the Psychological Laboratory of the University of Utrecht*, March, 9–15.

Johnson, M. (1973). A written academic exam as a disguised test of clairvoyance [Abstract]. In W.G. Roll, J.D. Morris, & R.L. Morris (Eds.), *Research in parapsychology 1972* (pp. 28–30). Metuchen, NJ: Scarecrow Press.

Johnson, M., & Haraldsson, E. (1984). Icelandic experiments IV and V with the defense mechanism test. *Journal of Parapsychology*, 48, 185–200.

Johnson, M., & Johannesson, G. (1972). An attempt to control scoring direction by means of treatment of the subjects. *Research Letter of the Parapsychological Division of the Psychological Laboratory of the University of Utrecht*, March, 1–18.

Johnson, M., & Kanthamani, B.K. (1967). The defense mechanism test as a predictor of ESP.

Johnson, M., & Nordbeck, B. (1972). Variation on the scoring behavior of a "psychic" subject. *Journal of Parapsychology*, 36, 122–132.

Jung, C.G. (1963). *Memories, dreams, reflection*. New York: Pantheon.

Jung, C.G. (1963). *Modern man in search of soul*. New York: Harcourt Brace Jovanovich [(1933). Princeton, N.J: Princeton University Press].

Jung. C.G. (1969). *The archetypes and the collective unconscious*. (R.F.C. Hall, trans.).

Jung, C.G. (1973). *Synchronicity: An acausal connecting principle*. (Trans. by R.F.C. Hull). Collected Works of C.G.

Jung, Vol. 8. Princeton, NJ: Princeton University Press.

Jung, C.G., & Pauli, W. (1955). *The interpretation of nature and the psyche: Synchronicity and the influence of archetypal ideas on the scientific theories of Kepler*. New York: Pantheon Books, 1955.

Kahn, S.D. (1976). "Myers' problem" revisited. In G.R. Schmeidler (Ed.), *Parapsychology: Its relation to physics, biology, psychology and psychiatry* (pp. 208–234). Metuchen, NJ: Scarecrow Press.

Kamiya, J. (1969). Operant control of the EEG alpha rhythm and some of its reported effects on consciousness. In C.T. Tart (Ed.), *Altered states of consciousness*. New York: Wiley.

Kanthamani, B.K. (1965a). A study of differential response in language ESP tests. *Journal of Parapsychology*, 29, 27–34.

Kanthamani, B.K. (1965b) The experimenter's role in language ESP tests. Paper read at the Eighth Annual Convention of the Parapsychological Association, New York.

Kanthamani, B.K., & Rao, K.R. (1972). Personality characteristics of ESP subjects: III Extraversion and ESP. *Journal of Parapsychology*, 36, 198–212.

Kanthamani, B.K., & Rao, H.H. (1974). A study of memory ESP relationship using linguistic forms. *Journal of Parapsychology*, 38, 286–300.

Kanthamani, B.K., & Rao, K.R. (1973a). Personality characteristics of ESP subjects: IV. Neuroticism and ESP. *Journal of Parapsychology*, 37, 37–50.

Kanthamani, B.K., & Rao, K.R. (1973b). Personality characteristics of ESP subjects: V. Graphic expansiveness and ESP. *Journal of Parapsychology*, 37, 119–129.

Kanthamani, H., & Kelly, E.F. (1974a). Card experiments with a special subject. Single-card clairvoyance. *Journal of Parapsychology*, 38, 16–26.

Kanthamani, H., & Kelly, E.F. (1974b). Awareness of success in an exceptional subject. *Journal of Parapsychology*, 38, 355–382.

Karagulla, S. (1967). *Breakthrough to creativity: Your higher sense perception*. Los Angeles: De Vorss.

Kasamatsu, A., & Hirai, T. (1969). An electroencephalographic study of Zen meditation. In C.T. Tart (Ed.), *Altered states of consciousness.* New York: John Wiley and Sons.

Kellogg, C.E. (1936). Dr. J.B. Rhine and extra-sensory perception. *Journal of Abnormal Social Psychology*, 31, 190.

Kelly, E.F., & Kanthamani, B.K. (1972). A subject's efforts toward voluntary control. *Journal of Parapsychology*, 36, 185–197.

Kelly, E.F., Kelly, E.W., & Myers, F.W.H. (2007). *Irreducible mind: Toward a psychology for the 21st century.* Lanham, MD: Rowman & Littlefield.

Kelly, E.W. (2007). F.W.H. Myers and the empirical study of the mind-body problem. In E. Kelly, E.W. Kelly, A. Crabtree, A. Gauld, M. Grosso, & B. Greyson, *Irreducible mind: Toward a psychology for the 21st century* (pp. 47–115). Lanham, MD: Rowman & Littlefield.

Kennedy, J.E. (1978). The role of task complexity in PK: A review. *Journal of Parapsychology*, 42, 89–122.

Kennedy, J.E. (1979). Consistent missing: A type of information-processing error in ESP. *Journal of Parapsychology*, 43, 113–128.

Kennedy, J.E. (1979). Redundancy in psi information: Implications for the goal-oriented psi hypothesis and for the application of psi. *Journal of Parapsychology*, 43, 290–314.

Kennedy, J.E. (2002). Commentary on "Experiments on distant intercessory prayer" in *Archives of Internal Medicine. Journal of Parapsychology*, 66 (pp. 177–182).

Kennedy, J.E. (2004). A proposal and challenge for proponents and skeptics of psi. *Journal of Parapsychology*, 68, 157–167.

Kennedy, J.E. (2004). What is the purpose of psi? *Journal of American Society for Psychical Research*, 98, 1–27.

Kennedy, J.E. (2006). Book Review of Irreducible mind: Toward a psychology for the 21 Century by Edward Kelly, Emily Williams Kelly, Adam Crabtree, Alan Gauld, Michael Grosso, & Bruce Greyson. *Journal of Parapsychology*, 70 (2), 373–377.

Kennedy, J.E. (2013). Can parapsychology move beyond the controversies of retrospective meta-analyses? *Journal of Parapsychology*, 77, 21–35.

Kennedy, J.E., & Taddonio, J.L. (1976). Experimenter effects in parapsychological research. *Journal of Parapsychology*, 40, 1–33.

Kennedy, J.L. (1938). The visual cues from the backs of the ESP cards. *Journal of Parapsychology*, 6, 149.

Kennedy, J.L. (1939). A critical review of discrimination shown between experimenters by subjects, by J.D. MacFarland. *Journal of Parapsychology*, 5: 213–225.

Koenig, H.G., Cohen, H.J., Blazer, D.G., Pieper, C., & Meador, K.G., Shelp, F., Goli, V., & DiPasquale, R. (1992). Religious coping and depression in elderly hospitalized medically ill men. *American Journal of Psychiatry*, 149, 1693–1700.

Koenig, H.G., Hays, J.C., Larson, D.B., George, L.K., Cohen, H.J., McCullough, M., Meador, K., & Blazer, D.G. (1999). Does religious attendance prolong survival?: A six year follow-up study of 3,968 older adults. *Journal of Gerontology* (medical sciences) 54A: M370–377.

Koenig H.G., Larson D.B., & Larson S.S. (2001) Religion and coping with serious medical illness. *Annals of Pharmacotherapy* 2001 Mar; 35(3):352–9.

Koenig, H.G., McCullough, M.E., & Larson, D.B. (2001). *Handbook of religion and health.* New York: Oxford University Press.

Koestler, A. (1972). *The roots of coincidence.* New York: Random House.

Kogan, I.M. (1966). Is telepathy possible? *Telecommunications and Radio Engineering*, 21 (pp. 75–81).

Koopman, B.G., & Blasband, R.A. (2002). Two case reports of distant healing: New paradigms at work? *Alternate Therapy Health Medicine*, 8(1), 116–120.

Kragh, U., & Smith, G. (1970). *Percept-Genetic Analysis.* Lund: Gleerups.

Kramer, J.K., & Terry, R.L. (1973). GESP and personality factors: A search for correlates. *Journal of Parapsychology*, 37, 74–75.

Kreitler, H., & Kreitler, S. (1972). Does extrasensory perception affect psychological experiments? *Journal of Parapsychology*, 36, 1–45.

Kreitler, H., & Kreitler, S. (1973). Subliminal perception and extrasensory perception. *Journal of Parapsychology*, 37, 163–188.

Kreitler, H., & Kreitler, S. (1974a). ESP and cognition. *Journal of Parapsychology*, 38, 267–285.

Kreitler, H., & Kreitler, S. 1974(b). Optimization of experimental ESP. *Journal of Parapsychology*, 38, 383–392.

Krieger, D. (1986). *The therapeutic touch. How to use your hands to help or to heal.* New York: Prentice-Hall.

Krippner, S. (1969). Investigations of extrasensory phenomena in dreams and other altered states of consciousness. *Journal of American Society for psychosomatic Dentistry and Medicine*, 16, 7–14.

Krippner, S. (Ed.) (1978). *Advances in parapsychological research 2: Extrasensory perception.* New York: Plenum Press.

Krippner, S., Honorton, C., & Ullman, M. (1972). A second precognitive dream study with Malcolm Bessent. *Journal of the American Society for Psychical Research*, 66, 269–279.

Krippner, S., Honorton, C., & Ullman, M. (1973). An experiment in dream telepathy with the "Grateful Dead." *Journal of the American Society of Psychosomatic Dentistry and Medicine*, 20, 9–17.

Kripnner, S., Ullman, M., & Honorton, C. (1971). A precognitive dream study with a single subject. *Journal of the American Society for Psychical Research*, 65, 192–203.

Krishna, S.R., & Rao, K.R. (1991). Effect on ESP feedback on subjects responses to a personality questionnaire *Journal of Parapsychology*, 55, 147158.

Krucoff, M.W., Crater, S.W., & Lee, K.L. (2006). From efficacy to safety concerns: A STEP forward or a step back for clinical research and intercessory prayer? The Study of Therapeutic Effects of Intercessory Prayer (STEP). *American Heart Journal*, 151(4), 762–764 (April 2006).

Kuhn, T.S. (1970). *The structure of scientific revolutions.* Chicago: University of Chicago Press.

Kurtz, P. (1981). Is parapsychology a science? In K. Frazier (Ed.), *Paranormal borderlands of science* (pp. 5–23). Buffalo, NY: Prometheus Books.

Lakatos, I. (1974). Falsification and the methodology of scientific research programmes. In I. Lakatos & A.E. Musgrave (Eds.), *Criticism and growth of knowledge.* Cambridge: Cambridge University Press.

Lantz, N.O., Luke, W.L., & May, E.C. (1994). Target and sender dependencies in anomalous cognition experiments. *Journal of Parapsychology*, 58, 285–302.

Lawrence, T. (1993). Gathering in the sheep and goats: A meta-analysis of forced-choice sheep-goat ESP studies, 1947–1993. *Proceedings of the Parapsychological Association 36th Annual Convention* (pp. 75–86).

Lemmon, V.W. (1939). Symposium on ESP methods: The role of selection in ESP data. *Journal of Parapsychology*, 3, 104–105.

Lenington, S. (1979). Effect of holy water on the growth of radish plants. *Psychological Report*, 45, 381–382.

LeShan, L. (1974). *The medium, the mystic and the physicist.* London: Turnstone Press.

LeShan, L. (1976). *Alternate realities.* New York: Ballantine Books.

Leuba, C. (1938). An experiment to test the role of chance in ESP research. *Journal of Parapsychology*, 2, 217–221.

Leuret, F., & Bon, H. (1957). *Modern miraculous cures: A documented account of miracles and medicine in the 20th century.* New York: Farrar, Straus and Cudahy.

Lodge, O. (1916). *Raymond, or life and death.* London: Methuen.

Lodge, O.J. (1884). An account of some experiments in thought-transference. *Proceedings of the Society for Psychical Research*, 1, 189–200.

Lombroso, C. (1909). *After death what? Spiritistic phenomena and their interpretation.* Boston: Small, Maynard.

London Dialectical Society. (1871). *Report*

on spiritualism, of the Committee of the London Dialectical Society, together with the evidence, oral and written, and a selection from the correspondence. London: Longmans, Green, Reader, and Dyer.

Lovitts, B. (1981). The sheep-goat effect turned upside down. *Journal of Parapsychology*, 45, 293–310.

Lübke, C., & Rohr, W. (1975). Psi and subliminal perception. A replication of the Krietler and Krietler study. In J.D. Morris, W.G. Roll & R.L. Moris (Eds.), *Research in parapsychology 1974* (pp. 161–164). Metuchen, NJ: Scarecrow.

Lucadou, W. von. (1987). The model of pragmatic information (MPI). In R.L. Morris (Ed.), *The Parapsychological Association 30th Annual Convention, Proceedings of Presented Papers* (pp. 236–254).

Lucadou, W. von. (1995). The model of pragmatic information. *European Journal of Parapsychology*, 11, 58–75.

Lucadou, W. von. (2015). The model of pragmatic information. In E.C. May and S.B. Marwaha (Eds.). *Extrasensory perception: Support, skepticism, and science, volume II—theoretical frameworks*. Santa Barbara: Praeger.

MacFarland, J.D. (1938) Discrimination shown between experiments by subjects. *Journal of Parapsychology*, 2: 160–170.

Mackenzie, B. (1982). "Parapsychology's critics: A link with the past?" *Behavioural and Brain Sciences*, 10(4), 597.

Mackenzie, B., & Mackenzie, L. (1980). "Whence the enchanted boundary? Sources and significance of the parapsychological tradition." *Journal of Parapsychology*, 44, 125–166.

Marks, D. & Kammann, R. (1980). *The psychology of the psychic*. New York: Prometheus Brother.

Marks, D.F. (1986). Remote viewing revisited. In K. Frazier (Ed.), *Science confronts the Paranormal* (pp. 110–121). Buffalo, NY: Prometheus Books.

Marks, D.F., & Kammann, R. (1978). Information transmission in remote viewing experiments. *Nature*, 274, 680¬–681.

Marks, D.F. & Scott, C. (1986). Remote viewing exposed. *Nature*, 319, 414.

Markwick, B. (1978). The Soal-Goldney experiments with Basil Shackelton: New evidence of data manipulation. *Proceedings of the Society for Psychical Research*, 56, 250–277.

Marwaha, S.B., & May, E.C. (2015). Fundamental issues for psi theorists. In E.C. May and S.B. Marwaha (Eds.). *Extrasensory perception: Support, skepticism, and science, volume II—theoretical frameworks*. Santa Barbara: Praeger.

Mason, L.I., Patterson, R.P., & Radin, D.I. (2007). Exploratory study: The random number generator and group meditation. *Journal of Scientific Exploration*, 21, 295–317.

Masters, K.S., Spielmans, G.I., & Goodson, J.T. (2006). Are there demonstrable effects of distant intercessory prayer? A meta-analytic review. *Annals of Behavioral Medicine*, 32(1), 21–26. (Abstract). www.springerlink.com/content/x7rtu32722145572/

Mattlin, J., Wethington, E., & Kessler, R. (1990). Situational determinants of coping and coping effectiveness. *Journal of Health and Social Behavior*, 31 (March), 103–122.

Mattuck, R.D. (1977). Random fluctuation theory of psychokinesis: Thermal noise model. In J.D. Morris, W.G. Roll, & R.L. Morris (Eds.), *Research in parapsychology* (pp. 191–195). Metuchen, NJ: Scarecrow Press.

Mattuck, R.D. (1982). A model of the interaction between consciousness and matter using Bohm-Bub hidden variables. In W. Roll., R. Morris, & R. White (Eds.). *Research in parapsychology* (pp. 147–147). Metuchen, NJ: Scarecrow Press.

Mauskopf, S.H., & McVaugh, M.R. (1980). *The Elusive Science: Origins of Experimental Psychical Research*. Baltimore: Johns Hopkins University Press.

May, E.C. (1998). Response to "Experiment one of the SAIC remote viewing program: A critical re-evaluation. *Journal of Parapsychology*, 62, 309–318.

May, E.C. (2015). Experimenter psi: An expanded view of decision augmentation theory. In E.C. May and S.B. Marwaha (Eds.). *Extrasensory perception: Support, skepticism, and science, volume II—theoretical frameworks.* Santa Barbara: Praeger.

May, E.C., & Marwaha, S.B. (Eds.) (2014). *Anomalous cognition: Remote viewing research and theory.* Jefferson, NC: McFarland.

May, E.C., Utts, J.M., & Spottiswoode, S.J.P. (1995). Decision augmentation theory: Applications to the random number generator database. *Journal of Scientific Exploration*, 9, 453–488.

May, E.C., Utts, J.M., & Spottiswoode, S.J.P. (1995b). Decision augmentation theory: Toward a model of anomalous mental phenomena. *Journal of Parapsychology*, 59, 195–220.

May, E.C., Utts, J.M., & Spottiswoode, S.J.P. (2014). Decision augmentation theory: Toward a model of anomalous mental phenomena. In Edwin C. May and S.B. Marwaha, *Anomalous cognition: Remote viewing research and theory.* Jefferson, NC: McFarland.

McClenon, J. (1981). The rhetorical aspect of parapsychology's struggle with its critics. Paper presented at the Eighth Annual Convention of the Southeastern Parapsychological Association. *Journal of Parapsychology*, 45, 162 (Abstract).

McClenon, J. (1994). Surveys of anomalous experience: A cross-cultural analysis. *Journal of the American Society for Psychical Research*, 88, 117–135.

McConnell, R.A. (1968). The structure of scientific revolutions: An epitome. *Journal of the American Society for Psychical Research*, 62, 321–327.

McConnell, R.A., Snowden, R.J., & Powell, K.F. (1955). Wishing with dice. *Journal of Experimental Psychology*, 50(4), 269–275.

McCullough, M.E., Hoyt, W.T., Larson, D.B., Koenig, H.G., & Thoresen, C.E. (2000). Religious involvement and mortality: A meta-analytic review. *Health Psychology*, 19, 211–222.

McDougall, W. (1934). Foreword. In J.B. Rhine (Ed.), *Extrasensory perception* (pp. viii–xvi). Boston, MA: Boston Society for Psychical Research.

McMahan, E. (1946). Success in ESP as related to form of response drawings. II. GESP Experiments. *Journal of Parapsychology*, 10, 169–180.

McMahan, E.A., & Rhine, J.B. (1947). A second Zagreb Durham ESP experiment. *Journal of Parapsychology*, 11, 244–253.

McMoneagle, J. (1993). *Mind trek.* Charlottesville, VA: Hampton Roads.

McVaugh, M.R., & Mauskopf, S.H. (1976). J.B. Rhine's *Extrasensory perception* and its background in psychical research. *Isis*, 67, 160–189.

Mead, G.H. (1934). *Mind, self and society.* Chicago: University of Chicago Press.

Medhurst, R.G., Goldney, K.M., and Barrington, M.R. (1972). *Crookes and the spirit world.* New York: Taplinger.

Medhurst, R.G., & Scott, C. (1974). A reexamination of C.E.M. Hansel's criticism of the Pratt-Woodruff experiment. *JP*, 38, 163–184.

Mesmer, F.A. (1779). *Memoire sur la decouverte du magnetisme animal.* Paris: Didot.

Millar, B. (1978). The observational theories: A primer. *European Journal of Parapsychology*, 2, 304–332.

Miller, N.E., Barber, T.X., Dicara, L.V., Kamiya, J., Shapiro, D., & Stoyva, J. (Eds.). (1974). *Biofeedback and self-control 1973: An Aldine annual on the regulation of bodily processes and consciousness.* Chicago: Aldine.

Milton, J. (1993). Ordinary state ESP meta-analysis. In M.J. Schiltz (Ed.), *Proceedings of Presented Papers, 36 Annual Parapsychological Association* (pp. 87–104). Favihaves, MA: Parapsychology Association.

Milton, J., & Wiseman, R. (1999). Does psi exist? Lack of replication of an anomalous process of information transfer. *Psychological Bulletin*, 125, 387–391.

Miovic, M. (2004). *Initiation: Spiritual insights on life, art, and psychology.* Hyderabad (India): Sri Aurobindo Society.

Mishlove, J. (1993). *The roots of consciousness.* Tulsa, OK: Council Oak Books.

Moerman, D.E. (1981). Edible symbols: On the effectiveness of placebos. *Annals of* the *New York Academy of Sciences*, 364, 256–268.

Morris, R.L. (1970): Psi and animal behavior: A survey. *Journal of the American Society for Psychical Research*, 64, 242–260.

Morris, R.L. (1978): A survey of methods and issues in ESP research. Krippner, S. (Ed.), *Advances in parapsychological research. Volume 2: Extrasensory perception* (pp. 7–58). New York: Plenum Press.

Morris, R.L. (1982). An updated survey of methods and issues in ESP research. Krippner, S. (Ed.), *Advances in Parapsychological Research. Volume 2: Extrasensory Perception*, 7–58. New York: Plenum Press.

Morris, R.L., Roll, W.G., Klein, J., & Wheeler, G. (1972). EEG patterns and ESP results in forced-choice experiments with Lalsingh Harribance. *Journal of the American Society for Psychical Research*, 66, 253268.

Moss, S., & Butler, D.C. (1978). The scientific credibility of ESP. *Perceptual and Motor Skills*, 46, 1063–1079.

Mueller, P.S., Plevak, D.J., & Rummans, T.A. (2001) Religious involvement, spirituality, and medicine: implications for clinical practice. *Mayo Clinic Proceedings*, 76(12): 1189–91 [Pub Med Citation]

Mullen, B., & Rosenthal, R. (1985). *BASIC meta-analysis procedures and programs*. Hillsdale, NJ: Erlbaum.

Mundle, C.W.K. (1952). "Some philosophical perspectives for parapsychology." *Journal of Parapsychology*, 16, 257–272.

Mundle, C.W.K. (1976). Strange facts in search of a theory. In J.M.O. Wheatley, & H.L. Edge (Eds.) *Philosophical dimensions of parapsychology* (pp. 76–97). Springfield, IL: Charles C. Thomas.

Munson, R.J. (1979). The effects of PK on rye seeds. *Journal of Parapsychology*, 43–45.

Murphy, G. (1945). Field theory and survival. *Journal of the American Society for Psychical Research*, 39, 181–209.

Murphy, G. (1948). An approach to precognition. *Journal of American Society for Psychical Research*, 42: 3–14.

Murphy, G. (1949). The place of parapsychology among the sciences. *Journal of Parapsychology*, 13, 62–71.

Murphy, G. (1961/1970). *Challenge of psychical research: A primer of parapsychology*. New York: Harper Row.

Murphy, G., & Ballou, R.O. (Eds.). (1960). *William James on psychical research*. New York: Viking Press.

Musso, J.R. (1965). ESP experiments with primary school children. *Journal of Parapsychology*, 29, 115–121.

Myers, F.W.H. (1903/1915). *Human personality and its survival of death*. (2 Vols.). New York: Longmans, Green & Co.

Myers, F.W.H., O.J. Lodge, W. Leaf and W. James. (1889–1890). "A Record of observations of certain phenomena of trance." *Proceedings of the Society for Psychical Research*.

Nash, C.B. (1960). Can precognition occur diametrically? *Journal of Parapsychology*, 24:26–32.

Nash, C.B. (1968). Comparison of ESP run-score average of groups liked and disliked by the experimenter. *Journal of the American Society of Psychical Research*, 62, 411–414.

Nash, C.B. (1982). Hypnosis and transcendental meditation as inducers of ESP. *Parapsychology Review*, 13, 19–20.

Nash, C.B., & Durkin, M.G. (1959). Terminal salience with multiple digit targets. *Journal of Parapsychology*, 23, 49–53.

Nelson, R. (2001). Design and preliminary results of three on-line PSI experiments. *20th Annual SSE Meeting*, June 7–9, 2001, San Diego.

Nelson, R.D. (2015). Implicit physical psi: The global consciousness project. In E. Cardeña, J. Palmer, & D. Marcusson-Clavertz (Eds.), *Parapsychology: A handbook for the 21st century*, 282–292. Jefferson, NC: McFarland.

Nelson, R.D., Bradish, G.J., Dobyns, Y.H., Dunne, B.J., & Jahn, R.G. (1996). Field REG anomalies in group situations. *Journal of Scientific Exploration*, 10, 111–141.

Nelson, R.D., & Dunne, B.J. (1986). Attempted correlation of engineering anomalies with global geomagnetic activity. *Proceedings of Presented Papers: The 29th Annual Convention of the Parapsychological Society* (pp. 507–518).

Nelson, R.D., Jahn, R.G., Dunne, B.J., & Dobyns, Y.H. (1998). Field REG II: Conscious field effect: Replication and extensions. *Journal of Scientific Exploration,* 12, 425–454.

Nelson, R.D., & Radin, D.I. (1989). Statistically robust anomalous effects: Replication in random event generator experiments. In L.A. Henkel and R.E. Berger (Eds.), *Research in parapsychology, 1988* (pp. 23–27). Metuchen, NJ: Scarecrow Press.

Nichols, A.A. (2000). A water poltergeist in Florida. *International Journal of Parapsychology,* 11, 143–159.

Nicol, J.F., & Carington, W. (1947). Some experiments in willed die-throwing. *Proceedings of the Society for Psychical Research,* 48, 164–176.

Nicolas, C. (1977). The effects of loving attention on plant growth. *New England Journal of Parapsychology,* 1, 19–24.

Nielsen, W. (1956). Mental states associated with success in precognition. *Journal of Parapsychology,* 20, 96109.

Nilsson, N.J. (1975). *Artificial intelligence: Research and application.* Volume 2, Technical Note. AI Center, Stanford Research Institute.

Osis, K. (1952). A test of the occurrence of a psi effect between man and the cat. *Journal of Parapsychology, 16,* 233–256.

Osis, K., & Bokert, E. (1971) ESP and changed states of consciousness induced by meditation. *Journal of the American Society for Psychical Research,* 65, 17–65.

Osis, K., & Carlson, M.L. (1972). The ESP channel—Open or closed? *Journal of the American Society for Psychical Research,* 66, 310–320.

Osis, K., & Dean, D. (1964). The effect of experimenter differences and subjects belief level upon ESP scores. *Journal of the American Society for Psychical Research,* 58, 158–185.

Osis, K., & Foster, E.B. (1953). A test of ESP in cats. *Journal of Parapsychology,* 17, 168–186.

Osis, K., & McCormick, D. (1980). Kinetic effects at the ostensible location of an out-of-body projection during perceptual testing. *Journal of the American Society for Psychical Research,* 74, 319–329.

Osis, K., & Pienaar, D.C. (1956). ESP over a distance of seventy-five hundred miles. *Journal of Parapsychology,* 20, 229–33.

Osty E., & M. Osty. (1931). Les Pouvoirs inconnus de l'esprit sur la matière. *Revue Métapsychique,* No. 6, 393–427, No. 1, 1–59, No. 2, 81–122.

Otani, S. (1955). Relations of mental set and change of skin resistance to ESP score. *Journal of Parapsychology,* 1955, 19, 164. 14.

Otani, S. (1965). Some relations of ESP scores to change in skin resistance. In *Parapsychology: From Duke to FRNM.* Durham, NC: Parapsychology Press.

Owen, A.R.G. (1964). *Can we explain the poltergeist?* New York: Garrett Publications.

Palmer, J. (1971). Scoring in ESP tests as a function of belief in ESP, Part I: The sheep-goat effect. *Journal of American Society for Psychical Research,* 65, 373–408.

Palmer, J. (1972). Scoring in ESP tests as a function of belief in ESP, Part II: Beyond the sheep-goat effect. *Journal of American Society for Psychical Research,* 66, 1–26.

Palmer, J. (1978). Extrasensory perception: Research findings. In S. Krippner (Ed.), *Advances in parapsychological research,* 2, 59–243. New York: Plenum.

Palmer, J. (1978). The out-of-body experience: A psychological theory. *Parapsychology Review,* 9 (5), 19–22.

Palmer, J. (1982). Methodological objections to the case for psi: Are formal control conditions necessary for the demonstration of psi? *Journal of Parapsychology,* 4, 13–18.

Palmer, J. (1996). External psi influence on ESP task performance. *Journal of Parapsychology,* 60, 193–210.

Palmer, J. (1997). The challenge of experimenter psi. *European Journal of Parapsychology,* 13, 110–125.

Palmer, J. (2003). ESP in the ganzfeld: Analysis of a debate. *Journal of Consciousness Studies,* 10(6–7), 51–68.

Palmer, J. (2009). Editorial: Winning over the scientific mainstream. *Journal of Parapsychology*, 73, 3–8.

Palmer, J. (2015). Experimental methods in anomalous cognition and anomalous perturbation research. In E. Cardeña, J. Palmer, & D. Marcusson-Clavertz, *Parapsychology: A handbook for the 21st century* (pp. 49–61). Jefferson, NC: McFarland.

Palmer, J., & Carpenter, J.C. (1998). Comments on the extraversion-ESP meta-analysis by Honorton, Ferrari and Bem. *Journal of Parapsychology*, 62, 277–282.

Palmer, J., Khamashta, K., & Israelson, K. (1979). An ESP ganzfeld experiment with transcendental meditators. *Journal of the American Society for Psychical Research*, 73, 333–348.

Parapsychological Association. (1989). Terms and methods in parapsychological research. *Journal of Humanistic Psychology*, 29, 394–399.

Pargament, K.I., Koenig H.G., Tarakeshwar, N., & Hahn, J. (2001). Religious struggle as a predictor of mortality among medically ill elderly patients: A two-year longitudinal study. *Archives of Internal Medicine*, 161, 1881–1885.

Parker, A. (1975). Some findings relevant to the change in state hypothesis. In J.D. Morris, W.G. Roll, & R.L. Morris (Eds.), *Research in parapsychology 1974* (pp. 40–42). Metuchen, NJ: Scarecrow Press.

Parker, A., & Sjödén, B. (2010). Do some of us habituate to future emotional events? *Journal of Parapsychology*, 74, 99–115.

Parra, A., & Villanueva, J. (2003). Personality factors and ESP during ganzfeld sessions. *Journal of the Society for Psychical Research*, 67, 26–36.

Pauli, E.N. (1973). PK on living targets as related to sex, distance, and time. In W.G. Roll, R.L. Morris, & J.D. Morris (Eds.), *Research in parapsychology*, 68–70. Metuchen, NJ: Scarecrow Press.

Pegram, M.H. (1937). Some psychological relations of extra-sensory perception. *Journal of Parapsychology*, 1, 191–205.

Pekala, R.J., Kumar, V.K., & Marcano, G. (1995). Anomalous/paranormal experiences, hypnotic susceptibility, and dis-sociation. *Journal of American Society for Psychical Research*, 89, 313–332.

Penrose, R. (1989). *The emperor's new mind: Concerning computers, minds and the laws of physics*. Oxford: Oxford University Press.

Persinger, M.A. (1979). ELF field mediation in spontaneous psi events: Direct information transfer or conditional elicitation? In C.T. Tart, H.E. Puthoff, & R. Targ (Eds.), *Mind at large* (pp. 191–204). New York: Praeger.

Persinger, M.A. (1985). Geophysical variables and behavior: XXX. Intense paranormal experiences occur during days of quiet, global, geomagnetic activity. *Perceptual and Motor Skills*, 61, 320–322.

Persinger, M.A. (1989). Psi phenomena and temporal lobe activity: The geomagnetic factor. In L.A. Henkel & R.K. Berger (Eds.), *Research in parapsychology* (pp. 121–156). Metuchen, NJ: Scarecrow Press.

Persinger, M.A. (2015). Neuroscientific investigation of anomalous cognition. In E.C. May and S.B. Marwaha (Eds.), *Extrasensory perception: Support, skepticism and science*. Santa Barbara: Praeger.

Persinger, M.A., & Krippner, S. (1989). Dream ESP experiments and geomagnetic activity. *Journal of American Society for Psychical Research*, 83, 101–116.

Persinger, M.A., & Schaut, G.B. (1988). Geomagnetic factors in subjective telepathic, precognitive, and postmortem experiences. *Journal of the American Society for Psychical Research*, 82, 217–235.

Peterson, D.M. (1978). *Through the looking glass: An investigation of the faculty of extra-sensory detection of being stared at*. Unpublished Master's Thesis, University of Edinburgh.

Pinch, T. (1987). Some suggestions from the sociology of science to advance the psi debate. *Brain and Behavior*, 10(4), 603–605.

Podmore, F. (1894). *Apparitions and thought transference*. London: Scott.

Podmore, F. (1902). *Mediums of the 19th century*. New Hyde Park, NY: University Books, 1963. Orig. publ. under the title *Modern spiritualism*. London: Methuen.

Poincaré, H. (1952). *Science and hypothesis.* New York: Dover.

Polanyi, M. (1958). *Personal knowledge: Towards a post-critical philosophy.* Chicago: University of Chicago Press.

Polanyi, M. (1964). *Personal knowledge.* New York: Harper Torchbook

Poortaman, J.J. (1959). The feeling of being started at. *Journal of the Society for Psychical Research,* 40, 412.

Popper, K.R. (1959). *The logic of scientific discovery.* New York: Basic Books.

Popper, K.R. (1969). *Conjectures and refutations.* London: Routledge & Kegan Paul.

Pratt, J.G. (1947). Target preference in PK tests with dice. *Journal of Parapsychology,* 11, 26–45.

Pratt, J.G. (1953). A review of Kahn's "Studies in extrasensory perception." *Journal of Parapsychology,* 17.

Pratt, J.G. (1973). *ESP research today: A study of developments in parapsychology since 1960.* Metuchen, NJ: Scarecrow Press.

Pratt, J.G. (1974). Some notes for the future Einstein for parapsychology. *Journal of the American Society for Psychical Research,* 68, 133–155.

Pratt, J.G., & Price, M.M. (1938). The experimenter subject relationship in tests for ESP. *Journal of Parapsychology,* 2, 84–94.

Pratt, J.G., Rhine, J.B., Smith, B.M., & Stuart, C.E. (1940/1966). *Extrasensory perception after sixty years: A critical appraisal of the research in extrasensory perception.* New York: Henry Holt. (Reprinted, Boston: Bruce Humphries, 1966).

Pratt, J.G., & Woodruff, J.L. (1939). Size of stimulus symbols in extra-sensory perception. *Journal of Parapsychology,* 3, 121–158.

Price, A.D. (1973). Subjects' control of imagery, "agent's" mood, and position effects in a dual-target ESP experiment. *Journal of Parapsychology,* 37, 298–322.

Price, G.R. (1955). Science and the supernatural. *Science,* 122, 359–367.

Price, G.R. (1972). Apology to Rhine and Soal. *Science,* 175–359.

Price, H.H. (1940). Some philosophical questions about telepathy and clairvoyance. *Philosophy,* 15, 363–374.

Price, H.H. (1948). Psychical research and human personality. *Hibbert Journal,* 47, 105–113.

Price, H.H. (1949). Mind over mind and mind over matter. *Enquiry,* 2, 20–27.

Price, H.H. (1967). Psychical research and human personality. In J.R. Smythies (Ed.), *Science and ESP.* New York: Humanities Press.

Progoff, I. (1973). *Jung, synchronicity, & human destiny. Noncausal dimensions of human experience.* New York: The Julian Press.

Puthoff, H.E., & Targ, R. (1976). A perceptual channel for information transfer over kilometer distances: Historical perspective and recent research. *Proceedings of IEEE,* 64(3), 329–354.

Quinn, J.F. (1984). Therapeutic touch as energy exchange: Testing the theory. *Advances in Nursing Science,* 6 (2): 42–49.

Radin, D. (1997). *The conscious universe: The scientific truth of psychic phenomena,* New York: HarperCollins Publishers.

Radin, D. (2006). *Entangled minds: Extrasensory experiences in a quantum reality.* New York: Paraview Pocket Books.

Radin, D. (2008). Testing nonlocal observation as a source of intuitive knowledge. *Explore,* 4, 25–35.

Radin, D., Michel, L., Galdamez, K., Wendland, P., Rickenbach, R., & Delorme, A. (2012). Consciousness and the double-slit interference pattern: Six experiments, *Physics Essays,* 25, 157–171.

Radin, D., Nelson, R., Dobyns, Y., & Houtkooper, J. (2006a). Assessing the evidence for mind-matter interaction effects. *Journal of Scientific Exploration,* 20, 361–374.

Radin, D., Nelson, R., Dobyns, Y., & Houtkooper, J. (2006b). Re-examining psychokinesis: Comment on Bösch, Steinkamp and Boller (2006). *Psychological Bulletin,* 132, 523–532.

Radin, D., Stone, J., Levine, E., Eskandarnejad, Schlitz, M., Kozak, L., Mandel, D., & Hayssen, G. (2006). Effects of motivated distant intention on electrodermal activity. *Parapsychological Association 49th Annual Convention Proceedings of Presented Papers*, 176–178.

Radin, D.I. (1997a). Unconscious perception of future emotions: An experiment in presentiment. *Journal of Scientific Exploration*, 11 (2), 163–180.

Radin, D.I. (1997b). *The conscious universe: Truth of psychic phenomena.* San Francisco: HarperCollins.

Radin, D.I. (2004). Electrodermal presentiments of future emotions. *Journal of Scientific Exploration*, 18, 253–273.

Radin, D.I. (2004b). Event-related electroencephalographic correlation between isolated human subjects. *Journal of Alternative & Complementary Medicine*, 10, 315–323.

Radin, D.I., Rebman, J.M., & Mackwe, P.C. (1996). Anomalous organization of random events by group consciousness: Two exploratory experiments. *Journal of Scientific Exploration*, 10, 143–168.

Radin, D.I., Taylor, R.D., & Braud, W. (1995). Remote mental influence of human electrodermal activity: A pilot replication. *European Journal of Parapsychology*, 11, 19–34.

Ranganathan, S.R. (1967). *Ramanujan: The man and the mathematician.* London: Asia Publishing House.

Rao, K.R. (1955). Vedanta and the modus operandi of paranormal cognition. *Philosophical Quarterly* 29, 35–38.

Rao, K.R. (1957). *Psi cognition.* Tenali, India: Tagore Publishing House.

Rao, K.R. (1962). The preferential effect in ESP. *Journal of Parapsychology*, 26, 252–59.

Rao, K.R. (1963). Studies in the preferential effect II: A language ESP test involving precognition and "intervention." *Journal of Parapsychology*, 27, 23–32.

Rao, K.R. (1964). The differential response in three new situations. *Journal of Parapsychology*, 28, 81–92.

Rao, K.R. (1965). The bidirectionality of psi. *Journal of Parapsychology*, 29, 230–250.

Rao, K.R. (1966). *Experimental parapsychology: A review and interpretation.* Springfield, IL: Charles Thomas.

Rao, K.R. (1972). *Mystic awareness: Four lectures on the paranormal.* Mysore: Mysore University Press.

Rao, K.R. (1977a). Some frustrations and challenges in parapsychology. *Journal of Parapsychology*, 41, 119–135.

Rao, K.R. (1977b). On the nature of psi. *Journal of Parapsychology*, 41, 294–351.

Rao, K.R. (1978). Psi: Its place in nature. *Journal of Parapsychology*, 42, 276–303.

Rao, K.R. (1979). The scientific credibility of ESP. *Perceptual and Motor Skills*, 49, 415–429.

Rao, K.R. (1981). Correspondence. *Journal of the Society for Psychical Research*, 51, 191–194.

Rao, K.R. (1988). "Psychology of transcendence: A study in early Buddhistic psychology." In A.C. Paranjpe, D.G.F. Ho and R.W. Riebu (eds.), *Asian Contributions to Psychology*, 123–148. New York: Praeger.

Rao, K.R. (1991). Consciousness research and psi. *Journal of Parapsychology*, 55, 1–43.

Rao, K.R. (2001). Consciousness studies: A survey of perspectives and research. In J. Pandey (Ed.) *Psychology in India revisited: Developments in the discipline.* New Delhi: Sage Publications.

Rao, K.R. (2002). *Consciousness studies: Cross-cultural perspectives.* Jefferson, NC: McFarland.

Rao, K.R. (2011). *Cognitive anomalies, consciousness, and yoga.* New Delhi: Centre for Studies in Civilizations for the Project of History of Indian Science, Philosophy and Culture and Matrix Publishers.

Rao, K.R. (2017). *Foundations of yoga psychology.* New Delhi: Springer.

Rao, K.R. (Ed.). (1993). *Cultivating consciousness: Enhancing human potential, wellness, and healing.* Westport, CT: Praeger.

Rao, K.R., Dukhan, H., & Rao, P.V.K. (1978). Yogic meditation and psi scoring in forced-choice and free response tests. *Journal of Parapsychology*, 1, 160–175.

Rao, K.R., & Feola, J. (1979). Electrical activity of the brain and ESP: An exploratory study of alpha rhythm and ESP scoring. *Journal of Indian Psychology*, 2, 118–133.

Rao, K.R, Kanthamani, B.K., & Sailaja, P. (1968). ESP scores before and after a scheduled interview. *Journal of Parapsychology*, 32, 293.

Rao, K.R., Morrison, M., & Davis, J.W., & Freeman, J. (1977). The role of association in memory-recall and ESP. *Journal of Parapsychology*, 41, 190–197.

Rao, K.R., & Palmer, J. (1987). The anomaly called psi: Recent research and criticism. *Behavioral and Brain Sciences*, 10, 539–555.

Rao, K.R, & Puri, I. (1978). Subsensory perception (SSP), extrasensory perception (ESP) and transcendental meditation. *Journal of Indian Psychology*, 1, 69–74.

Rao, P.V.K., & Rao, K.R. (1982). Two studies of ESP and subliminal perception. *Journal of Parapsychology*, 46, 185–207.

Rao, K.R., & Sailaja, P. (1973). The role of test preparedness in psi experiments. In W.G. Roll, R.L. Morris, & J.D. Morris (Eds.), *Research in Parapsychology*, 1972, p. 151–153. Metuchen, NJ: Scarecrow Press.

Rauscher, E.A., & Rubik, B.A. (1980). Effects on mobility behaviour and growth rate on salmonella typhimurium in the presence of Olga Worrall. *Research in Parapsychology*. Metuchen, NJ: Scarecrow Press.

Reed, P.G. (1986). Religiousness among terminally ill and healthy adults. *Research in Nursing and Health*, 9, 3541.

Reed, P.G. (1987). Spirituality and well being in terminally ill hospitalized adults. *Research in Nursing and Health*, 10, 335–344.

Reichenbach, H. (1938). *Experience and prediction: An analysis of the foundations and the structure of knowledge by Hans Reichenbach*. Chicago: University of Chicago Press.

Rhine, J.B. (1934/1973). *Extrasensory perception*. Brookline Village, MA: Bradon Press.

Rhine, J.B. (1934a). *Extrasensory perception*. Boston, MA: Boston Society for Psychical Research.

Rhine, J.B. (1935). *Extrasensory perception*. Boston: Bruce Humphries.

Rhine, J.B. (1938a). Experiments bearing on the precognition hypothesis. *Journal of Parapsychology*, 2, 38–54.

Rhine, J.B. (1938b). *New frontiers of the mind*. London: Faber and Faber.

Rhine, J.B. (1941). Experiments bearing upon the precognition hypothesis: III. Mechanically selected cards. *Journal of Parapsychology*, 5, 1–58.

Rhine, J.B. (1945a). Telepathy and clairvoyance reconsidered. *Journal of Parapsychology*, 9, 176–193.

Rhine, J.B. (1945b). Early PK tests: Sevens and low-dice series. *Journal of Parapsychology*, 9, 106–115.

Rhine, J.B. (1946). Hypnotic suggestion in PK tests. *Journal of Parapsychology*, 10, 126–40.

Rhine, J.B. (1947). *The reach of the mind*. New York: Sloane.

Rhine, J.B. (1950). The shifting scene in parapsychology. *Journal of Parapsychology*, 14, 161–167.

Rhine, J.B. (1952). The problem of psi-missing. *Journal of Parapsychology*, 16, 90–120.

Rhine, J.B. (1953). *New world of the mind*. New York: William Sloane Associates.

Rhine, J.B. (1958). On the nature and consequences of the unconsciousness of psi. *Journal of Parapsychology*, 22, 175–186.

Rhine, J.B. (1965). Advancement toward control and application. In J.B. Rhine & Associates (Eds.) *Parapsychology from Duke to FRNM* (pp. 45–56). Durham, NC: Parapsychology Press.

Rhine, J.B. (1969). Position effects in psi test result. *Journal of Parapsychology*, 33(2).

Rhine, J.B. (1974). A new case of experimenter unreliability. *Journal of Parapsychology*, 38, 215–225.

Rhine, J.B. (1975). Comments: Second report on a case of experimenter fraud. *Journal of Parapsychology*, 39, 306–325.

Rhine, J.B. (1975b). Psi methods reexamined. *Journal of Parapsychology*, 39, 38–58.

Rhine, J.B. (1977). "Extra-sensory perception." In B.B. Wolman (Ed.), *Handbook of parapsychology*, Reprinted Jefferson, NC: McFarland, 1985.

Rhine, J.B., & Feather, S.R. (1957). The

study of psi-trailing in animals. *Journal of Parapsychology,* 21, 245–258.

Rhine, J.B., & Humphrey, B.M. (1942). The transoceanic ESP experiment. *Journal of Parapsychology,* 6, 52–74.

Rhine, J.B., & Humphrey, B.M. (1944). The PK effect: special evidence from hit patters. I. Quarter distributions of the page. *Journal of Parapsychology,* 8, 18–60.

Rhine, J.B., & Humphrey, B.M. (1945). The PK effect with sixty dice per throw. *Journal of Parapsychology,* 9, 203–18.

Rhine, J.B., & Pratt, J.G. (1957). *Parapsychology: Frontier science of the mind.* Springfield, IL: Charles C. Thomas.

Rhine, J.B., Pratt, J.G., Stuart, C.E., Smith, B.M., & Greenwood, J.A. (1940). *Extrasensory perception after sixty years.* New York: Henry Holt.

Rhine, L.E. (1961/1965). *Hidden channels of the mind.* New York: William Sloane Associates [New York: William Morrow].

Rhine, L.E. (1962). Psychological processing in ESP experiences. Part II. Dreams. *Journal of Parapsychology,* 26, 172–199.

Rhine, L.E. (1967). *ESP in life and lab: Tracing hidden channels.* New York: Macmillan.

Rhine, L.E. (1981). *The invisible picture: A study of psychic experiences.* Jefferson, NC: McFarland.

Rhine, L.E, & Rhine, J.B. (1943). The psychokinetic effect: I. The first experiment. *Journal of Parapsychology,* 7, 20–43.

Rice, G.E., & Townsend, J. (1962). Agent-percipient relationship and GESP performance. *Journal of Parapsychology,* 26, 211–17.

Richet, C. (1884). La Suggestion mentale et le clacul des probabilities. (*Revue Philosophique de la France et de l'Étranger* 18 [1884]: 609–74).

Richet, C. (1923). *Thirty years if psychical research.* New York: Macmillan.

Rilling, M.E., Adams, J.Q., & Pettijohn, C. (1962). A summary of some clairvoyance experiments conducted in classroom situations. *Journal of the Society for Psychical Research,* 56: 125–130.

Rilling, M.E., Pettijohn, C., & Adams, J.Q. (1961). A two-experimenter investigation of teacher-pupil attitudes and clairvoyance test results in the high-school classroom. *Parapsychology,* 25, 247–60.

Robinson, E. (2011). Not feeling the future: A failed replication of retroactive facilitation of memory recall. *Journal of the Society for Psychical Research,* 75, 142–147.

Rock, A.J., Storm, L., Harris, K., & Friedman, H.L. (2013). Shamanic-like journeying and psi signal detection: II. Phenomenological dimensions. *Journal of Parapsychology,* 77, 249–270.

Roll, W.G. (1961). The problem of precognition. *Journal of the Society for Psychical Research,* 41, 115–128.

Roll, W.G. (1966). ESP and memory. *International Journal of Neuropsychiatry.* 2, 505–521.

Roll, W.G. (1970). Poltergeist phenomena and interpersonal relations. *Journal of the American Society for Psychical Research,* 64, 66–99.

Roll, W.G. (1972). Recent research with Lalsingh Harribance: Physical aspects of the target. In W.G. Roll, R.L. Moris, & J.D. Morris (Eds.), *Proceedings of the Parapsychological Association,* No. 8 (pp. 67–69). Durham, NC: Parapsychological Association. (Abstract)

Roll, W.G. (1977). Poltergeists. In B.B. Wolman (Ed.), *Handbook of parapsychology.* New York: Van Nostrand Reinhold.

Roll, W.G. (1987). Memory and long body. *Theta,* 15, 1029.

Roll, W.G., & Pratt, J.G. (1971). The Miami disturbances. *Journal of the American Society for Psychical Research,* 65, 409–454.

Roll, W.G., Saroka, K.S., Mulligan, B.P., Hunter, M.D., Dotta, B.T., Gang, N., Scott, M.A., St-Pierre, L.S., & Persinger, M.A. (2012). Case report: A prototypical experience of "poltergeist" activity, conspicuous quantitative electroencephalographic patterns, and sLORETA profiles—suggestions for intervention. *Neurocase,* 18, 527–536.

Roll, W.G., Solfvin, G.F., Krieger, J., Ray, D., & Younts, L. (1980). Psi scoring on individual and group targets before and after meditation. In W.G. Roll (Ed.), *Re-*

search in parapsychology, 1979, p. 172–174. Metuchen, NJ: Scarecrow Press.

Roll, W.G., & Zill, R. (1981). Psi scoring on individual and group targets before and after meditation. In W.G. Roll and J. Beloff (Eds.), *Research in parapsychology,* 1980, p. 73–75. Metuchen, NJ: Scarecrow Press.

Roney-Dougal, S.M., Ryan, A., & Luke, D. (2014). The relationship between local geomagnetic activity and psychic awareness. *Journal of Parapsychology,* 78, 235–252.

Roney-Dougal, S.M., & Solfvin, J. (2002). Field study of enhancement effect on lettuce seeds—their germination rate, growth and health. *Journal of the Society for Psychical Research,* 66, 129–143.

Rose, R. (1957). *Living magic: The Realities underlying the psychical practices and beliefs of the Australian aborigines.* London: Chatto & Windus.

Rosenthal, R. (1966). *Experimenter effects in behavioral research.* New York: Appleton-Century-Crofts.

Rosenthal, R. (1976). *Experimenter effects in behavioral research.* New York: Irvington Publishers.

Rosenthal, R. (1979). The "file drawer problem" and tolerance for null results. *Psychological Bulletin,* 86, 638–641.

Rosenthal, R., & Rubin, D.B. (1978). Interpersonal expectancy effects: The first 345 studies. *Behavioral and Brain Sciences,* 3, 377–415.

Ross, C.A., & Joshi, S. (1992). Paranormal experiences in the general population. *Journal of Nervous and Mental Disease,* 180, 357–361.

Rush, J.H. (1986). Physics and quasi-physical theories of psi. In H.L. Edge et al. (Eds.), *Foundations of parapsychology: Exploring the boundaries of human capability* (pp. 276–292). London: Routledge & Kegan Paul.

Ryzl, M. (1962). Training the psi faculty by hypnosis. *Journal of the Society for Psychical Research,* 41, 234–252.

Ryzl, M. (1990). Correspondence. *Journal of Parapsychology,* 54, 282–284.

Ryzl, M., & Pratt, J.G. (1963a). A repeated-calling ESP test with sealed cards. *Journal of Parapsychology,* 27, 161–74.

Ryzl, M., & Pratt, J.G. (1963b). The focusing of ESP upon particular targets *Journal of Parapsychology,* 27, 22741.

Ryzl, M., & Ryzlova, J. (1962) a case of high-scoring ESP performance in the hypnotic state, *Journal of Parapsychology,* 26, 153–171.

Sailaja, P., & Rao, K.R. (1973). *Experimental studies of the differential effect in life setting.* Parapsychological Monographs (No. 13). New York: Parapsychology Foundation.

Sanders, J.T. (1987). Are there any "Communications Anomalies"? *Brain and Behavior,* 10(4), p. 608.

Sanders, M.S. (1962). A comparison of verbal and written responses in a precognition experiment. *Journal of Parapsychology,* 26, 23–34.

Sargent, C. (1980). A covert test of psi abilities of psiconducive and psi-inhibitory experimenters. In W.G. Roll (Ed.), *Research in parapsychology* (pp. 115–116). Metuchen, NJ: Scarecrow Press.

Sargent, C.L. (1981). Extraversion and performance in "extra-sensory perception" tasks. *Personality and Individual Differences,* 2, 137–143.

Sargent, E. (1869). Review of Planchette. In W. James (ed.), *Essays in psychical research.* Cambridge, MA: Harvard University Press.

Savva, L., Child, C., & Smith, M.D. (2004). The precognitive habituation effect: An adaptation using spider stimuli. *Proceedings of Presented Papers: The Parapsychological Association 47th Annual Convention,* 223–229.

Schechter, E.I. (1984). Hypnotic induction vs. control conditions. Illustrating an approach to the evaluation of replicability in parapsychological data. *Journal of the American Society for Psychical Research,* 78, 1–27.

Schlitz, M., & Braud, W.G. (1997). Distant intentionality and healing: Assessing the evidence. *Alternative Therapies,* 3(6), 62–73.

Schlitz, M., & Gruber, E. (1980). Transcontinental remote viewing. *Journal of Parapsychology,* 44, 305–317.

Schlitz, M., & Gruber, E. (1981). The appendix is from a subsequent paper "Transcontinental remote viewing." *Journal of Parapsychology*, 45, 233–237.

Schlitz, M.J., & LaBerge, S. (1997). Covert observation increases skin conductance in subjects unaware of when they are being observed: A replication. *Journal of Parapsychology*, 61, 185–196.

Schmeidler, G.R. (1954). Picture-frustration ratings and ESP scores for subjects who showed moderate annoyance at the ESP task. *Journal of Parapsychology*, 18, 137–52.

Schmeidler, G.R. (1958). Agent-percipient relationships. *Journal of the American Society for Psychical Research*, 52, 47–69.

Schmeidler, G.R. (1960). Structures of uncertainty. *International Journal of Parapsychology*, 4, 103–108.

Schmeidler, G.R. (1961). Are there two kinds of telepathy? *Journal of the American Society for Psychical Research*, 55, 87–97.

Schmeidler, G.R. (1964). An experiment on precognitive clairvoyance: I. The main results. *Journal of Parapsychology*, 28, 1–14.

Schmeidler, G.R. (1970). High ESP scores after a swami's brief instruction in meditation and breathing. *Journal of the Society for Psychical Research*, 64, 100–103.

Schmeidler, G.R. (1971). Respice, adspice, prospice. *Proceedings of the Parapsychological Association*, 8, 117–143.

Schmeidler, G.R. (1977a). Methods for controlled research on ESP and PK. In B. B, Wolman (Ed.), *Handbook of parapsychology*. New York: Van Nostrand Reinhold.

Schmeidler, G.R. (1982). PK research: Findings and theories. In S. Krippner (Ed.), *Advances in parapsychological research*, vol. 3, 115–146. New York: Plenum Press.

Schmeidler, G.R. (1991). Perceptual processing of psi: A model. *Journal of the American Society for Psychical Research*, 85, 217–236.

Schmeidler, G.R., & McConnell, R.A. (1958). *ESP and personality patterns*. New Haven, CT: Yale University Press.

Schmidt, H. (1969a). Precognition of a quantum process. *Journal of Parapsychology*, 33, 99–108.

Schmidt, H. (1969b). Clairvoyance tests with a machine. *Journal of Parapsychology*, 33, 300–306.

Schmidt, H. (1970). PK test with electronic equipment. *Journal of Parapsychology*, 34(3), 7.

Schmidt, H. (1970a). A PK test with electronic equipment. *Journal of Parapsychology*, 34, 175–181.

Schmidt, H. (1970b). The psi quotient: An efficiency measure for psi tests. *Journal of Parapsychology*, 34, 210–214.

Schmidt, H. (1974). Comparison of PK action on two different random number generators. *Journal of Parapsychology*, 36, 47–55.

Schmidt, H. (1975). Toward a mathematical theory of psi. *Journal of the American Society for Psychical Research*, 69, 301–319.

Schmidt, H. (1976). PK effect on prerecorded targets. *Journal of the American Society for Psychical Research*, 70, 267–291.

Schmidt, H. (1981). PK tests with prerecorded and pre-inspected seed numbers. *Journal of Parapsychology*, 45, 87–98.

Schmidt, H. (1984). Comparison of a teleological with a quantum mechanical theory of psi. *Journal of Parapsychology*, 48, 261–276.

Schmidt, H., Morris, R.L., & Rudolph, L. (1986). Channeling evidence for PK effects to independent observers. *Journal of Parapsychology*, 50, 1–16.

Schmidt, H., & Pantas, L. (1972). Psi tests with internally different machines. *Journal of Parapsychology*, 36, 222–232.

Schmidt, S., Schneider, R., Utts, J., & Walach, H. (2002). Remote intention on electrodermal activity—Two meta-analyses. *Paper presented at the 45TH Annual Parapsychological Association Convention, Paris*.

Schmidt, S., Schneider, R., Utts, J., & Walach, H. (2004). Distant intentionality and the feeling of stared at: Two meta-analysis. *British Journal of Psychology*, 95:235.

Schmidt, S., & Walach, H. (2000). Electrodermal activity (EDA)—State of the art measurement and techniques for parapsychological purposes. *Journal of Parapsychology*, 64, 139–163.

Schnabel, J. (1997). *Remote viewers: The secret history of America's psychic spies.* New York: Dell.

Schneider, R., Binder, M., & Walach, H. (2000). Examining the role of neutral versus personal experimenter—participant interactions. An EDA—DMILS experiment. *Journal of Parapsychology*, 64, 181–194.

Schouten, S.A. (1972). Psi in mice: Positive reinforcement. *Journal of Parapsychology*, 36, 261282.

Schrödinger, E.C. (1966). Is science a fashion of the times? In A. Vavoulis & A.W. Colver (Eds.), *Science and society: Selected essays.* San Francisco: Holden Day.

Schwartz, S.A. (1983). *The Alexandria project.* New York, N.Y.: Delacorte Press/ E. Friede.

Scriven, M. (1962). The frontiers of psychology: Psychoanalysis and parapsychology. In R.G. Colodny (Ed.), *Frontiers of science and philosophy.* (pp. 9–129). Pittsburgh, PA: University of Pittsburgh Press.

Scriven, M. (1976). The frontiers of psychology: Psychoanalysis and parapsychology. In J.M.O. Wheatley, & H.L. Edge (Eds.) *Philosophical dimensions of parapsychology* (pp. 46–75). Springfield, ILL: Charles C Thomas.

Seybert Commission. (1887). *Preliminary report of the Commission Appointed by the University of Pennsylvania to Investigate Modern Spiritualism in Accordance with the Request of the Late Henry Seybert.* Philadelphia: J.B. Lippincott.

Sharp, V., & Clark, C.C. (1937). Group tests for extrasensory perception. *Journal of Parapsychology*, 1, 123–42.

Sheehan, D.P. (2015). Remembrance of things future: A case for retrocausation and precognition. In E.C. May and S.B. Marwaha (Eds.). *Extrasensory perception: Support, skepticism, and science, volume II—theoretical frameworks.* Santa Barbara: Praeger.

Sheldrake, R. (1994). *Seven experiments that could change the world.* London: Fourth Estate.

Sheldrake, R. (2015). Experimental methods in anomalous cognition and anomalous perturbation research. In E. Cardeña, J. Palmer, & D. Marcusson-Clavertz (Eds)., *Parapsychology: A handbook for the 21st century*, 49–61. Jefferson, NC: McFarland.

Sherwood, S.J., & Roe, C.A. (2003). A review of dream ESP studies conducted since the Maimonides dream ESP programme. *Journal of Consciousness Studies*, 10(6–7), 85–109.

Shields, E. (1962). Comparison of children's guessing ability (ESP) with personality characteristics. *Journal of Parapsychology*, 26, 200–210.

Shoup, R. (2015). Physics beyond causality: Making sense of quantum mechanics and certain experimental anomalies. In E.C. May and S.B. Marwaha (Eds.). *Extrasensory perception: Support, skepticism, and science, volume II—theoretical frameworks.* Santa Barbara: Praeger.

Sidgwick, E. (1889). Some fundamental ethical controversies. *Mind*, 14: 473–87.

Sidgwick, H., Sidgwick, E.M., & Smith, G.A. (1889). Experiments in thought transference. *Proceedings of the Society for Psychical Research*, 6, 128–170.

Sinclair, U. (1930). *Mental Radio.* Monrovia, CA: Sinclair/New York: A. & C. Boni.

Skibinsky, M. (1950). A comparison of names and symbols in a distance ESP test. *Journal of Parapsychology*, 14, 140–56.

Skinner, B.F. (1937). Is sense necessary? *Saturday Review.* October 9, 1937, 5.

Smith, M. (2003). The psychology of the "psi-conducive" experimenter: Personality, attitudes towards psi, and personal psi experience. *Journal of Parapsychology*, 67, 117–128.

Smith, M.J. (1968). Paranormal effects on enzyme activity. *Journal of Parapsychology*, 32, 281 (Abstract).

Smith, M.J. (1972). Paranormal effects on enzyme activity through laying on of hands. *Human Dimensions*, 1(2), 15–19.

Smith, W.R., et al. (1963). *Testing for extrasensory perception with a machine.* Bedford: Air Force Cambridge Research Laboratories.

Spottiswoode, J. (1997a). Apparent association between effect size in free response anomalous cognition experiments and local sidereal time. *Journal of Scientific Exploration*, 11, 109–122.

Spottiswoode, J. (1997b). Geomagnetic fluctuations and free response anomalous cognition: A new understanding. *Journal of Parapsychology*, 61, 3–12.

Stanford, R.G. (1970). Extrasensory effects upon "memory." *Journal of American Society for Psychical Research*, 64, 161–186.

Stanford, R.G. (1971). EEG alpha activity and ESP performance: A replicative study. *Journal of American Society for Psychical Research*, 65, 144–154.

Stanford, R.G. (1972). The differential effect revisited: An interaction of personality and ESP tank? In W.G. Roll., R.L. Morris., & J.D. Morris (Eds.), *Proceedings of the Parapsychological Association, No. 7*, 1970 (pp. 12–13). Durham, NC: Parapsychology Association. (Abstract).

Stanford, R.G. (1973). Extrasensory effects upon associative processes in a directed free-response task. *Journal of American Society for Psychical Research*, 68, 147–190.

Stanford, R.G. (1974a). An experimentally testable model for spontaneous psi events. I. Extrasensory events. *Journal of the American Society for Psychical Research*, 68, 34–57.

Stanford, R.G. (1974b). An experimentally testable model for spontaneous psi events. II. Psychokinetic events. *Journal of the American Society for Psychical Research*, 68, 321–356.

Stanford, R.G. (1977a). Conceptual frameworks of contemporary psi research. In B.B. Wolman (Ed.), *Handbook of parapsychology* (pp. 823–858). New York: Van Nostrand Reinhold.

Stanford, R.G. (1977b). Experimental psychokinesis: A review from diverse perspectives. In B.B. Wolman (Ed.), *Handbook of parapsychology* (pp. 324–381). New York: Van Nostrand Reinhold.

Stanford, R.G. (1977c). Are parapsychologists paradigmless in psi-land? In B. Shapin & L. Coly (Eds.), *The philosophy of parapsychology*. New York: Parapsychology Foundation.

Stanford, R.G. (1978). Toward reinterpreting psi events. *Journal of the American Society for Psychical Research*, 72, 197–214.

Stanford, R.G., & Mayer, B. (1974). Relaxation as a psiconducive state: A replication and exploration of parameters. *Journal of American Society for Psychical Research*, 68, 182–191.

Stanford, R.G., & Palmer, J. (1973). Meditation prior to the ESP task: An EEG study with an outstanding ESP subject. In W.G. Roll, R.L. Morris, & J.D. Morris (Eds.), *Research in Parapsychology*. NJ: Scarecrow Press.

Stanford, R.G., & Stanford, B.E. (1969). Shifts in EEG alpha rhythm as related to calling patterns and ESP run-score variance, *Journal of Parapsychology*, 33, 39–47.

Stanford, R.G., & Stevenson, I. (1972). EEG correlates of free-response GESP in an individual subject, *Journal of American Society for Psychical Research*, 66, 357–368.

Stanford, R.G., Zenhausern, R., Taylor, A., & Dwyer, M.A. (1975). Psychokinesis as psi mediated instrumental response, *Journal of the American Society for Psychical Research*, 69, 127–133.

Steffen, P.R., Hinderliter, A.L., Blumenthal, J.A., & Sherwood, A. (2001). Religious coping, ethnicity, and ambulatory blood pressure. *Psychosomatic Medicine*, 63, 523–530

Steinkamp, F., Boller, E., & Bösch, H. (2002). Experiments examining the possibility of human intention interacting with random number generators: A preliminary meta-analysis. *Proceedings of Presented Papers: The Parapsychological Association 45th Annual Convention*, 256–272.

Steinkamp, F., Milton, J., & Morris, R.L. (1998). A metaanalysis of forced-choice experiments comparing clairvoyance and precognition. *Journal of Parapsychology*, 62, 193–218.

Stevenson, I. (1966). Twenty cases suggestive of reincarnation. *Proceedings of the American Society for Psychical Research*, 26, 1–362.

Stevenson, I. (1970). Telepathic impressions: A review and report of thirty-five new cases. *Proceedings of the American Society for Psychical Research*, 29, 1–198.

Stevenson, I. (1974). *Twenty cases suggestive of reincarnation* (2 Ed.). Charlottesville: University of Virginia Press.

Stevenson, I. (1977). Reincarnation: Field studies and theoretical issues. In B.B. Wolman, L.A. Dale, G.R. Schmeidler & M. Ullman (Eds.). *Handbook of parapsychology*, 631–663. Jefferson, NC: McFarland.

Stokes, D. (1977). Review of Mind-reach: Scientists look at psychic ability, by R. Targ & H. Puthoff. *Journal of the American Society for Psychical Research*, 1977, 71, 437–442.

Stokes, D.M. (1987). Theoretical parapsychology. In S. Krippner (Ed.), *Advance in parapsychological research, Volume 5* (pp. 77–189). Jefferson, NC: McFarland.

Stokes, D.M. (1997). *The nature of mind: Parapsychology and the role of consciousness in the physical world.* Jefferson, NC: McFarland.

Stokes, D.M. (1998). Book Review: K. Frazier (Ed.). Encounters with the paranormal: Science, knowledge and belief. *Journal of Parapsychology*, 62, 158–170.

Storm, L., & Thalbourne, M. (2000). A paradigm shift away from the ESP-PK dichotomy: The theory of psychopraxia. *Journal of Parapsychology*, 64, 279–300.

Storm, L., Tressoldi, P.E., & Di Risio, L. (2010). Meta-analysis of ESP studies, 1987–2010: Assessing the noise reduction model in parapsychology. *Psychological Bulletin*, 136, 471–485.

Storm, L., Tressoldi, P.E., & DiRisio, L. (2012). Meta-analysis of ESP studies, 1987–2010: Assessing the success of the forced-choice design in parapsychology. *Journal of Parapsychology*, 76, 242.

Stuart, C.E. (1938). A review of certain proposed hypotheses alternative to extrasensory perception. *Journal of Abnormal and Social Psychology*, 33, 57–70.

Stuart, C.E. (1940). An examination of Kennedy's study of the McFarland data. *Journal of Parapsychology*, 4, 135–141.

Stuart, C.E. (1946). GESP experiments with the free response method. *Journal of Parapsychology*, 10, 2135.

Stuart, C.E., Humphrey, B.M., Smith, B.M., & McMahan, K. (1947). Personality measurement and ESP tests with cards and drawings. *Journal of Parapsychology*, 11, 118–146.

Subbotsky, E., and Ryan, A. (2009). Motivation and belief in the paranormal in a remote viewing task. https://www.researchgate.net/publication/236984643_Motivation.

Sudhakar, U.V., & Rao, P.V.K. (1986). Belief and personality factors of participants. A study in an ESP/Ganzfeld setting. *Journal of Indian Psychology*, 5(2), 21–45.

Taddonio, J.L. (1976). The relationship of experimenter expectancy to performance on ESP tasks. *Journal of Parapsychology*, 40, 107–115.

Targ, R., & Harary, K. (1985). *The mind race: Understanding and using psychic abilities.* New York: Ballantine.

Targ, R., & Puthoff, H.E. (1977). *Mind reach.* New York: Delacorte Press/Eleanor Friede.

Targ, R., Puthoff, H.E., & May, E.C. (1979). Direct perception of remote geographic locations. In C.T. Tart, H.E. Puthoff, & R. Targ (Eds.). *Mind at large* (pp. 78–106). New York: Praeger.

Tart, C.T. (1968). A psychophysiological of out-of-body experiences in a selected subject. *Journal of the American Society for Psychical Research*, 62, 3–27.

Tart, C.T. (2009). *The end of materialism: How evidence of the paranormal is bringing science and spirit together.* Oakland, CA: Noetic Books, Institute of Noetic Sciences.

Tart, C.T. (2009). *The end of materialism: How evidence of the paranormal is bringing science and spirit together.* Oakland, CA: Noetic Books, Institute of Noetic Sciences.

Tart, C., Puthoff, H.E., & Targ, R. (1980). Information transmission in remote viewing experiments. *Nature*, 204, 191.

Tenny, K. (1962). Physiological responses during an ESP test. Abstract. *Journal of Parapsychology*, 13, 138.

Terry, J.C., & Honorton, C. (1976). Psi information retrieval in the ganzfeld: Two confirmatory studies. *Journal of the American Society for Psychical Research.* 70, 207–217.

Thouless, R.H. (1943). The present position of experimental research into telepathy and related phenomena. *Journal of Parapsychology*, 7, 158–171.

Thouless, R.H. (1946). On J.B. Rhine's "Telepathy and clairvoyance reconsidered," *Proceedings of the Society for Psychical Research*, v. 48, 15–17.

Thouless, R.H. (1949). A comparative study of performance in three psi tasks. *Journal of Parapsychology*, 1949, 13, 263–273.

Thouless, R.H. (1960). The empirical evidence for survival. *Journal of the American Society for Psychical Research*, 54: 23–32.

Thouless, R.H. (1963). *Mind and consciousness in experimental psychology.* London: Cambridge University Press.

Thouless, R.H., & Weisner, B.P. (1947). The psi-process in normal and "paranormal" psychology. *Proceedings of the Society for Psychical Research*, 48, 177–196.

Thouless, R.H., & Wiesner, B.P. (1948). The psi process in normal and "paranormal" psychology. *Journal of Parapsychology*, 12, 192–212.

Timm, U. (1969). Mixing-up of symbols in ESP card experiments (so-called consistent missing) as a possible cause for psi-missing. *Journal of Parapsychology*, 33, 109–124.

Townsend, M., Kladder, V., Ayele, H., & Mulligan, T. (2002) Systematic review of clinical trials examining the effects of religion on health. *South Medical Journal*, 95(12), 1429–34.

Tressoldi, P.E. (2011). Extraordinary claims require extraordinary evidence: The case of non-local perception. A classical and Bayesiau review of evidences. *Frontiers in Psychology*, 2, 117.

Tressoldi, P.E., & Del Prete, G. (2007). ESP under hypnosis: The role of induction instructions and personality characteristics. *Journal of Parapsychology*, 71, 125–137.

Tressoldi, P.E., & Utts, J. (2015). Statistical guideline for empirical studies. In *Parapsychology: A Handbook for the 21st century,* edited by E. Cardeña, J. Palmer, & D. Marcusson-Clavertz, 83–93. Jefferson, NC: McFarland.

Truzzi, M. (1980). A skeptical look at Paul Kurtz' analysis of the scientific status of parapsychology. *Journal of Parapsychology*, 44, 35–55.

Tyrrell, G.N.M. (1946). The modus operandi of paranormal cognition. *Proceedings of the Society for Psychical Research*, 48(173), 65–120.

Tyrrell, G.N.M. (1946a). On J.B. Rhine's "Telepathy and clairvoyance reconsidered," *Proceedings of the Society for Psychical Research*, v. 48, 17–19.

Tyrrell, G.N.M. (1946b). The modus operandi of paranormal cognition. *Proceedings of the Society for Psychical Research*, 1946–49, 48, 65–120.

Tyrrell, G.N.M. (1947a). The modus operandi of paranormal cognition. *Proceedings of the Society for Psychical Research*, 48, 65–120.

Tyrrell, G.N.M. (1947b). *The personality of man.* Liarmondswortli, England: Penguin.

Ullman, M. (1966). An experimental approach to dreams and telepathy: Methodology and preliminary findings. *Archives of General Psychiatry*, 14, 605–613.

Ullman, M., & Krippner, S. (1970). *Dream studies and telepathy: An experimental approach.* New York: Parapsychological Foundation.

Ullman, M., Krippner, S., & Feldstein, S. (1966). Experimentally induced telepathic dreams: Two studies using EEG-REM monitoring techniques. *International Journal of Neuropsychiatry*, 2, 420–437.

Ullman, M., Krippner, S., & Vaughan, A. (1973). *Dream telepathy: Experiments in nocturnal ESP.* New York: Macmillan.

Ullman, M., Krippner, S., & Vaughan, A. (1989). *Dream telepathy: Experiments in nocturnal ESP.* Jefferson, NC: McFarland.

Underwood, B. (1969). Attributes of memory. *Psychological Review*, 76, 559–573.

Utts, J. (2001). An assessment of the evidence of psychic functioning. In K.R. Rao (Ed.). *Basic Research in Parapsychology.* (pp. 110–141). Jefferson, NC: McFarland.

Utts, J. (2015). What constitutes replication in parapsychology? In Edwin C. May and S.B. Marwaha (Eds.). *Extrasensory perception: Support, skepticism and science.* Santa Barbara: Praeger.

Van Busschbach, J.G. (1955). A further report on an investigation of ESP in school children. *Journal of Parapsychology,* 19, 69–8 1.

Van Busschbach, J.G. (1956). An investigation of ESP between teacher and pupils in American Schools. *Journal of Parapsychology,* 20, 71–80.

Van Busschbach, J.G. (1958). Idem. *Tijdschrift voor parapsychologie,* 24, 1958, 172–177.

Van Busschbach, J.G. (1959). An investigation of ESP in first and second grades of Dutch schools. *Journal of Parapsychology,* 23, 227–237.

Van Busschbach, J.G. (1961). An investigation of ESP in first and second grades in American schools. *Journal of Parapsychology,* 25, 161–174.

Van de Castle, R.L. (1953). An exploratory study of some variables relating to individual ESP performance. *Journal of Parapsychology,* 17, 61–72.

Van de Castle, R.L. (1977). Sleep and dreams. In Benjamin B. Wolman (Ed.) *Handbook of parapsychology.* New York: Van Nostrand Reinhold, p. 473–499.

Varvoglis, M., & Bancal, A. (2015). Micro-Psychokinesis. In *Parapsychology: A Handbook for the 21st Century,* edited by E. Cardeña, J. Palmer, & D. Marcusson-Clavertz, 266–281. Jefferson, NC: McFarland.

Varvoglis, M., & Bancal, A. (2016). Micropsychokinesis: Exceptional or universal? *Journal of Parapsychology,* 80(1), 37–44.

Vasiliev, L.L. (1963/1976). *Experiments in distance influence.* New York: Dutton: Originally published in 1963.

Vasiliev, L.L. (1976). *Exploration of distant influences.* New York: Dutton.

Vassy, Z. (1979). Anomalous anticipatory response on randomized future conditions. In Bierman, D.J., & Radin, D.I. (1997), *Perceptual and Motor Skills,* 84, 689–690.

Vieten, C., Radin, D., Schlitz, M., & Delorme, A. (2013). *Psychophysiology of spiritual transmission: A preliminary investigation.* Final Report for the Bial Foundation. Unpublished report.

Wackermann, J., Seiter, C., Keibel, H., & Walach, H. (2003). Correlations between brain electrical activities of two spatially separated human subjects. *Neuroscience Letters,* 336, 60–64.

Wagner, M.W., & Monnet, M. (1979). Attitudes of college professors toward extrasensory perception. *Zetetic Scholar,* 5, 7–16.

Walach, H., & Stillfried, N.V. (2011). Generalised quantum theory—Basic idea and general intuition: A background story and overview. *Axiomathes,* 21(2), 185–209.

Walker, E.H. (1975). Foundations of paraphysical and parapsychological phenomena. In L. Oteri (Ed.). *Quantum physics and parapsychology* (pp. 1–53). New York: Parapsychology Foundation.

Walker, E.H. (2000). *The physics of consciousness: The quantum mind and the meaning of life.* Cambridge, MA: Perseus.

Warren, C.A., McDonough, B.E., & Don, N.S. (1992a). Event-related brain potential changes in a psi task. *Journal of Parapsychology,* 56, 1–30.

Warren, C.A., McDonough, B.E., & Don, N.S. (1992b). Partial replication of single subject event-related potential effects in a psi task. *Proceedings of Presented Papers: The Parapsychological Association 35th Annual Convention,* 169–181.

Watkins, G.K., & Watkins, A.M. (1971). Possible PK influence on the resuscitation of anesthetized mice. *Journal of Parapsychology,* 35, 257–272.

Watt, C., & Baker, I.S. (2002). Remote facilitation of attention focusing with psi-supportive versus psiunsupportive experimenter suggestions. *Journal of Parapsychology,* 66, 151–168.

Watt, C., & Brady, C. (2002). Experimenter effects and the remote facilitation of attention focusing: Two studies and the discovery of an artifact. *Journal of Parapsychology*, 66, 49–71.

Watt, C., & Ramakers, P. (2003). Experimenter effects with a remote facilitation of attention focusing task: A study with multiple believer and disbeliever experimenters. *Journal of Parapsychology*, 67, 99116.

Watt, C., & Wiseman, R. (2002). Experimenter differences in cognitive correlates of paranormal belief, and in psi. *Journal of Parapsychology*, 66, 371385.

Watt, C., Wiseman, R., & Schlitz, M. (2002). Tacit information in remote staring research: The Wiseman Schlitz interviews. *Paranormal Review*, 24, 18–25.

Watt, C.A., & Morris, R.L. (1995). The relationships among performance on a prototype indicator of perceptual defence/vigilance, personality, and extrasensory perception. *Personality and Individual Differences*, 19, 635–648.

Weiner, D.H., & Zingrone, N.L. (1986). The Checker Effect revisited. *Journal of Parapsychology*, 50, 155161.

Weserman, H.M. (1819). Versuche Willkürlicher träumbilung. *Archiv, f.d. Tierischen Magnnetismus*, 6, 135–142.

West, D.J. (1957). *Eleven Lourdes miracles*. London: Gerald Duckworth.

West, D.J., & Fisk, G.W. (1953). A dual ESP experiment with clock cards. *Journal of the Society for Psychical Research*, 37, 185–189.

White, R.A. (1964). A comparison of old and new methods of response to targets in ESP experiments. *Journal of the American Society for Psychical Research*, 58, 21–56.

White, R.A. (1976a). The influences of persons than the experimenter on the subject's scores in psi experiments. *Journal of the American Society for Psychical Research*, 70, 133–166.

White, R.A. (1976b). The limits of experimenter influence on psi test results: Can any be set? *Journal of the American Society for Psychical Research*, 70, 333–369.

White, R.A. (1977). The influence of experimenter motivation, attitudes and methods of handling subjects in psi test results. In B. Wolman (Ed.), *Handbook of Parapsychology* (pp. 273–301). New York: Van Nostrand Reinhold.

White, R.A., & Angstadt, J.A. (1961). Resume of research at the A.S.P.R. into teacher-pupil attitudes and clairvoyance test results, 1950–60. *Journal the American Society for Psychical Research*, 55, 142–147.

White, R.A., & Angstadt, J. (1965). A review of results and new experiments bearing on teacher-selection methods in the Anderson-White high school experiments. *Journal of the American Society for Psychical Research*, 59, 56–84.

Wilkinson, H.P., & Gauld, A. (1993). Geomagnetism and anomalous experience, 1868–1980. *Proceedings of the Society for Psychical Research*, 57, 275–310.

Willoughby, R.R. (1935). A critique of Rhine's "Extra-sensory perception." *Journal of Abnormal and Social Psychology*, 30(2), 202–203.

Wilson, S. (2002). Psi, perception without awareness and false recognition. *Journal of Parapsychology* 66 (3):271–289.

Winkleman, M. (1981). The effect of formal education on extrasensory abilities: The Ozolco study. *Journal of Parapsychology*, 45, 321–336.

Wiseman, R., & Milton, J. (1998). Experimenter effects and the remote detection of staring: An attempted replication. *The Parapsychological Association 42nd Annual Convention. Proceedings of Presented Papers*, 471–479. Durham, NC: The Parapsychological Association.

Wiseman, R., & Schlitz, M. (1997). Experimenter effects and the remote detecting of staring. *Journal of Parapsychology*, 61, 197–207.

Wiseman, R., & Schlitz, M.J. (1999). Experimenter effects and the remote detection of staring: An attempted replication. *The Parapsychological Association 42nd Annual Convention. Proceedings of Presented Papers* (pp. 471–479). Durham, NC: The Parapsychological Association.

Wiseman, R., & Smith, M.D. (1994). A further look at the detection of unseen gaze. *Proceedings of the Parapsycholog-*

ical Association 37 Annual convention, 480–492.

Wiseman, R., Smith, M.D., Freedman, D., & Hurst, C. (1995). Two further experiments concerning the remote detection of an unseen gaze. *Proceedings of the Parapsychological Association 38th Annual Convention*, 480–492.

Wolfle, D.L. (1938). Extrasensory perception. *The American Journal of Psychiatry*, 94, 4, January 1938, 947.

Woodruff, J.L, & George, R.W. (1937). Experiments in extrasensory perception. *Journal of Parapsychology*, 1, 18–30.

Woodruff, J.L., & Murphy, G. (1943). Effect of incentives on ESP and visual perception. *Journal of Parapsychology*, 7, 144–157.

Woods, J.H. (1927). *The yoga system of Patanjali*. Cambridge, MA: Harvard University Press.

Woodward, W. (1987). Commented on "The anomaly called psi: Recent research and criticism." In K.R. Rao & J. Palmer, *Behavioural and Brain Sciences*, 10, 539–551.

Zusne, L. (1982). *Anomalistic psychology: A study of extraordinary phenomena of behavior and experience*. Hillsdale, NJ: Erlbaum.

Index